THE BOOK

CW00540841

Renault 21
Service and Repair Manual

I M Coomber

Models covered

(1397-288-7Y5)

Renault 21 models with petrol engines and front-wheel-drive
Saloon (inc. Turbo), Hatchback and Estate (Savanna)
1721 cc & 1995 cc (inc. 12-valve)

Does not cover Diesel engine or four-wheel-drive (Quadra) models

© Haynes Publishing 1997

A book in the **Haynes Service and Repair Manual Series**

ABCDE
FGHIJ
KLMNO
PQRST
2

ISBN **1 85960 275 4**

British Library Cataloguing in Publication Data
A catalogue record for this book is available from the British Library.

Printed by **J H Haynes & Co. Ltd, Sparkford, Nr Yeovil, Somerset BA22 7JJ**

Haynes Publishing
Sparkford, Nr Yeovil, Somerset BA22 7JJ, England

Haynes North America, Inc
861 Lawrence Drive, Newbury Park, California 91320, USA

Editions Haynes S.A.
147/149, rue Saint Honoré, 75001 PARIS, France

Haynes Publishing Nordiska AB
Fyrisborgsgatan 5, 754 50 Uppsala, Sverige

Contents

Contents

REPAIRS & OVERHAUL

Introduction to the Renault 21

The Renault 21 series was first introduced in June 1986 and filled the mid-range gap between the Renault 11 and Renault 25 models. Initially available only in Saloon form, in April 1987, an Estate version known as the Savanna was added to the range.

A 1.7 or 2.0 litre OHC, water-cooled engine is used together with a five-speed manual transmission or a three-speed automatic transmission. On 1.7 litre models the engine and transmission are transversely-mounted whilst on 2.0 litre models the engine and transmission are mounted longitudinally.

Independent front suspension and rack and pinion steering (power assisted on some models) is used, but the layout and specifications differ according to engine type and model.

All 1.7 litre models are fitted with a carburettor, whilst 2:0 litre models have fuel injection, with a turbocharger on the top of the range 2.0 litre Turbo model. An electronic engine management system is employed, and the fuel and ignition systems are jointly controlled by a computer module in accordance with engine demands.

All models are well built and fully equipped. They provide a combination of comfort, reliability and economy.

Acknowledgements

Thanks are due to Champion Spark Plug who supplied the illustrations showing the spark plug conditions. Certain other illustrations are the copyright of Renault UK Limited, and are used with their permission. Thanks are also due to SykesPickavant, who supplied some of the workshop tools, and to all those people at Sparkford who helped in the production of this manual.

We take great pride in the accuracy of information given in this manual, but vehicle manufacturers make alterations and design changes during the production run of a particular vehicle of which they do not inform us. No liability can be accepted by the authors or publishers for loss, damage or injury caused by any errors in, or omissions from, the information given.

Project vehicles

The project vehicles used in the preparation of this manual, and appearing in many of the photographic sequences, were a Renault 21 GTX, Renault 21 Savanna TS and Renault 21 2.0 litre Turbo.

Renault 21 GTX

Renault 21 Savanna GTS

Working on your car can be dangerous. This page shows just some of the potential risks and hazards, with the aim of creating a safety-conscious attitude.

General hazards

Scalding

• Don't remove the radiator or expansion tank cap while the engine is hot.
• Engine oil, automatic transmission fluid or power steering fluid may also be dangerously hot if the engine has recently been running.

Burning

• Beware of burns from the exhaust system and from any part of the engine. Brake discs and drums can also be extremely hot immediately after use.

Crushing

• When working under or near a raised vehicle, always supplement the jack with axle stands, or use drive-on ramps. *Never venture under a car which is only supported by a jack.*

• Take care if loosening or tightening high-torque nuts when the vehicle is on stands. Initial loosening and final tightening should be done with the wheels on the ground.

Fire

• Fuel is highly flammable; fuel vapour is explosive.
• Don't let fuel spill onto a hot engine.
• Do not smoke or allow naked lights (including pilot lights) anywhere near a vehicle being worked on. Also beware of creating sparks (electrically or by use of tools).
• Fuel vapour is heavier than air, so don't work on the fuel system with the vehicle over an inspection pit.
• Another cause of fire is an electrical overload or short-circuit. Take care when repairing or modifying the vehicle wiring.
• Keep a fire extinguisher handy, of a type suitable for use on fuel and electrical fires.

Electric shock

• Ignition HT voltage can be dangerous, especially to people with heart problems or a pacemaker. Don't work on or near the ignition system with the engine running or the ignition switched on.

• Mains voltage is also dangerous. Make sure that any mains-operated equipment is correctly earthed. Mains power points should be protected by a residual current device (RCD) circuit breaker.

Fume or gas intoxication

• Exhaust fumes are poisonous; they often contain carbon monoxide, which is rapidly fatal if inhaled. Never run the engine in a confined space such as a garage with the doors shut.

• Fuel vapour is also poisonous, as are the vapours from some cleaning solvents and paint thinners.

Poisonous or irritant substances

• Avoid skin contact with battery acid and with any fuel, fluid or lubricant, especially antifreeze, brake hydraulic fluid and Diesel fuel. Don't syphon them by mouth. If such a substance is swallowed or gets into the eyes, seek medical advice.
• Prolonged contact with used engine oil can cause skin cancer. Wear gloves or use a barrier cream if necessary. Change out of oil-soaked clothes and do not keep oily rags in your pocket.
• Air conditioning refrigerant forms a poisonous gas if exposed to a naked flame (including a cigarette). It can also cause skin burns on contact.

Asbestos

• Asbestos dust can cause cancer if inhaled or swallowed. Asbestos may be found in gaskets and in brake and clutch linings. When dealing with such components it is safest to assume that they contain asbestos.

Special hazards

Hydrofluoric acid

• This extremely corrosive acid is formed when certain types of synthetic rubber, found in some O-rings, oil seals, fuel hoses etc, are exposed to temperatures above 400°C. The rubber changes into a charred or sticky substance containing the acid. *Once formed, the acid remains dangerous for years. If it gets onto the skin, it may be necessary to amputate the limb concerned.*
• When dealing with a vehicle which has suffered a fire, or with components salvaged from such a vehicle, wear protective gloves and discard them after use.

The battery

• Batteries contain sulphuric acid, which attacks clothing, eyes and skin. Take care when topping-up or carrying the battery.
• The hydrogen gas given off by the battery is highly explosive. Never cause a spark or allow a naked light nearby. Be careful when connecting and disconnecting battery chargers or jump leads.

Air bags

• Air bags can cause injury if they go off accidentally. Take care when removing the steering wheel and/or facia. Special storage instructions may apply.

Diesel injection equipment

• Diesel injection pumps supply fuel at very high pressure. Take care when working on the fuel injectors and fuel pipes.

⚠ *Warning: Never expose the hands, face or any other part of the body to injector spray; the fuel can penetrate the skin with potentially fatal results.*

Remember...

DO

• Do use eye protection when using power tools, and when working under the vehicle.

• Do wear gloves or use barrier cream to protect your hands when necessary.

• Do get someone to check periodically that all is well when working alone on the vehicle.

• Do keep loose clothing and long hair well out of the way of moving mechanical parts.

• Do remove rings, wristwatch etc, before working on the vehicle – especially the electrical system.

• Do ensure that any lifting or jacking equipment has a safe working load rating adequate for the job.

DON'T

• Don't attempt to lift a heavy component which may be beyond your capability – get assistance.

• Don't rush to finish a job, or take unverified short cuts.

• Don't use ill-fitting tools which may slip and cause injury.

• Don't leave tools or parts lying around where someone can trip over them. Mop up oil and fuel spills at once.

• Don't allow children or pets to play in or near a vehicle being worked on.

Dimensions

Overall length:
Saloon (except RS, RX and Turbo) .... 4462 mm (175.6 in)
Saloon RS and RX .... 4465 mm (175.7 In)
Turbo .... 4498 mm (177.0 in)
Savanna .... 4644 mm (182.8 in)
Overall width:
Saloon and Savanna (except TL, TS and Turbo) .... 1715 mm (67.5 in)
Saloon and Savanna TL and TS .... 1706 mm (67.1 in)
Turbo .... 1714 mm (67.4 in)
Overall height:
Saloon (except Turbo) .... 1414 mm (55.6 in)
Turbo .... 1385 mm (54.5 in)
Savanna (except GTX and TXE) .... 1427 mm (56.1 in)
Savanna GTX and TXE .... 1430 mm (56.2 in)
Ground clearance (at kerb weight):
All models .... 120 mm (4.7 in)
Wheelbase:
Saloon (except RX, TXE and Turbo) .... 2695 mm (104.6 in)
Saloon RX and TXE .... 2600 mm (102.3 in)
Turbo .... 2597 mm (102.2 in)
Savanna (except GTX and TXE) .... 2809 mm (110.6 in)
Savanna GTX and TXE .... 2750 mm (108.2 in)
Front track:
Saloon (except RX, TXE and Turbo) and Savanna (except GTX
and TXE) .... 1429 mm (56.2 in)
Saloon RX and TXE .... 1454 mm (57.2 in)
Savanna GTX and TXE .... 1454 mm (57.2 in)
Turbo .... 1450 mm (57.0 in)
Rear track:
Saloon (except RX, TXE and Turbo) .... 1402 mm (55.2 in)
Saloon RX and TXE and ail Savanna models .... 1406 mm (55.3 in)
Turbo .... 1402 mm (55.2 in)

Weights

Kerb weight:
Saloon models:
TL .... 985 kg (2172 lb)
TS, GTS, RS and TSE .... 1040 kg (2293 lb)
RX and TXE .... 1130 kg (2491 lb)
Turbo .... 1190 kg (2624 lb)
5-seat Savanna models*:
TL .... 1015 kg (2238 lb)
TS .... 1030 kg (2271 lb)
GTS .... 1040 kg (2293 lb)
GTX .... 1135 kg (2502 lb)
TXE .... 1155 kg (2546 lb)
*For 7-seat Savanna models add 20 kg (44 lb)
Maximum roof rack load:
Saloon .... 60 kg (132 lb)
Savanna .... 70 kg (154 lb)
Maximum towing weight .... Consult a Renault dealer

Capacities*

Engine oil:
1.7 litre engine (excluding filter) .... 4.7 litres (8.0 pints)
2.0 litre engine (excluding filter) .... 5.7 litres (10.0 pints)
Oil filter .... 0.5 litre (0.88 pint)
Cooling system:
1.7 litre models .... 5.2 litres (9.2 pints)
2.0 litre non-Turbo models .... 6.8 litres (12.0 pints)
2.0 litre Turbo model .... 6.2 litres (11.0 pints)
Fuel tank:
All models .... 66 litres (14.5 gals)
Manual transmission oil:
JB3 type .... 3.4 litres (6.0 pints)
NG9 type .... 2.2 litres (4.0 pints)
UN1 type .... 3.0 litres (5.2 pints)
Automatic transmission fluid:
Fluid renewal .... 2.5 litres (4.4 pints)
Dry fill .... 6.0 litres (10.6 pints)
*For information applicable to later models, see Supplement at end of manual

Jump starting

HAYNES HINT *Jump starting will get you out of trouble, but you must correct whatever made the battery go flat in the first place. There are three possibilities:*

1 *The battery has been drained by repeated attempts to start, or by leaving the lights on.*

2 *The charging system is not working properly (alternator drivebelt slack or broken, alternator wiring fault or alternator itself faulty).*

3 *The battery itself is at fault (electrolyte low, or battery worn out).*

When jump-starting a car using a booster battery, observe the following precautions:

✔ Before connecting the booster battery, make sure that the ignition is switched off.

✔ Ensure that all electrical equipment (lights, heater, wipers, etc) is switched off.

✔ Make sure that the booster battery is the same voltage as the discharged one in the vehicle.

✔ If the battery is being jump-started from the battery in another vehicle, the two vehcles MUST NOT TOUCH each other.

✔ Make sure that the transmission is in neutral (or PARK, in the case of automatic transmission).

1 Connect one end of the red jump lead to the positive (+) terminal of the flat battery

2 Connect the other end of the red lead to the positive (+) terminal of the booster battery.

3 Connect one end of the black jump lead to the negative (-) terminal of the booster battery

4 Connect the other end of the black jump lead to a bolt or bracket on the engine block, well away from the battery, on the vehicle to be started.

5 Make sure that the jump leads will not come into contact with the fan, drive-belts or other moving parts of the engine.

6 Start the engine using the booster battery, then with the engine running at idle speed, disconnect the jump leads in the reverse order of connection.

Identifying leaks

Puddles on the garage floor or drive, or obvious wetness under the bonnet or underneath the car, suggest a leak that needs investigating. It can sometimes be difficult to decide where the leak is coming from, especially if the engine bay is very dirty already. Leaking oil or fluid can also be blown rearwards by the passage of air under the car, giving a false impression of where the problem lies.

 Warning: Most automotive oils and fluids are poisonous. Wash them off skin, and change out of contaminated clothing, without delay.

 The smell of a fluid leaking from the car may provide a clue to what's leaking. Some fluids are distinctively coloured. It may help to clean the car carefully and to park it over some clean paper overnight as an aid to locating the source of the leak.
Remember that some leaks may only occur while the engine is running.

Sump oil

Engine oil may leak from the drain plug...

Oil from filter

...or from the base of the oil filter.

Gearbox oil

Gearbox oil can leak from the seals at the inboard ends of the driveshafts.

Antifreeze

Leaking antifreeze often leaves a crystalline deposit like this.

Brake fluid

A leak occurring at a wheel is almost certainly brake fluid.

Power steering fluid

Power steering fluid may leak from the pipe connectors on the steering rack.

Jacking, towing and wheel changing

To avoid repetition, the procedure for raising the vehicle, in order to carry out work under it, is not included before each relevant operation described in this Manual.

It is to be preferred, and it is certainly recommended, that the vehicle is positioned over an inspection pit or raised on a lift. Where these facilities are not available, use ramps or jack up the vehicle strictly in accordance with the following guide. Once the vehicle is raised, supplement the jack with axle stands.

Wheel changing

To change a roadwheel, remove the jack and wheelbrace from their compartment under the luggage area floor.

Where a wheel trim is fitted, prise it free using a screwdriver inserted in the lever opening on its outer rim. Some models are fitted with an anti-theft type wheel and in this instance the trim can only be removed using the special key supplied for this purpose.

Place the car in gear (preferably 1st or reverse), or on automatic transmission model engage 'P'.

Make sure that the handbrake is fully applied and if possible chock the roadwheel opposite to the one being removed.

Release but do not remove the roadwheel bolts.

Locate the jack under the sill jacking point nearest to the wheel being changed. If the ground is soft, a base plate should be located under the jack.

Using the wheelbrace, turn the jack screw and raise the wheel off the floor.

Remove the bolts and wheel, and bolt on the spare wheel.

If a smaller emergency only type wheel is fitted, or if a steel type roadwheel is fitted as a replacement for an alloy type, the vehicle speed should not exceed 50 mph (80 kph) during their use. The normal roadwheel should be repaired and put back into service as soon as possible.

When the spare wheel is fitted, moderately tighten the bolts, lower the vehicle, then fully tighten the bolts. Refit the trim where applicable.

Jacking

When raising the car for repair or maintenance work, preferably use a trolley jack, or a hydraulic bottle or heavy screw type jack.

Place the jack under the sill jacking points using a shaped wooden block with a groove into which the weld flange of the sill will locate.

The front end may be raised if a substantial wooden baulk of timber is placed transversally under the subframe as shown. Place the jack under the centre of the timber.

Never attempt to jack the car under the front crossmember or front or rear suspension arms, or the rear axle unit.

Rear end jacking points (arrowed)

Jacking and support points for axle stands (1)

Front end jacking point under subframe using support beam located as shown - transverse engine models

Front and jacking point - note use of shaped wooden block (arrowed), between jack and sill

Front end jacking point under subframe using support beam located as shown - longitudinal engine models

Towing

The towing hooks may be used for towing or being towed on normal road surfaces.

When being towed, remember to unlock the steering column by turning the ignition key to the 'M' position.

Vehicles equipped with automatic transmission should preferably be towed with the front wheels off the ground. However, towing with the front wheels on the ground is permissible if an extra 2.0 litres (3.5 pints) of the specified transmission fluid is poured into the transmission, the speed is restricted to 30 km/h (18 mph) and the distance towed kept below 50 km (30 miles).

Keep the selector lever in 'M' during towing and remove the surplus fluid after the vehicle has been made serviceable again; a syphon is the best way to do this.

Rear towing eye

Front towing eye

Maintenance is essential for ensuring safety, and desirable for the purpose of getting the best in terms of performance and economy from your car. Over the years the need for periodic lubrication – oiling, greasing and so on – has been drastically reduced, if not totally eliminated. This has unfortunately tended to lead some owners to think that because no such action is required, components either no longer exist, or will last forever. This is a serious delusion. It follows therefore that the largest initial element of maintenance is visual examination and a general sense of awareness. This may lead to repairs or renewals, but should help to avoid roadside breakdowns.

Although fluid levels and brakepad wear are monitored by sensors, there is still no real substitute for visual inspection. This is a precautionary operation to be able to anticipate the illumination of a warning lamp which may well otherwise occur at a time when topping-up, rectification of a leak, or brake overhaul may at least be inconvenient if not expensive or dangerous.

The following service schedules are a list of the maintenance requirements and the intervals at which they should be carried out, based on the schedule recommended by the manufacturers. Where applicable these procedures are covered in greater detail throughout this manual, near the beginning of each Chapter.

Every 250 miles (400 km) or weekly, whichever comes first

- [ ] Check engine oil level (Chapter 1)
- [ ] Check coolant level (Chapter 2)
- [ ] Check tyre pressures (Chapter 8)
- [ ] Check operation of all lights and horn (Chapter 12)
- [ ] Check washer bottle level (Chapter 12)

After first 1000 miles (1600 km) – new cars or after major engine overhaul

- [ ] Renew engine oil and filter (Chapter 1)
- [ ] Adjust valve clearances (after overhaul only) (Chapter 1)
- [ ] Check torque of cylinder head bolts (after overhaul only) (Chapter 1)
- [ ] Renew manual transmission oil (Chapter 6)

Every 6 000 miles (10 000 km) or 6 months, whichever comes first

- [ ] Renew the engine oil and filter (Chapter 1)
- [ ] Check the cooling system hoses for condition and security (Chapter 2)
- [ ] Check and clean the crankcase ventilation system hoses and jets (Chapter 1)
- [ ] Check the condition and tension of the drivebelts (Chapter 2)
- [ ] On Turbo models, have the Turbo boost pressure circuits checked for leaks. This task must be entrusted to a Renault dealer
- [ ] Renew the spark plugs (Chapter 4)
- [ ] Check the manual transmission oil level (Chapter 6)
- [ ] Check the automatic transmission fluid level (Chapter 7)
- [ ] Check the fluid level in the brake/clutch master cylinder and top up if necessary (Chapter 9)
- [ ] Inspect the front brake pads for excessive wear and renew if necessary (Chapter 9)
- [ ] Check the fluid level in the power steering fluid reservoir and top up if necessary (Chapter 10)

- [ ] Check the brake system circuits for damage, corrosion and signs of leakage (Chapter 9)
- [ ] Check the battery terminals for security and signs of corrosion
- [ ] Where applicable, check the battery electrolyte level and top up if required (Chapter 12)
- [ ] Check the headlamps for satisfactory operation and adjustment (Chapter 12)
- [ ] Check the windscreen wipers and washers for satisfactory operation and the wiper blades for condition (Chapter 12) Check all the instruments for satisfactory operation

Every 12 000 miles (20 000 km) or annually, whichever comes first

- [ ] Renew the air filter element (Chapter 3)
- [ ] Check the rear brake linings (or pads if applicable) for wear (Chapter 9)
- [ ] Check the driveshaft bellows for condition (Chapter 8)
- [ ] Check the underbody for corrosion (Chapter 11)

Every 30 000 miles (50 000 km) or 2 1/2 years whichever comes first

- [ ] Renew the fuel filter (Chapter 3)
- [ ] Drain and renew the manual transmission oil (Chapter 6)
- [ ] Drain and renew the automatic transmission fluid. Renew the gauze filter (Chapter 7)
- [ ] Drain and renew the brake fluid (Chapter 9)
- [ ] Check and if necessary adjust the handbrake (Chapter 9)
- [ ] Check the condition of the steering and suspension components (Chapter 10)
- [ ] Check the wheel alignment (Chapter 10)
- [ ] Drain and renew the engine coolant (Chapter 2)

Every 72 000 miles (115 000 km)

- [ ] Renew the timing belt (Chapter 1)

Engine and underbonnet component locations - 1.7 litre model

1 Engine oil dipstick
2 Radiator and cooling fan
3 Oil filter
4 Radiator expansion tank cap
5 Alternator
6 Vehicle identification plates
7 Oil filler cap
8 Fuel filter
9 Brake master cylinder reservoir
10 Air cleaner
11 Coolant/heater feed and return hoses
12 Ignition distributor
13 Shock absorber turret
14 Ignition control module
15 Battery
16 Washer reservoir
17 Gearbox
18 Gearbox breather
19 Clutch cable

Engine and underbonnet component locations - 2.0 litre non-Turbo model

1 Engine oil dipstick
2 Battery
3 Vehicle identification plates
4 Shock absorber turret
5 Brake master cylinder reservoir
6 Steering gear unit
7 Engine oil filler cap
8 Ignition coil module
9 Heater coolant hose and bleed valve
10 Cooling system expansion bottle
11 Power steering fluid reservoir
12 Engine management computer
13 Air cleaner
14 Throttle casing
15 Throttle control linkage
16 Cooling system top hose/bleed valve/thermostat
17 Washer reservoir

Engine and underbonnet component locations - 2.0 litre Turbo model (turbocharger heat shield removed for clarity)

1 Engine oil dipstick
2 Turbocharger
3 Air cleaner
4 Engine oil filter mounting
5 Vehicle identification plates
6 Shock absorber turret

7 Brake/clutch master cylinder
   reservoir
8 Ignition coil module and
   distributor
9 ABS relays

10 Cooling system expansion
   bottle
11 Power steering fluid reservoir
12 Engine management computer
13 Engine oil filler cap
14 Battery

15 Washer reservoir
16 Throttle casing
17 Throttle control linkage
18 Coolant top hose/bleed
   valve/thermostat

Front underside view - 1.7 litre model (undershield removed)

1 Exhaust
2 Subframe
3 Steering gear

4 Driveshaft
5 Sump drain plug
6 Transmission undershield

7 Brake caliper
8 Suspension lower arm
9 Anti-roll bar

10 Steering arm
11 Gearchange rod

Front underside view - 2.0 litre model (undershield removed)

1 Washer reservoir
2 Sump and drain plug
3 Power steering pump unit
4 Alternator

5 Air cleaner intake hose
6 Driveshaft
7 Suspension lower arm
8 Subframe

9 Transmission mounting
10 Reverse selector cable
11 Exhaust
12 Gearchange selector

13 Transmission (undershield
   removed)
14 Brake caliper
15 Anti-roll bar

Rear underside view - 1.7 litre model

1 Fuel tank	4 Brake compensator unit	6 Rear axle beam	8 Heat shield
2 Shock absorber	5 Handbrake cables	7 Rear axle mounting	9 Exhaust
3 Torsion bar			

Rear underside view - 2.0 litre model

1 Fuel tank
2 Shock absorber
3 Rear axle beam
4 Fuel pump
5 Fuel pulse damper
6 Fuel filter
7 Brake compensator unit
8 Handbrake cables
9 Torsion bar
10 Exhaust
11 Rear axle mounting
12 Heat shield

Tyre conditon and pressure

It is very important that tyres are in good condition, and at the correct pressure - having a tyre failure at any speed is highly dangerous. Tyre wear is influenced by driving style - harsh braking and acceleration, or fast cornering, will all produce more rapid tyre wear. As a general rule, the front tyres wear out faster than the rears. Interchanging the tyres from front to rear ("rotating" the tyres) may result in more even wear. However, if this is completely effective, you may have the expense of replacing all four tyres at once!

Remove any nails or stones embedded in the tread before they penetrate the tyre to cause deflation. If removal of a nail does reveal that the tyre has been punctured, refit the nail so that its point of penetration is marked. Then immediately change the wheel, and have the tyre repaired by a tyre dealer.

Regularly check the tyres for damage in the form of cuts or bulges, especially in the sidewalls. Periodically remove the wheels, and clean any dirt or mud from the inside and outside surfaces. Examine the wheel rims for signs of rusting, corrosion or other damage. Light alloy wheels are easily damaged by "kerbing" whilst parking; steel wheels may also become dented or buckled. A new wheel is very often the only way to overcome severe damage.

New tyres should be balanced when they are fitted, but it may become necessary to re-balance them as they wear, or if the balance weights fitted to the wheel rim should fall off. Unbalanced tyres will wear more quickly, as will the steering and suspension components. Wheel imbalance is normally signified by vibration, particularly at a certain speed (typically around 50 mph). If this vibration is felt only through the steering, then it is likely that just the front wheels need balancing. If, however, the vibration is felt through the whole car, the rear wheels could be out of balance. Wheel balancing should be carried out by a tyre dealer or garage.

1 Tread Depth - visual check

The original tyres have tread wear safety bands (B), which will appear when the tread depth reaches approximately 1.6 mm. The band positions are indicated by a triangular mark on the tyre sidewall (A).

2 Tread Depth - manual check

Alternatively, tread wear can be monitored with a simple, inexpensive device known as a tread depth indicator gauge.

3 Tyre Pressure Check

Check the tyre pressures regularly with the tyres cold. Do not adjust the tyre pressures immediately after the vehicle has been used, or an inaccurate setting will result.

Tyre tread wear patterns

Shoulder Wear

Underinflation (wear on both sides)
Under-inflation will cause overheating of the tyre, because the tyre will flex too much, and the tread will not sit correctly on the road surface. This will cause a loss of grip and excessive wear, not to mention the danger of sudden tyre failure due to heat build-up.
Check and adjust pressures
Incorrect wheel camber (wear on one side)
Repair or renew suspension parts
Hard cornering
Reduce speed!

Centre Wear

Overinflation
Over-inflation will cause rapid wear of the centre part of the tyre tread, coupled with reduced grip, harsher ride, and the danger of shock damage occurring in the tyre casing.
Check and adjust pressures

If you sometimes have to inflate your car's tyres to the higher pressures specified for maximum load or sustained high speed, don't forget to reduce the pressures to normal afterwards.

Uneven Wear

Front tyres may wear unevenly as a result of wheel misalignment. Most tyre dealers and garages can check and adjust the wheel alignment (or "tracking") for a modest charge.
Incorrect camber or castor
Repair or renew suspension parts
Malfunctioning suspension
Repair or renew suspension parts
Unbalanced wheel
Balance tyres
Incorrect toe setting
Adjust front wheel alignment
Note: *The feathered edge of the tread which typifies toe wear is best checked by feel.*

Component or system	Lubricant type/ specification	Duckhams recommendation
1 Engine	Multigrade engine oil, viscosity SAE 10W/40, 15W/50, or 20W/50	Duckhams QXR, QS, Hypergrade Plus or Hypergrade
2 Manual transmission JB3 and NG9	Hypoid gear oil, viscosity SAE 80W to API GL5	Duckhams Hypoid 80W/90S
UN1	Hypoid gear oil, viscosity SAE 75W/90	Duckhams Hypoid 75W/90S
3 Automatic transmission	Dexron type ATF	Duckhams Uni-Matic
4 Brake/clutch fluid reservoir	Hydraulic fluid to SAE J1703F, DOT3 or DOT4	Duckhams Universal Brake and Clutch Fluid
5 Cooling system	Ethylene glycol based antifreeze with corrosion inhibitor to BS 3151, 3152, or 6580	Duckhams Antifreeze and Summer Coolant
6 Power steering fluid reservoir	Dexron type ATF	Duckhams Uni-Matic

Choosing your engine oil

Oils perform vital tasks in all engines. The higher the engine's performance, the greater the demand on lubricants to minimise wear as well as optimise power and economy. Duckhams tailors lubricants to the highest technical standards, meeting and exceeding the demands of all modern engines.

HOW ENGINE OIL WORKS

• Beating friction

Without oil, the surfaces inside your engine which rub together will heat, fuse and quickly cause engine seizure. Oil, and its special additives, forms a molecular barrier between moving parts, to stop wear and minimise heat build-up.

• Cooling hot spots

Oil cools parts that the engine's water-based coolant cannot reach, bathing the combustion chamber and pistons, where temperatures may exceed 1000°C. The oil assists in transferring the heat to the engine cooling system. Heat in the oil is also lost by air flow over the sump, and via any auxiliary oil cooler.

• Cleaning the inner engine

Oil washes away combustion by-products (mainly carbon) on pistons and cylinders, transporting them to the oil filter, and holding the smallest particles in suspension until they are flushed out by an oil change. Duckhams oils undergo extensive tests in the laboratory, and on the road.

OIL CARE
FOLLOW THE CODE
OIL BANK LINE
0800 66 33 66

Note: It is antisocial and illegal to dump oil down the drain. To find the location of your local oil recycling bank, call this number free.

Engine oil types

Mineral oils are the "traditional" oils, generally suited to older engines and cars not used in harsh conditions. *Duckhams Hypergrade Plus* and *Hypergrade* are well suited for use in most popular family cars.
Diesel oils such as *Duckhams Diesel* are specially formulated for Diesel engines, including turbocharged models and 4x4s.
Synthetic oils are the state-of-the-art in lubricants, offering ultimate protection, but at a fairly high price. One such is *Duckhams QS*, for use in ultra-high performance engines.
Semi-synthetic oils offer high performance engine protection, but at less cost than full synthetic oils. *Duckhams QXR* is an ideal choice for hot hatches and hard-driven cars.

For help with technical queries on lubricants, call Duckhams Oils on 0181 290 8207

DUCKHAMS

Chapter 1 Engine

For modifications, and information applicable to later models, see Supplement at end of manual

Contents

Degrees of difficulty

Easy, suitable for novice with little experience 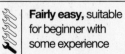 **Fairly easy,** suitable for beginner with some experience   **Fairly difficult,** suitable for competent DIY mechanic **Difficult,** suitable for experienced DIY mechanic **Very difficult,** suitable for expert DIY or professional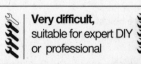

Specifications

Part A - 1721 cc (1.7 litre) engines

General

Type	Four cylinder, in-line, belt-driven overhead camshaft. Engine transversely mounted
Engine type designation	F2N

Engine code numbers and maximum power output:

F2N 712	76 bhp at 5000 rpm
F2N 710	90 bhp at 5500 rpm

Compression ratio:

F2N 712	9.2 : 1
F2N 710	10 : 1
Firing order	1-3-4-2 (No 1 cylinder at flywheel end)
Bore	81.0 mm
Stroke	83.5 mm
Capacity	1721 cc

Crankshaft

Number of main bearings	5
Main journal diameter	54.794 mm
Main journal minimum regrind diameter	54.545 mm
Crankpin journal diameter	48 mm
Crankpin journal minimum regrind diameter	47.75 mm
Crankshaft endfloat	0.07 to 0.23 mm
Thrust washer thicknesses available	2.30, 2.35, 2.40, 2.45 and 2.50 mm

Connecting rods

Connecting rod endfloat	0.22 to 0.40 mm

Pistons

Piston fitted direction	V or arrow on crown towards flywheel
Gudgeon pin fit in piston	Hand push-fit
Gudgeon pin fit in connecting rod	Interference
Gudgeon pin length	64.7 to 65.0 mm
Gudgeon pin outside diameter	21 mm
Piston clearance in cylinder bore	0.023 to 0.047 mm

Piston rings

Number	Three (two compression, one oil control)

Compression ring thickness:

Top ring	1.75 mm
Second ring	2.0 mm
Oil control ring thickness	3.0 mm
Piston ring end gaps	Supplied pre-set

Valves

Seat included angle:

Inlet	120°
Exhaust	90°

Head diameter:

Inlet	38.1 mm
Exhaust	32.5 mm
Stem diameter	8.0 mm
Valve seat width in cylinder head	1.5 to 1.9 mm
Valve head-to-cylinder head face recess depth (inlet and exhaust)	0.8 to 1.1 mm

Valve guides:

Bore diameter in cylinder head	12.99 mm
Fitted height above joint face	42.8 to 43.2 mm

Valve springs:

Free height	44.9 mm

Valve clearances (cold):

Inlet	0.20 mm (0.0079 in)
Exhaust	0.40 mm (0.0158 in)

Camshaft
Number of bearings 5
Endfloat . . . . 0.048 to 0.133 mm

Auxiliary shaft
Bush diameter:
    Inner . . . . 39.5 mm
    Outer . . . . 40.5 mm
Endfloat . . . . 0.07 to 0.15 mm

Tappets
Diameter . . . . 34.99 to 35.04 mm

Cylinder head
Maximum permitted warp . . . . 0.05 mm
Cylinder head height . . . . 169.3 to 169.7 mm

Lubrication system
Oil pump:
    Gear-to-body clearance . . . . 0.02 mm (maximum)
    Gear endfloat . . . . 0.085 mm (maximum)
System pressure (at 80°C):
    Idling . . . . 2.0 bar (29.0 lbf/in²)
    Running (at 3000 rpm) . . . . 3.5 bar (50.8 lbf/in²)
Oil type/specification . . . . Multigrade engine oil, viscosity SAE 10W/40, 15W/50, or 20W/50
Oil capacity (with filter renewal) . . . . 5.2 litres (9.15 pints)
Oil filter . . . . Champion F103

Torque wrench settings

	Nm	lbf ft
Cylinder head bolts:		
1st tightening	30	22
2nd tightening	70	52
1st retightening - wait 3 minutes, slacken all bolts then tighten to	20	15
2nd retightening	Turn through 123°	Turn through 123°
Main bearing cap bolts	65	48
Big-end bearing cap bolts	50	37
Flywheel retaining bolts	55	41
Camshaft bearing cap bolts:		
8 mm diameter	20	15
6 mm diameter	10	7
Camshaft sprocket bolt	50	37
Idler pulley bolt	20	15
Tensioner pulley nut	40	30
Auxiliary shaft sprocket bolt	50	37
Crankshaft pulley bolt	95	70
Oil pump-to-crankcase retaining bolts	25	18
Sump retaining bolts	15	11
Engine mounting nuts and bolts	40	30
Piston cooler oil jet bolts	30	22

Part B - 1995 cc (2.0 litre) engines

General
Type . . . . Four-cylinder, in-line, belt-driven overhead camshaft, light alloy construction with wet cylinder liners. Engine and transmission longitudinally mounted at the front of vehicle
Engine type designation J7R
Engine code numbers and maximum power output:
    J7R 750 and J7R 751 . . . . 120 bhp at 5500 rpm
    J7R 752 (Turbo model) . . . . 175 bhp at 5200 rpm
Compression ratio:
    J7R 750 and J7R 751 . . . . 10 : 1
    J7R 752 . . . . 8 : 1
Firing order . . . . 1-3-4-2 (No 1 cylinder at the flywheel end)
Bore . . . . 88.0 mm
Stroke . . . . 82.0 mm
Capacity . . . . 1995 cc
Compression pressure:
    Minimum . . . . 10.3 bar (149.4 lbf/in²)
    Maximum difference between cylinders . . . . 1.4 bar (20.3 lbf/in²)

Cylinder block
Material .... Light alloy
Overall depth .... 149.25 to 149.75 mm

Cylinder liners
Height .... 143.5 mm
Bore .... 88.0 mm
Base locating diameter .... 93.6 mm
Protrusion without O-ring .... 0.08 to 0.150 mm

Crankshaft
Number of main bearings 5
Main bearing journal diameter .... 62.880 mm
Main bearing journal minimum regrind diameter .... 62.630 mm
Crankpin diameter .... 52.296 mm
Crankpin minimum regrind diameter .... 52.046 mm
Crankshaft endfloat .... 0.07 to 0.25 mm

Connecting rods and gudgeon pins
Small-end play .... 0.31 to 0.57 mm
Gudgeon pins:
    Length .... 75.0 mm
    Diameter .... 23.0 mm

Piston rings
Piston ring thickness:
    Top compression .... 1.75 mm
    Second compression .... 2.0 mm
    Oil control .... 4.0 mm

Camshaft
Number of bearings 5
Endfloat .... 0.07 to 0.13 mm

Cylinder head
Material .... Light alloy
Overall height .... 111.6 mm
Maximum permitted surface distortion .... 0.05 mm

Timing belt
Deflection at midway point between auxiliary shaft sprocket and
camshaft sprocket:
    For belts with square tooth profile .... 5.5 to 7.0 mm
    For belts with round tooth profile .... 6.0 to 8.0 mm

Valves
Stem diameter .... 8.0 mm
Head diameter:
    Inlet .... 44.0 mm
    Exhaust .... 38.5 mm
Valve seat included angle:
    Inlet .... 120°
    Exhaust .... 90°
Valve seat width:
    Inlet .... 1.8 mm
    Exhaust .... 1.6 mm
Valve guides:
    Bore .... 8.0 mm
    Outside diameter (nominal) .... 13.0 m
    Repair oversizes:
        With one groove .... 13.10 mm
        With two grooves .... 13.25 mm
Valve springs:
    Free height .... 46.0 mm
Valve clearances (cold):
    Inlet .... 0.10 to 0.15 mm (0.004 to 0.006 in)
    Exhaust .... 0.20 to 0.25 mm (0.008 to 0.010 in)

Lubrication system

Oil pump:

Type .... Gear, driven from auxiliary shaft

Clearances:

Gear teeth to body .... 0.05 to 0.12 mm

Gear endfloat .... 0.02 to 0.10 mm

Oil pressure (at 80°C 176°F):

At idle:

J7R 750 and J7R 751 .... 0.8 bar (11.6 lbf/in²)

J7R 752 .... 1.0 bar (14.5 lbf/in²)

At 3000 rpm .... 3.0 bar (43.5 lbf/in²)

Oil type/specification .... Multigrade engine oil, viscosity SAE 10W/40, 15W/50, or 20W/50

Oil capacity (with filter renewal) .... 6.2 litres (10.9 pints)

Oil filter .... Champion F102

Torque wrench setting

	Nm	lbf ft
Cylinder head bolts:		
Stage 1	49	36
Stage 2	79	58
Stage 3 - slacken half a turn then tighten to	95	70
Run engine for 20 minutes, allow to cool fully then retighten bolts as described in Section 88		
Main bearing cap bolts	95	70
Big-end cap nuts	49	36
*Flywheel bolts	60	44
*Driveplate-to-crankshaft bolts	68	50
Driveplate-to-torque converter bolts	30	22
Crankshaft pulley bolt:		
Bolt shank length of 45 mm	80	59
Bolt shank length of 55 mm or greater	125	92
Auxiliary shaft sprocket bolt	49	36
Camshaft sprocket bolt	49	36
Oil pump fixing bolts	44	32
Oil pump cover bolts	12	9
Timing belt tensioner bolt and nut	25	18
Sump pan bolts	16	12
Flywheel or torque converter housing-to-engine bolts	54	40
Rocker shaft filter bolt	20	15
Engine mounting nuts and bolts	40	30

Smear bolt threads with locking fluid

PART A: 1721 CC (1.7 LITRE) ENGINE

1 General description

The engine is of four-cylinder, in-line overhead camshaft type, mounted transversely at the front of the car.

The crankshaft is supported in five shell type main bearings. Thrust washers are fitted to No 2 main bearing to control crankshaft endfloat. The connecting rods are attached to the crankshaft by horizontally split shell type big-end bearings, and to the pistons by interference fit gudgeon pins. The aluminium alloy pistons are of the slipper type and are fitted with three piston rings; two compression rings and a scraper type oil control ring.

The overhead camshaft is mounted directly in the cylinder head, and is driven by the crankshaft via a toothed rubber timing belt. The camshaft operated the valves via inverted bucket type tappets which operate in bores

Fig. 1.1 Cutaway view of the 1.7 litre engine (Sec 1)

Fig. 1.2 Sectional view of the 1.7 litre engine (Sec 1)

Fig. 1.3 Lubrication circuit with lower cylinder bore jets shown inset (Sec 1)

machined directly in the cylinder head. Valve clearance adjustment is by selected shims located externally between the tappet bucket and the cam lobe. The inlet and exhaust valves are mounted vertically in the cylinder head and are each closed by a single valve spring.

An auxiliary shaft located alongside the crankshaft is also driven by the toothed timing belt, and actuates the oil pump via a skew gear.

A semi-closed crankcase ventilation system is employed, and crankcase fumes are drawn from an oil separator on the cylinder block and passed via a hose to the inlet manifold.

Engine lubrication is by pressure feed from a gear type oil pump located beneath the crankshaft. Engine oil is fed through an externally-mounted oil filter to the main oil gallery feeding the crankshaft auxiliary shaft and camshaft. Oil jets are fitted to the lower end of each cylinder bore to lubricate and cool the pistons.

The distributor rotor and the fuel pump are driven by the camshaft; the rotor directly and the fuel pump via an eccentric and plunger.

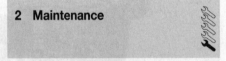

2 Maintenance

Carry out the following procedures at the intervals specified in the *'Routine*

maintenance' Section at the start of this manual.

General checks

1 At weekly intervals, check the engine oil level, preferably when the engine is cold.
2 Withdraw the dipstick, wipe it clean and re-insert it. Withdraw it for the second time and read off the oil level which should be between the low and high marks.
3 Top up if necessary through the cap on the camshaft cover.
4 Visually inspect the engine joint faces, gaskets, seals and related hoses for any sign of oil or water leaks. Pay particular attention to the areas around the camshaft cover, crankshaft oil seal carrier and sump joint faces. Rectify any leaks by referring to the appropriate Sections of this Chapter.

Engine oil and filter renewal

5 Run the engine for a few minutes to warm the oil, enabling it to drain more easily. Switch off, and remove the cap from the camshaft cover.
6 Position a suitable container underneath the engine sump drain plug. Unscrew and remove the plug using an 8 mm square head key as shown (photo).
7 When the oil has drained, unscrew and discard the oil filter. A filter removal tool (strap wrench) will be required for this. If one is not available, drive a large screwdriver through

Fig. 1.4 Engine oil level dipstick location (1) and oil filler cap (3) (Sec 2)

2.6 Sump plug removal using 8 mm square head key

2.7 Oil filter removal using a strap wrench

2.9 Topping-up the engine oil level

6 Engine and transmission - removal

the filter canister and use it as a lever to unscrew the filter (photo).

8 Smear the rubber sealing ring of the new filter with clean engine oil and tighten it fully by hand only.

9 Refit and tighten the sump drain plug. Refill the engine with the specified type and quantity of oil (photo), and refit the cap to the camshaft cover.

10 Start the engine, and run it for a few minutes to allow time for the new filter to fill with oil. Check for signs of any oil leaks from the filter joint.

11 Switch off, wait a few minutes and check the oil level on the dipstick. Top up as necessary to the full mark.

3 Major operations possible with the engine in the car

The following operations can be carried out without having to remove the engine from the car:

(a) Removal and refitting of the timing belt
(b) Removal and refitting of the camshaft
(c) Removal and refitting of the cylinder head
(d) Removal and refitting of the sump
(e) Removal and refitting of the oil pump
(f) Removal and refitting of the connecting rod and piston assemblies
(g) Removal and refitting of the engine mountings

Warning: Vehicles equipped with air conditioning:

Whenever overhaul of a major nature is being undertaken to the engine, and components of the air conditioning system obstruct the work, and such items of the system cannot be unbolted and moved aside sufficiently far within the limits of their flexible connecting pipes, before any components are disconnected or removed the system should be discharged by your dealer or a competent refrigeration engineer.

As the system must be completely evacuated before recharging, the necessary vacuum equipment to do this is

only likely to be available at a specialist establishment.

The refrigerant fluid is Freon 12 and although harmless under normal conditions, contact with the eyes or skin must be avoided. If Freon comes into contact with a naked flame, then a poisonous gas will be created which is injurious to health.

4 Major operations requiring engine removal

The following operations can only be carried out after removal of the engine from the car:

(a) Removal and refitting of the flywheel
(b) Removal and refitting of the crankshaft and main bearings
(c) Removal and refitting of the crankshaft rear oil seal
(d) Removal and refitting of the auxiliary shaft

Warning: Vehicles equipped with air conditioning. Refer to the warning note at the end of the previous Section.

5 Methods of engine removal

The engine and gearbox assembly can be lifted from the car as a complete unit, as described in the following Section, or the gearbox may first be removed, as described in Chapter 6.

Although it may be feasible to remove the engine leaving the transmission in position, it is not considered practical. The reason for this is that most of the transmission fittings and attachments will need to be disconnected in order to allow the engine and transmission to be separated (and subsequently reconnected). It is therefore considered more practical to remove the two units as an assembly and then to separate them.

Warning: Vehicles equipped with air conditioning. Refer to the warning note at the end of Section 3.

1 Disconnect the battery negative terminal, then remove the bonnet, as described in Chapter 11.
2 Remove the radiator, as described in Chapter 2.
3 Remove the air cleaner, as described in Chapter 3.
4 Drain the engine oil into a suitable container for disposal. An 8 mm square head key is required to remove the sump drain plug. When the oil has drained, refit and tighten the drain plug and remove the container.
5 Unbolt and detach the undershield from the transmission, then unscrew the gearbox drain plug and drain the oil into a suitable container. When the oil has drained, refit and tighten the drain plug.
6 Improved access to some components may be gained by unbolting and removing the front undershield from the underside of the vehicle.
7 Slacken the hose clips and disconnect the two heater hoses at their connections on the engine.
8 Release the clip securing the choke cable to its support bracket on the carburettor and disconnect the cable end loop from the stud on the linkage.
9 Open the throttle and slip the accelerator cable out of the slot on the linkage bellcrank. Release the outer cable from its support bracket and move the cable to one side.
10 Disconnect the fuel feed and return pipes at the fuel pump and plug their ends (photo).
11 Disconnect the ignition HT cable from the centre of the distributor cap.
12 Detach the ignition vacuum pipe at the carburettor.
13 Detach the brake servo vacuum hose from the rear of the inlet manifold.
14 Note the locations of the wiring at the rear of the alternator and disconnect the wires.
15 Note the wiring locations at the starter

6.10 Detach the hoses from the fuel pump (arrowed)

6.15 Disconnect the starter motor solenoid wires (arrowed)

6.16 Detach the lead from the oil temperature sensor

6.17 Engine angular position sensor and retaining bolts

Fig. 1.5 Drive the roll pins from the right-hand driveshaft using a pin punch (arrowed) (Sec 6)

Fig. 1.6 Undo the three retaining bolts (arrowed) to detach the left-hand driveshaft (Sec 6)

motor solenoid and disconnect the wires (photo).

16 Disconnect the lead at the water temperature gauge sender unit on the cylinder head, and the lead at the oil temperature sensor on the front facing side of the cylinder block (photo).

17 Undo the two shouldered bolts and remove the angular position/speed sensor from its location at the top of the bellhousing (photo). Unclip the sensor lead from the transmission breather hose, then fold the lead back out of the way.

18 Disconnect the engine and transmission earth straps (photos).

19 Disconnect the reversing light switch lead from the transmission.

20 All the wiring to the engine and transmission should now have been disconnected and, after releasing the clips and ties, it should be possible to move the complete wiring harness to one side.

21 Withdraw the spring wire and retaining clip securing the speedometer cable to the transmission at the rear, and remove the cable. Note the fitted direction of the clip (photos).

22 Disconnect the clutch cable from the release fork and the bracket on the bellhousing.

23 Apply the handbrake, and raise and support the front end of the vehicle on axle stands. Unbolt and remove the front roadwheels.

24 Undo the two retaining nuts and detach the exhaust downpipe from the manifold (photo).

6.18A Earth strap connection to transmission

6.18B Earth strap connection to transmission mounting

6.21A Extract the retaining clip (arrowed) . . .

6.21B . . . and withdraw the speedometer cable

6.24 Exhaust downpipe connection to manifold (arrowed)

25 Disconnect the gearchange rod from the fork control shaft. To do this, cut free the nylon retainer strap from the gaiter (taking care not to damage the gaiter), fold back the gaiter, then undo the link nut (photo).

26 Drive out the roll pin securing the right-hand driveshaft inner joint to the differential stub shaft, using a pin punch. Note that there are in fact two roll pins, one inside the other.

27 Undo the three bolts securing the left-hand driveshaft inner joint bellows and retaining plate to the side of the transmission.

28 Disconnect the steering arm outer balljoints as described in Chapter 10.

29 On each side of the vehicle, undo the two retaining nuts securing the shock absorber to the hub carrier, and remove the upper bolt. This will allow the hub carrier to pivot sufficiently to enable the driveshaft to be withdrawn from the transmission, leaving it attached to the hub carrier at its outboard end. Take care not to strain the brake hydraulic hoses. Allow for oil leakage from the transmission as the driveshafts are disengaged.

30 Temporarily reconnect the shock absorbers and the steering arm balljoints to the hub carriers to enable the vehicle to rest on its roadwheels during engine and transmission removal. Refit the front roadwheels.

31 Lower the car to the ground and make a final check that all cables, pipes and components likely to impede removal have been detached and moved aside.

32 Attach a crane or hoist to the engine using chain or rope slings, or secure the chains or ropes to the engine lifting brackets.

33 Undo the retaining nuts and detach the engine stabilizer from the front of the subframe.

34 Unbolt and detach the rear engine mounting.

35 Unbolt and detach the right-hand engine mounting (underneath the alternator).

36 Unbolt and detach the left-hand engine/transmission mounting.

37 Check that all engine and transmission fittings and associated attachments are disconnected and out of the way.

38 Slowly lift the engine and transmission assembly, moving it around as necessary to clear all obstructions. When high enough, lift it over the front body panel and lower the unit to the ground (photo).

7 Engine - separation from transmission

1 Unbolt and remove the 'U'-shaped support bar from the underside of the sump. It is secured by five bolts, one on each side of the crankcase, one on each side of the transmission housing, and one underneath the transmission housing (photos).

2 Unbolt and remove the starter motor heat

6.25 Fold back gaiter and disconnect the gearchange rod

shield. Unbolt and remove the starter motor.

3 Undo the retaining bolts and remove the cover plate from the base of the transmission bellhousing.

4 Unscrew and remove the remaining engine-to-transmission bellhousing bolts, noting the bolt lengths and locations, also the location of wiring retainer clips and the rear engine mounting bracket.

5 Support the engine and withdraw the transmission from it, supporting its weight so that the input shaft is not strained. The transmission may initially be stuck on the location dowels, in which case tap it free using a piece of wood.

8 Engine dismantling - general

1 If possible, mount the engine on a stand for the dismantling procedure, but, failing this, support it in an upright position with blocks of wood placed under each side of the sump or crankcase.

2 Drain any remaining oil into a suitable container before cleaning the engine for major dismantling.

3 Cleanliness is most important, and if the engine is dirty it should be cleaned with paraffin or a suitable solvent while keeping it in an upright position.

4 Avoid working with the engine directly on a concrete floor, as grit presents a real source of trouble.

7.1A Undo the support bar mounting bolts at the side (arrowed) . . .

6.38 Engine and transmission removal

5 As parts are removed, clean them in a paraffin bath. However, do not immerse parts with internal oilways in paraffin as it is difficult to remove, usually requiring a high pressure hose.

HAYNES HiNT *Clean oilways with nylon pipe cleaners.*

6 It is advisable to have suitable containers to hold small items, as this will help when reassembling the engine and also prevent possible losses.

7 Always obtain complete sets of gaskets when the engine is being dismantled, but retain the old gaskets with a view to using them as a pattern to make a replacement if a new one is not available. Note that in many instances a gasket is not used, but instead the joints are sealed with an RTV sealant. It is recommended that a tube of CAF 4/60 THIXO paste, obtainable from Renault dealers, be obtained as it is specially formulated for this purpose.

8 When possible, refit nuts, bolts and washers in their location after being removed, as this helps to protect the threads and will also be helpful when reassembling the engine.

9 Retain unserviceable components in order to compare them with the new parts supplied.

10 The operations described in this Chapter are a step by step sequence, assuming that the engine is to be completely dismantled for major overhaul or repair. Where an operation

7.1B . . . and underneath (undershield shown still fitted)

1

Fig. 1.7 Typical 'Torx' socket bits required for engine overhaul (Sec 8)

can be carried out with the engine in the car, the dismantling necessary to gain access to the component concerned is described separately.

11 Socket-headed multi-point 'Torx' bolts and screws are used extensively in the construction of the engine, and a set of suitable wrenches will be essential.

9 Ancillary components - removal

With the engine separated from the gearbox or transmission the externally-mounted ancillary components, as given in the following list, can be removed. In most cases removal is straightforward, but further information will be found in the relevant Chapters.

Inlet and exhaust manifolds and carburettor
  (Chapter 3)
Fuel pump (Chapter 3)
Alternator (Chapter 12)
Spark plugs (Chapter 4)
Distributor (Chapter 4)
Water pump (Chapter 2)
Clutch (Chapter 5)

10.2 Timing belt cover removal

Oil filter (Section 2 of this Chapter)
Engine front mounting bracket (Section 23 of
  this Chapter)

10 Timing belt - removal

1 If the engine is in the car, first carry out the following operations:
(a) Disconnect the battery negative lead
(b) Remove the air cleaner
(c) Remove the alternator drivebelt
(d) Pull free the fuel filter from its mounting clip on the side face of the timing belt cover, and position it out of the way, leaving the fuel lines attached

2 Undo the four bolts and lift off the timing belt cover (photo).

3 Note the location of the timing mark on the outer edge of the camshaft sprocket. Using a socket or spanner on the crankshaft pulley bolt, turn the crankshaft until the camshaft sprocket timing mark is uppermost and in line with a corresponding mark or notch on the metal plate behind the sprocket.

4 Again using a socket or spanner, undo the crankshaft pulley retaining bolt and withdraw

the pulley. If the engine is in the car, the crankshaft can be prevented from turning by engaging top gear and firmly applying the handbrake. If the engine is out of the car, lock the flywheel ring gear using a wide-bladed screwdriver or strip of angle iron between the ring gear teeth and the long stud on the side of the cylinder block.

5 Remove the plug on the lower front facing side of the engine, at the flywheel end, and obtain a metal rod which is a snug fit in the plug hole. Turn the crankshaft slightly as necessary to the TDC position then push the rod through the hole to locate in the slot in the crankshaft web. Make sure that the crankshaft is exactly at TDC for No 1 piston by aligning the timing notch on the flywheel with the bellhousing mark, or the mark on the camshaft sprocket with the corresponding mark on the metal plate. If the crankshaft is not positioned accurately, it is possible to engage the rod with a balance hole in the crankshaft web which is not the TDC slot (Fig. 1.9).

Fig. 1.9 Timing marks on belt and sprocket must align with those on backing plate when crankshaft is at TDC (No 1 cylinder on compression). Note metal rod used to locate crankshaft (Sec 10)

Fig. 1.8 Timing belt, sprocket and pulley components (Sec 10)

11.11 Hose support plate on the side of the cylinder head (securing nuts arrowed)

Fig. 1.10 Using a hexagonal socket bit to remove the cylinder head retaining bolts (Sec 11)

Fig. 1.11 Remove the cylinder head by tapping upwards using a block of wood or a plastic mallet (Sec 11)

6 Double check that the camshaft sprocket timing mark is aligned with the corresponding mark on the metal plate. If the plate does not have a mark, make one now using paint or by accurately scribing a line aligned with the mark on the sprocket. Also check that there are arrows indicating the running direction of the belt, located between the auxiliary shaft sprocket and the idler pulley. Some belts also have their own timing marks and if so these marks should also be aligned with the marks on the sprocket and plate.

7 Slacken the tensioner pulley retaining nut and rotate the tensioner body until the belt is slack.

8 Slip the timing belt off the sprockets and pulleys and remove it from the engine.

11 Cylinder head - removal (engine in car)

1 Disconnect the battery earth (negative) lead.

2 Drain the engine coolant as described in Chapter 2.

3 Remove the air cleaner unit as described in Chapter 3.

4 Detach the HT leads from the spark plugs, then detach and remove the distributor cap.

5 Remove the timing belt as described in the previous Section.

6 Disconnect the lead at the water temperature gauge sender on the cylinder head.

7 Disconnect the fuel feed and return pipes at the fuel pump and plug their ends.

8 Open the throttle linkage by hand and slip the accelerator cable end out of the slot on the linkage bellcrank connector. Release the accelerator cable from its support bracket and move the cable clear.

9 Release the choke cable looped end from the stud on the linkage and detach the support clip from the carburettor bracket.

10 Disconnect the brake servo vacuum hose from the inlet manifold.

11 Disconnect the heater hoses, crankcase ventilation hoses and the two nuts securing the support plate to the rear facing side of the cylinder head (photo).

12 Disconnect the radiator top hose from the thermostat housing.

13 Undo the two bolts and withdraw the tension springs securing the exhaust front section to the manifold.

14 Undo the three domed nuts, lift off the washers and withdraw the the camshaft cover

from the cylinder head. Recover the gasket.

15 Undo the top retaining bolt securing the timing case backing plate to the end face of the cylinder head.

16 Using a suitable hexagon-headed socket bit, slacken the cylinder head retaining bolts, half a turn at a time in the reverse order to that shown in Fig. 1.32. When the tension has been relieved, remove all the bolts.

17 Lift the cylinder head, complete with manifolds and carburettor upwards and off the engine. If it is stuck, tap it upwards using a hammer and block of wood (Fig. 1.11). Do not try to turn it as it is located by two dowels and make no attempt whatsoever to prise it free using a screwdriver inserted between the block and head faces.

12 Cylinder head - removal (engine on bench)

The procedure for removing the cylinder head with the engine on the bench is similar to that for removal when the engine is in the car, with the exception of disconnecting the controls and services Remove the timing belt, as described in Section 10, then refer to Section 11 and follow the procedure given in paragraphs 11, then 14 to 17.

13 Camshaft and tappets - removal

1 If the engine is in the car, first carry out the following operations:
(a) Remove the timing belt
(b) Remove the distributor cap (Chapter 4)
(c) Remove the camshaft cover
(d) Remove the fuel pump (Chapter 3)

2 Undo the bolt securing the camshaft sprocket to the camshaft and withdraw the sprocket. The camshaft may be prevented from turning during this operation by holding it between the cam lobes using grips or, preferably, by wrapping an old timing belt around the sprocket, clamping the belt tight and holding securely (Fig. 1.13). With the

Fig. 1.12 Cylinder head, camshaft and associated components (Sec 11)

Fig. 1.13 Hold the camshaft sprocket with an old timing belt, then remove the sprocket retaining bolt followed, if necessary, by the idler pulley (Sec 13)

1

Fig. 1.14 Undo the two bolts and remove the sprocket metal backing plate. Also remove the Woodruff key if loose (Sec 13)

Fig. 1.15 Mark the camshaft bearing caps, then remove the retaining bolts (Sec 13)

Fig. 1.16 Keep the tappet buckets and shims in strict order of removal (Sec 13)

sprocket removed, check whether the locating Woodruff key is likely to drop out of its camshaft groove and if it is, remove it and store it safely.

3 Undo the two bolts securing the metal sprocket backing plate to the cylinder head and remove the plate.

4 Number the camshaft bearing caps 1 to 5 with No 1 nearest the flywheel, and also mark them with an arrow pointing towards the flywheel, to indicate their fitted direction.

5 Progressively slacken all the camshaft bearing cap retaining bolts and, when all are slack, remove them from the caps.

6 Lift off the five bearing caps and then remove the camshaft complete with oil seals from the cylinder head.

7 Withdraw the tappet buckets, complete with shims, from their bores in the head. Lay the buckets out on a sheet of cardboard numbered 1 to 8 with No 1 at the flywheel end. It is a good idea to write the shim thickness size on the card alongside each bucket in case the shims are accidentally knocked off their buckets and mixed up. The size is stamped on the shim bottom face.

14 Cylinder head - dismantling

1 If the cylinder head has been removed with the engine in the car, remove the following associated components from it, referring to the appropriate Chapter for further details where necessary.

Fig. 1.17 Oil pump retaining bolt locations (Sec 16)

(a) Carburettor, inlet and exhaust manifolds (Chapter 3)
(b) Fuel pump (Chapter 3)
(c) Water temperature gauge sender unit
(d) Hose support bracket on the side face of the cylinder head
(e) Camshaft and tappets (see previous Section)
(f) Thermostat (Chapter 2)

2 Using a valve spring compressor, compress each valve spring in turn until the split collets can be removed. Release the compressor and lift off the cap, spring and spring seat.

 HAYNES HiNT *If, when the valve spring compressor is screwed down, the valve spring cap refuses to free and expose the split collets, gently tap the top of the tool, directly over the cap with a light hammer. This will free the cap.*

3 Withdraw the oil seal off the top of the valve guide, and then remove the valve through the combustion chamber.

4 It is essential that the valves are kept in their correct sequence unless they are so badly worn that they are to be renewed. If they are going to be kept and used again, place them in a sheet of card having eight

Fig. 1.18 Auxiliary shaft housing retaining bolt locations, oil pump driveshaft and cover plate (Sec 17)

holes numbered 1 to 8 - corresponding to the relative fitted positions of the valves. Note that No 1 valve is nearest to the flywheel end of the engine.

15 Sump - removal

1 If the engine is in the car, first carry out the following operations:

(a) Unscrew the drain plug and drain the engine oil into a suitable container for disposal
(b) Detach and remove the undertray just forward of the engine for improved access (if necessary)
(c) Undo the retaining bolts and remove the 'U'-shaped support bracket from the underside of the sump (see Section 7, paragraph 1)

2 Undo and remove the bolts securing the sump to the crankcase. Tap the sump with a hide or plastic mallet to break the seal between sump flange and crankcase, and remove the sump. Note that a gasket is not used, only a sealing compound.

16 Oil pump - removal

1 If the oil pump is to be removed with the engine in the car, first remove the sump (see previous Section).

2 Undo the four retaining bolts at the ends of the pump body and withdraw the pump from the crankcase and drivegear. Note that no gasket is fitted between the mating faces of the pump and crankcase.

17 Auxiliary shaft - removal

1 The engine must be removed from the car for this operation to allow clearance for the withdrawal of the auxiliary shaft.

Fig. 1.19 Crankshaft front plate retaining bolt locations (Sec 18)

Fig. 1.20 Number the connecting rods and caps before removal (Sec 19)

Fig. 1.21 Removing the No 1 main bearing cap bolts (Sec 21)

2 Remove the timing belt as described in Section 10.
3 Undo the retaining bolt and remove the washer securing the sprocket to the auxiliary shaft. Hold the sprocket with an old timing belt, tightly clamped and securely held while undoing the bolt.
4 Withdraw the sprocket using two screwdrivers as levers to ease it off. If it is very tight use a two-legged puller. Recover the Woodruff key if it is not securely located in its groove.
5 Undo the retaining bolts and remove the timing case backing plate.
6 Undo the four bolts and withdraw the auxiliary shaft housing.
7 At the top undo the two bolts and withdraw the oil pump drivegear cover plate. Screw a suitable bolt into the oil pump drivegear or use a tapered wooden shaft and withdraw the drivegear from its location.
8 Undo the two bolts and washers and lift out the auxiliary shaft retaining plate and the auxiliary shaft.

18 Crankshaft front plate - removal

1 If the engine is in the car, first carry out the following operations:
(a) *Remove the timing belt (Section 10) and the timing case backing plate*
(b) *Remove the sump (Section 15)*
2 Withdraw the crankshaft sprocket using two screwdrivers carefully as levers, or by using a suitable puller. Remove the Woodruff key.
3 Undo the bolts securing the front plate to the cylinder block and withdraw the plate, noting that it is located by dowels in the two lower bolt hole locations (Fig. 1.19).

19 Pistons, connecting rods and big-end bearings - removal

1 If the engine is in the car, first carry out the following operations:
(a) *Remove the sump (Section 15)*

(b) *Remove the oil pump (Section 16)*
(c) *Remove the cylinder head (not necessary if only the big-end bearings are to be removed) (Section 11 or 12)*
2 Rotate the crankshaft so that No 1 big-end cap (nearest the flywheel) is at the lowest point of its travel. Using a centre punch, number the cap and rod on the auxiliary shaft side to indicate the cylinder to which they are fitted.
3 Undo and remove the big-end bearing cap bolts and withdraw the cap, complete with shell bearing from the connecting rod. If only the bearing shells are being attended to, push the connecting rod up and off the crankpin then remove the upper bearing shell. Keep the bearing shells and cap together in their correct sequence if they are to be refitted.
4 Push the connecting rod up and withdraw the piston and connecting rod assembly from the top of the cylinder block.
5 Now repeat these operations on the remaining three piston and connecting rod assemblies.

20 Flywheel - removal

1 Lock the crankshaft using a strip of angle iron between the ring gear teeth and the engine dowel bolt, or a block of wood between one of the crankshaft counterweights and the crankcase.
2 The flywheel retaining bolt holes are not symmetrical so there is no need to mark the fitting position of the flywheel. Undo the retaining bolts and withdraw the flywheel.

21 Crankshaft and main bearings - removal

1 Before removing the crankshaft and bearings, first check the endfloat of the crankshaft to assess for excessive wear. This procedure is described in Section 28.
2 Identification numbers should be cast onto the base of each main bearing cap, but if not, number the cap and crankcase using a centre punch.

3 Undo and remove the main bearing cap retaining bolts, noting that a hexagonal socket bit will be needed for No 1 main bearing cap bolts. Withdraw the caps and the bearing shell lower halves.
4 Carefully lift the crankshaft from the crankcase.
5 Remove the thrust washers from each side of No 2 main bearing then remove the bearing shell upper halves from the crankcase. Place each shell with its respective bearing cap.
6 Oil jets are located within the crankcase at the lower end of each cylinder bore. These can be unbolted and removed for cleaning in petrol if necessary, but note the fitted position of each jet (see inset in Fig. 1.3).

22 Crankshaft rear oil seal - renewal

1 With the engine removed from the car and separated from the gearbox (if applicable), remove the flywheel.
2 Clean the area around the crankshaft rear oil seal, then use a screwdriver to prise it from the block and bearing cap.
3 Wipe clean the oil seal recess. Dip the new oil seal in clean engine oil and carefully install it over the crankshaft rear journal. Take great care not to damage the delicate lip of the seal and make sure that the seal open face is towards the engine.

HAYNES HiNT

A polythene shim can be temporarily used to protect the crankshaft rear oil seal when fitting.

23.3A Engine mounting bracket removal

23.3B Transmission mounting

23.4A Engine stabilizer bracket removal from subframe

23.4B Engine stabilizer and retaining bolts

4 Using a tube of suitable diameter, a block of wood or the old seal, install the new seal squarely into its location until the outer face is flush with the block and bearing cap. If the original seal has worn a groove in the journal, drive the seal in a further 3 mm (0.12 in).
5 Refit the flywheel and the engine, as described in the applicable Sections of this Chapter.

23 Engine/transmission mountings - renewal

1 The engine and transmission flexible mountings may be renewed with the units in the car.

2 Support the engine or transmission securely on a jack using a block of wood as an insulator.
3 Renew only one mounting at a time by unscrewing the through-bolt nuts and unbolting the mounting bracket from the crankcase, transmission casing or body member (photos).
4 A stabilizer/bracket is fitted, and is located at the front between engine and subframe. Removal is simply a matter of undoing the retaining bolts (photos).
5 Refitting is the reverse sequence to removal.

24 Crankcase ventilation system - description

The layout of the crankcase ventilation system is shown in the accompanying illustration (Fig. 1.22).
When the engine is idling, or under partial load conditions, the high depression in the inlet manifold draws the crankcase fumes (diluted by air from the air cleaner) through the calibrated restrictor and into the combustion chambers.
The system ensures that there is always a partial vacuum in the crankcase, and so prevents a build-up of pressure which could cause oil contamination, fume emission and

oil leakage past seals. An oil separator unit is fitted between the crankcase (to which it is attached) and the main hose to the three-way union.
The only maintenance required on this system is to ensure that the hoses and connections are in good condition, secure and clean.

25 Examination and renovation

1 With the engine completely stripped, clean all the components and examine them for wear. Each part should be checked and where necessary, renewed or renovated, as described in the following Sections.

Cylinder block and crankcase

2 The cylinder bores must be examined for taper, ovality, scoring and scratches. Start by examining the top of the bores; if these are worn, a slight ridge will be found which marks the top of the piston ring travel. If the wear is excessive, the engine will have had a high oil consumption rate accompanied by blue smoke from the exhaust.
3 If available, use an inside dial gauge to measure the bore diameter just below the ridge and compare it with the diameter at the bottom of the bore, which is not subject to wear. If the difference is more than 0.152 mm the cylinders will normally require boring with new oversize pistons fitted.
4 Provided the cylinder bore wear does not exceed 0.203 mm, special oil control rings and pistons can be fitted to restore compression and stop the engine burning oil.
5 If new pistons are being fitted to old bores it is essential to roughen the bore walls slightly with fine glasspaper to enable the new piston rings to bed in properly. Only a crosshatch diagonal honing pattern must be used (not vertical).
6 Thoroughly examine the crankcase and cylinder bores for cracks and damage and use a piece of wire to probe all oilways and waterways to ensure they are unobstructed.

1 Oil separator
2 Hose from oil separator to 3-way union
3 Air filter unit
4 Filter to 3-way union hose
5 Hose from 3-way union to carburettor
6 3-way union
7 1.7 mm diameter jet
8 7.0 mm diameter jet

Fig. 1.22 Engine crankcase ventilation system (Sec 24)

Fig. 1.23 Piston diameter measuring point – A = 53.8 mm (Sec 25)

Pistons and connecting rods

7 Examine the pistons for ovality, scoring and scratches, and for wear of the piston ring grooves.

8 If the pistons or connecting rods are to be renewed it is necessary to have this work carried out by a Renault dealer or suitable engineering works who will have the necessary tooling to remove the gudgeon pins.

9 If a single piston only is being renewed, ensure that the replacement has identical type markings on its crown to the piston it replaces (photo). The piston diameter is measured at the point indicated in Fig. 1.23.

10 If new rings are to be fitted to the original pistons, expand the old rings over the top of the pistons (photo). The use of two or three old feeler blades will be helpful in preventing the rings dropping into empty grooves.

11 Before fitting the new rings, ensure that the ring grooves in the piston are free of carbon by cleaning them using an old ring. Break the ring in half to do this.

12 Install the new rings by fitting them over the top of the piston, starting with the oil control scraper ring. Note that the second compression ring is tapered and must be fitted with the word TOP uppermost (photo).

13 With all the rings in position, space the ring gaps at 120° to each other (Fig. 1.24).

Crankshaft

14 Examine the crankpin and main journal surfaces for signs of scoring or scratches, and check the ovality and taper of the crankpins

Fig. 1.24 Piston ring fitting diagram (Sec 25)

1 Top compression ring
2 Second compression ring
3 Oil control ring

and main journals. If the bearing surface dimensions do not fall within the tolerance ranges given in the Specifications at the beginning of this Chapter, the crankpins and/or main journals will have to be reground.

15 Big-end and crankpin wear is accompanied by distinct metallic knocking, particularly noticeable when the engine is pulling from low revs, and some loss of oil pressure.

16 Main bearing and main journal wear is accompanied by severe engine vibration rumble - getting progressively worse as engine revs increase and again by loss of oil pressure.

17 If the crankshaft requires regrinding take it to an engine reconditioning specialist, who will machine it for you and supply the correct undersize bearing shells.

Big-end and main bearing shells

18 Inspect the big-end and main bearing shells for signs of general wear, scoring, pitting and scratches. The bearings should be matt grey in colour. With lead-indium bearings, should a trace of copper colour be noticed, the bearings are badly worn as the lead bearing material has worn away to expose the indium underlay. Renew the bearings if they are in this condition or if there are any signs of scoring or pitting.

19 The undersizes available are designed to correspond with crankshaft regrind sizes. The bearings are in fact, slightly more than the stated undersize as running clearances have been allowed for during their manufacture.

20 Main and big-end bearing shells can be identified as to size by the marking on the back of the shell. Standard size shell bearings are marked STD or.00, undersize shells are marked with the undersize such as 0.020 u/s. This marking method applies only to replacement bearing shells and not to those used during production.

Camshaft and tappets

21 Examine the camshaft bearing surfaces and cam lobes for wear ridges, pitting or scoring. Renew the camshaft if any of these conditions are apparent.

22 The oil seals at each end of the camshaft should be renewed as a matter of course. To change the oil seal at the flywheel end of the camshaft, the distributor rotor and endplate must first be removed. Unfortunately the rotor is bonded to the end of the camshaft with a special adhesive and can only be removed by breaking it. Having done this the seal and endplate can be slid off. With two new oil seals, new rotor and a quantity of the special adhesive, available from Renault dealers, the new seals can be fitted. Lubricate their seal lips, then carefully slip them over the camshaft journals, ensuring that their open sides face the camshaft. Refit the endplate, then bond the new rotor to the camshaft. After fitting the new oil seals, store the camshaft in such a way that the weight of the camshaft is not resting on the oil seals.

23 Examine the camshaft bearings and bearing caps in the cylinder head. The camshaft runs directly in the aluminium housings and separate bearing shells are not used. Check the housings and caps for signs of wear ridges or deep scoring. Any excessive

25.9 Marks on piston crown

25.10 Remove the piston rings from the top of the pistons

25.12 The word TOP (arrowed) indicates the second compression ring upper face

25.25 Auxiliary shaft components

25.27 Auxiliary shaft housing and oil seal

25.28 Prising out oil seal from crankshaft front plate

25.29 Oil seal installed in crankshaft front plate. Note orientation

wear in these areas will mean a new cylinder head.

24 Finally, inspect the tappet buckets and the shims for scoring, pitting, especially on the shims, and wear ridges. Renew any components as necessary. Note that some scuffing and discoloration of the tappets is to be expected and is acceptable providing that the tappets are not scored.

Auxiliary shaft and bearings

25 Examine the auxiliary shaft and oil pump driveshaft for pitting, scoring or wear ridges on the bearing journals and for chipping or wear of the gear teeth. Renew as necessary (photo).

26 Check the auxiliary shaft bearings in the

cylinder block for wear and, if worn, have these renewed by your Renault dealer or a suitably equipped engineering works.

27 Clean off all traces of old gasket from the auxiliary shaft housing and tap out the oil seal using a tube of suitable diameter. Install the new oil seal using a block of wood and tap it in until it is flush with the outer face of the housing. The open side of the seal must be towards the engine (photo).

Crankshaft front plate

28 Check the front plate for signs of distortion or damage to the threads. If serviceable, clean off all traces of sealant and prise or tap out the oil seal using a tube of suitable diameter (photo).

29 Fit a new seal so that it is flush with the outer face of the front plate using a block of wood. Ensure that the open side of the seal is fitted towards the engine (photo).

Timing belt, sprockets and tensioner

30 Examine the timing belt carefully for any signs of cracking, fraying or general wear, particularly at the roots of the teeth. Renew the belt if there is any sign of deterioration of this nature, or if there is any oil or grease contamination.

31 Also inspect the timing sprockets for cracks or chipping of the teeth. Handle the sprockets with care as they may easily fracture if they are dropped or sharply knocked. Renew the sprockets if they are in any way damaged.

32 Check that the idler and tensioner pulleys rotate freely with no trace of roughness or

harshness and without excessive free play. Renew if necessary.

Oil pump

33 Undo the retaining bolts and lift off the pump cover.

34 Withdraw the idler gear and the drivegear and shaft.

35 Extract the retaining clip and remove the oil pressure relief valve spring retainer, spring, spring seat and plunger.

36 Clean the components and carefully examine the gears, pump body and relief valve plunger for any signs of scoring or wear. Renew the pump if these conditions are apparent.

37 If the components appear serviceable, measure the clearance between the pump body and the gears and also the gear endfloat using feeler gauges. If the clearances exceed the specified tolerance. the pump must be renewed (Figs. 1.26 and 1.27).

38 If the pump is satisfactory, reassemble the components in the reverse order of removal, fill the pump with oil and refit the cover.

Flywheel

39 Examine the flywheel for scoring of the clutch face and for chipping of the ring gear teeth. If the clutch face is scored, the flywheel may be machined until flat, but renewal is preferable. If the ring gear is worn or damaged it may be renewed separately, but this job is best left to a Renault dealer or engineering works. The temperature to which the new ring gear must be heated for installation is critical, and if not done accurately the hardness of the teeth will be destroyed.

Fig. 1.26 Check clearance between the gears and oil pump body (A) (Sec 25)

Fig. 1.27 Check the oil pump gear endfloat (B) (Sec 25)

Fig. 1.25 Exploded view of the oil pump components (Sec 25)

26 Cylinder head and pistons - decarbonizing, valve grinding and renovation

1 The operation will normally only be required at comparatively high mileages. However, if persistent pinking occurs and performance has deteriorated, even though the engine adjustments are correct, decarbonizing and valve grinding may be required.

2 With the cylinder head removed, use a scraper to remove the carbon from the combustion chambers and ports. Remove all traces of gasket from the cylinder head surface, then wash it thoroughly with paraffin.

3 Use a straight-edge and feeler blade to check that the cylinder head surface is not distorted. If it is, it must be resurfaced by a suitably equipped engineering works.

4 If the engine is still in the car, clean the piston crowns and cylinder bore upper edges, but make sure that no carbon drops between the pistons and bores. To do this, locate two of the pistons at the top of their bores and seal off the remaining bores with paper and masking tape. Press a little grease between the two pistons and their bores to collect any carbon dust; this can be wiped away when the piston is lowered.

HAYNES HiNT *To prevent carbon buildup, polish the piston crown with metal polish, but remove all traces of polish afterwards.*

5 Examine the heads of the valves for pitting and burning, especially the exhaust valve heads. Renew any valve which is badly burnt. Examine the valve seats at the same time. If the pitting is very slight, it can be removed by grinding the valve heads and seats together with coarse, then fine grinding paste.

6 Where excessive pitting has occurred, the valve seats must be recut or renewed by a suitably equipped engineering works.

7 Valve grinding is carried out as follows: place the cylinder head upside down on a bench with a block of wood at each end to give clearance for the valve stems.

8 Smear a trace of coarse carborundum

Fig. 1.28 Valve seat profile (Sec 26)

A *Valve seating surface*
B *Seat step – lower*
C *Seat step – upper*

paste on the seat face and press a suction grinding tool onto the valve head. With a semi-rotary action, grind the valve head to its seat, lifting the valve occasionally to redistribute the grinding paste. When a dull matt even surface is produced on both the valve seat and the valve, wipe off the paste and repeat the process with fine carborundum paste. A light spring placed under the valve head will greatly ease this operation. When a smooth unbroken ring of light grey matt finish is produced on both the valve and seat, the grinding operation is complete.

9 Scrape away all carbon from the valve head and stem, and clean away all traces of grinding compound. Clean the valves and seats with a paraffin-soaked rag, then wipe with a clean rag.

10 When each valve head has been ground to the required finish, insert it into its location in the cylinder head and check the amount the valve head is recessed beneath the cylinder head face, using a feeler gauge and steel rule across the head face and valve. It is important to retain the valve head recessing within the specified limits, as the valve seats have a step (C in Fig. 1.28) which must be kept intact. If the valve and/or seat are worn beyond the specified limit, they will need renewal, in which case consult a Renault dealer.

11 If the valve guides are worn, indicated by a side-to-side motion of the valve, new guides must be fitted. To do this, use a suitable mandrel to press the worn guides downwards and out through the combustion chamber. Press the new guides into the cylinder head in the same direction until they are at the specified fitted height.

12 Check that all valve springs are intact. If any one is broken, all should be renewed. Check the free height of the springs against new ones. If some springs are not within specifications, replace them all. Springs suffer from fatigue and it is a good idea to renew them even if they look serviceable.

27 Engine reassembly - general

1 To ensure maximum life with minimum trouble from a rebuilt engine, not only must everything be correctly assembled, but it must also be spotlessly clean. All oilways must be clear, and locking washers and spring washers must be fitted where indicated. Oil all bearings and other working surfaces thoroughly with engine oil during assembly.

2 Before assembly begins, renew any bolts or studs with damaged threads and have all new components at hand ready for assembly.

3 Gather together a torque wrench, oil can, clean rags and a set of engine gaskets, together with a new oil filter. A tube of RTV sealing compound will also be required for the joint faces that are fitted without gaskets. It is recommended that CAF 4/60 THIXO paste, obtainable from Renault dealers, is used, as it is specially formulated for this purpose.

28 Crankshaft and main bearings - refitting

1 If they were removed, refit the oil jets to their positions in the crankcase, at the bottom end of each cylinder bore (photo). Ensure that the fitted position of each is as noted during removal, otherwise it is possible for contact to occur between the jets and pistons as the pistons reach the bottom of their strokes. Tighten the retaining bolts to the specified torque wrench setting.

2 Before fitting the crankshaft or main bearings, it is necessary to determine the correct thickness of side seals to be fitted to No 1 main bearing cap. To do this, place the bearing cap in position without any seals and secure it with the two retaining bolts. Locate a twist drill, dowel rod, or any other suitable implement which will just fit, in the side seal groove. Now measure the implement, and this dimension is the side seal groove size. If the dimension is less than or equal to 5 mm, a 5.1 mm thick side seal is needed. If the dimension is more than 5 mm, a 5.3 mm thick side seal is required. Having determined the side seal size and obtained the necessary seals, proceed as follows.

3 Clean the backs of the bearing shells and the bearing recesses in both the cylinder block and main bearing caps.

4 Press the bearing shells without oil holes

28.1A Oil jet and retaining bolt

28.1B Oil jet in position

Fig. 1.29 Exploded view of cylinder block and related components (Sec 28)

28.4 Main bearing shells without oil holes fit to caps

into the caps, ensuring that the tag on the shell engages in the notch in the cap (photo).

5 Press the bearing shells with the oil holes into the recesses in the cylinder block (photo).

6 If the original bearing shells are being refitted, these must be placed in their original locations.

7 Using a little grease, stick the thrust washers to each side of No 2 main bearing, so that the oilway grooves on each thrust washer face outwards (photo).

8 Lubricate the lips of a new crankshaft rear oil seal and carefully slip it over the crankshaft journal. Do this carefully as the seal lips are very delicate. Ensure that the open side of the seal faces the engine.

9 Liberally lubricate each bearing shell in the cylinder block and lower the crankshaft into position (photo).

10 Fit all the bearing caps, with the exception of No 1, in their numbered or previously noted locations, so that the bearing shell locating notches in the cap and block are both on the same side (photo). Fit the retaining bolts and tighten them hand tight at this stage.

11 Check the crankshaft endfloat using a dial gauge or feeler gauges inserted between the thrust washers and the side of the bearing journal (photos). If new thrust washers have been fitted, the endfloat should be in accordance with the dimension given in the Specifications. If the original washers have been refitted and the endfloat is excessive,

28.5 Main bearing shells with oil grooves and holes fit to block

28.7 Locate the thrust washers each side of No 2 main bearing – note oilway grooves face outwards

28.9 Lowering the crankshaft into position

28.10 Fit the main bearing caps (except No 1)

28.11A Check the crankshaft endfloat using a dial gauge . . .

28.11B . . . or feeler gauges

28.12 Fit the side seals to No 1 main bearing cap

28.16 Tighten the main bearing cap bolts to the specified torque

28.17 Trim the side seals flush with the block face

new thrust washers must be obtained. These are available in a number of oversizes.

12 Fit the side seals to No 1 main bearing cap with their seal groove facing outwards. Position the seals so that approximately 0.2 mm (0.008 in) of seal protrudes at the bottom facing side (the side towards the crankcase) (photo).

13 Apply some CAF 4/60 THIXO paste to the bottom corners of the cap and then place the retaining bolts through the cap bolt holes.

14 Place the cap in position and just start the bolts two or three turns into their threads. These will now serve as guide studs.

15 Press the cap firmly into place taking care not to displace the side seals. When the cap is nearly home, check that the side seals are still protruding at the bottom, push the cap down fully and tighten the bolts hand tight to hold it.

16 Position the oil seal so that its face is flush with the bearing cap and block, then tighten all the retaining bolts to the specified torque (photo). Check that the crankshaft is free to turn.

17 When all components have been fitted and tightened, trim off the protruding ends of the side seals, flush with the block face (photo).

29 Pistons, connecting rods and big-end bearings - refitting

1 Clean the backs of the bearing shells and the recesses in the connecting rods and big-end caps If new shells are being fitted, ensure

that all traces of the protective grease are cleaned off using paraffin (photo).

2 Press the big-end bearing shells into the connecting rods and caps in their correct positions and oil them liberally.

3 Lubricate the pistons and rings with engine oil, then fit a ring compressor to No 1 piston. Insert the piston and connecting rod into No 1 cylinder (at the flywheel end). With No 1 crankpin at its lowest point, drive the piston carefully into the cylinder with the wooden handle of a hammer and at the same time guide the connecting rod onto the crankpin (photo). Make sure that the V mark on the piston crown, or arrow, is facing the flywheel end of the engine.

4 Fit the big-end bearing cap in its previously noted position, then tighten the bolts to the specified torque (photos).

29.1 Piston, connecting rod, bearing shells, cap and bolts ready for refitting

29.3 Using a piston ring compressor and a wooden drift to refit the piston and connecting rod assembly

29.4A Locate the connecting rod big-end bearing cap . . .

29.4B . . . and fit and tighten the retaining bolts

30.2 Tighten the flywheel retaining bolts to the specified torque

31.1 Apply sealant to the front plate. Do not block the oilway in zone C

5 Check that the crankshaft turns freely.
6 Repeat the procedure given in paragraphs 3 to 5 for No 4 piston and connecting rod, then turn the crankshaft through half a turn and repeat the procedure on No 2 and No 3 pistons.
7 If the engine is in the car, refit the oil pump, sump and cylinder head.

30 Flywheel - refitting

1 Clean the flywheel and crankshaft faces, then fit the flywheel. The flywheel retaining bolts are not symmetrical, so the flywheel can only be fitted in one position.

2 Apply a few drops of thread locking compound to the retaining bolt threads, fit the bolts and tighten them in a diagonal sequence to the specified torque (photo).

31 Crankshaft front plate - refitting

1 Apply a bead of CAF 4/60 THIXO paste to the mating face of the front plate and liberally lubricate the oil seal lips (photo).
2 Refit the front plate and the retaining bolts. Do not fit the two bolts around the oil seal opening at the 2 o'clock and 8 o'clock positions at this stage, as they also secure the timing case backing plate.

3 Tighten the retaining bolts in a progressive sequence.

32 Auxiliary shaft - refitting

1 Liberally lubricate the auxiliary shaft and slide it into its bearings (photo).
2 Place the retaining plate in position with its curved edge away from the crankshaft and refit the two retaining bolts (photo). Tighten the bolts fully.
3 Place a new gasket in position over the dowels of the cylinder block (photo). If a gasket was not used previously, apply a bead of CAF 4/60 THIXO paste to the housing mating face.
4 Liberally lubricate the oil seal lips and then locate the housing in place (photo). Refit and tighten the housing retaining bolts progressively in a diagonal sequence.
5 Lubricate the oil pump drivegear and lower the gear into its location.
6 Position a new O-ring seal on the drivegear cover plate, fit the plate and secure with the two retaining bolts.
7 Fit the drivebelt tensioner pulley unit to the front face of the block.
8 Refit the timing case backing plate. The two bolts around the crankshaft front plate oil seal opening at the 2 o'clock and 8 o'clock positions should also have a small quantity of

Fig. 1.30 Fit a new O-ring seal (arrowed) to the cover plate (Sec 32)

32.1 Insert the auxiliary shaft . . .

32.2 . . . and fit the retaining plate

32.3 Fit the auxiliary shaft housing gasket over the dowels . . .

32.4 . . . then locate the housing

32.8 Fit the timing case backing plate. Note the special spacer bolt location (A). Apply sealant to bolts (B)

the sealant paste applied to their threads, as they protrude into the crankcase (photo).
9 Locate the special spacer bolt at the 7 o'clock position under the auxiliary shaft.
10 With the Woodruff key in place, refit the auxiliary shaft sprocket, washer and retaining bolt. Hold the sprocket using the method employed for removal, and tighten the bolt to the specified torque.
11 If the engine is in the car, refit the timing belt and, if removed, the engine undertray.

33 Oil pump - refitting

1 Place the oil pump in position with its shaft engaged with the drivegear.
2 Refit the retaining bolts and tighten them securely (photo).
3 If the engine is in the car, refit the sump.

Fig. 1.31 Valve components (Sec 35)

1	Oil seal	4 Spring
2	Valve	5 Cap
3	Spring seat	6 Split collets

33.2 Refit the oil pump and tighten the retaining bolts

34 Sump - refitting

1 Ensure that the mating faces of the sump and crankcase are clean and dry.
2 Apply a bead of CAF 4/60 THIXO paste to the sump face and place the sump in position (photo). Refit the retaining bolts and tighten them progressively in a diagonal sequence.
3 Refit the 'U'-shaped support bracket to the underside of the sump.
4 Refit the undertray, and fill the engine with oil.

35.1A Using a socket . . .

35.2 Inserting a valve . . .

34.2 Refit the sump

35 Cylinder head - reassembly

1 Using a suitable tube, fit new oil seals to each of the valve guides (photos).
2 Lubricate the stems of the valves and insert them into their original locations. If new valves are being fitted, insert them into the locations to which they have been ground (photo).
3 Working on the first valve, fit the spring seat to the cylinder head followed by the valve spring and cap (photos).
4 Compress the valve spring and locate the

35.1B . . . to fit the valve oil seals (arrowed)

35.3A . . . valve spring seat . . .

1

35 3B . . . and valve spring

35.4 Using a valve spring compressor

36.1A Underside of a tappet bucket

split collets in the recess in the valve stem (photo). Release the compressor, then repeat the procedure on the remaining valves.

5 With all the valves installed, lay the cylinder head on one side and tap each valve stem with a plastic mallet to settle the components.

6 If the cylinder head has been removed with the engine in the car, refit the camshaft and tappets, the fuel pump, carburettor and manifolds, water temperature gauge sender unit, hose support bracket, and thermostat.

36 Camshaft and tappets - refitting

1 Lubricate the tappet buckets and insert

them into their respective locations as noted during removal. Make sure that each bucket has its correct tappet shim in place on its upper face (photos).

2 Lubricate the camshaft bearings, then lay the camshaft in position. Position the oil seals so that they are flush with the cylinder head faces and refit the bearing caps. Ensure that the caps are fitted facing the same way as noted during removal and in their original locations (photos).

3 Apply a thread locking compound to the bearing cap retaining bolts, refit the bolts and progressively tighten them to the specified torque (photo).

4 Refit the camshaft sprocket backing plate to the cylinder head and secure with the retaining bolts (photo).

5 With the Woodruff key in its groove, fit the camshaft sprocket and retaining bolts. Prevent the camshaft turning using the same method as for removal and tighten the sprocket retaining bolt to the specified torque (photo).

6 If the engine is in the car, refit the fuel pump, timing belt and distributor cap, then check the valve clearances before refitting the camshaft cover.

37 Cylinder head - refitting

1 Ensure that the mating faces of the cylinder block and head are spotlessly clean, that the

36.1B Underside of tappet shim showing the thickness identification number

36.1C Refitting a tappet bucket

36.2A Refit the camshaft to the cylinder head

36.2B Fit the camshaft oil seals and bearing caps

36.3 Camshaft bearing cap and retaining bolts

36.4 Fit the camshaft sprocket backing plate

36.5 Camshaft sprocket bolt tightening method

Fig. 1.32 Cylinder head bolt tightening sequence (Sec 37)

37.2 Insert bolts through TDC locating hole in cylinder block

retaining bolt threads are also clean and dry and that they screw easily in and out of their locations.

2 Turn the crankshaft as necessary to bring No 1 piston to the TDC position. Retain the crankshaft in this position using a metal rod in the TDC locating hole in the cylinder block (photo).

3 Place a new gasket on the block face and located over the studs. Do not use any jointing compound on the gasket (photo).

4 Turn the camshaft sprocket until the mark on its outer face is aligned with the mark on the sprocket backing plate.

5 Lower the cylinder head into position on the block and engage the dowels (photo).

6 Lightly lubricate the cylinder head retaining bolt threads and under the bolt heads with clean engine oil and screw in the bolts finger tight.

7 Tighten the retaining bolts in the sequence shown in Fig. 1.32 to the 1st tightening setting given in the Specifications. Now repeat the sequence, but this time to the 2nd tightening setting.

8 Wait 3 minutes then loosen all the bolts completely. Tighten them again this time to the 1st retightening setting, still in the correct sequence.

9 The final, or 2nd, retightening is done using an angular measurement. Ideally, an angle gauge, obtainable at modest cost from accessory outlets, should be used (photo).

The following method is an alternative if an angle gauge is not available Draw two lines at 123° to each other on a sheet of card and punch a hole for the socket bit at the point where the lines intersect. Starting with bolt No 1, engage the socket through the card and into the bolt head. Position the first line on the card under, and directly in line with, the socket extension bar. Hold the card, and in one movement tighten the bolt until the extension bar is aligned with the second line on the card. Repeat this procedure for the remaining bolts in the correct sequence.

10 Fit and tighten the bolt securing the top end of the timing case backing plate to the end face of the cylinder head.

11 Refit the timing belt and check the valve clearances. If the engine is in the car, refit the control cables and services using the reverse of the removal procedure described in Section 11, but bearing in mind the following points:

(a) Tighten the exhaust front section-to-manifold retaining bolts so that the tension springs are compressed and coil bound (see Chapter 3)
(b) Adjust the choke and accelerator cables, as described in Chapter 3
(c) Adjust the drivebelt tension, as described in Chapter 2
(d) Refill the cooling system, as described in Chapter 2

37.3 Locate the cylinder head gasket over the studs

38 Timing belt - refitting

1 Check that the crankshaft is at the TDC position for No 1 cylinder and that the crankshaft is locked in this position using the metal rod through the hole in the crankcase (photo 37.2).

2 Check that the timing mark on the camshaft sprocket is in line with the corresponding mark on the metal backing plate (photo).

3 Align the timing marks on the belt with those on the sprockets, noting that the running direction arrows on the belt should be

37.5 Refitting the cylinder head

37.9 Cylinder head bolt tightening method using an angle gauge

38.2 Align timing marks on camshaft sprocket and backing plate

1

38.3A Fit the timing belt, aligning the timing marks . . .

38.3B . . . and ensure correct running direction (indicated by arrows which must point in direction of normal rotation)

38.5 Timing belt tensioner

positioned between the auxiliary shaft sprocket and the idler pulley (photos).

4 Hold the belt in this position and slip it over the crankshaft, auxiliary shaft and camshaft sprockets in that order, then around the idler tensioner pulleys.

5 Check that all the timing marks are still aligned, then temporarily tension the belt by turning the tensioner pulley anti-clockwise and tightening the retaining nut (photo).

6 Remove the TDC locating rod.

7 Refit the crankshaft pulley and retaining bolt. Prevent the crankshaft turning by whichever method was used during removal and tighten the pulley bolt to the specified torque.

8 Using a socket or spanner on the pulley bolt, turn the crankshaft at least two complete turns in the normal direction of rotation; then return it to the TDC position with No 1 cylinder on compression.

9 Check that the timing marks are still aligned. If not, slacken the tensioner, move the belt one tooth as necessary on the camshaft sprocket and check again.

10 With the timing correct, tension the belt by turning the tensioner as necessary so that under moderate pressure applied at a point midway between the auxiliary sprocket and idler pulley, the belt deflects by 7.5 mm (0.3 in). When the tension is correct, tighten the tensioner pulley retaining nut.

11 Refit the timing belt cover and secure with the four retaining bolts.

12 If the engine is in the car, refit the alternator drivebelt, air cleaner, and fuel filter, then reconnect the battery.

39 Valve clearances - adjustment

1 If the engine is in the car, remove the air

cleaner and disconnect the choke cable, as described in Chapter 3. Undo the three domed retaining nuts and lift off the camshaft cover and gasket.

2 Using a socket or spanner on the crankshaft pulley bolt, turn the engine until the peak of the cam lobe for valve No 1 (nearest the flywheel) is uppermost. Using feeler gauges measure and record the clearance between the heel of the cam lobe and the shim on the top of the tappet bucket. Repeat this procedure for the remaining valves in turn.

3 Once all the clearances have been recorded, compare the figures with the specified valve clearances given in the Specifications, noting that valve Nos 2, 4, 5 and 7 are inlet and valve Nos 1, 3, 6 and 8 are exhaust.

4 If the clearance of any of the valves differs from the specified value, then the shim for that valve must be replaced with a thinner or thicker shim accordingly. The size of shim required can be calculated as follows: If the measured clearance is less than specified, subtract the measured clearance from the specified clearance. A shim thinner by this amount from the one now in place is needed. If the measured clearance is greater than specified, subtract the specified clearance from the measured clearance. A shim thicker by this amount than the one now in place, is needed. The shim size is stamped on the bottom face of the shim.

5 The shims can be removed from their locations on top of the tappet buckets without removing the camshaft if the Renault tool shown in the accompanying illustrations can be borrowed, or a suitable alternative fabricated. To remove the shim the tappet bucket has to be pressed down against valve spring pressure just far enough to allow the shim to be slid out. Theoretically this could be done by levering against the camshaft between the cam lobes with a suitable pad to push the bucket down, but this is not recommended by the manufacturers. Alternatively an arrangement similar to the Renault tool can be made by bolting a bar to the camshaft bearing studs and levering down against this with a stout screwdriver. The contact pad should be a triangular-shaped

Fig. 1.33 Arrangement of the timing belt, sprockets, timing marks and belt direction arrows – A (Sec 38)

Fig. 1.34 Renault tool for compressing tappet buckets to change tappet shims (Sec 39)

Fit slots (A) at right-angles to the camshaft

Mot. 992

Mot. 992-01

A

metal block with a lip filed along each side to contact the edge of the bucket. Levering down against this will open the valve and allow the shim to be withdrawn. Make sure that the cam lobe peaks are uppermost when doing this and rotate the buckets so that the notches are at right angles to the camshaft centreline.

6 If the Renault tool cannot be borrowed or a suitable alternative made up then it will be necessary to remove the camshaft, as described in Section 13 to gain access to the shims.

7 When refitting the shims ensure that the size markings face the tappet buckets (ie downwards).

8 On completion refit the camshaft cover using a new gasket. If the engine is in the car refit the air cleaner and choke cable with reference to Chapter 3.

40 Ancillary components - refitting

Refer to Section 9, and refit all the components listed with reference to the Chapters indicated.

41 Engine - attachment to transmission

Refer to Section 7 and attach the engine using the reverse of the removal procedure. Apply a trace of molybdenum disulphide grease to the end of the transmission input shaft before fitting.

42 Engine and transmission - refitting

Refitting the engine is a reverse of the removal procedure contained in Section 6, but bear in mind the following additional points:

(a) Tighten the exhaust front section-to-manifold retaining bolts so that the tension springs are compressed and coil bound (see Chapter 3)

(b) Reconnect the driveshafts and front steering/suspension components as described in Chapters 8 and 10 respectively

(c) Refill the cooling system with reference to Chapter 2

(d) Adjust the choke and accelerator cables with reference to Chapter 3

(e) Refill the transmission with oil, as described in Chapter 6, and the engine, as described in Section 2 of this Chapter.

43 Engine - adjustments after major overhaul

1 With the engine and transmission refitted to the car, make a final check to ensure that everything has been reconnected and that no rags or tools have been left in the engine compartment.

2 Make sure that the oil and water levels are topped up and then start the engine; this may take a little longer than usual as the fuel pump and carburettor float chamber may be empty.

3 As soon as the engine starts, watch for the oil pressure light to go out and check for any oil, fuel or water leaks. Don't be alarmed if there are some odd smells and smoke from parts getting hot and burning off oil deposits.

4 If new pistons, rings or crankshaft bearings have been fitted, the engine must be run-in for the first 500 miles (800 km). Do not exceed 45 mph (72 kph), operate the engine at full throttle or allow it to labour in any gear.

1

PART B: 1995 CC (2.0 LITRE) ENGINE

44 General description

The 2.0 litre engine is a four-cylinder in-line unit mounted at the front of the vehicle. It incorporates a crossflow design head, having the inlet valves and manifold on the left-hand side of the engine and the exhaust on the right. The inclined valves are operated by a single rocker shaft assembly which is mounted directly above the camshaft. The rocker arms have a stud and locknut type of adjuster for the valve clearances, providing easy adjustment. No special tools are required to set the clearances. The camshaft is driven via its sprocket from the timing belt, which in turn is driven by the crankshaft sprocket.

This belt also drives an auxiliary shaft, which in turn drives the oil pump by means of a short driveshaft geared to it.

The distributor is driven from the rear end of the camshaft by means of an offset dog.

A spring-loaded jockey wheel assembly provides the timing belt tension adjustment. A single, twin or triple pulley is mounted on the front of the crankshaft and this drives the alternator/water pump drivebelt, the power

steering pump drivebelt and the air conditioning compressor drivebelt, as applicable. The crankshaft runs in the main bearings which are shell type aluminium/tin material. The crankshaft endfloat is taken up by side thrust washers. The connecting rods also have aluminium/tin shell bearing type big-ends.

Aluminium alloy pistons are employed, the gudgeon pins being a press fit (non-turbo engines) or sliding fit (turbo engines) in the

connecting rod small ends, and a sliding fit in the pistons on all engines. The No 1 piston is located at the flywheel end of the engine (at the rear).

Removable wet cylinder liners are employed, each being sealed in the crankcase by a flange and O-ring. The liner protrusion above the top surface of the crankcase is crucial; when the cylinder head and gasket are tightened down they compress the liners to provide the upper and lower seal of the engine

Fig. 1.35 Cutaway view of the 2.0 litre (J7R 750 and J7R 751) engine (Sec 44)

Fig. 1.36 Cutaway view of the 2.0 litre Turbo (J7R 752) engine (Sec 44)

Fig. 1.37 Engine lubrication circuit (Sec 44)

(c) *Removal and refitting of the cylinder head*
(d) *Removal and refitting of the sump*
(e) *Removal and refitting of the auxiliary shaft*
(f) *Removal and refitting of the oil pump*
(g) *Removal and refitting of the connecting rod and piston assemblies*
(h) *Removal and refitting of the engine/transmission mountings*
(l) *Removal and refitting of the cylinder liners*

⚠ **Warning: Vehicles equipped with air conditioning: Refer to the warning note in Part A, Section 3 of this Chapter.**

47 Major operations requiring engine removal

The following operations can only be carried out after removal of the engine from the car:
(a) *Removal and refitting of the flywheel*
(b) *Removal and refitting of the crankshaft and main bearings*

⚠ **Warning: Vehicles equipped with air conditioning. Refer to the warning note in Part A, Section 3 of this Chapter.**

48 Methods of engine removal

The engine may be removed on its own or withdrawn complete with transmission for separation later.

If the transmission is not in need of overhaul, it will be easier to remove the engine and leave the transmission in the car.

Suitable lifting equipment will be required, also a trolley jack to support the units during removal. An assistant will also be required to assist with the actual removal of the units.

Where applicable, additional items for disconnection and/or removal on Turbo models are included in the removal instructions.

coolant circuit within the engine. The cylinder head and crankcase are manufactured in light alloy.

This engine is available in both normally aspirated and turbocharged forms.

45 Maintenance

1 The engine servicing procedures for 2.0 litre models are much the same as those outlined for the 1.7 litre engine variants. Reference should therefore be made to Section 2 in Part A of this Chapter for details. As with the 1.7 litre engine, the maintenance intervals are

given in the *'Routine maintenance'* Section at the start of this manual.
2 The accompanying photos illustrate the main items for servicing on the 2.0 litre engine.

46 Major operations possible with the engine in the car

The following operations are possible without the need to remove the engine from the car:
(a) *Removal and refitting of the timing belt*
(b) *Removal and refitting of the camshaft*

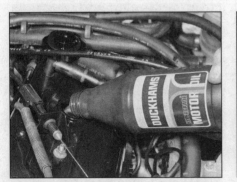

45.2A Topping up the engine oil – 2.0 litre engine

45.2B Engine oil drain plug – 2.0 litre engine

45.2C Engine oil filter renewal using a strap wrench – 2.0 litre engine

Fig. 1.38 Front grille retaining screw locations – arrowed (Sec 49)

Fig. 1.39 Upper front panel front retaining bolt locations – arrowed (Sec 49)

Fig. 1.40 Upper front panel top retaining bolt locations – arrowed (Sec 49)

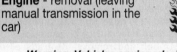

49 Engine - removal (leaving manual transmission in the car)

Warning: Vehicles equipped with air conditioning: Refer to the warning note in Part A, Section 3 of this Chapter.

1 Open the bonnet, mark the position of the hinges on its underside using a pencil or masking tape and with the help of an assistant, unbolt and remove the bonnet.
2 Disconnect the battery.
3 Drain the engine oil.

4 Drain the cooling system, and then remove the radiator as described in Chapter 2. On Turbo models it will also be necessary to detach and remove the following items. Refer to the accompanying illustrations for details:
(a) Front grille panel
(b) Upper front panel
(c) Upper crossmember and intercooler
(d) Headlight units (refer to Chapter 12)
(e) Front grille mounting
5 Disconnect the throttle cable as described in Chapter 3.
6 Disconnect and remove the air cleaner unit as described in Chapter 3.
7 Disconnect the clutch cable from the operating lever as described in Chapter 5.
8 Unbolt and remove the engine angular position/speed sensor from the top of the

clutch bellhousing (photo). Disconnect the HT lead from the coil.
9 Undo the retaining nut and remove the protective cover from the computer unit on the inner left-hand wing panel. Undo the computer unit retaining screw at the bottom and release the retaining clip at the top. Detach the appropriate wiring connections. and then move the computer unit and rest it on top of the engine. The computer unit can then be removed together with the engine.
10 Disconnect the fuel feed and return hoses at the bulkhead, and plug them to prevent leakage (photo).
11 Disconnect the appropriate heater coolant hoses and the coolant hose to the expansion bottle (photo).

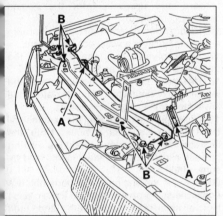

Fig. 1.41 Upper crossmember bolts (B) and intercooler clips (A) (Sec 49)

Fig. 1.42 Front grille mounting bolts (E) (Sec 49)

Fig. 1.43 Unbolt engine mountings at points 'A' (Sec 49)

49.8 Engine angular position/speed sensor location on clutch bellhousing

49.10 Detach the fuel hoses at the bulkhead

49.11 Detach the heater coolant hoses

49.13A Wiring connector to oil level indicator

49.13B Wiring connector to coolant temperature sensor (arrowed)

12 Disconnect the vacuum hose to the brake servo unit at the manifold.

13 Disconnect the various wiring connectors to the engine sensors, switches, starter motor and alternator (photos). Note and label the wiring runs and connections to avoid confusion during reassembly.

14 Remove the starter motor - see Chapter 12 for details.

15 Raise and support the front of the vehicle on axle stands.

16 Detach and remove the engine undershield.

17 Disconnect the power steering hoses at the pump. Clamp the hoses and plug the ports to prevent fluid leakage.

18 Unbolt and disconnect the exhaust downpipe at the exhaust manifold. On Turbo models also remove the turbocharger heat shield and the intercooler hoses (see Chapter 3). Unbolt the downpipe at the lower end and remove it.

19 Disconnect the engine earth lead.

20 Attach a suitable hoist and lifting gear to the engine lifting lugs, using the inner hole of the front lug, and just take the weight of the engine. The computer unit should be securely tied to the engine to avoid any possibility of damage during the subsequent lifting operation.

21 Position a jack to support the weight of the transmission.

22 Unbolt and remove the engine mountings at the points indicated in Fig. 1.43.

23 Unscrew the bolts which hold the reinforcement brackets and cover plate to the lower face of the clutch bellhousing.

24 Unscrew and remove the engine-to-transmission connecting bolts. Note the locations of the various brackets, wiring harness clips and other attachments held by some of the bolts.

25 Make a final check to ensure that any components, hoses, etc, affecting engine removal have been removed or disconnected as applicable.

26 Carefully raise the engine to clear the mounting brackets, then withdraw it forwards, swivelling the engine slightly about the crankshaft axis to enable the clutch release fork to be released from its bearing. As the two units are separated, support the weight of

the transmission with the jack to prevent any unnecessary force being applied to the Input shaft.

27 Lift the engine carefully from the engine compartment.

50 Engine and manual transmission - removal and separation

⚠️ *Warning: Vehicles equipped with air conditioning. Refer to the warning note in Part A, Section 3 of this Chapter.*

1 Proceed as described in paragraphs 1 to 19 inclusive of the previous Section, then continue as follows.

2 Remove the transmission undershield, then drain the transmission oil.

3 Apply the handbrake, then raise and support the vehicle at the front on axle stands so that there is sufficient clearance to work underneath the transmission. Unbolt and remove the front roadwheels.

4 Disconnect the gearchange link rods and reverse interlock operating cable, as described in Chapter 6.

5 Disconnect the reversing light switch leads.

6 Disconnect the speedometer cable by pulling the nylon retainer pin downwards using suitable pliers, and disengaging the cable from the transmission.

Fig. 1.44 Engine and transmission lift angle (Sec 50)

7 Using a suitable pin punch, drive out the roll pins which secure the driveshafts to the transmission (see Chapter 8).

8 On each side of the vehicle, loosen, but do not remove at this stage, the two nuts securing the front shock absorber-to-hub carrier bolts. Drive each bolt rearwards so that the splined section under its head is clear of the hub carrier, then remove the nut from the upper bolt only.

9 Withdraw the upper bolt to enable the hub carrier to be pivoted outwards sufficiently to allow the driveshaft on the side concerned to be withdrawn. Take care not to strain the brake hydraulic hoses. If necessary, detach the steering arm outer balljoint as described in Chapter 10.

10 Position a trolley jack under the transmission to support its weight.

11 Undo the retaining bolts, and remove the transmission mountings on each side.

12 Unbolt and remove the transverse bar from the subframe.

13 Attach a suitable hoist and lifting gear to the engine lifting lugs. Use the inner hole of the front lug. Arrange the lifting gear to give a lift angle of 15° from the horizontal - see Fig. 1.44.

14 Take the weight of the engine and transmission, then unbolt and remove the engine mountings.

15 Withdraw the engine/transmission forward and upwards from the engine compartment (photo).

16 Clean away external dirt using paraffin and a stiff brush or a water soluble solvent.

17 To separate the engine from the transmission, proceed as follows.

18 Unscrew the bolts which hold the reinforcement brackets and cover plate to the lower face of the clutch bellhousing.

19 Unscrew and remove the engine-to-transmission connecting bolts. Note the location of the various brackets, wiring harness clips and other attachments held by some of the bolts.

20 Support the engine with wooden blocks under the sump pan so that the transmission has a clear gap underneath, and then withdraw the transmission from the engine. **Do not** allow the weight of the transmission to hang upon the input shaft while the latter is

50.15 Engine and transmission removal

still engaged with the clutch driven plate. As the two units are separated, swivel the gearbox slightly about the input shaft axis to enable the clutch release fork to be released from its bearing.

51 Engine - removal (leaving automatic transmission in the car)

Warning: Vehicles equipped with air conditoning. Refer to the warning note in Part A, Section 3 of this Chapter.

1 Carry out the operations described in paras 1 to 6 and 8 to 19 of Section 49.
2 Working through the starter motor aperture, lock the teeth of the ring gear using a suitable tool and unscrew the driveplate-to-torque converter fixing bolts.
3 In order to bring each bolt into view, the crankshaft will have to be turned by means of a socket on its pulley bolt while the ring gear locking tool is temporarily removed.
4 Unscrew and remove the bolts which hold the torque converter lower cover plate. The cover plate will drop off its dowels only after the engine and transmission are separated.
5 Unscrew and remove the engine-to-transmission bolts.
6 Attach a hoist to the engine lifting lugs and just take the weight of the engine.
7 Place a jack under the transmission.
8 Unscrew the engine mounting through-bolt nuts.
9 Raise the engine to clear the mounting brackets, then withdraw it forward to disconnect it from the transmission and lift it up and out of the engine compartment. Ensure that the torque converter remains on the transmission.
10 Bolt a retaining bar to one of the torque converter housing flange bolts in order to retain the converter in full engagement with the transmission and to prevent damage to the oil seal.

Fig. 1.45 Camshaft sprocket timing notch aligned with pointer in timing belt cover. No 1 piston at TDC (Sec 55)

52 Engine and automatic transmission - removal and separation

Warning: Vehicles equipped with air conditioning. Refer to the warning note in Part A, Section 3 of this Chapter.

1 Carry out the operations described in paras 1 to 6 and 8 to 18 of Section 49.
2 Disconnect the earth straps.
3 Remove the transmission dipstick tube.
4 Disconnect the fluid hoses from the transmission fluid cooler and plug them.
5 Disconnect reversing lamp switch lead.
6 Disconnect the speedometer cable.
7 Disconnect the driveshafts from the transmission as described in paragraphs 7 to 9 of Section 50.
8 Disconnect the speed selector control cable and kick-down cable after reference to Chapter 7, also the vacuum pipe and computer wiring plugs.
9 With a hoist attached to the lifting lugs and taking the weight of the engine and transmission, remove the transmission mountings and unscrew the nuts from the engine mounting through-bolts. Prepare to guide the computer out with the transmission.
10 Withdraw the engine/transmission forward and upwards out of the engine compartment.
11 Clean away external dirt using paraffin and a stiff brush or a water soluble solvent.
12 Separate the transmission from the engine as described in paragraphs 2 to 8 of Section 51. Pull the transmission from the engine and then fit a torque converter retaining bar as described in paragraph 10 of Section 51.

53 Engine dismantling - general

Refer to Part A, Section 8 of this Chapter.

55.4 Remove the power steering pump and alternator drivebelts

54 Ancillary components - removal

Before complete engine dismantling begins, remove the following ancillary items:
Exhaust manifold and where applicable.
Turbocharger unit (Chapter 3)
Power steering unit (Chapter 10)
Alternator (Chapter 12)
Distributor cap and plug leads (Chapter 4)
Engine mounting and reinforcement brackets
Timing belt cover
Coolant pump (Chapter 2)
Clutch (Chapter 5)
Injection and induction manifold (Chapter 3)
Coolant hoses and thermostat housing (Chapter 2)
Starter motor (Chapter 12)

55 Timing belt - removal

1 Disconnect the battery earth lead.
2 Raise and support the front of the vehicle on axle stands.
3 Detach and remove the engine undertray.
4 Remove the power steering pump and alternator drivebelts as described in Chapter 2 (photo).
5 Detach the HT leads and remove the spark plugs.
6 Turn the crankshaft using a suitable spanner on the crankshaft pulley bolt until No 1 piston (flywheel end) is at TDC on its compression stroke. The correct position can be established by feeling for compression being generated in No 1 cylinder (place a finger over the spark plug hole) then checking that the flywheel TDC notch is aligned with the 'O' mark on the graduated scale at the clutch housing aperture (photo). With the crankshaft in this position the distributor rotor arm will be pointing toward the No 1 cylinder HT segment in the distributor cap and the notch on the camshaft sprocket will be aligned with the pointer in the viewing aperture on the front face of the timing belt cover (Fig. 1.45).

55.6 Flywheel timing mark at TDC position (arrowed)

1

55.7A Remove the brass plug (arrowed) from the crankcase . . .

55.7B . . . and insert a suitable rod (arrowed) to retain the crankshaft at TDC

55.7C Timing rod slot in crankshaft counterbalance weight (sump removed)

7 To keep the crankshaft in the TDC position, remove the brass plug from the crankcase, located just forward of the starter motor (photo). Insert a dowel rod of suitable diameter to engage in the slot provided for this purpose in the crankshaft counterbalance weight (photos). It may be necessary to move the crankshaft very slightly back and forth to check for positive engagement of the dowel rod in the crankshaft slot.

8 Undo the four nuts and remove the timing belt cover.

9 Slacken the timing belt tensioner retaining bolt and nut, push the tensioner against spring pressure to relieve tension on the belt and retighten the upper nut (photo). Take care, if completely removing the tensioner, that the tension spring and piston do not fly out of their apertures at high speed.

55.9 Timing belt tensioner retaining bolt and nut (arrowed)

10 Slip the timing belt off the sprockets and remove it from the engine. Store the belt on its side while removed if it is to be re-used.

56 Cylinder head - removal (engine in car)

1 Disconnect the battery earth lead.

2 On Turbo models, unbolt and remove the heat shield from the top of the turbocharger unit/exhaust manifold assembly (photo).

3 Disconnect the throttle cable from the pivot quadrant on top of the camshaft cover. Detach the cable adjuster at the retaining bracket on top of the cover and prise free the throttle connecting rod from the balljoint at the throttle housing.

4 Drain the cooling system as described in Chapter 2.

5 Unclip and detach the air intake duct from the throttle case cover. For improved access underneath the manifolds, remove the air filter (Chapter 3) and on Turbo models, the battery (Chapter 12).

6 Disconnect the appropriate cooling system hoses, vacuum hoses, and wiring connections to the cylinder head and its associated components. Take note of and label their respective connections as they are detached to avoid confusion on refitting. Note that the thermostat is positioned within the cylinder head end of the coolant top hose.

7 Disconnect and plug the fuel hoses to

prevent leakage and the ingress of dirt.

8 Unbolt and disconnect the exhaust downpipe at its connection to the manifold or turbocharger unit, as applicable (Chapter 3). If the turbocharger and exhaust are to be removed as a unit together with the cylinder head, detach the turbocharger support bracket, working from underneath. If required, the manifolds can be removed with reference to Chapter 3.

9 Detach the distributor cap and HT leads from the cylinder head, and remove the rotor arm (Chapter 4). Position the cap and leads out of the way.

10 Remove the timing belt as described in Section 55.

11 Unbolt and remove the camshaft cover. Disconnect the coolant hose, vacuum hose and HT lead support brackets as applicable (photos).

12 The cylinder head retaining bolts can now be progressively loosened, and with the exception of the front right-hand bolt, removed. Loosen off the bolts in the reverse sequence to that shown in Fig. 1.46.

Fig. 1.46 Cylinder head bolt tightening sequence (Sec 56)

56.2 Remove the heat shield from the turbocharger and exhaust manifold

56.11A Detach the hoses and support brackets . . .

56.11B . . . and the HT leads support bracket from the camshaft cover

56.15 Fabricated liner clamps

13 The cylinder head is now ready for removal from the block, and it is essential that it is detached in the correct manner. Do not lift the head directly upwards from the block. The head must be swivelled from the rear in a horizontal manner, pivoting on the remaining head dowel and bolt at the front. You will probably have to tap the head round on its rear corner, using a soft-headed mallet or wood block to break the seal between the head, gasket and block. Once the head is pivoted round and the seal broken, it can be lifted clear. This action is necessary because if the head were to be lifted directly from the block, the seal between the head gasket and block would be unbroken and the liners would thus be disturbed. Each liner has a seal around its lower flange; where the liners are not being removed, it is essential that this seal is not broken or disturbed. If the liners are accidentally disturbed they must be removed and new lower seals fitted.
14 The rocker shaft assembly and final bolt can be removed from the cylinder head once it is withdrawn from the engine.
15 To prevent the possibility of movement by the respective cylinder liners whilst the head is removed, it is advisable to place a clamp-plate over the top edges of the liners. A suitable plate (or bar) can be fastened temporarily in position using the existing head bolt holes, using shorter bolts of the desired thread and diameter with large, flat washers under the heads. Alternatively, use a block of wood with two bolts and spacers, clamping it in position in diagonal fashion (photo).
16 Refer to Section 69 for details of dismantling and decarbonising the cylinder head.

57 Cylinder head - removal (engine on bench)

1 Carry out the operations described in paragraph 9 onwards of the previous Section.
2 If required, the manifolds and associated components can be removed from the cylinder head prior to its removal, as described in Chapter 3.

58 Camshaft - removal

1 Remove the cylinder head as described in Section 56 or 57, as applicable.
2 To remove the camshaft sprocket, pass a suitable rod through one of the sprocket holes and jam it against the top surface of the cylinder head to prevent the camshaft from turning. Place a thin strip of wood under the rod to avoid damaging the cylinder head.
3 Unscrew the camshaft sprocket retaining bolt and remove the washer and sprocket. Take great care as the sprocket is manufactured of sintered metal and is therefore relatively fragile. With the sprocket removed, prise out the Woodruff key from the camshaft slot.
4 Unbolt and remove the distributor body.
5 Unbolt and remove the timing belt rear cover plate.
6 Carefully prise out the camshaft front oil seal from its location. Take great care not to damage the seal location bore in the cylinder head.
7 The camshaft can now be carefully withdrawn through the oil seal aperture in the front of the cylinder head. Take care during its removal not to snag any of the lobes on the bearings as they are passed through the cylinder head.

59 Cylinder head - dismantling

1 With the cylinder head removed to the bench, dismantle in the following way.

1 Oil filler cap
2 Camshaft cover
3 Gasket
4 Rocker shaft
5 End plug and oil filter
6 Rocker arm
7 Rocker shaft pedestal
8 Camshaft retaining plate
9 Camshaft
10 Sprocket
11 Split collets
12 Spring retaining cap
13 Valve spring
14 Spring seat
15 Cylinder head bolt
16 Exhaust valve
17 Inlet valve
18 Cylinder head
19 Gasket

Fig. 1.47 Cylinder head and associated components (Sec 59)

Fig. 1.48 Sectional view of valve components (Sec 59)

1 Split collets
2 Spring retaining cap
3 Valve spring
4 Spring seat
5 Oil seal

2 If not already done, remove the manifolds, as described in Chapter 3.

3 Unscrew and remove the spark plugs.

4 Remove the distributor body from the rear of the cylinder head (Chapter 4).

5 Remove the camshaft sprocket and key.

6 Extract the camshaft front oil seal, and remove the rocker assembly.

7 Lift the camshaft from the cylinder head.

8 Using a valve spring compressor, compress the first valve spring and remove the split collets.

9 Gently release the compressor and remove it.

10 Take off the spring retainer, the spring and the spring seat.

11 Remove all the other valves in a similar way, keeping them in their original fitted sequence together with their associated components. Remove and discard the valve stem oil seals.

12 Bearing in mind that the cylinder head is of light alloy construction and is easily damaged, use a blunt scraper or rotary wire brush to clean all traces of carbon deposits from combustion spaces and the ports. The valve stems and valve guides should also be freed from any carbon deposits. Wash the combustion spaces and ports down with paraffin and scrape the cylinder head surface free of any foreign matter with the side of a steel rule, or a similar article.

60 Sump - removal

1 If the engine has been removed from the car, proceed from paragraph 5.

2 Drain the engine oil as described in Section 45.

Fig. 1.49 Using a valve spring compressor (Sec 59)

3 Apply the handbrake, and raise and support the car at the front end on axle stands.

4 Detach and remove the engine undertray. This is secured by screws and clips. Loosen the engine mountings and raise the engine slightly using a hoist and lifting gear attached to the inner hole of the front engine lifting lug.

5 Unscrew the securing screws and remove the sump pan. If it is stuck tight, tap it gently with a wooden or plastic-faced hammer.

6 Remove the original gasket and clean the mating surfaces.

7 Note that, on Turbo models, bolt A shown in Fig. 1.50 cannot be fully withdrawn from its location until after the sump has been removed from the engine.

61 Oil pump - removal

1 If the engine is in the car, remove the sump as described in Section 60.

2 Unbolt and remove the cover plate from the left-hand side of the crankcase.

3 Withdraw the drive pinion and then the oil pump driveshaft, noting that the circlip is at its lower end.

4 Unbolt and remove the oil pump. The pump flange is located on dowels, so pull it straight off.

62 Auxiliary shaft - removal

1 If the engine is in the car, disconnect the battery earth lead then remove the radiator, as described in Chapter 2. For increased access it may be advantageous to remove the bonnet and radiator grille as described in Chapter 11.

2 Remove the timing belt as described in Section 55.

3 Unscrew the auxiliary shaft sprocket retaining bolt, passing a screwdriver shaft or rod through one of the holes in the sprocket to

Fig. 1.50 On Turbo models, bolt 'A' cannot be withdrawn from the sump (Sec 60)

lock against the front of the block and prevent the sprocket turning.

4 Withdraw the sprocket and remove the Woodruff key from the shaft.

5 Unbolt and remove the auxiliary shaft housing cover.

6 Unbolt and remove the auxiliary shaft forked lockplate.

7 Unbolt and remove the oil pump drive gear cover plate from the left-hand side of the crankcase.

8 Withdraw the oil pump drivegear from its location. When removing the gear, place a thin screwdriver or, alternatively, a length of welding rod through the centre of the gear and retain the pump driveshaft in its location. If this is not done. the shaft may drop off the gear as it is withdrawn and fall into the sump.

9 The auxiliary shaft can now be removed from the front of the crankcase.

10 If required, the oil seal in the front of the housing cover can be removed by carefully prising it out with a screwdriver or by drifting it out from the rear.

Fig. 1.51 Auxiliary shaft components (Sec 62)

1 Bolt
2 Sprocket
3 Front housing cover
4 Forked lockplate
5 Shaft

63 Flywheel (or driveplate) - removal

1 Jam the flywheel teeth and unscrew the flywheel bolts (or driveplate automatic transmission). The flywheel bolt holes are offset so it can only be fitted one way.
2 It should be noted that the flywheel retaining bolts must be renewed when refitting.

64 Crankshaft and main bearings - removal

1 Remove the cylinder head as described in Section 57, and the flywheel as described in Section 63.
2 Turn the engine on its side and remove the sump as described in Section 60, and the oil pump as described in Section 61. Unbolt and remove the crankshaft pulley, using a block of wood between the crankshaft counterweights and crankcase to prevent crankshaft rotation.
3 The main and big-end bearing caps are numbered from 1 to 4, from the flywheel end of the block. The main bearing cap numbers are read from the oil filter side of the crankcase (photo).
4 The big-end bearing caps and their connecting rods are not very clearly marked, so it is best to centre punch them at adjacent points and on the oil filter side so that there is no doubt as to their position and orientation in the block.
5 The connecting rod big-ends will not pass out through the cylinder liners, so each liner/piston/connecting rod must be removed as an assembly out of the top of the cylinder block. Before doing this however, centre punch each liner rim and adjacent surface on the top of the cylinder block so that they will be refitted in their original position and orientation if of course they are not being renewed completely.
6 Unbolt the big-end bearing caps, keeping the bearing shells taped to their original cap or connecting rod if they are to be used again, although this is not to be recommended

(see Section 68 for bearing renewal).
7 Withdraw the cylinder liner/piston/connecting rod assemblies.
8 Unbolt and remove the main bearing caps, again keeping their bearing shells with their respective caps if they are to be refitted, again not to be recommended.
9 Note that the front and rear main bearing caps are located on dowels so if they are tight, tap them straight off, **not** in a sideways direction.

10 Withdraw the crankshaft, noting the two semi-circular thrust washers located in the crankcase. Remove the bearing shells and identify them by marking with numbered tape if they are to be used again.
11 Using two screwdrivers inserted at opposite points, lever off the crankshaft sprocket. Extract the Woodruff key and remove the belt guide.
12 Remove the crankshaft front and rear oil seals and discard them.

Fig. 1.52 Exploded view of cylinder block (Sec 64)

1 Dipstick
2 Coolant pump
3 Timing belt cover
4 Timing belt
5 Timing belt tensioner
6 Gudgeon pin
7 Piston
8 Cylinder liner
9 O-ring seal
10 Crankcase
11 Oil seal
12 Connecting rod
13 Flywheel (manual transmission)
14 Driveplate (automatic transmission)
15 Auxiliary shaft
16 Sprocket
17 Housing
18 Oil pump drive gear
19 Oil pump driveshaft
20 Oil pump
21 Crankshaft pulley
22 Crankshaft timing belt sprocket
23 Crankshaft
24 Gasket
25 Sump pan

64.3 Crankshaft main bearing cap identification number

66.3A Left-hand engine mounting

66.3B Transmission mounting

67 Crankcase ventilation system - description

The system is designed to extract oil fumes and blow-by gas from within the crankcase and burn them in the combustion chambers. This ensures that there is always a partial vacuum in the crankcase, and so prevents a build-up of pressure which could cause oil contamination, fume emission, and oil leakage past seals.

Periodically clean out the connecting hoses and jets and make sure that the hoses are a tight fit on their connectors.

The system layouts for non-Turbo and Turbo models are shown in Fig. 1.53 and 1.54.

65 Piston/connecting rod/cylinder liner assembly - removal

1 These assemblies can be removed with the engine in the car once the cylinder head, sump and oil pump have been removed, as described in previous Sections.
2 Rotate the crankshaft, using a spanner on the crankshaft pulley, so that No 1 big-end (nearest the flywheel) is at the lowest point of its travel.
3 The remainder of the procedure is as described in Section 64, paragraphs 4 to 7.

66 Engine/transmission mountings - renewal

1 The procedure for the 2.0 litre engine variants is similar to that for the 1.7 litre variants described in Part A, Section 23 of this Chapter.
2 The engine undertray will have to be removed for access to the mountings, and to allow the engine/transmission to be supported with a jack.
3 Refer to the accompanying photos. Note that there is no stabilizer bracket fitted to 2.0 litre models.

68 Examination and renovation

1 With the engine stripped down and all parts thoroughly clean, it is now time to examine everything for wear. The following items should be checked and where necessary renewed or renovated as described in the following Sections.

Fig. 1.53 Crankcase ventilation system hoses – non-Turbo (Sec 67)

1 2- way union
2 Calibrated connector-to-2-way union hose
3 Calibrated connector (red)
4 Calibrated connector-to-air intake casing hose
5 Air intake casing
6 2-way union with internal restrictor
7 2- way union-to-mixer casing hose
8 Mixer casing

Fig. 1.54 Crankcase ventilation system hoses – Turbo (Sec 67)

1 Turbocharger
2 Restrictor
3 Restrictor
4 Valve
5 Downstream circuit
6 Inlet manifold
7 Upstream circuit

Cylinder block and crankcase

2 Clean away all old gasket material and then examine the casting for cracks particularly about bolt holes. If they are found, specialist welding or cold repair will be required.

3 Clean out the oilways and galleries with compressed air or wire.

4 If the cylinder bores are worn, this will be evident by the emission of exhaust smoke and general deterioration in engine performance together with increased oil consumption. A good way to test the condition of the engine when it is still in the car is to have it at normal operating temperature with the spark plugs removed. Screw a compression tester (available from most modern accessory stores) into the first plug hole. Hold the accelerator pedal fully depressed and crank the engine on the starter motor for several revolutions. Record the reading. Zero the tester and check the remaining cylinders in the same way. All four compression figures should be approximately equal and within the tolerance given in the Specifications. If they are all low, suspect piston ring or cylinder bore wear. If only one reading is down, suspect a valve not seating.

5 The cylinder bores must be checked for taper, ovality, scoring and scratching. Start by examining the top of the cylinder bores. If they are at all worn, a ridge will be felt on the thrust side. This ridge marks the limit of piston ring travel.

6 An internal micrometer or dial gauge can be used to check bore wear and taper against Specifications, but this is a pointless operation if the engine is obviously worn as indicated by excessive oil consumption.

7 The engine is fitted with renewable 'wet' cylinder liners and these are supplied complete with piston, rings and gudgeon pin.

Pistons and connecting rods

8 On non-Turbo models the gudgeon pin is an interference fit in the connecting rod small end and removal or refitting and changing a piston should be left to a dealer or engine reconditioner. This is due to the need for a press and special tooling, and careful heating of the connecting rod. On Turbo models the gudgeon pin is retained in the piston and connecting rod by circlips and, once removed, the components can be separated for renewal.

9 Removal and refitting piston rings is described in the following paragraphs.

10 Remove the piston rings from the top of the piston. To avoid breaking a ring either during removal or refitting, slide two or three old feeler blades at equidistant points behind the top ring and slide it up them. Remove the other rings in a similar way.

11 Clean carbon from the ring grooves, a segment of old piston ring is useful for this purpose.

12 Clean out the oil return holes in the piston ring grooves and fit the new piston rings.

13 If proprietary rings are being fitted to old pistons, the top ring will be supplied stepped so that it does not impinge on the wear ridge.

14 Insert each piston ring in turn squarely into its bore. New rings supplied as part of Renault piston/liner sets are pre-gapped and must not be altered.

15 Now check each compression ring in its groove and measure the clearances with a feeler gauge. If it is tight the ring may be rubbed flat on a sheet of wet and dry paper laid flat on a piece of plate glass.

16 Fit the rings to the piston using the feeler blade method as described for removal. Work from the top of the piston, fitting the oil control ring first.

17 Lubricate the piston rings and locate their end gaps at 120° apart.

Crankshaft

18 Examine the crankpin and main journal surfaces for signs of scoring or scratches, and check for ovality and taper of the crankpins and main journals. If the bearing surface dimensions do not fall within the tolerance ranges given in the Specifications at the beginning of this Chapter, the crankpins and/or main journals will have to be reground.

19 Big-end and crankpin wear is accompanied by distinct metallic knocking, particularly noticeable when the engine is pulling from low revs, and some loss of oil pressure.

20 Main bearing and main journal wear is accompanied by severe engine vibration rumble - getting progressively worse as engine revs increase again by loss of oil pressure.

21 If the crankshaft requires regrinding, take it to an engine reconditioning specialist, who will machine it for you and supply the correct undersize bearing shells.

Big-end and main bearing shells

22 Inspect the big-end and main bearing shells for signs of general wear, scoring, pitting and scratches. The bearings should be matt grey in colour. With lead-indium bearings, should a trace of copper colour be noticed, the bearings are badly worn as the lead bearing material has worn away to expose the indium underlay. Renew the bearings if they are in this condition or if there are any signs of scoring or pitting.

HAYNES HiNT *You are strongly advised to renew the main and big-end bearings - regardless of their condition at time of major overhaul. Refitting used bearings is a false economy.*

23 The undersizes available are designed to correspond with crankshaft regrind sizes. The bearings are in fact, slightly more than the stated undersize as running clearances have been allowed for during their manufacture.

24 Main and big-end bearing shells can be identified as to size by the marking on the back of the shell. Standard size shell bearings are marked STD or.00, undersize shells are marked with the undersize such as 0.020 u/s. This marking method applies only to replacement bearing shells and not to those used during production.

Flywheel/driveplate and starter ring gear

25 If the starter ring gear teeth on the flywheel (manual transmission) or torque converter driveplate (automatic transmission) are excessively worn, it will be necessary to obtain complete new assemblies. It is not possible to obtain separate ring gears.

26 On manual transmission models, examine the clutch mating surface of the flywheel and renew the flywheel if scoring or cracks are evident.

27 On automatic transmission models, the driveplate face should be checked for run-out, using a dial gauge. The maximum permissible run-out is 0.3 mm (0.012 in). Renew the plate if this figure is exceeded.

28 The flywheel/driveplate retaining bolts must be renewed on reassembly.

Camshaft

29 Check the bearings in the cylinder head. If worn, a new head will be required.

30 Inspect the camshaft journals and lobes.

Fig. 1.65 Rocker gear. Note oil filter (A) (Sec 68)

68.50A Oil pump gear

68.50B Removing the oil pump drive gear

Scoring or general wear will indicate the need for new parts.

31 The camshaft sprocket teeth should be unchipped and free from wear.

32 The camshaft thrust plate should be free from scoring otherwise camshaft endfloat will be excessive.

Auxiliary shaft

33 Check the journals and gear teeth for wear, chipping or scoring.

34 The sprocket teeth should be free from wear and damage.

35 The forked thrust plate should be unworn, otherwise excessive shaft endfloat will occur.

36 Wear in the shaft bearings can only be rectified by the purchase of a new crankcase.

Timing belt and tensioner

37 The belt should be without any sign of fraying, cuts or splits and no deformation of the teeth.

38 Even if the timing belt appears to be in good condition, it is recommended that it is renewed at the intervals specified in the Routine Maintenance Section at the beginning of the Manual.

39 Check the belt tensioner pulley. It should spin freely without noise. If it does not, renew it.

Rocker gear

40 Slight wear in the heels of the rocker arms can be removed using an oilstone, but ensure that the contour is maintained.

41 Scoring or wear in the components can only be rectified by dismantling and renewing the defective components.

42 Unscrew the end plug from the shaft and extract the plug and filter. This filter must be renewed at the specified intervals, or whenever it is removed.

43 Number the rocker arms and pedestals/bearings. Note that bearing No 5 has two threaded holes to retain the thrust plate which controls the camshaft endfloat, and a hole for the roll pin which locates the shaft and pedestal. Renew the roll pin if it is not the solid type.

44 Keep the respective parts in order as they are removed from the shaft and note their respective locations. Note also that the machined flat section on top of pedestals 1 to 4 all face towards the camshaft sprocket.

45 Lubricate each component as it is assembled with engine oil. Lay the pedestals, spacers, springs and rockers out in order.

46 Support the rocker shaft in a soft-jawed vice and insert the new filter into the end of it, fit the retaining bolt and tighten it to the specified torque.

47 Assemble the respective pedestals, rocker arms, springs and spacers onto the shaft. When the shaft assembly is complete, compress the last pedestal to align the retaining pin hole in the shaft and pedestal. Drive a new pin into position to secure it. Early models fitted with a hollow type roll pin should have the later solid type pin fitted on reassembly.

Oil pump

48 All parts of the pump must be in good condition for the pump to work effectively.

49 To dismantle the pump, remove the cover retaining bolts and detach the cover.

50 Extract the gears and clean the respective components (photos).

51 Inspect for any signs of damage or excessive wear. Use a feeler gauge and check the clearance between the rotor (gear) tips and the inner housing.

52 Also, check the rotor endfloat using a straight-edge rule laid across the body of the pump and feeler gauge inserted between the rule and gears.

53 Compare the clearances with the allowable tolerances given in the Specifications at the start of this Chapter and, if necessary, renew any defective parts, or possibly the pump unit.

54 Do not overlook the relief valve assembly. To extract it, remove the split pin and withdraw the cup, spring, guide and piston. Again, look for signs of excessive wear or damage and renew as applicable.

55 Check the pump driveshaft for signs of wear or distortion and renew if necessary.

69 Cylinder head and pistons - decarbonizing, valve grinding and renovation

1 Proceed as described in Part A, Section 26 of this Chapter, but ignore the instructions given in paragraph 10.

2 The valve seat profile should be as shown in Fig. 1.59.

Fig. 1.66 Oil pump rotor-to-body clearance (A) (Sec 68)

Fig. 1.57 Oil pump rotor endfloat (B) (Sec 68)

Fig. 1.58 Oil pump pressure relief valve (Sec 68)

Fig. 1.59 Valve seat profile (Sec 69)

1 *Valve seating surface*
2 *Upper seat step*
3 *Lower seat step*
X = *1.8 mm for inlet valve, 1.6 mm for exhaust valve*
α = *120° for inlet valve, 90° for exhaust valve*

70 Piston rings - renewal (engine in car)

1 The piston rings can be renewed with the engine in the car, but a ring compressor and some suitable liner clamps will be required unless the liner seals are to be renewed also. In the latter instance, remove the pistons and liners as an assembly as described in Section 65.

2 Although the pistons cannot be withdrawn through the top of the block independently of the cylinder liners, new piston rings can be fitted, but the normal process of cylinder bore glaze removal cannot be carried out to enable the new rings to bed in properly. Despite this, the procedure is useful if a broken ring has to be renewed.

3 Remove the cylinder head (Section 56).

4 Remove the sump and oil pump (Sections 60 and 61).

5 Disconnect the big-end bearing caps (Section 64).

6 Before pushing the piston and rod assemblies up their respective bores, ensure that the cylinder liners are clamped down to prevent the liner seals from being disturbed. Refer to Section 56 for details.

Fig. 1.60 Cylinder liner clamp arrangement (Sec 70)

7 Push each connecting rod upwards until the piston rings are out of the bore. If a wear ridge is evident, then this must be removed by careful scraping or using a ridge reamer.

8 Remove the piston rings by sliding two or three feeler blades behind the top ring and removing it upwards using a twisting motion. Refit using the same method.

9 If the top compression ring is being renewed, a stepped replacement should be obtained to prevent it making contact with the wear ridge.

10 A piston ring compressor should be fitted to the rings (well lubricated with engine oil) and the wooden handle of a hammer placed on the piston crown while the head of the hammer is given a sharp blow with the hand. This will drive the piston/rod assembly down the cylinder bore out of the compressor which will be left standing on the liner rim.

11 Reconnect the big-ends, remove the liner clamps and refit the cylinder head (see Sections 73 and 80). Refit the oil pump and sump with reference to Sections 76 and 77.

71 Engine - reassembly (general)

1 To ensure maximum life with minimum trouble from a rebuilt engine, not only must everything be correctly assembled, but everything must be spotlessly clean, all the

72.1 Locate the main shells into position in the block

oilways must be clear, locking washers and spring washers must always be fitted where indicated and all bearing and other working surfaces must be thoroughly lubricated during assembly.

2 Before assembly begins renew any bolts or studs the threads of which are in any way damaged, and whenever possible use the new spring washers.

3 Apart from your normal tools, a supply of clean rag, an oil can filled with engine oil (an empty plastic detergent bottle, thoroughly cleaned and washed out, will do just as well), a new supply of assorted spring washers, a set of new gaskets and a torque wrench should be collected together.

72 Crankshaft and main bearings - refitting

1 Invert the block and locate the main bearing upper shells into position, engaging the lock tabs into the cut-outs in the bearing recesses. Note that the bearing shells for bearings Nos 1, 3 and 5 are identical and have two oil holes in them whilst the Nos 2 and 4 bearing shells have three holes and an oil groove in them. However, all new shells incorporate grooves (photo).

2 Lubricate the shells with clean engine oil (photo), fit the thrust washers to No 2 main bearing so that the oil grooves are visible (photo) and lower the crankshaft into position.

72.2A Lubricating main bearing shell

72.2B Crankshaft thrust washer

72.2C Lowering the crankshaft into position

72.4 Fitting a main bearing cap. Note the locating dowel (arrowed)

72.5 Checking crankshaft endfloat using a feeler gauge

72.7 Tightening a main bearing cap bolt

3 Locate the shells in the main bearing caps in a similar manner to that of the block, and lubricate.

4 Fit the bearing caps into position, and torque tighten the retaining bolts (photo).

5 Now check the crankshaft endfloat using a dial gauge or feeler gauge (photo). Select a thrust washer of suitable thickness to provide the correct endfloat (see Specifications).

6 Remove the main bearing caps and crankshaft, and insert the selected thrust washers, with their grooved side towards the crankshaft.

7 Refit Nos 2, 3 and 4 main bearing caps again and tighten their bolts to the specified torque (photo).

8 The grooves at the sides of the front and rear main bearing caps may be sealed using an RTV silicone sealant (CAF 4/60 THIXO available from Renault parts stockists) or alternatively, and preferably, by using butyl rubber sealing strips (also available from Renault parts stockists). If the silicone sealant is being used, ensure that all contact areas on the bearing cap and cylinder block are clean and degreased. Apply sealant sparingly to the lower face of the cylinder block, fit the cap and tighten the bolts to the specified torque. Fill the side grooves with sealant ensuring that the sealant is forced in under sustained pressure to prevent any air pockets. Cease injecting when the sealant begins to seep from the joints (photo). Repeat this procedure on the other main bearing cap. If butyl side seals are being used, follow the procedure described in Part A, Section 28, paragraph 1, and paragraphs 12 to 17 for both main bearing caps.

9 Lubricate the new front and rear crankshaft oil seals and carefully locate them into their apertures tapping them fully into position using a tubular drift of a suitable diameter. Ensure that the seals face the correct way round with the cavity/spring side towards the engine.

Should the seal lip accidentally become damaged during fitting, remove and discard it and fit another new seal (photos).

10 If a new clutch spigot bearing is being fitted, now is the time to do it. Drive it home using a suitable diameter tubular drift. **Note:** *When fitting this bearing to the crankshaft smear the outer bearing surface with a suitable thread locking compound.* To the crankshaft front end fit the belt guide, the Woodruff key and sprocket (rollpins visible) (photos) and the pulley and retaining bolt.

72.8 Sealing main bearing cap groove

72.9A Locate a new crankshaft front oil seal

72.9B Locate a new crankshaft rear oil seal

72.10A Clutch spigot bearing in crankshaft rear flange

72.10B Timing belt guide

72.10C Crankshaft sprocket Woodruff key

72.10D Fitting crankshaft sprocket

73.8A Fitting a piston/connecting rod into cylinder liner

73.8B Fitting a cylinder liner/piston/ connecting rod assembly into the block

73 Piston/connecting rod/cylinder liner assembly

1 Before fitting the piston and connecting rod assemblies into the liners, the liners must be checked in the crankcase for depth of fitting. This is carried out as follows.

2 Although the cylinder liners fit directly onto the crankcase inner flange, O-ring seals are fitted between the chamfered flange and the lower cylinder section, as shown in Fig. 1.61. New O-rings must always be used once the cylinders have been disturbed from the crankcase.

3 First, insert a liner into the crankcase without its O-ring and measure how far it protrudes from the top face of the crankcase. Lay a straightedge rule across its top face and measure the gap to the top face of the cylinder block with feeler gauges. It should be as given in the Specifications.

4 Now check the height on the other cylinders in the same way and note each reading. Check that the variation in protrusion on adjoining liners does not exceed 0.0016 in (0.04 mm).

5 New liners can be interchanged for position to achieve this if necessary, and when in position should be marked accordingly 1 to 4 from the flywheel end.

6 Remove each liner in turn and position an O-ring seal onto its lower section so that it butts into the corner, taking care not to twist or distort it (see Fig. 1.61).

7 Wipe the liners and pistons clean and smear with clean engine oil, prior to their respective fitting.

8 Refit the pistons to the liners, using a piston ring compressor tightened around well oiled rings to install the piston into the lower end of the cylinder liners. Fit the liners/pistons into the cylinder block. Fit the big end caps with shells (photos).

9 Observe the following important points:
(a) the arrows on top of the pistons must point towards the flywheel (photo)
(b) the connecting rod and cap bolts must be tightened to the specified torque with the numbered markings in alignment (photo)
(c) When assembled, reclamp the liners and rotate the crankshaft to ensure it rotates smoothly

74 Flywheel (or driveplate) - refitting

1 Locate the flywheel or driveplate on the crankshaft mounting flange. The bolt holes are offset so it will only go on one way (photo).
2 Use new fixing bolts, and having cleaned their threads, apply thread locking fluid to them. Refit the clutch (Chapter 5) (photos).

73.8C Fitting a big-end cap

Fig. 1.61 Cylinder liner protrusion (Sec 73)
J   O-ring seal
X   Protrusion above block face

73.9A Piston directional arrow

73.9B Tightening a big-end cap bolt

74.1 Fitting the flywheel

74.2A Applying thread locking fluid to a flywheel bolt

74.2B Tightening a flywheel bolt

75.1 Insert the auxiliary shaft . . .

75.2A . . . fit the locking plate . . .

75.2B . . . and its retaining bolt and washer

75 Auxiliary shaft - refitting

1 Lubricate the shaft and insert it through the front of the crankcase (photo).

2 Slide the lockplate fork into the protruding shaft location groove and secure the plate with the bolt and washer. Check that the shaft is free to rotate on completion (photos).

3 Fit the new oil seal into the auxiliary shaft front cover and lubricate its lips. Locate the new gasket onto the cover face.

4 Refit the auxiliary shaft cover (photos).

5 Fit the Woodruff key into its groove in the shaft and carefully locate the auxiliary shaft drive sprocket into position with its large offset inner face towards the crankcase. Use a suitable diameter drift to tap the sprocket into position over the key (photo).

6 Prevent the sprocket from rotating by inserting a screwdriver blade or similar through a sprocket hole, and tighten the retaining nut (complete with flat washer) to the specified torque (photo).

7 The oil pump drive pinion and shaft can now be inserted through the side cover hole in the crankcase. Make sure that the limiting circlip is in position on the oil pump end of the shaft (photos).

8 Once in position lubricate with engine oil to

75.4A Auxiliary shaft cover and gasket

75.4B Fitting auxiliary shaft cover and retaining bolts

75.5 Fitting the auxiliary shaft sprocket . . .

75.6 . . . and its retaining bolt and washer

75.7A Oil pump driveshaft and circlip

75.7B Oil pump drive pinion

75.9 Crankcase cover plate being fitted

Fig. 1.62 Auxiliary shaft sprocket orientation. Large offset (d) must face towards crankcase (Sec 75)

prevent pinion 'pick-up' on restarting the engine.

9 Ensure that the auxiliary shaft and oil pump drive rotate freely then refit the cover plate. This should be sealed by applying a thick bead of RTV sealant (instant gasket) to its underside flange edge (photo).

76 Oil pump - refitting

1 Lubricate the respective parts of the oil pump and reassemble.

2 Insert the rotors and refit the cover. No gasket is fitted on this face.

3 Tighten the retaining bolts to secure the cover.

4 Insert the oil pressure relief valve assembly, fitting the piston into the spring and the cup over the spring at the opposing end. Compress into the cylinder and insert a new split pin to retain the valve assembly in place.

5 Fit the assembled pump into position. Tighten the retaining bolts (photos).

6 If not already done, refit the oil pump drive pinion and driveshaft, ensuring that the circlip is in position on the lower end of the shaft. Refit the cover plate.

76.5A Locate the oil pump . . .

76.5B . . . and tighten its retaining bolts

77 Sump - refitting

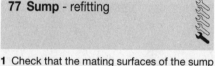

1 Check that the mating surfaces of the sump and crankcase are perfectly clean, with no sections of old gasket remaining.

2 Locate the new sump gasket, which should be fitted dry (photo).

3 Fit the sump carefully into position and locate the retaining bolts. Note that three

types of retaining bolts are used on the aluminium sumps fitted to non-Turbo models, and these should be located as shown in Fig. 1.62. On Turbo models, two types of retaining bolts are used, and these should be located as shown in Fig. 1.63. Tighten the three bolts securing the sump to the clutch housing first, then tighten the remaining bolts. On Turbo models, remember to tighten the captive bolt ('A' in Fig. 1.50).

4 Fit and tighten the sump drain plug.

77.2 Sump gasket located

Fig. 1.63 Sump retaining bolt identification and location – non-Turbo models (Sec 77)

Fig. 1.64 Sump retaining bolt identification and location – Turbo models (Sec 77)

78.1 Fitting a valve into its guide

78.2A Valve stem oil seal and spring seat

78.2B Fitting a valve spring

78 Cylinder head - reassembly

1 Commence reassembly by oiling the stem of the first valve and pushing it into its guide which should have been fitted with a new oil seal (photo).
2 Fit the spring seat, the valve spring so that the close coils are towards the cylinder head and then the spring retaining cap (photos).
3 Compress the valve spring and using a little grease locate the split collets in the valve stem cut-out (photo).
4 Gently release the compressor, checking to see that the collets are not displaced.

5 Fit the remaining valves in the same way.
6 Tap the end of each valve stem with a plastic or copper-faced hammer to settle the components.
7 Refit the camshaft to the cylinder head as described in Section 79.

79 Camshaft - refitting

1 Check that the respective camshaft location bearings in the cylinder head are perfectly clean and lubricate with some engine oil. Similarly lubricate the camshaft journals and lobes.

2 Insert the camshaft carefully into the cylinder head, guiding the cam sections through the bearing apertures so as not to score the bearing surfaces (photo).
3 With the camshaft in position, the front oil seal can be carefully drifted into position. Lubricate the seal lips with oil and drive into its location using a suitable tube drift (photo).
4 Bolt on the timing belt rear cover plate (photo).
5 Refit the distributor body.
6 Refit the Woodruff key (photo) followed by the camshaft sprocket. Note that, on some models, the sprocket can be fitted in either of two ways according to engine type. With reference to the sprocket and to Fig. 1.65, it can be seen that there are two keyways in the

78.2C Valve spring retaining cap

78.3 Compressing a valve spring

79.2 Inserting the camshaft into the cylinder head

79.3 Camshaft front oil seal

79.4 Timing belt rear cover plate

79.6 Camshaft sprocket Woodruff key

Fig. 1.65 Camshaft sprocket identification (Sec 79)

A Timing notch (Turbo engines)
D Identifying bosses (Turbo engines)
E Square hole
F Keyway for use with Turbo engines
G Timing notch (non-Turbo engines)
H Identifying boss (non-Turbo engines)
I Keyway for use with non-Turbo engines

Fig. 1.66 Camshaft sprocket orientation. Offset (d) must face towards cylinder head (Sec 79)

79.7 Tightening the camshaft sprocket bolt

1

sprocket hub. Adjacent to one keyway there is a square hole and two identifying bosses, adjacent to the other keyway there is a round hole and one identifying boss. On non-Turbo engines fit the sprocket so that the camshaft Woodruff key engages with the keyway adjacent to the round hole and single boss. On Turbo engines fit the sprocket so that the Woodruff Key engages the keyway adjacent to the square hole and two bosses. In all cases the sprocket must be fitted so that the offset 'd' in Fig. 1.66 is toward the cylinder head.

7 Refit the retaining bolt and washer, hold the sprocket to prevent rotation and tighten the bolt to the specified torque (photo).

8 Refit the cylinder head as described in Section 80.

80 Cylinder head - refitting

1 Before refitting the cylinder head, check that all the mating surfaces are perfectly

clean. Loosen the rocker arm adjuster screws fully back. Also ensure that the cylinder head bolt holes in the crankcase are clean and free of oil. Syringe or soak up any oil left in the bolt holes, and in the oil feed hole on the rear left-hand corner of the block. This is most important in order that the correct bolt tightening torque can be applied.

2 Prior to removing the liner clamps, rotate the crankshaft to locate the pistons halfway down the bores. Check that the location dowel is in position at the front right-hand corner.

3 Remove the liner clamps.

4 Fit the cylinder head gasket onto the cylinder block upper face and ensure that it is exactly located (photo). If possible, screw a couple of guide studs into position. They must be long enough to pass through the cylinder head so that they can be removed when it is in position.

5 Lower the cylinder head into position, engaging with the location dowel, and then locate the rocker assembly (photos).

6 Lubricate the cylinder head bolt threads and washers sparingly with engine oil, then screw them into position. Tighten them progressively in the sequence given in Fig. 1.46. Tighten all the bolts to the Stage 1 setting then to the Stage 2 setting as given in the Specifications at the beginning of this Chapter (photo). Slacken each bolt one at a time, in the sequence given, by half a turn

then immediately retighten to the Stage 3 setting before moving on to the next bolt. Further tightening of the cylinder head bolts will be necessary once the engine has been started and run for an initial period of twenty minutes, then allowed to cool for at least two and a half hours - see Section 88. With the cylinder head and rocker assembly secure, refit the camshaft thrust plate (photo).

7 Refit the timing belt as described in Section 81 and check the valve clearances as described in Section 82.

8 Reconnect the coolant hose, vacuum hose and HT lead brackets as applicable, and refit the camshaft cover.

9 Refit the rotor arm, distributor cap and HT leads.

80.4 Locating the cylinder head gasket

80.5A Lowering the cylinder head onto the block

80.5B Locating the rocker assembly

80.6A Tighten the cylinder head bolts

80.6B Tightening the camshaft thrust plate bolt

81.1A Timing belt tensioner spring and plunger

81.1B Fitting tensioner pulley

81.1C Tensioner pulley fully retracted

81.5 Tightening the belt tensioner nut

Fig. 1.67 Timing sprockets set with No 1 piston at TDC (Sec 81)

10 If the engine is in the car, refer to Section 56, and refit or reconnect as applicable the items removed or disconnected in paragraphs 1 to 8.

81 Timing belt - refitting

1 Locate the timing belt tensioner by inserting the spring into its housing in the side of the crankcase. and locate the plunger over it. Compress the spring and locate the tensioner pulley arm, retaining it with the bolt and nut. The spring tension is quite strong and an assistant will probably be required here. Fully retract the tensioner (photos).

2 Temporarily refit the timing belt cover and set the crankshaft and camshaft to the TDC position for No 1 piston on compression as described in Section 55, paragraph 6. Note that the camshaft sprocket has two TDC markings 180° apart; one being for non-Turbo engines and the other for Turbo versions. Ensure that the correct mark is aligned with the timing cover pointer according to engine type (see Section 79 and Fig. 1.65). Check also that the notch on the auxiliary shaft sprocket is aligned with the pointer in the lower viewing aperture on the timing belt cover.

3 Slip the belt over the sprocket teeth, making sure that it is taut from the crankshaft sprocket

around the intermediate shaft sprocket and camshaft sprocket - see Fig. 1.69.

4 Refit the crankshaft pulley.

5 Release the tensioner bolt and nut so that the tensioner pulley is spring-loaded against the timing belt, retighten the tensioner bolt and nut (photo).

6 Now turn the crankshaft two complete turns in a clockwise direction, never turn it anti-clockwise.

Fig. 1.68 TDC pointers in the timing belt cover (Sec 81)

Upper arrow indicates camshaft sprocket timing pointer
Lower arrow indicates auxiliary shaft sprocket timing pointer

Fig. 1.69 The timing belt must be taut at points A and B (Sec 81)

81.8 Fitting the timing belt cover

7 Release the tensioner bolt and nut about a quarter of a turn each, then retighten them to the specified torque (bolt first).
8 Check that the drivebelt deflection at the mid-way point between the camshaft and auxiliary shaft pulleys is as specified, then refit the timing belt cover (photo).
9 Refit the spark plugs and reconnect the battery earth terminal.
10 Refit the camshaft cover.
11 Refit the alternator and power steering pump drivebelts.

82 Valve clearances - adjustment

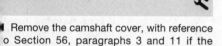

1 Remove the camshaft cover, with reference to Section 56, paragraphs 3 and 11 if the engine is in the car.
2 The precise adjustment of the valve/rocker clearances is of utmost importance for two main reasons. The first, to enable the valves to be opened and fully closed at the precise moment required by the cycle of the engine. The second, to ensure quiet operation and minimum wear of the valve gear components.
3 Settings made when the engine is on the bench will require rotation of the engine and this may be done by turning the exposed crankshaft pulley bolt. If the engine is in the car and a manual gearbox fitted, remove the spark plugs, select top gear, then jack up the front so that one front wheel is clear of the ground and can be turned. With automatic transmission, this method is not possible and 'inching' the engine using the starter motor will have to be resorted to. Alternatively the crankshaft pulley bolt can be turned as described previously.
4 Turn the crankshaft using one of the methods described until No 1 piston (nearest the flywheel) is at TDC on compression. With the crankshaft in this position the notch on the camshaft sprocket will be aligned with the pointer in the viewing aperture on the front face of the timing belt cover (Fig. 1.45) and the camshaft lobes for No 1 cylinder will be facing away from their respective rocker arms.
5 Slowly turn the crankshaft a further 90° in the normal direction of rotation until the first mark

82.6 Adjusting a valve clearance

on the rear face of the camshaft sprocket is aligned with the pointer on the timing belt cover backplate (Fig. 1.70). The clearance for No 2 cylinder inlet valve and No 4 cylinder exhaust valve can now be checked using feeler blades and, if necessary, adjusted to the figures given in the Specifications.
6 If the clearance requires adjustment, loosen the locknut and with the feeler in position turn the adjuster screw until the feeler blade is nipped and will not move. Now unscrew the adjuster until the feeler blade is a stiff sliding fit. Tighten the locknut and recheck the clearance (photo).
7 Turn the crankshaft in the normal direction of rotation until the second mark on the sprocket is aligned with the pointer. Repeat the adjustment procedure as shown in the following chart.

Camshaft sprocket mark aligned with pointer:	Inlet valve to adjust on cylinder:	Exhaust valve to adjust on cylinder:
1st mark	2	4
2nd mark	1	2
3rd mark	3	1
4th mark	4	3

Note that the inlet valves are on the inlet manifold side of the cylinder head and the exhaust valves are on the exhaust manifold side.
8 Should it be found that there are no marks on the rear face of the camshaft sprocket, make up a gauge out of cardboard, marked as shown in Fig. 1.71. Position the crankshaft at

Fig. 1.70 Camshaft sprocket valve clearance mark aligned with pointer in timing belt cover backplate (Sec 82)

TDC for No 1 piston on compression then make a reference mark on the timing belt cover using a dab of white paint. Stick the gauge on the crankshaft pulley so that the letter 'A' is aligned with the reference mark on the timing belt cover. Turn the crankshaft until the letter 'B' is aligned with the reference mark then check and adjust the valves as shown in the following chart. Repeat the procedure, turning the crankshaft in the normal direction of rotation, to each letter in turn, until all the valves have been checked and, if necessary, adjusted.

Gauge letter aligned with reference mark:	Inlet valve to adjust on cylinder:	Exhaust valve to adjust on cylinder:
B	2	4
C	1	2
B	3	1
C	4	3

9 On completion refit the camshaft cover and remove the gauge.

83 Ancillary components - refitting

1 Depending on the extent of the engine overhaul, refit the applicable items listed in Section 54, referring to the appropriate Sections in the Chapters concerned for details.
2 Where applicable, use new gaskets and seals and if specified, apply the recommended sealant.
3 Tighten the various components to the specified torque wrench settings (where given).
4 Adjust the drivebelt(s) as described in Chapter 2.
5 Arrange the wiring and hoses so that they will not interfere with the engine refitting procedures.
6 The starter motor can be bolted in position before refitting the engine, and held by its support bracket (see Chapter 12).
7 Oil the sealing ring of a new engine oil filter and screw it into position using hand pressure only.

Fig. 1.71 Valve clearance adjustment template for engines without camshaft sprocket markings (Sec 82)

Dimensions in mm

84 Engine - refitting (manual transmission in car)

1 The operations are reversals of those described in Section 49, but observe the following points.

2 Make sure that the clutch driven plate has been centralised, and smear the clutch shaft splines with a little molybdenum disulphide grease.

3 Refill the engine with oil and coolant.

4 Ensure that all wires and hoses have been reconnected in their correct positions.

5 Reconnect the exhaust downpipe to the manifold, fitting a new Thermoplastic seal, and tighten the clamp bolts/nuts to the point where the coil springs are fully compressed (coil bound). Refer to Chapter 3 for details.

85 Engine and manual transmission - reconnection and refitting

1 The operations are reversals of those described in Section 50, but observe the following points. Refer to the relevant Sections and Chapters where necessary for refitting details.

2 Make sure that the clutch driven plate has been centralised, and smear the input shaft splines with molybdenum disulphide grease.

3 As the engine/transmission units are lowered into the engine bay, the transmission must be raised and supported with a jack, as the engine is lowered onto its mouldings. Initially, only loosely fit the engine mounting nuts to allow for minor adjustments when connecting the transmission mountings. Fit the transmission mountings to the subframe first, then move the transmission as required to align the retaining bolts and holes. When all of the mounting bolts are located, tighten them to the specified torque wrench setting.

4 Lubricate the gearchange linkage, and reconnect as described in Chapter 6.

5 Reconnect the driveshafts as described in Chapter 8 and, if applicable, the steering arm outer balljoints as described in Chapter 10.

6 Reconnect the exhaust system as described in Chapter 3, ensuring that the coil springs at the joint are coil bound.

7 Top up the cooling system, the engine oil and transmission oil with reference to Chapters 2, 1 and 6 respectively.

8 Check that all connections are secure. Leave fitting the bonnet and undershields until the engine has been started, so that checks can be made for any leaks.

86 Engine - refitting (automatic transmission in car)

1 Apply a smear of molybdenum disulphide grease to the locating boss on the torque converter.

2 Remove the temporary holding bar from the torque converter.

3 Lower the engine into the car, making sure that the torque converter does not move forward as the engine is connected and bolted to the transmission. The upper bellhousing bolts must be in position before the engine is connected to the transmission as they cannot be fitted afterwards.

4 The bellhousing lower cover must be located on the dowels before the engine and transmission are brought together, and the alignment mark on the driveplate must be between the two marks on the torque converter.

5 The remaining reconnection and refitting operations are reversals of removal and separation (Section 51) but observe the following points.

6 Reconnect the vacuum pipe and the control linkage before connecting the transmission mountings. The control cable must have the notches towards the balljoint.

7 Refill the engine with oil and coolant and top up the transmission fluid if necessary.

87 Engine/automatic transmission - reconnection and refitting

1 The reconnection operations are as described in the preceding Section.

2 Once the engine/automatic transmission has been installed, refill with oil and coolant and adjust controls and cables as described in Chapter 7.

3 Top up the transmission fluid if necessary.

88 Engine - adjustments after major overhaul

1 Before starting the engine, check that all hoses, controls and electrical leads have been connected.

2 Make sure that tools and rags have been removed from the engine compartment.

3 If the majority of internal components have been renewed, treat the engine as a new one and restrict speed for the first 500 miles (800 km).

4 Once the engine has been restarted, run it for a period of twenty minutes, then switch off and allow it to cool for at least two and a half hours. Remove the valve cover and retighten the cylinder head bolts using the following procedure.

5 Refer to Fig. 1.46 and slacken each bolt one at a time in the sequence shown by half a turn, then immediately retighten to the Stage 3 torque wrench setting given in the Specifications before moving on to the next bolt,

6 On completion, refit the valve cover.

Fault finding - all engines

Engine fails to start

☐ Discharged battery
☐ Loose battery connection
☐ Loose or broken ignition leads
☐ Moisture on spark plugs, distributor cap, or HT leads
☐ Incorrect spark plug gaps
☐ Cracked distributor cap or rotor
☐ Other ignition system fault
☐ Dirt or water in carburettor (if applicable)
☐ Empty fuel tank
☐ Faulty fuel pump
☐ Other fuel system fault
☐ Faulty starter motor
☐ Low cylinder compressions

Engine idles erratically

☐ Inlet manifold air leak
☐ Leaking cylinder head gasket
☐ Worn rocker arms, timing belt or gears
☐ Worn camshaft lobes
☐ Faulty fuel pump
☐ Incorrect valve clearances
☐ Loose crankcase ventilation hoses
☐ Carburettor adjustment incorrect (if applicable)
☐ Uneven cylinder compressions

Engine misfires

☐ Spark plugs worn or incorrectly gapped
☐ Dirt or water in carburettor (if applicable)
☐ Carburettor adjustment incorrect (if applicable)
☐ Burnt out valve
☐ Leaking cylinder head gasket
☐ Distributor cap cracked
☐ Incorrect valve clearances
☐ Uneven cylinder compressions
☐ Worn carburettor (if applicable)

Engine stalls

☐ Carburettor adjustment incorrect (if applicable)
☐ Inlet manifold air leak
☐ Ignition timing incorrect

Excessive oil consumption

☐ Worn pistons, cylinder bores or piston rings
☐ Valve guides and valve stem seals worn
☐ Oil leaking from rocker cover, camshaft cover, engine gaskets or oil seals

Engine backfires

☐ Carburettor adjustment incorrect (if applicable)
☐ Ignition timing incorrect
☐ Incorrect valve clearances
☐ Inlet manifold air leak
☐ Sticking valve

1

Notes

Chapter 2
Cooling, heating and air conditioning systems

For modifications, and information applicable to later models, see Supplement at end of manual

Contents

2

Degrees of difficulty

Easy, suitable for novice with little experience	**Fairly easy,** suitable for beginner with some experience	**Fairly difficult,** suitable for competent DIY mechanic	**Difficult,** suitable for experienced DIY mechanic	**Very difficult,** suitable for expert DIY or professional

Specifications

System type .... Pressurized, pump assisted thermosyphon system with electric cooling fan(s)

Filler cap
Blow-off pressure:
  1.7 and 2.0 litre non-Turbo .... 1.2 bar (17.4 lbf/in²)
  2.0 litre Turbo .... 1.6 bar (23.2 lbf/in²)

Thermostat
Starts to open .... 89°C
Fully open .... 101°C

Coolant
Type/specification .... Ethylene glycol based antifreeze with corrosion inhibitor to BS 3151, 3152, or 6580

Capacity:
  1.7 litre .... 5.2 litres (9.2 pints)
  2.0 litre non-Turbo .... 6.8 litres (11.9 pints)
  2.0 litre Turbo .... 6.2 litres (10.9 pints)

1 General description

The system is of pressurised semi-sealed type with the inclusion of an expansion bottle or chamber to accept coolant displaced from the system when hot and to return it when the system cools.

Coolant is circulated by thermosyphon action and is assisted by means of the impeller in the belt-driven coolant pump.

A thermostat is fitted. When the engine is cold, the thermostat valve remains closed so that the coolant flow which occurs at normal operating temperatures through the radiator matrix is interrupted.

As the coolant warms up, the thermostat valve starts to open and allows the coolant flow through the radiator to resume.

The engine temperature will always be maintained at a constant level (according to the thermostat rating) whatever the ambient air temperature.

The coolant circulates around the engine block and cylinder head and absorbs heat as it flows, then travels out into the radiator to pass across the matrix. As the coolant flows across the radiator matrix, air flow created by the forward motion of the car cools it, and it returns via the bottom tank of the radiator to the cylinder block. This is a continuous process, assisted by the coolant pump impeller.

All models are fitted with an electric cooling

1 Engine	7 Bleed screws
2 Radiator	8 Temperature
3 Expansion	switch
chamber	11 Carburettor inlet
4 Heater	heating
5 Thermostat	14 Calibrated orifice
6 Coolant pump	15 Syphon loop

Fig. 2.1 Cooling system layout – 1.7 litre model (Sec 1)

Fig. 2.2 Cooling system layout – 2.0 litre non-Turbo model (Sec 1)

1 Engine	5 Coolant pump	8 Temperature
2 Radiator	6 Thermostat	switch
3 Expansion bottle	7 Bleed screws	14 Calibrated orifice
4 Heater		16 Bypass

Fig. 2.3 Cooling system layout – Turbo models (Sec 1)

1 Engine	6 Intercooler	9 Electric coolant
2 Radiator	(oil-to-water)	pump
3 Expansion bottle	7 Thermostat	14 Calibrated orifice
4 Heater	8 Temperature	15 Turbocharger
5 Coolant pump	switch	

fan which is actuated by the thermostat switch according to coolant temperature. Certain models are equipped with two cooling fans.

The car interior heater operates by means of coolant from the engine cooling system. Coolant flow through the heater is constant, as there is no coolant on/off valve fitted to the system. This improves engine cooling.

On carburettor models, the system incorporates coolant connections to permit coolant from the cooling system to circulate to the carburettor base. Coolant also circulates to the automatic choke operating mechanism.

On models with automatic transmission, a fluid cooler is built into the cooling system circuit.

An additional coolant pump is fitted in the cooling system circuit on Turbo models. This pump is electrically-operated and is located adjacent to the right-hand shock absorber turret within the engine compartment. This pump supplies coolant to the turbocharger unit when activated by a timed relay in the computer casing.

The cooling system circuits are shown in Figs. 2.1, 2.2 and 2.3.

2 Maintenance

1 Apart from renewing the coolant at the prescribed intervals, maintenance is mainly confined to checking the coolant level in the expansion bottle.
2 Check the level when cold. It should be maintained between the MINI and MAXI marks on the expansion bottle or radiator expansion chamber, as applicable (photos).
3 If topping-up is required, use only coolant made up in similar proportions to the original mixture.
4 Only very infrequent topping-up should be required, anything more will indicate a leak in the system which should be rectified immediately.
5 The hoses and their clamps should also be inspected regularly for security and good condition.
6 The radiator should be brushed periodically, or a compressed air jet or cold water hose directed onto it to remove insects and leaves from its cooling tubes and fins. This will ensure the maximum cooling effect from the radiator.
7 Blanking off the radiator or grille in very cold weather is not recommended. Provided the correct thermostat is used with a suitable antifreeze mixture in the system, the correct engine operating temperature will be maintained whatever the climatic conditions.
8 Check the condition and adjustment of the drivebelt(s) at the specified intervals, as described in Section 11.
9 If air conditioning is fitted, refer to Section 18 for maintenance procedures. If

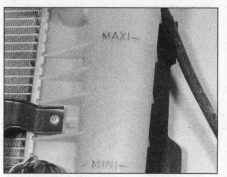

2.2A Coolant level markings – 1.7 litre model (radiator expansion chamber)

disconnecting any part of the air conditioning system any time, it is important that the precautionary notes given in Section 17 are adhered to.

3 Cooling system - draining, flushing and refilling

1 If the coolant is to be saved for further use, place a suitable container under the radiator bottom hose connection. If the coolant is to be renewed, it may be allowed to run to waste.
2 Remove the expansion bottle or chamber cap, as applicable.
3 Disconnect the radiator bottom hose and drain the coolant.
4 If the coolant has been renewed regularly,

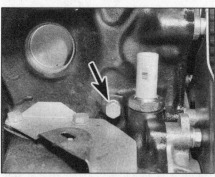

3.4A Cylinder block drain plug (arrowed) – 1.7 litre engine

3.6A Bleed screw in top hose (arrowed) – 2.0 litre engine

2.2B Topping up the cooling system – 2.0 litre model (expansion bottle)

then the system may be refilled immediately. If the cooling system has been neglected, remove the cylinder block drain plug (photos) and place a cold water hose in the radiator top hose. Flush the system through until the water comes out clear from the drain plug hole and the radiator hose. If contamination is severe, the radiator may have to be removed and cleaned out; see Section 7.
5 Reconnect the radiator hose and tighten its clip. Tighten the cylinder block drain plug if removed.
6 Open the system bleed screws. On 1.7 litre models, these are located in the radiator and heater hose. On 2.0 litre models, the bleed screws are located in the radiator top hose and the heater hose (photos). It should be noted that the bleed screw must not be opened with the engine running.

3.4B Cylinder block drain plug (arrowed) – 2.0 litre engine

3.6B Bleed screw in heater hose (arrowed) – 2.0 litre engine

2

Fig. 2.4 Bleed screw locations – 1.7 litre model (Sec 3)

A Radiator   B Heater hose

7 On 1.7 litre models, disconnect the syphon loop hose at the radiator and lay it out flat.

8 Fill the system slowly through the expansion bottle or tank opening. Use only coolant made up as an antifreeze mixture as described in the next Section.

9 As soon as coolant is ejected from the bleed screws, close them (photo). Proceed as described in the following paragraphs for 1.7 or 2.0 litre models, as applicable.

1.7 litre models

10 Start and run the engine at a speed of 1500 rpm.

11 Depress the accelerator 3 or 4 times to increase the engine speed to between 3000 and 4000 rpm, then top up the expansion chamber until it overflows.

12 Repeat this procedure for approximately 4 minutes, then switch off the engine and refit the expansion chamber cap and reconnect the syphon hose.

13 Run the engine for a further 10 minutes at 1500 rpm, until the cooling fan(s) have cut in at least 3 times (this is necessary for automatic degassing of the system).

14 Check that the coolant level is near the MAXI mark. It is permissible for the coolant level to be just above this mark.

2.0 litre models

15 Start and run the engine at a speed of 1500 rpm.

16 Run the engine at a constant 1500 rpm, and fill the expansion bottle until it overflows.

17 Continue this procedure for approximately 4 minutes, then switch off the engine and refit the expansion bottle cap.

18 Run the engine for a further 10 minutes at 1500 rpm until the cooling fan(s) cut in (this is necessary for automatic degassing of the system).

19 Check that the coolant level is near the MAXI mark.

4 Coolant mixtures

1 It is essential that an approved type of antifreeze is employed, in order that the necessary antifreeze and anticorrosion proportions are maintained.

2 The radiator matrix of some models is made of aluminium and it is essential to use an antifreeze product suitable for this material.

3 Whilst the life of the coolant originally used is stated to be 3 years or 40 000 miles (60 000 km), owners are advised to consider renewing the coolant yearly to ensure that all the essential properties of the solution are fully maintained.

4 Make up the solution, ideally using distilled water or rain water, in the proportions necessary to give protection in the prevailing climate. Percentages of antifreeze necessary are usually found on the container. Do not use too low a percentage of antifreeze, or the anti-corrosion properties will not be sufficiently effective.

5 If it is suspected that the coolant strength is unsatisfactory, a check may be made using a hydrometer. Employ the instrument as instructed by the manufacturer, and using the correction tables normally supplied. If the protection is found to be insufficient, drain off some of the coolant and replace it with pure antifreeze. Recheck the coolant with the hydrometer.

6 Even in territories where the climate does not require the use of antifreeze, never use plain water in the cooling system, always add a suitable corrosion inhibitor.

5 Thermostat (1.7 litre engine) - removal, testing and refitting

1 The thermostat is located in a housing bolted to the left-hand side of the cylinder head beneath the distributor (photo).

2 To remove the thermostat, first unscrew the expansion chamber filler cap. If the engine is hot, place a cloth over the cap and unscrew it slowly allowing all the pressure to escape before removing the cap completely.

3 Place a suitable container beneath the radiator bottom hose outlet. Disconnect the bottom hose and drain approximately 1 litre (1.76 pints) of the coolant. Reconnect the bottom hose and tighten the clip.

4 Slacken the clip securing the radiator top hose to the thermostat housing and remove the hose.

5 Undo the three bolts, lift off the housing and take out the thermostat (photo). Remove the thermostat rubber sealing ring.

3.9 Coolant bleeding from top hose – 2.0 litre engine

5.1 Thermostat housing location – 1.7 litre engine

5.5 Thermostat and housing removal – 1.7 litre engine

6.2 Thermostat removal from the top hose – 2.0 litre engine

7.2A Detach the radiator top and syphon hoses . . .

7.2B . . . and the bottom hose – 1.7 litre model

6 To test whether the unit is serviceable, suspend it on a string in a saucepan of cold water together with a thermometer. Heat the water and note the temperature at which the thermostat begins to open. Continue heating the water until the thermostat is fully open and then remove it from the water.

7 The temperature at which the thermostat should start to open is stamped on the unit. If the thermostat does not start to open at the specified temperature, does not fully open in boiling water, or does not fully close when removed from the water, then it must be discarded and a new one fitted.

8 Refitting is the reverse sequence to removal, but renew the thermostat rubber sealing ring if it shows any signs of deterioration. After fitting, fill the cooling system, with reference to Section 3.

6 Thermostat (2.0 litre engine) - removal, testing and refitting

1 The thermostat is located within the cylinder head end of the coolant top hose.

2 Proceed as described in paragraphs 2 to 4 of the previous Section. When the top hose is detached from the cylinder head, extract the thermostat from the hose (photo).

3 To test the thermostat, proceed as described in paragraphs 6 and 7 of the previous Section.

4 Refit in the reverse order of removal, then top up the cooling system as described in Section 3.

7 Radiator - removal and refitting

Note: *On Turbo models, remove the air-to-air intercooler above the radiator as described in Chapter 3 before proceeding*

1 Drain the engine coolant as described in Section 3.

2 Unclip and detach the top, bottom and, on 1.7 litre models, the syphon hose from the radiator (photos).

7.3A Remove the top crossmember bolts (arrowed) . . .

7.3B . . . and remove the crossmember – 1.7 litre model shown

3 Undo the four retaining bolts and remove the crossmember from above the radiator (photos).

4 Disconnect the wiring harnesses and connectors from the coolant temperature switches and the cooling fan(s), then lift out the radiator together with the cooling fan unit (photos).

5 If required, the cooling fan unit can be detached from the radiator as described in the following Section.

6 If the radiator is clogged, reverse flush it with a cold water hose. In severe cases of contamination, use a radiator cleaner but strictly in accordance with the manufacturer's instructions. The product must be suitable for aluminium radiators.

7 If the radiator is leaking, it may be

7.3C Top crossmember bolts (arrowed) – 2.0 litre model

7.4A Coolant temperature switch – 1.7 litre model

7.4B Coolant temperature switch – 2.0 litre non-Turbo model

2

7.4C Coolant temperature switch and associated wiring connections – Turbo model

7.4D Radiator and fan removal – 1.7 litre model

7.4E Radiator and fan removal – 2.0 litre model (fan is mounted on front face of radiator)

repairable using one of the numerous proprietary liquid sealants available. These sealants are usually diluted with water and run through the cooling system for a set period of time in accordance with the manufacturer's instructions. The radiator will need to be in position for this repair method. Failing this method, consult a radiator repair specialist for advice on any possible repairs, as it is not a task recommended for the home mechanic.

8 Do not leave the radiator empty for more than 48 hours or the aluminium will start to corrode.

9 Refitting is a reversal of removal, but ensure that the bottom locating pegs are engaged in their bushes (photos).

10 Refill and bleed the cooling system, as described in Section 3.

8 Cooling fan and switch - removal and refitting

Note: *On Turbo models, and those equipped with air conditioning, twin cooling fans are used as a means of dissipating the additional heat generated.*

1 The fan assembly and its mounting bracket may be clipped, bolted, screwed or riveted in position according to model and engine type. Once the radiator is removed (Sec 7) the fan assembly can be detached after removal of the relevant fastening (photos). Where the assembly is secured by rivets, these must be drilled out and the unit secured with new pop rivets on reassembly.

2 The temperature switch which regulates the operation of the electric cooling fan(s) is fitted into the radiator (see previous Section). Ideally, tests to the switch should be carried out after it has been removed from its location. If this is done, the cooling system will have to be drained and refilled, but the following alternative method may be used.

3 Connect a test light to the fan switch. When the engine is cold (ie switch contacts open), it should not light up.

4 Start the engine and blank off the radiator to ensure quick warming up.

5 When the temperature reaches the cut-in point, the lamp should light.

6 Switch off the engine and allow the temperature of the radiator to drop. When the cut-out temperature is reached the lamp should go out.

7 If the switch does not operate, renew it.

8 If the switch does operate correctly, then the fault must lie in the fan assembly or the connecting wiring or relay.

9 Refitting is a reversal of removal. Use a new seal when screwing in the temperature switch and avoid overtightening it.

9 Coolant temperature sensor - testing

1 Where an engine coolant temperature sensor unit is suspected of being faulty, the only simple way to test it is by substitution.

7.9A Engage location pegs when refitting radiator – 1.7 litre model

7.9B Radiator location peg and bush – 2.0 litre model

8.1A Radiator and cooling fan assembly – 1.7 litre model

8.1B Radiator and cooling fan assembly – 2.0 litre non-Turbo model

8.1C Radiator and twin cooling fan assembly – Turbo model

Fig. 2.5 Coolant pump retaining bolts (arrowed) – 1.7 litre model (Sec 10)

2 The temperature sensor unit is located in the side of the cylinder head near the thermostat housing (1.7 litre models), or in the front left-hand side of the cylinder head (2.0 litre models).

3 Removal necessitates partial draining of the cooling system, whilst the gauge removal necessitates removal of the instrument panel (see Chapter 12).

4 It is not possible to repair the gauge or temperature sensor unit and they must therefore be renewed if faulty.

5 A simple test of the gauge may be made by touching the temperature sensor unit wire to earth (ignition on) whilst an assistant observes the gauge. The gauge should read 'hot'; if not, either there is a break in the wiring or the gauge itself is at fault.

10 Coolant pump - removal and refitting

Note: *Coolant pump failure is indicated by water leaking from the gland at the front of the pump, or by rough and noisy operation. This is usually accompanied by excessive play of the pump spindle which can be checked by moving the pulley from side to side. Repair or overhaul of a faulty pump is not possible, as*

10.3 Coolant pump and pulley – 1.7 litre model

internal parts are not available separately. In the event of failure a replacement pump must be obtained.

1.7 litre engine

1 Disconnect the battery negative terminal and then refer to Section 3 and drain the cooling system.
2 Refer to Section 11 and remove the drivebelt.
3 Undo the three bolts and remove the pump pulley (photo).
4 Undo the bolts securing the pump to the cylinder block and withdraw the pump from its location. If it is stuck, strike it sharply with a plastic or hide mallet.
5 Refitting is the reverse sequence to removal, but note the following:
(a) Remove all traces of old gasket from the cylinder head and pump faces, and ensure that both mating surfaces are clean and dry.
(b) The gasket must be fitted dry, without jointing compound (photo)
(c) Adjust the drivebelt tension, as described in Section 11, and refill the cooling system, as described in Section 3

2.0 litre engine

6 Disconnect the battery negative lead.
7 Drain the cooling system as described in Section 3.
8 Remove the radiator as described in Section 7.
9 Disconnect the hoses from the coolant pump.

10.5 Refitting the coolant pump with new gasket – 1.7 litre model

10 Slacken the drivebelt and unbolt and remove the coolant pump pulley.
11 Unscrew the coolant pump fixing bolts, tap the pump gently to break its gasket seal and remove the pump, at the same time compressing the timing belt tensioner plunger spring.
12 The pump is of disposable type and if worn or leaking it must be renewed, no repair being possible (photo).
13 Clean away all old gasket material from the cylinder block and locate a new gasket in position. Bolt the pump into position, holding the timing belt tensioner spring compressed.
14 Refit the pulley, and the drivebelt. Tension the belt (Section 11).
15 Fill and bleed the cooling system. Reconnect the battery.

11 Drivebelts - tensioning, removal and refitting

1 Drivebelts are used to drive the coolant pump, alternator, and where applicable, the power steering pump and/or air conditioning compressor.
2 On 1.7 litre models, a single drivebelt is used to drive all ancillaries. On 2.0 litre models, a single, double, or triple drivebelt arrangement is used depending on equipment.
3 At the intervals specified in the *'Routine maintenance'* Section at the start of this

2

10.12 Rear view of coolant pump – 2.0 litre model

11.1 Dual drivebelt arrangement for coolant pump, alternator and power steering pump – 2.0 litre model

11.3 Checking drivebelt deflection

11.4A Alternator drivebelt tension adjuster – 2.0 litre model

11.4B Power steering pump drivebelt tension adjuster (viewed from underneath) – 2.0 litre model

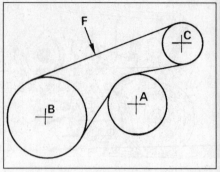

Fig. 2.6 Drivebelt deflection checking point – 1.7 litre models without power steering or air conditioning (Sec 11)

A   Coolant pump drive pulley
B   Crankshaft pulley
C   Alternator pulley
F = 3.0 mm (engine cold)

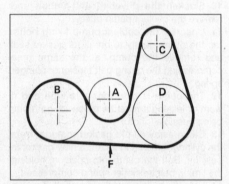

Fig. 2.7 Drivebelt deflection checking point – 1.7 litre models with power steering or air conditioning (Sec 11)

A   Coolant pump drive pulley
B   Crankshaft pulley
C   Alternator pulley
D   Power steering pump or air conditioning compressor pulley
F = 2.5 to 3.0 mm (engine cold)

manual, check the tension of the belt(s) by measuring the deflection at the relevant point(s) indicated in the accompanying figures (photo). Adjustment of the belt(s) will be necessary if the deflection is not as specified.

4 To adjust the tension of a drivebelt, loosen the adjuster and mounting bolts of an appropriate driven component (such as the alternator). Move the component to adjust the drivebelt tension as required, and tighten the adjuster and mounting bolts (photos).

5 Take care not to overtighten a drivebelt, as its life and that of the relevant component bearings will be reduced.

6 Check the belts regularly for cuts or fraying, and if evident, renew them.

7 To remove a drivebelt, release the driven component adjuster and mounting bolts and move the component fully in towards the engine. With the drivebelt slack, slip it off the pulleys. If there is any difficulty doing this, turn the crankshaft pulley and at the same time press the belt against the pulley rim when it will ride up and over the rim.

8 It will be obvious that before an inner belt

can be removed the outer one will have to be taken off.

9 Fit the new belt, again turning the crankshaft pulley if the belt is difficult to prise over the pulley rim.

10 Tension the belt as described earlier in this Section.

12 Electric coolant pump (Turbo models) - removal and refitting

1 Disconnect the battery earth lead.
2 Drain the cooling system as described in Section 3.
3 Disconnect the coolant inlet and delivery hoses from the pump unit, which is located next to the front right-hand suspension turret in the engine bay.
4 Detach the pump unit, disconnect the wiring to it, then remove it from the car.
5 Refitting is a reversal of the removal procedure, but ensure that the delivery pipe is vertical as shown in Fig. 2.10.
6 Refill the cooling system as described in Section 3.

Fig. 2.8 Drivebelt deflection checking point – 1.7 litre models with power steering and air conditioning (Sec 11)

A   Coolant pump pulley
B   Crankshaft pulley
C   Alternator pulley
D   Power steering pump pulley
E   Air conditioning compressor pulley
F   Tensioner pulley
F₁ = 4.0 to 5.0 mm (run engine for 5 minutes before checking)

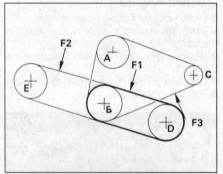

Fig. 2.9 Drivebelt deflection checking points – 2.0 litre models (Sec 11)

A   Coolant pump pulley
B   Crankshaft pulley
C   Alternator pulley
D   Power steering pump pulley
E   Air conditioning compressor pulley
F_1 = 3.0 to 3.5 mm (engine cold)
F_2 = 4.0 mm (engine cold)
F_3 = 4.5 to 5.0 mm (engine cold)

Fig. 2.10 Electric coolant pump fitted to Turbo models showing delivery pipe (A) and inlet pipe (B) (Sec 12)

13.6 Detaching a duct (arrowed) from the heater

13.7 Undo the heater retaining bolts

14.2 Heater control valve lever and return spring

13 Heater unit - removal and refitting

1 Disconnect the battery earth lead.
2 Drain the engine coolant as described in Section 3.
3 Remove the facia unit as described in Chapter 11.
4 Unclip and detach the coolant heater hoses at the engine compartment bulkhead. If the manufacturer's retaining clips are still fitted, they will need to be cut free and renewed when refitting.
5 Disconnect the control unit (Section 15).
6 Detach the ducts from each side of the heater unit (photo).
7 Undo the three heater retaining bolts and lower the heater unit, taking care not to spill any remaining coolant as the inlet and outlet pipes are passed through the bulkhead aperture (photo).
8 Refit in the reverse order of removal. Refill the cooling system as described in Section 3.

14 Heater matrix - removal and refitting

1 Remove the heater unit as described in Section 13.
2 Disconnect the control valve return spring from the end of the matrix (photo).
3 Undo the two retaining screws and withdraw the matrix from the heater unit (photo).
4 Refit in the reverse order of removal. Refit the heater unit as described in Section 13.

15 Heater and ventilation controls - removal and refitting

1 Disconnect the battery earth lead
2 Remove the lower facia panels for access to the underside of the heater/ventilation control unit.
3 Undo the three heater/ventilation control unit retaining screws.
4 Release the unit retaining clips (one each side), then lower the unit for withdrawal.
5 Disconnect the control cables and the wiring connector to fully remove the control unit (photo).

14.3 Withdrawing the heater matrix

6 Refit in the reverse order of removal. Check for satisfactory operation on completion.

16 Heater blower motor - removal and refitting

1 The blower motor can be removed from the heater unit leaving the heater in position. Proceed as follows.
2 Disconnect the battery earth lead.
3 Detach and remove the glovebox for access to the underside of the heater unit.
4 Prise free the insulator cover from the base of the heater unit casing.
5 Unscrew the three retaining bolts and lower the heater blower motor from the heater casing. Disconnect the wiring (photos).
6 Refit in the reverse order of removal.

15.5 Heater/ventilation control unit and connections

16.5A Undo the blower motor retaining screws . . .

16.5B . . . withdraw the motor/fan unit . . .

16.5C . . . and detach the wiring connector

2

17 Air conditioning system - description and precautions

1 When an air conditioning system is fitted, it is necessary to observe special precautions whenever dealing with any part of the system, its associated components and any items which necessitate disconnection of the system.

2 The refrigeration circuit contains a liquid refrigerant (Freon) and it is therefore dangerous to disconnect any part of the system without specialised knowledge and equipment. If for any reason the system must be disconnected (engine removal for example), entrust this task to your Renault dealer or a refrigeration engineer.

3 The layout of the air conditioning system is shown in Fig. 2.11. The air conditioner unit is located under the passenger side facia panel.

4 The refrigerant must not be allowed to come in contact with a naked flame or a poisonous gas will be created. Do not allow the fluid to come in contact with the skin or eyes.

5 Whenever the refrigerant lines are disconnected, all pipe lines and openings must be plugged or capped to prevent the entry of moisture.

6 After the system pipe lines have been reconnected, always have the system evacuated and recharged by your dealer or a competent refrigeration engineer.

18 Air conditioning system - maintenance

1 Regularly inspect the condition of hoses and the security of connections.

2 A sight glass is located on top of the receiver/dryer chamber. If bubbles are evident immediately after switching on the system, a fluid leak is indicated.

3 Keep the fins of the condenser free from flies and dirt and keep the compressor drivebelt in good condition and correctly tensioned (Section 11).

4 Water dripping or collecting on the floor under the car is quite normal, and is the result of condensation.

5 Run the system for a few minutes each week when it is not generally in use.

19 Air conditioning system - removal and refitting of main components

Note: *The system should be professionally discharged before carrying out any of the following work. Cap or plug the pipe lines as soon as they are disconnected. Refer to the precautions given in Section 17 before proceeding.*

Fig. 2.11 Layout of air conditioning system (Sec 17)

Fig. 2.12 Air conditioning system receiver/dryer chamber sight glass location (1) (Sec 18)

Fig. 2.13 Disconnect engine coolant hoses (C) at the radiator and air conditioning freon hoses (D) at the condenser (Sec 19)

Fig. 2.14 Heater/air conditioning unit showing mounting screw location points (B) and expansion valve-to-scuttle retaining nut locations (F) (Sec 19)

Fig. 2.15 Air conditioning system relays (B and C) and diodes (E) (Sec 19)

Fig. 2.16 Air conditioning system recycling flap solenoid valve (466) (Sec 19)

Fig. 2.17 Air conditioning system thermostat (T) (Sec 19)

Compressor

1 Disconnect the battery earth lead.
2 Disconnect the refrigerant lines from the compressor.
3 Unbolt and remove the compressor, slipping its pulley out of the drivebelt.
4 Refitting is a reversal of the removal procedure. Tension the belt as described in Section 11.

Condenser

5 Disconnect the battery earth lead.
6 Drain the engine cooling system as described in Section 3.
7 With reference to Fig. 2.13. disconnect the coolant hoses at the radiator, and the freon hoses at the condenser. Note that the condenser connections are easily damaged, so take care. Plug the condenser pipes and ports to prevent the ingress of dirt.
8 Unbolt and remove the crossmember from the top of the radiator.
9 Disconnect the wiring from the cooling fan unit, then carefully lift out the radiator and condenser unit.
10 Refitting is a reversal of the removal procedure. Top up and bleed the cooling system as described in Section 11. Have the refrigerant system recharged by a competent specialist.

Evaporator

11 This unit is combined with the heater/air conditioning unit, therefore refer to Section 13 and remove the heater unit. It will also be necessary to disconnect the following items:
(a) Detach the freon hoses from the expansion valve and the vacuum pipe from the vacuum reservoir small diameter connector. Plug the freon hoses and expansion valve ports
(b) Remove the expansion chamber and vacuum reservoir
(c) Unscrew the two expansion valve-to-scuttle retaining nuts (Fig. 2.14)
12 Refitting is a reversal of the removal procedure. Have the air conditioning circuit recharged by a competent specialist.

Air conditioning unit electrical components

13 The following electrical components of the system are attached to the heater/air conditioning unit and can be removed if required:
(a) Relays and diodes (Fig. 2.15)
(b) Recycling flap solenoid valve (Fig. 2.16)
(c) Thermostat - regulates temperature of air leaving the evaporator (Fig. 2.17)

2

Fault finding overleaf

Fault finding - cooling system

Overheating

- ☐ Insufficient coolant in system
- ☐ Pump ineffective due to slack drivebelt
- ☐ Radiator blocked either internally or externally
- ☐ Kinked or collapsed hose causing coolant flow restriction
- ☐ Thermostat not working properly
- ☐ Engine out of tune
- ☐ Ignition timing retarded or auto advance malfunction
- ☐ Cylinder head gasket blown
- ☐ Engine not yet run-in
- ☐ Exhaust system partially blocked
- ☐ Engine oil level too low
- ☐ Brakes binding
- ☐ Electric cooling fan or switch faulty

Engine running too cool

- ☐ Faulty, incorrect or missing thermostat
- ☐ Electric cooling fan switch faulty

Loss of coolant

- ☐ Loose hose clips
- ☐ Hoses perished or leaking
- ☐ Radiator leaking
- ☐ Expansion tank pressure cap defective
- ☐ Blown cylinder head gasket
- ☐ Cracked cylinder block or head

Fault finding - heater

Heater gives insufficient output

- ☐ Engine overcooled (see above)
- ☐ Heater matrix blocked
- ☐ Heater controls maladjusted or broken

Fault finding - air conditioner

Bubbles observed in sight glass of receiver drier

- ☐ Leak in system
- ☐ Low refrigerant level

No cooling

- ☐ No refrigerant

Expansion valve frosted over on evaporator

- ☐ Faulty or clogged expansion valve
- ☐ Thermal bulb leaking

Insufficient cooling

- ☐ Faulty expansion valve
- ☐ Air in refrigerant circuit
- ☐ Clogged condenser
- ☐ Receiver drier clogged
- ☐ Faulty compressor
- ☐ Compressor overfilled with oil

Chapter 3
Fuel and exhaust systems

For modifications, and information applicable to later models, see Supplement at end of manual

Contents

3

Degrees of difficulty

Easy, suitable for novice with little experience	**Fairly easy,** suitable for beginner with some experience	**Fairly difficult,** suitable for competent DIY mechanic	**Difficult,** suitable for experienced DIY mechanic	**Very difficult,** suitable for expert DIY or professional

Specifications

Part A: Fuel system - general

Fuel

Grade .... 98 octane (4-star) - for information on the suitability of unleaded fuel, refer to a Renault dealer
Fuel tank contents .... 66 litres (14.5 gals)

Air cleaner element

1.7 litre models .... Champion W190
2.0 litre non-Turbo models .... Champion W115
2.0 litre Turbo models .... Champion W230

Part B: Carburettor fuel system

General
Carburettor type .... Solex 28/34 Z10 twin choke
Code No application:
  F2N 712 engine .... 867 or 913
  F2N 710 engine 889/889D*
Non adjustable

Carburettor data

Type 867 and 913:	Primary	Secondary
Venturi	20	26
Main jet	97.5	122
Air correction jet	200	145
Idle jet	47	45
Econostat	-	120
Enrichener	50 (867) or 60 (913)	-
Accelerator pump injector	40	35
Needle valve	1.8	
Float level	33.0 to 34.0 mm	
Positive throttle opening	0.8 to 1.0 mm	
Mechanical initial opening	2.1 to 2.3 mm (867) or 1.6 to 2.0 mm (913)	
Degas valve	1.0 to 3.0 mm	
Idle speed	675 to 725 rpm	
CO mixture	0.5 to 1.5%	

Type 889/889D:	Primary	Secondary
Venturi	20	27
Main jet	100	145
Air correction jet	210	190
Idle jet	45 (889) or 47 (889D)	50
Econostat	-	120
Enrichener	50	-
Accelerator pump injector	40	35
Needle valve	1.8	1.8
Float level	33.0 to 34.0 mm	33.0 to 34.0 mm
Positive throttle opening	0.9 to 1.1 mm	0.9 to 1.1 mm
Mechanical initial opening	2.1 to 2.3 mm	2.1 to 2.3 mm
Degas valve	1.0 to 3.0 mm	1.0 to 3.0 mm
Idle speed	675 to 725 rpm	675 to 725 rpm
C0 mixture	1.0 to 2.0%	1.0 to 2.0%

Part C: Renix fuel injection system
Type .... Computer-controlled in conjunction with ignition system

Calibration and settings
Idle speed:
  Non-Turbo models .... 725 to 825 rpm
  Turbo .... 775 to 825 rpm
CO at idle .... 1.0 to 2.0%
Fuel injector resistance .... 2.0 to 3.0 ohms

Part D: Turbocharger
Type .... Garrett T3

Calibration
Boost pressure:
  At 2500 to 4000 rpm .... 850 to 950 mbar
  At max engine speed .... 750 to 850 mbar
Boost limiting pressostat operating pressure .... 1300 to 1480 mbar
Air bypass valve opening vacuum .... 180 to 220 mbar

Torque wrench settings

	Nm	lbf ft
Turbocharger mounting strut fixings	30	22
Turbocharger-to-exhaust manifold nuts	45	33
Turbocharger coolant pipe connections	35	26
Turbocharger oil pipe retainer clamp	20	15
Turbocharger oil pipe flange screws	20	15

Part A: Fuel and exhaust systems – general

1 General

The type of fuel system fitted is dependent on model. 1.7 litre models use a carburettor based system, whilst 2.0 litre models use a Renix fuel injection system, in the case of Turbo models in conjunction with a Garrett turbocharger. Both carburettor and fuel injection systems are electronically controlled by an engine management computer. The Renix system also has control over ignition advance characteristics.

The details of the carburettor, fuel injection and turbocharger systems will be found in Parts B, C and D respectively. Part A deals with general components which are applicable to all models, such as the fuel tank.

⚠ *Warning: Many of the procedures in this Chapter entail the removal of fuel pipes and connections which may result in some fuel spillage. Before carrying out any operation on the fuel system refer to the precautions given in Safety First! at the beginning of this manual and follow them implicitly. Petrol is a highly dangerous and volatile liquid and the precautions necessary when handling it cannot be over-stressed.*
Remember that fuel lines in the fuel injection system may contain fuel under pressure, even if the engine has not been running for some time. Do not smoke or allow any naked flame nearby when there is any risk of fuel spillage. Take care to avoid spilling fuel onto a hot engine, and keep a fire extinguisher handy.

2 Maintenance

1 At the service intervals shown in 'Routine maintenance' the following checks and adjustments should be carried out on fuel and exhaust system components.
2 With the car over a pit, raised on a vehicle lift or securely supported on axle stands, carefully inspect the underbody fuel pipes, hoses and unions for chafing, leaks and corrosion. Renew any pipes which are severely pitted with corrosion or in any way damaged. Renew any hoses which show signs of cracking or other deterioration.
3 Check the fuel tank for leaks, for any signs of corrosion or damage, and the security of the mountings.
4 Check the exhaust system condition, as described in Section Y.
5 From within the engine compartment, check the security of all fuel hose attachments and inspect them for chafing. kinks, leaks or deterioration.
6 Renew the air cleaner element as described in Section 3.
7 Check the operation of the accelerator and choke control linkages (as applicable) and lubricate the linkages, cables and accelerator pedal pivot with a few drops of a good quality multi-purpose oil (photos).
8 Renew the fuel filter, as described in Section 24 for fuel injection models, or as follows for carburettor models. On carburettor models the filter is a separate renewable unit held in a spring bracket next to the fuel pump (photo). Clamp and detach the hoses, then remove the filter from the bracket. When refitting, ensure that the direction of flow arrows on the filter body are correctly orientated.

3 Air cleaner - element renewal

1.7 litre models

1 To remove the air cleaner element, release the seven retaining clips around the cover rim, undo the three nuts and the single screw, and then lift the cover clear. Withdraw the element from the casing (photo).
2 Wipe clean the inside of the casing.
3 Insert the new element into the casing, refit the cover, and fasten it with the screw, nuts and clips.

2.0 litre non-Turbo models

4 Unscrew the wing nut, remove the nut and its flat washer, then lift clear the air cleaner

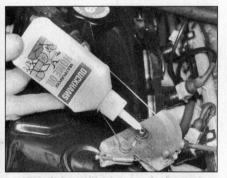

2.7 Lubricate the accelerator control linkage

2.8 Renew the in-line fuel filter – 1.7 litre model

3.1 Air cleaner element removal – 1.7 litre model

Fig. 3.1 Air cleaner cover securing clips (1) – 1.7 litre model (Sec 3)

Fig. 3.2 Air cleaner outer cover and retaining clips – 2.0 litre Turbo model (Sec 3)

3

3.4A Air cleaner unit cover and retaining nut – 2.0 litre non-Turbo model

3.4B Withdrawing the air cleaner element – 2.0 litre non-Turbo model

3.8A Detach the air intake hoses . . .

3.8B . . . and separate the air cleaner casing from the end cover – 2.0 litre Turbo model

3.14A Air cleaner casing removal – 1.7 litre model

3.14B Air cleaner casing retaining bolt and nut (arrowed) – 2.0 litre Turbo model

cover. Withdraw the element from the casing (photos).

5 Wipe clean the inside of the casing.

6 Insert the new element and refit the cover, fastening it with the nut and washer.

2.0 litre Turbo models

7 Release the retaining clips and remove the outer cover from the air cleaner casing.

8 Detach the air intake hoses from the air cleaner casing, release the four clips securing the end cover, then separate the end cover from the casing and withdraw the element (photos).

9 Wipe clean the inside of the casing.

10 Insert the new element and refit the covers in the reverse order of removal.

Air cleaner assembly (all models)

11 If it is necessary to remove the complete

air cleaner assembly at any time, the procedure is the same for all models, although the assemblies differ in appearance according to model.

12 Note their connections, and then detach the air intake and vacuum hoses and any wiring connectors from the air cleaner casing.

13 On some models it may be necessary to remove the cover(s) and/or element. as described earlier in this Section, to gain access to the casing fixings.

14 Undo the retaining nuts and/or bolts, and remove the casing (photos).

15 Refit in the reverse order to removal.

Ensure that all hose and wiring connections are securely made.

4 Accelerator cable - removal and refitting

1 Working from inside the car, release the cable end fitting by prising or pulling it free from the accelerator pedal rod (photo).

2 Detach the throttle return spring, open the throttle by hand, and withdraw the cable end from the linkage (photos).

4.1 Accelerator cable-to-pedal fitting

4.2A Accelerator cable and throttle linkage – 1.7 litre model

1 Throttle return spring
2 Cable end fitting
3 Outer cable adjuster support bracket
4 Pivot C-clip

4.2B Accelerator cable and throttle linkage – 2.0 litre non-Turbo model

1 Throttle return spring
2 Cable end fitting
3 Outer cable adjuster support bracket
4 Pivot C-clip

4.8A Accelerator cable adjuster and clip (arrowed) – 1.7 litre model

4.8B Accelerator cable adjuster – 2.0 litre non-Turbo model

3 Detach the outer cable adjuster from the support bracket by removing the retaining clip and unscrewing the adjuster. Take note of the set position of the adjuster in the bracket as a guide to general adjustment when refitting the cable.
4 According to model, the cable will be secured by a locating clip to the suspension strut turret or to the brake master cylinder. Detach the cable according to its method of retension, then withdraw it through the bulkhead from the engine compartment side.
5 If required, the throttle link rod can be removed by simply prising it free from the balljoints.
6 The accelerator pivot quadrant can be removed by releasing the C-clip using suitable circlip pliers, then lifting the pivot quadrant

from the pivot pin.
7 Refitting of the accelerator cable and its associated components is a reversal of the removal procedure. Lubricate the pivot points.
8 When securing the outer cable to the support bracket, adjust its position so that there is a small amount of slack in the cable when the throttle is closed (photos).

5 Accelerator pedal - removal and refitting

1 Working inside the car, release the accelerator cable end fitting, which is a push fit in the pedal rod.
2 Undo the bolt securing the pedal assembly

to the bulkhead and withdraw it from inside the car.
3 Refitting is the reverse sequence to removal.

6 Fuel tank - removal and refitting

Note: *Refer to the warning note in Section 1 before proceeding*
1 A drain plug is not provided on the fuel tank and it is therefore preferable to carry out the removal operation when the tank is nearly empty. Before proceeding, disconnect the battery negative terminal, and then syphon or hand pump the remaining fuel from the tank.
2 Jack up the rear of the car and securely support it on axle stands.
3 On models fitted with split rear seats, tilt the rear seats forward and fold back the luggage area carpet. On models fitted with a standard type bench seat, remove the seat as described in Chapter 11, then unfasten and fold back the luggage area carpet.
4 Prise free the circular plastic cover from the fuel level sender unit access hole in the floor.

Fig. 3.4 Fuel level sender unit connections (Sec 6)

1 Wiring connector   3 Return hose
2 Feed hose   4 Vent hose

Fig. 3.5 Fuel tank associated fittings (Sec 6)

1 Double connector
2 Vent pipes
3 Tank securing strap bolts
4 Protector plate
5 Protector plate securing bolts

1 Tank
2 Retaining straps
3 Strap securing bolts
4 Filler pipe hose
5 Double connector
6 Filler cap
7 Filler pipe
8 Vent hose (sender unit)
9 Vent hose (tank)
10 Sender unit lock ring
11 Vent hose (sender unit)
12 Sender unit gasket
13 Tank locating studs
14 Spacer

Fig. 3.3 Fuel tank and associated components (Sec 6)

6.5 Fuel tank sender unit and connections – 2.0 litre non-Turbo model shown

6.9 Fuel tank protector plate and securing nuts – 1.7 litre Savanna model shown

6.11A Rear fuel tank retaining strap and bolt

5 Disconnect the battery earth lead, then detach the wires from the fuel level sender unit (photo).

6 Disconnect the fuel feed, return and vent hoses from the top of the sender unit. Mark them for identification if necessary.

7 Remove the right-hand rear wheel.

8 Unclip and detach the two hoses from the double connector on the fuel tank - see Fig. 3.5.

9 Unbolt and remove the protector plate (photo).

10 Take the weight of the tank on a suitable jack, with a block of wood interposed to prevent damage.

11 Undo the tank retaining strap bolts and detach the fuel filler pipe connector hose (photos). An assistant may be required at this point to help in steadying the tank as it is lowered.

12 Carefully lower the fuel tank and withdraw it from under the vehicle.

13 If the tank is contaminated with sediment or water, remove the fuel level sender unit as described in Section 7 and swill out the tank with clean fuel. If the tank is damaged, or leaks, it should be repaired by a specialist or renewed. Do not under any circumstances solder or weld the tank.

14 Refit the tank in the reverse sequence to removal. Check for any signs of leaks when topping-up the fuel level.

6.11B Front fuel tank retaining strap and bolt

7 Fuel level sender unit - removal and refitting

1 Refer to the previous Section, observe the warning note and then proceed as described in paragraphs 1 to 6 inclusive.

2 Twist the sender unit body to disengage the retaining pegs. The judicious use of a suitable screwdriver or similar implement will be required to turn the unit. Withdraw the sender unit with care as it is easily damaged. On some models it may be necessary to lower the fuel tank slightly in order to allow the sender unit to be withdrawn. Tie a length of string to the lock ring to prevent it from getting lost between the body and tank.

3 If the sender unit is to be removed for an extensive period, seal off the tank and fuel hoses to prevent petrol fumes escaping.

4 Two types of sender unit are fitted depending on whether conventional or electronic instrumentation is fitted. If an ohmmeter is available, the sender unit can be tested by measuring the resistance produced

Fig. 3.6 Fuel level sender unit showing float height dimension (H) (Sec 7)

against the corresponding float heights as follows (see Fig. 3.6):

Float height (H) (electronic instrument panel)	Resistance at terminals 1 and 4
Highest point (31.5 mm)	310 to 350 ohms
Intermediate point (96 mm)	210 to 250 ohms
Lowest point (216 mm)	0 to 40 ohms

Float height (H) (conventional instrument panel)	Resistance at terminals 2 and 4
Highest point (31.5 mm)	6 to 8 ohms
Intermediate point (122.5 mm)	80 to 120 ohms
Lowest point (216 mm)	270 to 330 ohms

6 The minimum fuel level detector on the conventional type sender unit can be checked by holding the unit vertically with an ohmmeter connected to terminals 3 and 4. The resistance reading should be 0 to 30 ohms. If the unit is inverted, the ohmmeter should read infinity.

7 The movable gauze filter can be checked on the electronic type sender unit as follows. Connect the ohmmeter to terminals 1 and 4, hold the float in its highest position and progressively press down the filter. A resistance reading of 20 to 30 ohms should be produced.

8 Renew the sender unit with a replacement of the correct type if necessary.

9 Refitting is a reversal of the removal procedure. Renew the seal and ensure that the sender unit engages in its notch. Ensure that all connections are securely made.

8 Fuel filler pipe - removal and refitting

Note: *Refer to the warning note in Section 1 of this Chapter before proceeding*

1 The upper section of the fuel filler pipe (filler neck) is secured to the body by pop rivets. These rivets are 4.8 mm in diameter and will need to be drilled out for removal.

Fig. 3.7 Fuel filler pipe components (Sec 8)

1 Vent pipes
2 Double connector
3 Filler neck
4 Filler pipe
5 Connector hose
6 Clips

2 Raise and support the vehicle at the rear. Remove the rear right-hand roadwheel for access.

3 Unbolt and remove the protector plate from under the wing.

4 Release the hose clips and detach the connector hose from the filler pipe. The filler pipe can then be withdrawn.

5 Refitting is a reversal of the removal procedure. The four aluminium pop rivets required to secure the pipe at the top end should be 4.8 mm in diameter, 12 mm long, with 12 mm diameter heads.

9 Exhaust system

1 The exhaust system differs in design according to the engine used.

2 The complete system or just part of it can be removed for repair or renewal. The respective pipe section joints will either be of the flanged type, such as the manifold-to-

9.3 Exhaust system flanged joint connection – 1.7 litre model shown

Fig. 3.8 Exhaust system components – 1.7 litre models (Sec 9)

1 Downpipe
2 Flange clamp
3 Intermediate section
4 Thermo-fusing seal
5 Downpipe (alternative)
6 Rear silencer

downpipe joint, or a collared sleeve and clamp joint such as the downpipe-to-secondary expansion box pipe joint.

3 The flanged type joints can normally easily be separated by simply removing the clamping nuts of the joint and withdrawing the pipe from the manifold or mating pipe as the case may be. It may, however, be necessary to apply some rust penetrating fluid to the nuts and joints to ease removal (photo).

4 The collared sleeve joint is not so easily separated and a certain amount of heat from a gas torch may be required to separate the two pipes after the clamp has been removed. In this instance special care must be taken to guard against fire whenever working

Fig. 3.9 Exhaust system components – 2.0 litre non-Turbo models (Sec 9)

2 Downpipe
3 Thermo-fusing seal
4 Intermediate section
5 Flange clamp
6 Rear silencer

3

Fig. 3.10 Spring-loaded flange joint –
tighten nuts so that springs are coilbound
as shown (Sec 9)

9.6A Exhaust system forward mounting
bracket

9.6B Exhaust system rear mounting
bracket

underneath the vehicle, particularly at the petrol tank end or near fuel lines!

5 If a pipe section is being renewed it is usually far quicker to cut it through close to the joint concerned to ease removal.

6 The system is suspended in position by means of brackets and rubber mounting straps or rings and these can be levered from their mounting brackets when necessary (photo).

7 The foregoing operations should be followed if only certain sections of the system are to be renewed. If the complete system must be renewed, then it will be much easier if the old pipes are sawn through with a hacksaw in short lengths for removal.

8 When fitting the new system de-burr the connecting sockets and smear the pipe ends with an exhaust system sealant. New mounting clips and rubber suspension rings should be fitted, also new pipe clamps.

9 Do not fully tighten the retaining clamps and joint clamp/flange nuts until the complete system is in position and fully suspended.

10 The downpipe joint has a spring-loaded flange joint at the manifold on 1.7 litre models, or at the lower end of the downpipe on 2.0 litre models (photo). When assembling this joint, a new thermo-fusing seal must be used and the joint retaining nuts must be tightened to the point where

the springs are coilbound as shown in Fig. 3.10 (photos).

11 On Turbo models, access to the exhaust downpipe-to-turbocharger elbow flange joint will necessitate the removal of the heat shield mounted above the turbocharger unit. An additional heat shield is also attached to the downpipe-to-turbocharger joint (photo).

12 Check that the pipes do not foul any electrical leads or other components before final tightening of the fastenings.

13 Run the engine on completion and check for any signs of leakage.

10 Manifolds (1.7 litre engine) - removal and refitting

1 The inlet and exhaust manifolds on this engine share a common gasket and they must therefore be removed and refitted as a combined unit.

2 Remove the carburettor as described in Part B, Section 17 of this Chapter.

3 Disconnect the exhaust downpipe from the manifold as described in Section 9.

4 Unbolt and remove the hot air duct from the exhaust manifold (photo).

5 Unbolt and remove the throttle linkage support plate from the top of the inlet manifold (photo).

9.10A Spring-loaded flange joint at the
lower end of the downpipe – 2.0 litre non-
Turbo model

9.10B Manifold joint thermo-fusing seal –
1.7 litre model

9.11 Downpipe-to-turbocharger elbow
flange joint and heat shield

10.4 Remove the hot air duct from the
exhaust manifold – 1.7 litre engine

10.5 Throttle linkage support plate
retaining bolts (arrowed) – 1.7 litre engine

10.6 Remove the baseplate from the inlet manifold. Note inlet-to-exhaust manifold retaining screws (arrowed) – 1.7 litre engine

10.9 Refitting the inlet and exhaust manifolds with a new gasket – 1.7 litre engine

11.3 Exhaust manifold and retaining nuts – 2.0 litre non-Turbo model

6 Unbolt and remove the baseplate from the inlet manifold (photo).

7 Undo the retaining nuts and withdraw the inlet and exhaust manifolds from the cylinder head.

8 To separate the inlet and exhaust manifolds, undo the retaining screws on the top face of the inlet manifold.

9 Refitting is a reversal of the removal procedure. but ensure that the joint faces are perfectly clean and always use a new gasket (photo).

10 Refit the carburettor as described in Part B, Section 17 of this Chapter.

11 Reconnect the exhaust downpipe to the manifold as described in Section 9.

11 Manifolds (2.0 litre engine) - removal and refitting

Inlet manifold

1 Refer to Part C, Section 31.

Exhaust manifold (non-Turbo models)

2 Unbolt and disconnect the downpipe from the manifold.

3 Undo the retaining nuts and withdraw the manifold (photo).

4 Ensure that the joint faces are perfectly clean and renew the gasket.

5 Refitting is a reversal of the removal procedure. Refit the downpipe to the manifold with reference to Section 9.

Exhaust manifold (Turbo models)

6 Remove the turbocharger unit as described in Part D, Section 37 of this Chapter.

7 The exhaust manifold can now be removed and refitted as described in paragraphs 3 to 5 of this Section.

8 Refit the turbocharger unit and associated fittings as described in Part D, Section 37 of this Chapter.

Part B: Carburettor and associated fuel system components

12 Automatic air temperature system - removal, checking and refitting

This system is fitted in the air cleaner intake duct on carburettor engine models. Its function is to regulate the air temperature

Fig. 3.11 Air cleaner automatic air temperature control system (Sec 12)

A Cold air intake
B Hot air intake
C Flap valve
D Air cleaner body intake spout
2 Wax capsule

entering the carburettor, thereby assisting in the air/fuel mixture control.

2 A mixer flap directs hot or cold air as required into the air cleaner, the flap valve position being regulated by a wax element thermostat. The hot air is drawn from the area around the exhaust manifold through a hot air duct.

3 This system requires no maintenance, but if suspected of malfunction it can be tested and if necessary renewed as follows.

4 Remove the air cleaner and take out the element as described in Section 3.

5 Immerse the air cleaner body in water at 26°C (79°F) or less, ensuring that the wax capsule in the intake spout is completely submerged. After 5 minutes observe the position of the flap valve which should be blanking off the cold air intake.

6 Now repeat the test in water at 36°C (97°F) and after 5 minutes check that the flap is blanking off the hot air intake. If the flap valve does not operate as described at the specified temperatures, the wax capsule control assembly is faulty and must be renewed.

7 After completing the tests, dry off the air cleaner body and refit the hot air duct.

8 Refit the element and the air cleaner as described in Section 3.

13 Solex 28/34 Z10 carburettor - description

1 The Solex 28/34 Z10 carburettor is a twin choke downdraught carburettor mounted direct on the top of the inlet manifold (photos).

2 The carburettor base is heated or cooled according to prevailing conditions, and the

13.1A Top view of Solex 28/34 Z10 carburettor

A 1st choke barrel
B 2nd choke barrel
C Air correction, main and idle jets

3

13.1B Side view of Solex 28/34 Z10
carburettor

A Idle speed adjustment screw
B Choke control linkage
C Full load enrichment unit

13.1C Side view of Solex 28/34 Z10
carburettor

A Accelerator pump
B Cold start diaphragm
C Coolant pipe

Fig. 3.12 Additional items fitted to later
Solex 28/34 Z10 carburettor (Sec 13)

a Vacuum connection
1 Cold start diaphragm unit
2 Idle cut-off solenoid
3 Circuit heating resistor
4 Anti-stall valve (where applicable)

design of the carburettor is such that optimum fuel flow is obtained over extreme temperature variations. The throttle butterfly valve in the second stage venturi opens later than that in the first, giving improved fuel consumption. The carburettor is fitted with an idle solenoid which cuts off the fuel supply when the ignition is turned off. To aid cold starting a manual choke, operated by cable, is fitted.

3 Later models from (1987), are fitted with an electrically heated primary idle circuit in place of the coolant heated system used on previous models. To prevent stalling, a cold start diaphragm is also fitted to later models.

An idle cut-off solenoid is also fitted which cuts off the fuel supply when the ignition is switched off.

4 Models fitted with power steering and/or air conditioning have an anti-stall valve fitted to increase the idle speed when additional loading is placed on the engine (eg when the steering is moved to full lock at idle speed).

5 Another improvement made to later models is the fitting of an antipercolation chamber between the carburettor and the fuel pump. This device improves starting performance when the engine is hot. For more details on this system, refer to the Supplement at the end of this manual.

14 Carburettor - maintenance

1 Before blaming the carburettor for any shortcomings in engine performance, remember that there is no reason why the carburettor should lose tune, and in fact what usually happens is that, as the engine gets older and less efficient, more or less fruitless attempts are made to restore performance by interfering with the carburettor. In those parts of the world where exhaust emission is regulated by law it is inadvisable and may be

illegal to alter carburettor settings without monitoring exhaust emission levels using special equipment.

2 The ultimate cause of most carburettor problems is wear in moving parts or dirt in the jets. The Solex carburettors have no continuously moving parts, except for the float and the throttle spindle, which makes it a very reliable device so long as dirt does not get in.

3 Periodically unscrew the plug and extract the integral fuel filter. Wash it in clean petrol and refit it to the carburettor (photo).

4 Check the fuel feed and return hoses, the vacuum and the coolant hoses and connections at the carburettor for condition and security.

5 Occasionally apply a drop of oil to the various linkages and the throttle spindle to ensure that they do not wear prematurely.

Fig. 3.13 Carburettor fuel line connections
and layout on later models (Sec 13)

1 Feed hose (from tank to pump)
2 Fuel pump-to-anti-percolation chamber hose
3 Anti-percolation chamber
4 Anti-percolation chamber-to-carburettor hose
5 Return hose (to fuel rank)
6 Carburettor
7 Fuel pump
8 Cold start diaphragm vacuum chamber

14.3 Inspecting the carburettor integral
fuel filter

15 Carburettor - idle speed and mixture adjustments

1 Generally speaking, unless the carburettor is obviously out of tune or is malfunctioning it is not advisable to tamper with it.

2 Correct adjustment can only be achieved provided that the engine is in generally good condition. The valve clearances must be correct and the ignition system must also be in good condition.

3 An independent tachometer is necessary to make accurate adjustment and it should be connected to the engine in accordance with the maker's instructions. The air filter must be fitted. Run the engine at 2000 rpm until warm as indicated by the engagement of the cooling fan. On automatic transmission models engage P. Allow the engine to run; when the cooling fan cuts out, adjustments can be

15.6 Carburettor idle speed adjustment through air cleaner housing aperture

15.8 Carburettor mixture adjustment screw location (arrowed)

made. During prolonged adjustments take care as the cooling fan will cut-in again periodically.

4 Check and ensure that the manual choke is in the fully retracted position (off).

5 During the adjustment checks, all electrical consumers should be switched off, including the thermally switched radiator fan.

6 Check the idling speed is as given in the Specifications. Adjust using a thin screwdriver inserted through the hole in the air cleaner housing (photo) which allows access to the idle screw.

7 Mixture adjustment can only be made accurately using an exhaust gas analyser. If this is available, connect it to the vehicle exhaust in accordance with the manufacturer's instructions, and proceed as follows if the CO percentage is not as specified.

8 If fitted, remove the tamperproof plug for access to the mixture adjustment screw. Slowly turn the mixture screw in the required direction to weaken or richen the mixture (photo). The engine idle speed will change as this adjustment is made and this should therefore be readjusted as described previously in paragraph 6. Alternate the adjustments in this manner until the specified idle speed and CO percentage readings are obtained. During a prolonged adjustment, it will be necessary to occasionally blip the throttle to clear excess fuel in the inlet manifold so that correct readings can be obtained.

9 If an exhaust gas analyser is not available, but mixture adjustment is necessary, an approximate adjustment can be made as follows.

10 Turn the mixture screw to the position which provides the highest engine speed. Now reduce the engine speed to approximately 50 rpm above the specified idle speed.

11 Repeat the procedures outlined in paragraph 10, then screw in the mixture control screw to reduce the engine speed by 40 to 50 rpm. Further minor adjustment to the idle speed may be necessary to bring the engine speed to within the idle speed range specified.

16 Anti-stall system - checking and adjustment

1 This system is fitted to models from 1987 on fitted with power steering and/or air conditioning, the function of the system being to prevent the engine from stalling when under additional loading from these systems (eg steering moved to full lock at idle speed). The system operation and adjustment is as described below according to type.

Models with power steering

2 A pressostat mounted in the steering hydraulic circuit activates a solenoid valve, and this supplies manifold pressure to a butterfly opening device which increases the engine speed and prevents stalling. To check the system operation, use the following test method.

3 Detach the wiring connector from the pressostat unit, located in the fluid pipe at the rear of the power steering pump, then connect a length of wire between the female terminals of the wiring connector. The engine speed should increase to between 1000 and 1100 rpm. If necessary, adjust to this speed by turning the adjuster screw (VA) shown in Fig. 3.15, then remove the bridging wire and reconnect the wiring connector to the pressostat.

Models with air conditioning

4 The system is similar to that used on models with power steering, but the solenoid valve is mounted on the compressor. When the compressor is started, the solenoid valve supplies manifold pressure to the butterfly opening device on the carburettor to increase engine speed and prevent stalling.

5 If the operation of the system is suspect, check and if necessary adjust the opening device as follows.

6 Disconnect the wiring connectors from the solenoid valve, then connect the valve directly to the battery earth and positive terminals and check that the engine speed increases to between 1400 and 1600 rpm. If this speed is

Fig. 3.14 Carburettor idle speed (A) and mixture (B) adjustment points (Sec 15)

not obtained, turn the adjusting screw on the opening device as necessary.

7 Disconnect the leads from the battery, and reconnect the original wiring connections on completion.

Models with power steering and air conditioning

8 On these models, a two-stage butterfly opening device is used, each stage being separately controlled by its own solenoid in the system concerned. The two-stage device

Fig. 3.15 Single-stage butterfly opening device components (Sec 16)

V   Single-stage opening device
VA Opening device adjustment screw
K   Solenoid valve mounting plate
E   Solenoid valve
E₃ Solenoid valve air filter
B   Carburettor
A   Inlet manifold
a₁ Manifold vacuum

3

Fig. 3.16 Single-stage butterfly opening device system layout (schematic) (Sec 16)

V   Single stage opening
    device
VA Opening device
    adjustment screw
V₂ Hose (marked blue)

E   Solenoid valve
E₁ Hose (marked blue)
E₂ Hose (marked red)
E₃ Air filter

F   Power steering and/or air
    conditioning data
B   Carburettor
b   Hose (marked red)

Fig. 3.17 Two-stage butterfly opening
device components (Sec 16)

V   Two-stage opening device
VA Air conditioning system adjustment screw
VB Power steering system adjustment screw
V₁ Take-off (for air conditioning)
V₂ Take-off (for power steering)

and its associated components are shown in Fig. 3.17.

9 When checking and adjusting either system, both systems must be checked as previously described in this Section, starting with the power steering system, then the air conditioning system.

10 The anti-stall speeds for the two systems should be as follows:

Power steering system - 1000 to 1100 rpm
Air conditioning system - 1400 to 1600 rpm

11 When checking the power steering system speed, disconnect the vacuum hose from the air conditioning system (V1 in

Fig. 3.17). When checking the air conditioning system speed, disconnect the vacuum hose from the power steering system (V2 in Fig. 3.17).

17 Carburettor – removal and refitting

Note: *Refer to the warning note in Section 1 before proceeding*

1 Remove the air cleaner unit as described in Part A, Section 3 of this Chapter.

2 Disconnect the throttle link rod (photo).
3 Disconnect the choke cable from the carburettor as described in Section 19.
4 Disconnect the fuel supply hose to the carburettor. Plug or clamp the hose to prevent leakage.
5 Disconnect the vacuum and coolant hoses from the carburettor. Clamp the coolant hoses to prevent leakage (photo).
6 Disconnect the crankcase breather hose.
7 Where applicable, disconnect the idle solenoid lead.

17.2 Disconnect the throttle link rod (arrowed)

Fig. 3.18 Two-stage butterfly opening device system layout (schematic) (Sec 16)

V   Two-stage opening device
VA Air conditioning system
    adjustment screw
VB Power steering system
    adjustment screw
V₁ Take-off for air
    conditioning (marked
    grey)

V₂ Take-off for power
    steering (marked blue)
E   Power steering solenoid
    valve
E₁ Hose (marked blue)
E₂ Hose (marked red)
E₃ Air filter
F   Power steering data
G   Air conditioning data

D   Air conditioning solenoid
    valve
D₁ Hose (marked grey)
D₂ Hose (marked white)
D₃ Air filter
B   Carburettor
A   Inlet manifold
b   Hose (marked red)

17.5 Disconnect the hoses from the carburettor

17.11A Locate the new gasket piece over the dowels on the manifold face . . .

17.11B . . . then refit the carburettor

19.2 Release the choke outer cable from its support bracket (retaining clip arrowed)

8 Remove the gasket from the air cleaner mating face on the top of the carburettor.
9 Undo and remove the four bolts securing the carburettor to the inlet manifold.
10 Lift the carburettor from the inlet manifold.
11 Refitting is a reversal of removal. A new gasket piece must be fitted between the manifold and the carburettor. Ensure that both mating surfaces are clean (photos).

18 Solex 28/34 Z10 carburettor - diagnosis and overhaul

1 If a carburettor fault is suspected, always check first that the ignition timing is correct, and that the spark plugs are in good condition and correctly gapped. The accelerator and choke cables should be correctly adjusted, and the air filter element clean. If the engine is running very roughly, check the valve clearances. If the engine appears to be misfiring, check the ignition system as described in Chapter 4, Section 9. If the engine will not run above a certain speed, or runs poorly on full throttle, check the fuel pump (Section 20) and fuel filter (besides the filter mesh in the carburettor inlet pipe, a separate canister-type filter in the fuel line is fitted to some models).
2 If careful checking of all the above produces no improvement, the carburettor

should be removed (Section 17) for cleaning and overhaul.
3 Note that, in the rare event of a complete carburettor overhaul being necessary, it may prove more economical to renew the carburettor as a complete unit. Check the price and availability of a replacement unit, compared to its component parts, before starting work. Most sealing washers, screws and gaskets are usually available in kits, as are some of the major sub-assemblies. In most cases, however, it should be sufficient to dismantle the carburettor and to clean out the jets and internal passages.
4 To overhaul the carburettor, proceed as described in Chapter 13, Section 9.

19 Choke cable - removal and refitting

1 Remove the air cleaner unit for improved access to the cable at the carburettor end. Refer to Section 3 for details.
2 Release the choke outer cable from its support bracket on the carburettor by carefully prising the retaining clip tangs out of the bracket slots (photo).
3 Disconnect the cable end from the carburettor by prising the spring loop off the stud on the linkage (photo).
4 Undo the two retaining screws at the choke

knob end, pull the cable through from inside the vehicle and disconnect the 'choke-on' warning light lead. An assistant may be required to help feed the cable through the bulkhead (photo).
5 Refitting is the reverse sequence to removal. Adjust the position of the outer cable in its carburettor support bracket clip as necessary so that the choke linkage opens fully when the knob is pushed in, and closes fully when the knob is pulled out.

20 Fuel pump - removal, testing and refitting

3

Note: *Refer to the warning note in Section 1 before proceeding*
1 Disconnect the battery negative terminal.
2 Note the location of the fuel inlet, outlet and return pipes and disconnect them from the pump.
3 Undo the two nuts and washers securing the pump to the engine and withdraw it from its location (photo).
4 Remove the insulating block and gaskets from the underside of the pump.
5 If the pump is suspected of malfunctioning, it can be tested as follows. If found to be faulty, the pump is not repairable and must therefore be renewed.
6 Refit the fuel inlet pipe to the pump and

19.3 Prise the ring loop off the stud on the linkage

19.4 Choke cable removal

20.3 Fuel pump removal (fuel filter removed for clarity)

hold a wad of rag near the outlet. Operate the pump lever by hand and if the pump is in a satisfactory condition a strong jet of fuel should be ejected from the pump outlet as the lever is released. If this is not the case, check that fuel will flow from the inlet pipe when it is held below tank level; if so the pump is faulty.

7 Before refitting the pump, thoroughly clean the pump and cylinder head mating faces.

8 Locate the gaskets and the insulator block over the pump studs on the cylinder head, then refit the pump and secure with the two nuts and washers.

9 Reconnect the fuel pipes to their original positions, as noted during removal. If crimp type retaining clips were used to secure the fuel pipes, these should be replaced by screw type clips.

21 Fault finding - carburettor fuel system

Unsatisfactory engine performance and excessive fuel consumption are not necessarily the fault of the fuel system. In fact they more commonly occur as a result of ignition and timing faults. Before acting on the following it is necessary to check the ignition system first. Even though a fault may lie in the fuel system it will be difficult to trace unless the ignition is correct. The faults below, therefore, assume that this has been attended to first (where appropriate).

Smell of petrol when engine is stopped

- [ ] Leaking fuel lines or unions
- [ ] Leaking fuel tank

Smell of petrol when engine is idling

- [ ] Leaking fuel line unions between pump and carburettor
- [ ] Overflow of fuel from float chamber due to wrong level setting,
- [ ] ineffective needle valve or punctured float

Excessive fuel consumption for reasons not covered by leaks or float chamber faults

- [ ] Worn jets
- [ ] Over-rich setting
- [ ] Sticking mechanism
- [ ] Dirty air cleaner element
- [ ] Sticking air cleaner thermostatic mechanism

Difficult starting, uneven running, lack of power, cutting out

- [ ] One or more jets blocked or restricted
- [ ] Float chamber fuel level too low or needle valve sticking
- [ ] Fuel pump not delivering sufficient fuel
- [ ] Faulty idle cut-off solenoid
- [ ] Induction leak

Difficult starting when cold

- [ ] Choke malfunction
- [ ] Weak mixture

Difficult starting when hot

- [ ] Choke malfunction
- [ ] Accelerator pedal pumped before starting
- [ ] Vapour lock (especially in hot weather or at high altitude)
- [ ] Rich mixture

Engine does not respond properly to throttle

- [ ] Faulty accelerator pump
- [ ] Blocked jet(s)
- [ ] Slack in accelerator cable

Engine idle speed drops when hot

- [ ] Overheated fuel pump

Engine runs on

- [ ] Faulty idle cut-off solenoid

Part C: Renix fuel injection system

22 Description

This fuel system is of the pressure/speed type. The quantity of fuel injected is determined by both the vacuum in the inlet manifold and the engine speed.

The inlet vacuum pressure controls the basic injection time which is then corrected to suit other engine conditions and requirements. These include coolant temperature, air temperature, battery voltage and atmospheric pressure.

The Renix system also calculates the ignition advance requirements to suit any particular set of engine conditions.

A computer controls both the fuel injection and ignition systems.

A warning light on the instrument panel will illuminate should a fault develop in the Renix system.

1 Coolant temperature sensor
2 Engine angular position/speed sensor
3 Computer
4 Computer casing
5 Air cleaner unit
6 Throttle casing
7 Throttle switch
8 Air temperature sensor
9 Idle speed air regulator valve
10 Diagnostic socket
11 Ignition module
12 Distributor (ignition)

Fig. 3.19 General view of engine compartment showing positions of main injection and ignition system components (Sec 22)

Fig. 3.20 Renix injection circuit diagram (Sec 22)

BP	Throttle casing	PSE	Coolant outlet pipe
CP	Absolute pressure sensor	TCE	Thermistor
RIE	Injection manifold	TCT	Temperature switch
RER	Idle speed air regulator valve	STE	Coolant temperature sensor
RPE	Fuel pressure regulator	STA	Air temperature sensor
RR	Idle mixture potentiometer	DC	Pre-ignition detector
AR	Air cleaner		

23 Maintenance

Renew the air cleaner element at the specified intervals given in the 'Routine maintenance' Section at the start of this manual. Refer to Part A, Section 3 of this chapter for details.

Remove and renew the fuel filter at the specified intervals. Refer to Section 24 for details.

Periodically inspect the fuel injection system lines and hoses (fuel, air and vacuum) to ensure that they are in good condition and securely attached.

24 Fuel filter - removal and refitting

Note: Refer to the warning note in Section 1 before proceeding

The fuel filter is located adjacent to the electric fuel pump on the underside of the vehicle, inboard of the right-hand rear suspension mounting. For access, raise the vehicle at the rear and support on safety stands (photo).

Disconnect the battery earth lead.

Clamp the inlet and outlet hose each side of the filter to prevent fuel leakage, then disconnect the hoses from the filter by releasing their retaining clips.

4 Undo the retaining clamp nut, release the clamp and remove the filter.

5 Fit the new filter making sure that the direction of flow arrow marked on its body is pointing towards the engine, and the plastic sleeve is fitted between the filter and the clamp.

25 Fuel pump - removal and refitting

1 The fuel pump unit is mounted on the same plate as the fuel filter (see paragraph 1 of the previous Section).

24.1 Underside view of the fuel filter (1), fuel pump (2) and pulse damper (3)

2 The removal procedure is similar to that described previously for the fuel filter, but in addition, fold back the rubber covers and disconnect the wiring connectors.

3 Refitting is a reversal of the removal procedure. Ensure that the wiring connections are secure. Renew the hoses if they are perished or in poor condition.

4 If required, the fuel pulse damper, located between the pump and the filter, can be removed and refitted in the same manner as that described for the filter in Section 24.

26 Fuel injection system - adjustments

1 As mentioned previously, the Renix type fuel injection system is managed by the computer unit and therefore no manual adjustments are normally required. However the following checks and adjustments are possible if required. If checking the idle mixture adjustment, an exhaust gas analyser will be required.

Idle speed

2 The idle speed cannot be altered as it is controlled by an air regulating solenoid valve monitored by a power module and throttle switch to form an electronic idling system.

3 Main components of this system comprise a computer, an air regulating valve located at the front left-hand side of the engine near the alternator, and a three-position throttle switch.

4 The computer incorporates an integrated idling adjustment circuit.

5 The air regulating (idle speed adjusting) valve consists of two coils which are fed by signals which position the valve between the closed and fully open position according to requirements.

6 The computer controls the idle speed - faster at cold start and then reducing it as the engine warms up.

Fig. 3.21 Idle speed air regulator valve location (1) (Sec 26)

3

Fig. 3.22 Fuel mixture potentiometer adjustment screw (Sec 26)

Fig. 3.23 Air temperature sensor removed (Sec 27)

27.8 Air temperature sensor and wiring connector

Idle mixture

7 The engine must be at its normal running temperature for this check and an exhaust gas analyser (CO meter) should be connected in accordance with the manufacturer's instructions.
8 Remove the cover from the computer unit, then detach the idle mixture adjustment potentiometer (see Fig. 3.22).
9 Remove the tamperproof cap by prising it free, then using a suitable screwdriver, turn the adjustment screw as required to set the idle mixture at the specified CO level.
10 Refit the potentiometer and the computer cover.

27 Component testing

Note: *An ohmmeter will be needed for full component testing*

Fuel injectors

⚠️ *Warning: The following injector test procedure is the method recommended by the manufacturers for use in the controlled conditions of their dealer workshops. There is a very great risk of fire or explosion when carrying out these tests in less than ideal conditions and you are strongly advised to have this work carried out by a dealer or fuel injection specialist*

1 Disconnect the wiring plugs from the injectors.
2 Remove the injection manifold (see Section 30), leaving the fuel hoses connected, and place each injector in turn over a small container. Ensure that the manifold is held securely.
3 Switch on the ignition; there should be no ejection of fuel. Now apply battery voltage to each injector in turn; fuel should be ejected.
4 Refit the injection manifold, and reconnect the wiring plugs.

Coolant temperature sensor

5 Remove the sensor from the engine and leave it to stabilise for ten minutes (refer to Section 33 for removal details).
6 Using an ohmmeter, check the resistance using the following table:

Temperature	Resistance (ohms)
20 ± 1°C (68 ± 2°F)	283 to 297
80 ± 1°C (176 ± 2°F)	383 to 397
90 ± 1°C (194 ± 2°F)	403 to 417

Air temperature sensor

7 Place an accurate thermometer in the air cleaner air intake as a means of measuring the sensor temperature level.
8 Using an ohmmeter, check the resistance using the following table (photo).

Temperature	Resistance (ohms)
0 ± 1°C (32 ± 2°F)	254 to 266
20 ± 1°C (68 ± 2°F)	283 to 297
40 ± 1°C (104 ± 2°F)	315 to 329

Absolute pressure sensor

9 First check the vacuum pipe and its connections, also make sure that the calibrated jet is correctly located.
10 Check for continuity between terminal (A) on the sensor connector and terminal (17) on the computer connector (Fig. 3.24).
11 Check the computer earth between terminals 1, 2 and 10 and a good earth.

28 Three position throttle switch - removal, refitting and adjustment

1 The switch can be removed if the wiring plug is pulled off and the two fixing screws removed (photo).
2 When refitting, align the flat on the switch to coincide with the flat on the throttle butterfly spindle and then move it in the direction of the arrow until the light throttle 'click' is heard.
3 Tighten the fixing screws.
4 A check of the throttle switch operation can be made using an ohmmeter and a set of feeler gauges as follows.
5 When the throttle is set at the normal idle speed position the clearance 'X' in Fig. 3.25 should be 1 mm (0.039 in). With the throttle in this position, use the ohmmeter to measure the resistance across the switch terminals. The resistance across terminals A and B should be 0, and the resistance across terminals B and C should be infinite.
6 Move the throttle to the part open position. The clearance 'X' should be 1.2 mm (0.047 in).

Fig. 3.24 Absolute pressure sensor and terminals (Sec 27)

A Earth   B Output voltage   C +5V

28.1 Three position throttle switch

Fig. 3.25 Checking the throttle switch operation (Sec 28)

For X see text

29.1 Disconnect the throttle link rod at the balljoint

and the resistance across terminals A and B, and terminals B and C should be infinite.

7 Fully open the throttle. With the upper throttle plate open by 70°, the throttle plate-to-body clearance should be 22 mm (0.858 in). Use a gauge rod or twist drill to check this clearance. The resistance across terminals A and B should be infinite. and the resistance across terminals B and C should be 0.

8 If in any of the preceding tests the resistance measured is not as specified, then the switch is faulty and should be renewed.

29 Throttle casing - removal and refitting

1 Detach the throttle link rod by carefully prising it free at the balljoint (photo). Disconnect the throttle switch wire connector.
2 Unclip and remove the air intake duct and the crankcase ventilation hose from the throttle casing.
3 Undo the three retaining screws and remove the air intake casing and the throttle casing.
4 Clean the mating surfaces and refit in the reverse order of removal. New sealing gaskets must always be fitted during reassembly and the crankcase ventilation hose should be inspected before refitting to ensure that its orifice is clear.

30 Fuel rail and injectors - removal and refitting

Note: Refer to the warning note in Section 1 before proceeding
1 Disconnect the wiring plugs from the fuel injectors (photo).
2 Disconnect the fuel hoses from the injection manifold.
3 Unscrew the manifold fixing bolts and remove the manifold.
4 The injectors are held to the fuel rail by a clamp for each pair of injectors. Remove the clamps.
5 When refitting, fit new 'O'-ring seals (4), and also new caps (5 Fig. 3.28) if necessary.

Fig. 3.26 Throttle casing and attachments – 2.0 litre Turbo model (Sec 29)

1 Throttle link rod
2 Air temperature sensor connector
3 Air intake ducts
4 Throttle casing cover
5 Throttle casing

31 Inlet manifold - removal and refitting

1 Disconnect the battery earth lead.
2 Detach the throttle link rod at the balljoint.
3 Remove the fuel rail and injectors as described in Section 30.
4 Remove the throttle casing as described in Section 29.
5 Unbolt and remove the air regulating valve from the front end face of the manifold.
6 Detach the clutch cable and grommet from their location bracket on the manifold.
7 Disconnect the remaining hoses and wires from the manifold. Note the connection point of each to avoid the possibility of confusion when reassembling.
8 Unbolt and remove the manifold.
9 Refit the manifold in the reverse order of removal. Ensure that the mating surfaces are perfectly clean and be sure to use a new gasket. Ensure that all hoses and wires are connected in their previously noted locations.

Fig. 3.27 Fuel rail and injectors (Sec 30)

1 Injectors
2 Securing clamps
3 Fuel pressure regulator

Fig. 3.28 Sectional view of fuel injector (Sec 30)

4 O-rings   5 Cap

3

32 Fuel pressure regulator - removal and refitting

Note: Refer to the warning note in Section 1 before proceeding
1 This is located on the inlet manifold side of the engine, just below the front of the throttle housing (photo).
2 If available, fit suitable clamps to the fuel hoses to prevent fuel leakage when the hoses are disconnected from the regulator. Failing this, the hoses will need to be plugged as they are detached, so have suitable plugs ready.
3 Unclip and detach the fuel and vacuum hoses from the regulator unit, then undo the

30.1 Fuel injectors, fuel rail and injector wiring plugs

32.1 Fuel pressure regulator (arrowed)

33.4 Coolant temperature sensor location (arrowed)

Fig. 3.29 Absolute pressure sensor (1), 4-way union (2), and idle mixture adjustment potentiometer (3) (Sec 33)

Fig. 3.30 Pre-ignition detector (1) (Sec 33)

retaining screws and remove the regulator unit.
4 Refit in the reverse order of removal.

33 Sensors - removal and refitting

Coolant temperature sensor

1 This should only be removed when the engine is cold.
2 Disconnect the electrical leads.
3 Remove the expansion tank cap to release any pressure in the cooling system.
4 Unscrew the sensor and quickly plug the hole to minimise coolant loss (photo).
5 Smear the threads with a little gasket cement before screwing in the new sensor.

Air temperature sensor

6 Disconnect the wiring plug from the sensor.
7 Remove the air intake duct from the throttle casing.
8 Remove the sensor.
9 Refitting is a reversal of removal.

Absolute pressure sensor

10 Remove the cover from the computer.
11 Disconnect the wiring harness connector, then withdraw the absolute pressure sensor from the support. Detach the pipe at the four-way union and then lever off the pipe at the sensor. Do not pull on the pipe to detach it.
12 Refitting is a reversal of removal.

Engine angular position/speed sensor

13 This sensor is located on the transmission bellhousing, and measures the flywheel angular position and speed (see Chapter 1, photo 49.8).
14 To remove the sensor, disconnect the wiring plug, and remove the two sensor retaining bolts.
15 Refitting is a reversal of removal. No adjustment is necessary.

Pre-ignition detector

16 Disconnect the wiring from the air temperature sensor.

17 Detach the air cleaner-to-air intake casing duct and remove the air cleaner.
18 Disconnect the wiring, then unscrew the pre-ignition detector.
19 Refit in the reverse order of removal.

34 Idle mixture potentiometer - removal and refitting

1 This device is located with the absolute pressure sensor under the computer cover (see Fig. 3.29).
2 Remove the cover from the computer, undo the idle mixture potentiometer retaining screw, detach the wiring connector and remove the potentiometer.
3 Refit in the reverse order of removal. Ensure that the potentiometer is positioned correctly with the tamperproof cap on the opposite side to that of the retaining lug.
4 After refitting, adjust the idle mixture as described in Section 26.

35 Fault finding - Renix fuel injection system

Engine will not start or starts then stops

☐ Defective injection system relay
☐ Faulty fuel pump
☐ Leak in intake system
☐ Defective fuel injectors
☐ Defective absolute pressure sensor
☐ Defective engine angular position/speed sensor
☐ Defective ignition power module
☐ Defective coolant temperature sensor
☐ Defective computer
☐ Wiring fault

Uneven idling

☐ Throttle not closing
☐ Low fuel pressure
☐ Defective fuel injector
☐ Leak in air intake system
☐ Defective or incorrectly adjusted idle mixture potentiometer

Poor acceleration

☐ Defective or incorrectly adjusted idle mixture potentiometer
☐ Leak in air intake system
☐ Defective computer
☐ Wiring fault

Misfiring

☐ Poor central earth connection

Excessive fuel usage

☐ Defective injectors
☐ High fuel pressure
☐ Defective coolant temperature sensor
☐ Defective computer
☐ Wiring fault
☐ Defective air temperature sensor

Part D: Turbocharger

36 Description

1 A Garrett T3 turbocharger is used on the engine fitted to 2.0 litre Turbo models. The turbocharger uses the exhaust gas pressure to drive a turbine which pressurises the intake system. This increases engine efficiency and power.

2 The turbocharger is mounted directly above the exhaust manifold. A cooling circuit operating under pressure from the main cooling system passes coolant through the turbocharger unit to assist in cooling the central turbine bearing. When the engine is switched off, a separate electric coolant pump switches on for a few minutes to prevent the turbine bearing from overheating.

3 To assist the main engine cooling system, an additional electric cooling fan is fitted in front of the radiator. The two units are thermostatically-controlled and run in unison.

4 The air intake system incorporates two air-to-air intercoolers, one located at the bottom of the air cleaner, the other adjacent to the radiator.

5 Regulation of boost pressure is achieved by an exhaust system wastegate operated by a pressure sensor in the intake manifold.

6 A bypass circuit prevents the turbocharger supplying boost during deceleration (photo).

7 A safety feature is the provision of a

Fig. 3.31 Turbocharger and associated components (Sec 36)

1 Coolant temperature sensor	6 Throttle casing	10 Diagnostic socket
2 Boost pressure regulating solenoid valve	7 Throttle switch	11 Ignition module
3 Computer unit	8 Air temperature sensor	12 Distributor
5 Air cleaner	9 Idle speed air regulator valve	13 Turbocharger
		16 Air bypass valve

3

1 Throttle casing
2 Absolute pressure sensor
3 Fuel injection manifold
4 Idle speed air regulator valve
5 Fuel pressure regulator
6 Idle mixture adjustment potentiometer
7 Air cleaner
8 Coolant outlet pipe
9 Thermistor
10 Coolant temperature sensor
11 Air temperature sensor
12 Pre-ignition sensor
13 Valve
14 Boost pressure solenoid valve
15 Boost pressure limiting pressostat
76 Air bypass valve
17 Restrictor (7.5 mm diameter)
18 Air cleaner resonator

Fig. 3.32 Turbocharger system hoses and sensors (schematic) (Sec 36)

36.6 Deceleration air bypass valve

36.8 Engine oil filter and oil cooler connections

36.10 Boost pressure limiting presso-stat (1), absolute pressure sensor (2), mixture adjustment potentiometer (3) and electric cooling pump timer relay (4) (computer cover removed)

pressure sensor to cut the fuel supply off if boost pressure becomes excessive.

8 Engine oil is cooled by passing it through a cooler incorporated in the oil filter base (photo).

9 The fuel system used on Turbo versions is the Renix Type described in Part C of this Chapter.

10 The locations of the system main components are shown in Fig. 3.31 and the accompanying photo. The system hoses and sensors are shown in Figs. 3.32 and 3.33.

11 Testing and adjustment of the turbocharger system can only be carried out by a Renault dealer, as special gauges and adaptors are required.

37 Turbocharger - removal and refitting

1 Remove the air cleaner unit with reference to Part A, Section 3 of this Chapter.

2 Unbolt and remove the heat shield (photo).

3 Detach the remove the turbocharger air intake and outlet hoses.

4 Drain the cooling system (Chapter 2), or clamp the coolant hoses securely so that they cannot leak when disconnected. Unclip and detach the coolant hoses from the turbocharger unit (photo).

Fig. 3.33 Fuel injection and turbocharger system layout (Sec 36)

1 Air cleaner	15 Pre-ignition sensor
2 Turbocharger compressor	16 Air bypass valve
3 Air-to-air intercooler	17 Exhaust manifold
4 Air-to-air intercooler	18 Turbocharger turbine
5 Throttle casing	19 Turbocharger wastegate
6 Inlet manifold	20 Boost pressure regulating solenoid valve
7 Air pressure sensor	21 Variable 'leak' from solenoid valve 20
8 Boost pressure limiting pressostat	22 Coolant temperature sensor
9 Boost pressure gauge	23 Air temperature sensor
10 Computer	24 Turbocharger bearing cooling system
11 Idle speed air regulator valve	25 Electric coolant pump
12 Fuel pressure regulator	26 Distributor
13 Injectors	27 Radiator
14 Engine angular position/speed sensor	28 Oil cooler

Air at atmospheric pressure
Compressed intake air
Cooled compressed intake air
Air-fuel mixture
Exhaust gas

Atmospheric air intake

Exhaust outlet

Fuel intake

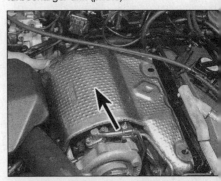

37.2 Remove the heat shield (arrowed)

37.4 Turbocharger unit hose connections coolant hoses (1 and 2), air intake hose (3) and oil feed pipe (4)

37.5 Underside view of turbocharger unit showing oil return pipe (1), mounting strut (2) and wastegate actuator (3)

5 Disconnect the oil feed and return pipes, and the turbocharger mounting strut (photo).
6 Undo the retaining nuts and detach the right-angled elbow from the exhaust downpipe and the turbocharger.
7 To unscrew the turbocharger nuts it will be necessary to modify a 17 mm ring spanner by grinding off the ring end as shown in Fig. 3.35. Undo the nuts and remove the turbocharger.
8 Prior to refitting the turbocharger, ensure that the joint faces of the turbocharger and manifold are thoroughly clean.
9 The following items must be renewed when refitting the turbocharger unit:
(a) The turbocharger-to-manifold nuts
(b) The turbocharger-to-manifold joint face O-ring seal
(c) The oil feed and return pipe seals

Fig. 3.36 Turbocharger wastegate actuator (Sec 38)

1 *Wastegate actuator*
2 *Circlip*
3 *Threaded rod*
4 *Fixing bolt*
5 *Locknut*
6 *Wastegate operating arm*

Fig. 3.34 Right-angled elbow connection to turbocharger and exhaust (Sec 37)

9, 10 and 11 Elbow retaining nuts
12 Right-angled elbow
13 Turbocharger retaining nuts

10 Refit the turbocharger in the reverse order of removal, tightening the retaining bolts to the specified torque.
11 Before reconnecting the oil feed pipe, prime the turbocharger unit with engine oil through the inlet aperture. Disconnect the three-way connector from the ignition power module and then operate the starter motor until oil starts to run out of the hole. Reconnect the oil feed pipe union with a new sealing gasket.
12 Reconnect the three-way connector and then run the engine at idling speed for a few minutes to re-establish the oil flow.
13 Never run the engine with the air intake system disconnected.

38 Turbocharger wastegate actuator - adjusting, removal and refitting

1 The wastegate actuator, when correctly adjusted, is vital to the correct operation of the turbocharger.
2 Due to the need for special gauges, it is not

Fig. 3.37 Boost pressure solenoid valve hose connections (Sec 39)

1 *Air outlet*
2 *Air-to-air intercooler outlet*
3 *Wastegate actuator outlet*

Fig. 3.35 Suitably modified 17 mm spanner for turbocharger retaining nuts (Sec 37)

possible for the home mechanic to adjust it, but for information purposes, if the wastegate actuator adjusting rod locknut is released and the end fitting screwed further onto the rod, the turbocharger pressure is increased. If it is unscrewed, the pressure is reduced.
3 To remove the wastegate actuator, first disconnect the oil supply and return pipes from the turbocharger as described in the preceding Section.
4 Disconnect the hose from the wastegate actuator.
5 Extract the circlip (2 - Fig. 3.36) and disconnect the adjusting rod (3) from the valve operating arm (6).
6 Unscrew and remove the mounting bolts (4) and withdraw the wastegate actuator by rotating it and passing it downwards beside the turbocharger.
7 Refitting is a reversal of the removal procedure.

39 Boost pressure solenoid valve - removal and refitting

1 Remove the air cleaner outer cover.
2 Detach the wiring connector and the air hoses from the valve unit. Mark and take note of the hose positions as they are disconnected to ensure correct refitting (photo).
3 Detach the solenoid valve and remove it together with its mounting.
4 Refit in the reverse order of removal, ensuring that the hoses are correctly reconnected as noted during removal.

39.2 Detach the wiring connector from the boost pressure solenoid valve

3

40 Air-to-air intercoolers -
removal and refitting

1 Two air-to-air intercoolers are fitted, one located under the air cleaner, the other adjacent to the radiator.
2 To remove the intercooler from under the air cleaner, first remove the air cleaner unit and mounting, then detach the air ducts, unclip the retaining strap and withdraw the intercooler from the housing (photo).
3 Refit in the reverse order of removal.
4 To remove the intercooler from adjacent to the radiator, first remove the front grill and the upper crossmember for access.
5 Undo the retaining clips, detach the unit and lift it clear.
6 Refit in the reverse order of removal.

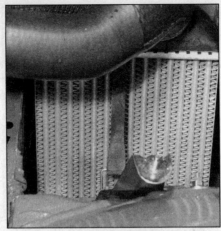

40.3 Intercooler mounted under air cleaner

Fig. 3.38 Air-to-air intercooler location adjacent to radiator (Sec 40)

41 Fault finding - turbocharger

Noisy operation
☐ Worn bearings
☐ Intake or exhaust leaks
☐ Poor lubrication

Blue smoke in exhaust
☐ Internal oil seals leaking

Poor acceleration
☐ Air filter clogged
☐ Wastegate actuator faulty
☐ Leaks in manifold or ducts

Chapter 4 Ignition system

For modifications, and information applicable to later models, see Supplement at end of manual

Contents

Degrees of difficulty

Easy, suitable for novice with little experience	Fairly easy, suitable for beginner with some experience	Fairly difficult, suitable for competent DIY mechanic	Difficult, suitable for experienced DIY mechanic	Very difficult, suitable for expert DIY or professional

Specifications

System type .... Breakerless, computer controlled

Distributor
Make .... Renix
Direction of rotation .... Anti-clockwise
Firing order .... 1-3-4-2 (No 1 cylinder nearest flywheel)

Ignition timing (vacuum disconnected)*
1.7 litre engine:
  F2N 712 .... 3° to 5° BTDC at idling speed
  F2N 710 .... 5° to 9° BTDC at idling speed
2.0 litre engine .... Computer controlled
*Non-adjustable, for checking purposes only

Spark plugs
Type
  1.7 litre engine .... Champion RN7YCC or N279YC
  2.0 litre engine .... Champion S6YCC or S6YC
Electrode gap** .... 0.8 mm (0.031 in)
**Electrode gap setting applicable to Champion spark plugs only

Torque wrench settings

	Nm	lbf ft
Spark plugs:		
1.7 litre engine	20	15
2.0 litre engine	25	18

1 General description

The electronic ignition system operates on an advanced principle whereby the main functions of the distributor are replaced by a computer module.

The system consists of three main components, namely the computer module which incorporates an ignition coil and a vacuum advance unit, the distributor, which directs the HT voltage received from the coil to the appropriate spark plug, and an angular position/speed sensor which determines the position and speed of the crankshaft by sensing special teeth on the flywheel periphery.

The computer module receives information on crankshaft position relative to TDC and BDC and also engine speed from the angular position/speed sensor, and receives information on engine load from the vacuum advance unit. From these constantly changing variables, the computer calculates the precise instant at which HT voltage should be supplied and triggers the coil accordingly. The voltage then passes from the coil to the appropriate spark plug, via the distributor in the conventional way. The functions of the centrifugal and vacuum advance mechanisms, as well as the contact breaker points normally associated with a distributor, are all catered for by the computer module, so that the sole purpose of the distributor is to direct the HT voltage from the coil to the appropriate spark plug.

Depending on model, the computer also receives information on the engine coolant temperature and the engine oil temperature. and this information is then collated together with the other factors to control the ignition advance as required.

On Turbo models, a pre-ignition sensor is fitted in the cylinder head. In the event of pre-ignition ('pinking'), the ignition timing is retarded by the computer to compensate.

4 Sensor winding
5 Sensor winding
6 Coil + terminal and suppressor capacitor terminal
7 Coil – terminal
8 Coil + switch
9 Coil – switch
11 Computer + input
12 Secondary pin
21 Computer earth
31 Rev counter output
41 Sensor information
51 Sensor information
M Distributor cap
HT Coil
C Vacuum capsule
E Computer
P Angular position/speed sensor
V Flywheel
A Feed connector
B Sensor connector
Z Coolant and engine oil temperature sensor information (not all models)

Terminals 8 and 11 are directly interconnected within the unit

Fig. 4.1 Electronic ignition system components – 1.7 litre models (Sec 1)

2 Electronic ignition system - precautions

Note: *Due to the sophisticated nature of the electronic ignition system the following precautions must be observed to prevent damage to the components and reduce the risk of personal injury.*

1 Ensure that the ignition is switched off before disconnecting any of the ignition wiring.
2 Ensure that the ignition is switched off before connecting or disconnecting any ignition test equipment such as a timing light.
3 Do not connect a suppression condenser or test lamp to the ignition coil negative terminal.
4 Do not connect any test appliance or stroboscopic timing light requiring a 12 volt supply to the ignition coil positive terminal.
5 Do not allow an HT lead to short out or spark against the computer module body.

3 Maintenance and inspection

1 The only components of the electronic ignition system which require periodic maintenance are the distributor cap, HT leads and spark plugs. These should be treated in

the same way as on a conventional system and reference should be made to Section 8.
2 At the intervals specified in *'Routine maintenance'* at the start of this manual, clean or renew the spark plugs and check the high tension (HT) leads.
3 Remove the distributor cap and inspect it for cracks, and the condition of the centre carbon brush.
4 Check the rotor contact end and the cap contacts for erosion. They may be cleaned carefully to remove deposits but, if badly eroded, renew the components.
5 On this system dwell angle and ignition timing are a function of the computer module and there is no provision for adjustment. It is possible to check the ignition timing on 1.7 litre models using a stroboscopic timing light, but this should only be necessary as part of a fault finding procedure, as any deviation from the specified setting would indicate a possible fault in the computer module.

4 Distributor - removal and refitting

1 On all models, the distributor simply comprises a rotor arm driven from the end of the camshaft, and a distributor cap attached to the end face of the cylinder head.
2 To remove the distributor cap, undo the retaining screws and withdraw it together with the HT leads (photos).
3 The rotor arm and shield can now be pulled free and removed (photos).

4.2A Distributor cap – 1.7 litre model

4.2B Distributor cap – 2.0 litre model

4.3A Rotor arm and shield – 1.7 litre model

4.3B Rotor arm and shield – 2.0 litre model

4.3C Removing the shield – 2.0 litre model

4.4 Rotor housing retaining screws (arrowed) – 2.0 litre model

4.7 Rotor engagement slot in camshaft (arrowed) – 1.7 litre model

5.3 Ignition computer unit location (coil arrowed) –1.7 litre model

4 On 2.0 litre models. undo the three retaining screws to remove the rotor housing if required (photo). If necessary renew the O-ring seal.

5 Wipe clean the cap and leads. If the camshaft oil seal requires renewal, refer to Chapter 1.

6 Carefully inspect the HT leads and cap for signs of deterioration. Check the cap for hairline cracks, and the electrodes for excessive wear. Renew if necessary.

7 Refit in the reverse order of removal. When fitting the rotor arm, ensure that its single inner tooth engages with the slot in the end of the camshaft (photo).

5 Computer unit - removal and refitting

1 The computer unit is located in the engine compartment on the left-hand side just forward of the suspension turret. Whenever the computer unit is removed, handle it with care as it is fragile and easily damaged.

2 Disconnect the battery earth lead.

3 On 1.7 litre models proceed as follows. Disconnect the vacuum hose and the wiring connectors, noting their respective locations. Undo the retaining nuts and remove the unit (photo). If required the coil can be removed as described in Section 7. Do not attempt to remove the vacuum unit.

4 On 2.0 litre models proceed as follows.

Undo the retaining screw and remove the outer casing from the computer unit. Release the retaining clip at the top and undo the retaining screw at the bottom, then withdraw the plastic case containing the computer unit (photos).

5 On all models, if removing the unit completely from the car, trace the routeings of the wiring harnesses and disconnect their connectors. Note the positions of the harnesses and connectors to avoid confusion when refitting.

6 Refitting is a reversal of the removal procedure.

6 Engine angular position/ speed sensor - description, removal and refitting

1 An angular position/speed sensor is used to monitor the TDC and BDC positions of the crankshaft from the tooth gaps on the periphery of the flywheel (or driveplate).

2 The sensor is secured to the bellhousing by special shouldered bolts and its position is preset in production to provide the required clearance. No adjustment of this clearance is necessary or possible.

3 To remove the sensor, proceed as follows.

4 Disconnect the battery negative terminal.

5 Disconnect the smaller of the two wiring multi-plugs from the front of the computer unit (1.7 litre models), from the front of the ignition coil (2.0 litre models) or, where applicable, from the wiring connector near the sensor.

6 Undo and remove the two bolts securing the sensor to the top of the clutch bellhousing and lift off the sensor. Note that the two retaining bolts are of the shouldered type and must not be replaced with ordinary bolts. When handling the sensor, take care not to damage it.

7 Refitting is the reverse sequence to removal.

7 Ignition coil - removal and refitting

1 The location of the ignition coil is dependent on model. On 1.7 litre models it is attached to the computer unit mounted forward of the left-hand suspension turret (see Section 5). Whilst on 2.0 litre models it is attached to the engine compartment bulkhead. In each case the removal procedure is the same (photos).

Fig. 4.2 Angular position/speed sensor (P) and special bolt (Sec 6)

4

5.4A Removing the computer unit outer casing – 2.0 litre model

5.4B Computer unit location within plastic case – 2.0 litre model

7.1A Ignition coil – 2.0 litre non-Turbo model

7.1B Ignition coil (arrowed) – 2.0 litre Turbo model

8.2 Spark plug removal – 2.0 litre engine

8.9 Spark plug installation – 1.7 litre engine

2 Disconnect the HT and LT wires from the coil unit, then undo the retaining nuts or bolts (as applicable) and remove the coil units from its location.
3 Refit in the reverse order of removal. Ensure that the wiring connections are securely made.

8 Spark plugs and HT leads - general

1 The correct functioning of the spark plugs is vital for the correct running and efficiency of the engine. It is essential that the plugs fitted are appropriate for the engine, and the suitable type is specified at the beginning of this chapter. If this type is used and the engine is in good condition, the spark plugs should not need attention between scheduled replacement intervals. Spark plug cleaning is rarely necessary and should not be attempted unless specialised equipment is available as damage can easily be caused to the firing ends.
2 To remove the plugs, first mark the HT leads to ensure correct refitment, and then pull them off the plugs. Using a spark plug spanner, or suitable deep socket and extension bar, unscrew the plugs and remove them from the engine. It will be noted that on 2.0 litre models the plugs are of the tapered seat type and therefore no washers are fitted (photo).

3 The condition of the spark plugs will also tell much about the overall condition of the engine.
4 If the insulator nose of the spark plug is clean and white, with no deposits, this is indicative of a weak mixture, or too hot a plug. (A hot plug transfers heat away from the electrode slowly - a cold plug transfers it away quickly).
5 If the tip and insulator nose are covered with hard black-looking deposits, then this is indicative that the mixture is too rich. Should the plug be black and oily, then it is likely that the engine is fairly worn, as well as the mixture being too rich.
6 If the insulator nose is covered with light tan to greyish brown deposits, then the mixture is correct and it is likely that the engine is in good condition.
7 The spark plug gap is of considerable importance as, if it is too large or too small, the size of spark and its efficiency will be seriously impaired. The spark plug gap should be set to the figure given in the Specifications at the beginning of this Chapter.
8 To set it, measure the gap with a feeler gauge, and then bend open, or close, the *outer* plug electrode until the correct gap is achieved. The centre electrode should **never** be bent as this may crack the insulation and cause plug failure, if nothing worse.
9 To refit the plugs, screw them in by hand initially and then fully tighten to the specified torque. If a torque wrench is not available,

tighten the plugs until initial resistance is felt as the sealing washer or plug taper (as applicable) contacts its seat and then tighten by a further eighth of a turn. Refit the HT leads in the correct order, ensuring that they are a tight fit over the plug ends. Periodically wipe the leads clean to reduce the risk of HT leakage by arcing (photo).

HAYNES HiNT

It's often difficult to insert spark plugs into their holes without cross-threading them. To avoid this possibility, fit a short piece of rubber hose over the end of the spark plug. The flexible hose acts as a universal joint, to help align the plug with the plug hole. Should the plug begin to cross-thread, the hose will slip on the spark plug, preventing thread damage.

Fig. 4.3 Ignition HT lead connections – 1.7 litre engine (Sec 8)

Fig. 4.4 Ignition HT lead connections – 2.0 litre engine (Sec 8)

Fault finding - electronic ignition system

1 Problems associated with the electronic ignition system can usually be grouped into one of two areas, those caused by the more conventional HT side of the system, such as spark plugs, HT leads, rotor arm and distributor cap, and those caused by the LT circuitry including the computer module and its related components.

Prior to making any diagnostic checks on the system, observe the precautionary notes given in Section 2 of this Chapter.

Engine fails to start

2 If the engine fails to start and the car was running normally when it was last used, first check that there is fuel in the petrol tank. If the engine turns over normally on the starter motor and the battery is evidently well charged, then the fault may be in either the high or low tension circuits. First check the HT circuit. If the battery is known to be fully charged, the ignition light comes on, and the starter motor fails to turn the engine, check the tightness of the leads on the battery terminals and also the security of the earth lead to its connection on the body. It is quite common for the leads to have worked loose, even if they look and feel secure. If one of the battery terminal posts gets very hot when trying to work the starter motor this is a sure indication of a faulty connection to that terminal.

3 Check the wiring connections at the plug sockets A and B shown in Fig. 4.1. The terminal connections must be clean and secure. Detach and reconnect them several times to overcome a poor contact.

4 One of the commonest reasons for bad starting is wet or damp spark plug leads and distributor. Remove the distributor cap. If condensation is visible internally, dry the cap with a rag and also wipe over the leads. Refit the cap.

5 If the engine still fails to start, check that the current is reaching the plugs, by disconnecting each plug lead in turn at the spark plug end, and holding the end of the cable about 5 mm (0.2 in) away from the cylinder block. Spin the engine on the starter motor.

6 Sparking between the end of the cable and the block should be fairly strong with a good, regular blue spark. (Hold the lead with rubber insulated pliers to avoid electric shocks.) If current is reaching the plugs, then remove them and clean and regap them. The engine should now start.

7 If there is no spark at the plug leads, take off the HT lead from the centre of the distributor cap and hold it to the block as before. Spin the engine on the starter once more. A rapid succession of blue sparks between the end of the lead and the block indicates that the coil is in order and that the distributor cap is cracked, the rotor arm faulty, or the carbon brush in the top of the distributor cap is not making good contact with the rotor arm.

8 If there are no sparks from the end of the lead from the coil, check the connections at the coil end of the lead. If no fault is apparent in the HT circuit, it is likely that the fault lies in the computer unit which can only be checked by a suitably equipped dealer.

Engine misfires

9 If the engine misfires regularly, run it at a fast idling speed. Pull off each of the plug caps in turn and listen to the note of the engine. Hold the plug cap in a dry cloth or with a rubber glove as additional protection against a shock from the HT supply.

10 No difference in engine running will be noticed when the lead from the defective circuit is removed. Removing the lead from one of the good cylinders will accentuate the misfire.

11 Remove the plug lead from the end of the defective plug and hold it about 5 mm (0.2 in) away from the block. Restart the engine. If the sparking is fairly strong and regular the fault must lie in the spark plug.

12 The plug may be loose, the insulation may be cracked, or the electrodes may have burnt away, giving too wide a gap for the spark to jump. Worse still, one of the electrodes may have broken off.

13 If there is no spark at the end of the plug lead, or if it is weak and intermittent, check the ignition lead from the distributor to the plug. If the insulation is cracked or perished, renew the lead. Check the connections at the distributor cap.

14 If there is still no spark, examine the distributor cap carefully for tracking. This can be recognised by a very thin black line running between two or more electrodes, or between an electrode and some other part of the distributor. These lines are paths which now conduct electricity across the cap, thus letting it run to earth. The only answer is a new distributor cap.

4

Notes

Chapter 5 Clutch

Contents

Degrees of difficulty

Easy, suitable for novice with little experience	**Fairly easy,** suitable for beginner with some experience	**Fairly difficult,** suitable for competent DIY mechanic	**Difficult,** suitable for experienced DIY mechanic	**Very difficult,** suitable for expert DIY or professional

Specifications

Type .... Single dry plate with diaphragm spring. Sealed release bearing in constant contact with the diaphragm spring fingers.

Actuation
Turbo model .... Hydraulic
Non-Turbo models .... Cable

Driven plate (disc) diameter
1.7 litre models .... 200 mm (7.8 in)
2.0 litre non-Turbo models .... 215 mm (8.4 in)
2.0 litre Turbo models .... 228 mm (8.9 in)

Torque wrench settings	**Nm**	**lbf ft**
Clutch cover-to-flywheel bolts	24	18
Clutch master and slave cylinder retaining nuts	15	11

1 Description

The clutch is of single dry plate type with a diaphragm spring pressure plate.

The driven plate incorporates torsion springs to give resilience to the hub.

The release bearing is of sealed ball type, self-centring and in constant contact with the diaphragm spring fingers.

Clutch actuation may be hydraulic or by cable according to model; refer to Specifications. On hydraulic clutches, the master cylinder is fed by fluid from the brake fluid reservoir.

On 1.7 litre models, the clutch release mechanism has conventional push-type actuation, whilst on 2.0 litre models, the clutch can have either a push-type actuation or a pull-type actuation (depending on model). On 2.0 litre models, the type of release mechanism can be determined from the position of the release fork. On models with

Fig. 5.1 Sectional view of clutch unit on 1.7 litre models (Sec 1)

Fig. 5.2 Sectional view of clutch unit on 2.0 litre non-Turbo models (Sec 1)

Fig. 5.3 Sectional view of clutch unit on 2.0 litre Turbo models (Sec 1)

Fig. 5.6 Remove screws from positions indicated to remove lower facia trim panels (Sec 2)

'push-type' mechanism, the release lever is on the right-hand side of the transmission, whereas on models with a 'pull-type' mechanism, the lever is on the left-hand side of the bellhousing.

Fig. 5.4 Push-type actuation clutch mechanism – 1.7 litre models (Sec 1)

Fig. 5.5 Pull-type actuation clutch mechanism – 2.0 litre models (Sec 1)

2 Clutch cable - removal and refitting

1 Disconnect the battery earth lead.
2 Detach the cable end from the release fork and disengage the outer cable from the bracket on the bellhousing (photos).
3 With reference to Fig. 5.6, undo the retaining screws from the positions indicated and remove the lower facia trim panels on the driver's side. With the panel released, detach the fusebox from the hinged lid, and remove the cigar lighter (Chapter 12). Disconnect the heater ventilation duct if necessary for improved access.
4 Pull on the cable by pressing down on the pedal, hold the cable, then release the pedal and extract the cable end fitting from the pedal quadrant to free the cable (photo). Withdraw the cable through the scuttle from the engine side.
5 Refit in the reverse order of removal. Ensure that the outer cable end stop is in correct alignment with the scuttle. The outer cable is clipped into the scuttle by depressing the pedal. Adjustment is automatic.
6 Before refitting the lower facia trim panels, check that the clutch operates in a satisfactory manner. The toothed cam of the automatic adjuster must pivot on its shaft and there must be at least 20 mm (0.78 in) free play at the clutch operating fork when the cable is pulled.

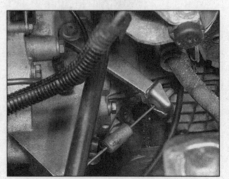

2.2A Detach the clutch cable from the release fork – 1.7 litre model

2.2B Detach the clutch cable from the release fork – 2.0 litre model

2.4 Clutch cable end fitting (arrowed) and pedal quadrant

Fig. 5.7 Clutch free play automatic adjuster mechanism at clutch pedal (Sec 2)

R *Spring*
S *Toothed quadrant section*
C *Toothed cam*

3 Hydraulic clutch master cylinder - removal and refitting

1 The clutch master cylinder cannot be overhauled; if defective it must be renewed.
2 Remove the clutch spring capsule as described in Section 11.
3 Fit a suitable clamp to the hydraulic hose at the brake master cylinder end as shown in Fig. 5.8.
4 Detach the fluid feed hose and the fluid outlet pipe at the master cylinder. Note the location of the seal and flat washer in the cylinder outlet pipe bore.
5 Undo the two nuts and remove the master cylinder.
6 Refitting is the reverse sequence to removal bearing in mind the following:
(a) Ensure that the outlet pipe seal and flat washer are correctly positioned in the cylinder bore (as noted during removal)
(b) Use a new seal on the master cylinder pushrod
(c) Tighten the retaining nuts to the specified torque
(d) Bleed the hydraulic system as described in Section 5 on completion

4 Hydraulic clutch slave cylinder - removal and refitting

1 The clutch slave cylinder cannot be overhauled: if defective it must be renewed.
2 Before proceeding, fit a suitable clamp onto the hydraulic hose at the brake master cylinder end as shown in Fig. 5.8. This will prevent excessive fluid spillage when the pipe is detached from the cylinder.
3 Unbolt and remove the turbocharger heat shield.
4 Unbolt and remove the heat shield from the clutch slave cylinder (see Fig. 5.9).

Fig. 5.8 Clamp the hydraulic hose at the brake master cylinder (Sec 4)

5 Unscrew and detach the hydraulic fluid feed pipe from the slave cylinder, then undo the mounting bolts and withdraw the slave cylinder unit.
6 Refitting is a reversal of the removal procedure. When the slave cylinder is bolted in position and the hydraulic hose reconnected, release the clamp from the hydraulic hose and top up the hydraulic fluid level in the fluid reservoir, then bleed the clutch hydraulic system as described in Section 5.
7 On completion ensure that the clutch pedal returns to its full height position and that the operating lever travel is as shown in Fig. 5.11.

5 Clutch hydraulic system - bleeding

Note: *Bleeding of the hydraulic system is necessary whenever air has entered the system, after disconnecting any component or as a result of leakage (which should first be rectified).*
1 Gather together a clean jar, a length of rubber or plastic tubing which fits tightly over the bleed nipple on the slave cylinder and a supply of fresh hydraulic fluid. An assistant will also be required to operate the clutch

Fig. 5.11 Clutch operating lever travel (Sec 4)

C = 11.0 mm (0.429 in)

Fig. 5.9 Unbolt the heat shield (arrowed) from the clutch slave cylinder (Sec 4)

Fig. 5.10 Hydraulic fluid feed pipe to the clutch slave cylinder (Sec 4)

pedal and to keep the fluid level in the master cylinder topped up.
2 Check that the master cylinder reservoir is full - if not, fill it, using the procedure given in Chapter 9. Section 2 - and also cover the bottom inch of the jar with hydraulic fluid. Note that the ignition must be switched on when checking the fluid level in the reservoir. When the fluid level reaches the 'MAXI' mark, the reservoir is full.
3 Remove the dust cap (if present) from the bleed nipple on the slave cylinder and place one end of the tube securely over it (photo). Place the other end of the tube in the jar, ensuring that the tube orifice is below the level of the fluid.
4 Using a ring or open-ended spanner, unscrew the bleed nipple approximately one turn and then slowly depress the clutch pedal.

5.3 Clutch slave cylinder bleed nipple fitted with dust cap (arrowed)

5

6.6 Clutch disc orientation – 2.0 litre non-Turbo model

6.8A Tightening the clutch cover bolts – 1.7 litre model

6.8B Tightening the clutch cover bolts – 2.0 litre non-Turbo model

5 Tighten the bleed nipple while the pedal is held in the fully depressed position.

6 Release the clutch pedal slowly. allowing it to return fully. After waiting four seconds to allow the master cylinder to recuperate, repeat the above procedure.

7 Keep the master cylinder reservoir topped up throughout this bleeding operation, otherwise further air will be introduced into the system.

8 When clean hydraulic fluid free from air bubbles can be seen coming from the end of the tube, tighten the bleed nipple, remove the rubber tube and refit the dust cap.

9 Finally top up the master cylinder reservoir and refit the cap. Discard the old hydraulic fluid as it is contaminated and must not be re-used in the system.

10 Reference should be made to Chapter 9, Section 15 for details of bleeding using one-way valve or pressure bleeding equipment which is also suitable for the clutch hydraulic system.

6 Clutch unit - removal and refitting

Removal - all models

1 Access to the clutch may be gained in one of two ways. Either the engine, or

Fig. 5.12 Clutch disc orientation on 2.0 litre Turbo models larger offset side (A) must face towards gearbox (Sec 6)

engine/transmission unit, can be removed, as described in Chapter 1, and the transmission separated from the engine, or the engine may be left in the car and the transmission unit removed independently, as described in Chapter 6.

2 Having separated the transmission from the engine, undo and remove the clutch cover retaining bolts, working in a diagonal sequence and slackening the bolts only a few turns at a time.

3 Ease the clutch cover off its locating dowels and be prepared to catch the clutch disc which will drop out as the cover is removed. Note which way round the disc is fitted.

4 It is important that no oil or grease is allowed to come into contact with the friction material of the clutch disc or the pressure plate and flywheel faces during inspection and refitting. The inspection procedures are outlined in Section 7.

5 It is advisable to refit the clutch assembly with clean hands and to wipe down the pressure plate and flywheel faces with a clean dry rag before assembly begins.

Refitting - 1.7 litre and 2.0 litre non-Turbo models

6 Fit the clutch disc into its cover orientated so that the central hub is as shown in Fig. 5.1 or 5.2 according to model (photo). As the clutch disc is a snug fit within its cover, it is virtually self-centralising.

7 Fit the combined disc and cover assembly to the flywheel, align the cover plate over the dowels on the flywheel, then locate the cover plate retaining bolts.

8 Align the disc so that it is central within the cover, with reference to paragraphs 13 to 16 of this Section if necessary, then tighten the retaining bolts to the specified torque wrench setting (photos). Tighten the bolts progressively in a diagonal sequence.

9 The transmission can now be mated to the engine by referring to the relevant Sections and Chapters.

Refitting - 2.0 litre Turbo models

10 The clutch disc must be fitted so that its hub is orientated as shown in Figs. 5.3 and 5.12.

11 Locate the disc, then place the clutch cover over the dowels, refit the retaining bolts and tighten them finger tight so that the clutch disc is gripped, but can still be moved.

12 The clutch disc must now be centralised so that, when the engine and transmission are mated, the splines of the gearbox primary shaft will pass through the splines in the centre of the clutch disc hub.

13 Centralisation can be carried out quite easily by inserting a round bar or long screwdriver through the hole in the centre of the clutch disc so that the end of the bar rests in the hole in the end of the crankshaft containing the primary shaft support bearing.

14 Using the support bearing as a fulcrum, moving the bar sideways or up and down will move the clutch disc in whichever direction is necessary to achieve centralisation.

15 Centralisation is easily judged by removing the bar and viewing the clutch disc hub in relation to the support bearing. When the support bearing appears exactly in the centre of the clutch disc hub, all is correct.

16 An alternative and more accurate method of centralisation is to use a commercially available clutch aligning tool obtainable from most accessory shops.

17 Once the clutch is centralised, progressively tighten the cover bolts in a diagonal sequence to the torque setting given in the Specifications.

7 Clutch unit - inspection

1 With the clutch assembly removed, clean off all traces of asbestos dust using a dry cloth. This is best done outside or in a well ventilated area; asbestos dust is harmful, and must not be inhaled.

2 Examine the linings of the clutch disc for wear and loose rivets, and the disc rim for distortion, cracks, broken torsion springs and worn splines. The surface of the friction linings may be highly glazed, but, as long as the friction material pattern can be clearly seen, this is satisfactory. If there is any sign of oil contamination, indicated by a continuous, or patchy, shiny black discoloration, the disc

7.3 Examine the machined contact face of the pressure plate – 2.0 litre non-Turbo model

8.2 Clutch release bearing – 1.7 litre model

Fig. 5.13 Clutch release bearing. Lug (A) must engage with release fork – 1.7 litre models (Sec 8)

Fig. 5.14 Clutch release fork spring retainer (1) and ball stud (2) – 1.7 litre models (Sec 8)

must be renewed and the source of the contamination traced and rectified. This will be either a leaking crankshaft oil seal or gearbox primary shaft oil seal - or both. Renewal procedures are given in Chapter 1 and Chapter 6 respectively. The disc must also be renewed if the lining thickness has worn down to, or just above, the level of the rivet heads.

3 Check the machined faces of the flywheel and pressure plate. If either is grooved, or heavily scored, renewal is necessary (photo). The pressure plate must also be renewed if any cracks are apparent, or if the diaphragm spring is damaged or its pressure suspect.

4 With the gearbox removed it is advisable to check the condition of the release bearing, as described in the following Sections.

8 Clutch release bearing (1.7 litre models) - removal, inspection and refitting

1 To gain access to the release bearing it is necessary to separate the engine and transmission either by removing the engine or transmission individually, or by removing both units as an assembly and separating them after removal. Depending on the method chosen, the appropriate procedures will be found in Chapter 1 or Chapter 6.

2 With the transmission removed from the engine, tilt the release fork and slide the bearing assembly off the gearbox input shaft guide tube (photo).

3 To remove the bearing from its holder, release the four tags of the spring retainer, lift off the retainer and remove the bearing.

4 Check the bearing for smoothness of operation and renew it if there is any roughness or harshness as it is spun.

5 To remove the release fork, disengage the rubber cover and then pull the fork upwards to release it from its ball pivot stud.

6 Refitting the release fork and release bearing is the reverse sequence to removal, but note the following points:

(a) Lubricate the release fork pivot ball stud and the release bearing-to-diaphragm spring contact areas sparingly with molybdenum disulphide grease

(b) Ensure that the release fork spring retainer locates behind the flat shoulder of the ball pivot stud

9 Clutch release bearing (2.0 litre models) - removal, inspection and refitting

Pull-type clutch

1 The release bearing is attached to the clutch cover/pressure plate diaphragm springs and, if renewal is necessary, the two must be obtained as a unit part (photo).

2 Check the bearing for smoothness of operation. If any harshness is felt when the bearing is spun, it must be renewed.

3 If required, the release fork can be removed by driving out the retaining roll pins. It is recommended that Renault special tools B Vi 606 and Cor 41 are used for this operation.

4 When refitting the release fork, lubricate the fork shaft with a liberal amount of grease and fit it with its seal rubber. Locate the fork with the plastic spacers and ensure that it is correctly orientated before fitting the new roll pins. Double roll pins are fitted, and they must be orientated as shown in Fig. 5.15 when refitting.

Push-type clutch

5 Proceed as described in Section 8.

Fig. 5.15 Release fork retaining roll pin orientation – 2.0 litre non-Turbo models (Sec 9)

10 Clutch pedal - removal and refitting

1 The clutch and brake pedals share a common mounting and pivot shaft. Remove the clutch pedal as follows.

2 Detach the battery earth lead. For improved access, remove the driver's seat or at least move it fully rearwards.

3 Undo the fastenings and remove the trim panels from the lower facia on the driver's side. Unclip the fuse holder and remove the ventilation duct.

4 Disconnect the clutch cable from the pedal with reference to Section 2.

9.1 Clutch release bearing location in clutch cover – 2.0 litre non-Turbo model

5

10.6 Pedal shaft retaining clip (arrowed)

Emb. 1 082

Fig. 5.18 Spring compressor tool located on spring capsule (Sec 11)

Fig. 5.16 Clutch spring capsule location – Turbo models (Sec 11)

A Pedal pivot
B Spring capsule lower pivot
C Spring capsule upper pivot

Fig. 5.17 Sectional view of spring capsule (Sec 11)

B Spring capsule lower pivot pin
C Spring capsule upper pivot pin (connected to pushrod and pedal)

5 On Turbo models, detach the spring capsule as described in Section 11.

6 Withdraw the pedal shaft retaining clip on the clutch pedal end of the shaft, then carefully withdraw the shaft from the brake pedal side just enough to allow the clutch pedal to be removed (photo). If the shaft is withdrawn too far, the brake pedal will become detached as well, so take care.

7 Refit in the reverse order of removal. Lubricate the pedal, and cable or spring capsule pivots (as applicable). Check the clutch pedal for satisfactory operation before refitting the ventilation duct, fuse holder, and lower facia trim panels.

11 Clutch spring capsule (Turbo models) - description, removal and refitting

1 This device is mounted between the clutch pedal mounting and the pedal, and serves the purpose of a clutch pedal return spring. As the pedal is depressed beyond the dotted line shown in Fig. 5.16, the pedal pressure required to operate the clutch is reduced by approximately 18%. This results in a 'lighter' clutch pedal.

2 When removing the spring capsule, a special spring compressor tool (Renault No Emb 1082) or similar will be required to secure the unit in the compressed position during removal.

3 Detach the battery earth lead. For improved access in the car, remove the driver's seat or at least move it fully rearwards.

4 Undo the fastenings and remove the trim panels from the lower facia on the driver's side. Unclip the fuse holder and remove the ventilation duct.

5 With the clutch pedal now accessible, locate the special spring compressor tool as shown in Fig. 5.18.

6 Extract the circlip retaining the capsule lower pivot pin and the roll pin securing the upper pivot pin to the pedal and pushrod.

7 Press the pedal downwards and withdraw the lower pivot pin. Remove the capsule unit complete with the spring compressor tool.

8 To remove the spring compressor tool from the capsule unit, locate the unit in a vice, release the tool, then slowly unscrew the vice and remove the capsule unit from it.

9 Refitting is a reversal of removal. Lubricate the pivot pins with grease. If fitting a new capsule, locate the unit in a vice and fit the spring compressor tool.

10 When fitting the capsule, ensure that its larger diameter is at the pushrod end. Locate the pushrod (and plastic bushes) into the capsule and pedal, fit the upper pivot pin and roll pin, then slightly depress the pedal to enable the lower pivot pin to be fitted. Ensure that the circlip is correctly fitted on the lower pivot pin.

Fault finding - clutch

Judder when taking up drive

☐ Loose or worn engine/gearbox mountings
☐ Clutch disc contaminated or linings worn
☐ Clutch cable sticking or frayed (where applicable)
☐ Faulty pressure plate assembly
☐ Worn primary shaft or clutch disc splines

Clutch fails to disengage

☐ Clutch self-adjusting mechanism faulty or inoperative (where applicable)
☐ Air in hydraulic system (where applicable)
☐ Hydraulic master or slave cylinder faulty (where applicable)
☐ Clutch disc sticking on primary shaft splines
☐ Clutch disc linings sticking on flywheel or pressure plate
☐ Faulty pressure plate assembly
☐ Cable broken (where applicable)

Clutch slips

☐ Clutch self adjusting mechanism faulty or inoperative (where applicable)
☐ Clutch disc contaminated or linings worn
☐ Faulty pressure plate
☐ Diaphragm spring broken

Noise when depressing clutch pedal

☐ Worn release bearing
☐ Faulty pressure plate assembly
☐ Diaphragm spring broken
☐ Worn or dry cable (where applicable) or pedal bushes

Noise when releasing clutch pedal

☐ Faulty pressure plate assembly
☐ Broken clutch disc cushioning springs
☐ Gearbox internal wear

Chapter 6 Manual transmission

For modifications, and information applicable to later models, see Supplement at end of manual

Contents

Degrees of difficulty

| Easy, suitable for novice with little experience | | Fairly easy, suitable for beginner with some experience | | Fairly difficult, suitable for competent DIY mechanic | 🔧 | Difficult, suitable for experienced DIY mechanic | 🔧 | Very difficult, suitable for expert DIY or professional | 🔧 |

Specifications

Part A: JB3 transmission

General

Application	1.7 litre models	
Ratios	**JB3**	**JB3S***
1st	3.72 : 1	3.09 : 1
2nd	2.05 : 1	1.85 : 1
3rd	1.32 : 1	1.32 : 1
4th	0.96 : 1	0.96 : 1
5th	0.79 : 1	0.75 : 1
Reverse	3.54 : 1	3.54 : 1
Final drive	3.56 : 1	4.06 : 1

*RS model only

Differential bearing preload (see text)

Used bearings	0 to 16 N (0 to 3.6 lbf)
New bearings	16 to 32 N (3.6 to 7.2 lbf)

Lubrication

Capacity	3.4 litres (6.0 pints)
Lubricant type/specification	Hypoid gear oil, viscosity SAE 80W to API GL5

Torque wrench settings	Nm	lbf ft
Mounting nuts	40	30
Selector rod bolt	30	22
Primary shaft nut	135	100
Secondary shaft bolt:		
10 mm diameter	80	59
8 mm diameter	20	14
Housing bolts	25	18
5th gear detent unit	19	14
Crownwheel nut (taper bearing type)	130	95

Part B: NG9 transmission

General

Application	2.0 litre non-Turbo models
Ratios:	
1st	4.09 : 1
2nd	2.17 : 1
3rd	1.40 : 1
4th	1.03 : 1
5th	0.86 : 1
Reverse	3.54 : 1
Final drive	3.44 : 1

Differential bearing preload (see text)   10 to 13 N (2.3 to 2.9 lbf)

Crownwheel-to-pinion backlash   0.12 to 0.25 mm (0.005 to 0.010 in)

Lubrication

Capacity	2.2 litres (4.0 pints)
Lubricant type/specification	Hypoid gear oil, viscosity SAE 80W to API GL5

Torque wrench settings	Nm	lbf ft
Mounting nuts	40	30
Primary shaft nut	130	95
Secondary shaft (speedometer drive) nut	150	110
Rear casing bolts	15	11
Half-casing bolts	25	18
Reverse cable locknut	20	15
Crownwheel bolts	125	92

Part C: UN1 transmission

General

Application	2.0 litre Turbo models
Ratios:	
1st	3.36 : 1
2nd	2.05 : 1
3rd	1.38 : 1
4th	1.03 : 1
5th	0.89 : 1
Reverse	3.54 : 1
Final drive	3.44 : 1

Differential bearing preload (see text)   45 to 65 N (10.1 to 14.6 lbf)

Lubrication

Capacity	3.0 litres (5.2 pints)
Lubricant type/specification	Hypoid gear oil, viscosity SAE 75W/90

Torque wrench settings	Nm	lbf ft
Primary shaft nut	135	100
Secondary shaft nut	200	147
Rear casing bolts	25	18
Half-casing bolts:		
8 mm diameter	25	18
10 mm diameter	50	37
Spacer plate bolts	50	37
Clutch bellhousing bolts	50	37
Reverse shaft swivel bolt	25	18
Crownwheel bolts	122	90

3.3A Removing the JB3 transmission drain plug

3.3B Remove the undershield from the NG9 and UN1 transmission . . .

3.3C . . . for access to the drain plug (arrowed)

1 General description

JB3 transmission

The JB3 transmission has five forward gears and one reverse gear. All forward gears have baulk ring synchromesh units fitted for ease of engagement.

The final drive (differential) unit is integral with the main gearbox and is located between the mechanism casing and clutch and differential housing. The gearbox and differential both share the same lubricating oil.

Gearshift is by means of a floor-mounted lever connected by a remote control housing and gearchange rod to the gearbox fork contact shaft.

If transmission overhaul is necessary, due consideration should be given to the costs involved, since it is often more economical to obtain a service exchange or good second-hand transmission rather than fit new parts to the existing unit.

NG9 and UN1 transmission

These transmissions are located behind the engine in a similar manner to rear-wheel-drive cars but power is transmitted to the front roadwheels through driveshafts. The driveshafts are splined to the side gears of the differential/final drive which is integrated into the transmission casing.

Five forward synchromesh gears are provided with a reverse gear.

The gearchange control is of floor-mounted type.

The transmission casing is of four section type: the clutch bellhousing, the rear cover (which houses the selector finger and 5th gear), and the two main casing sections which are split longitudinally.

If transmission overhaul is necessary, due consideration should be given to the costs involved, since it is often more economical to obtain a service exchange or good second-hand transmission rather than fit new parts to the existing unit.

2 Maintenance

1 At the intervals specified in *Routine maintenance*, inspect the transmission joint faces and oil seals for any signs of damage, deterioration or oil leakage.
2 At the same service interval, check and, if necessary, top up the transmission oil using the procedure described in Section 3.
3 At less frequent intervals (see '*Routine maintenance*') the transmission should be drained and refilled with fresh oil, and this procedure is also described in Section 3.
4 It is also advisable to check for excess free play or wear in the gear linkage joints and rods and check the gear lever adjustment, as described in Section 6.

3 Transmission - draining and refilling

1 When draining the transmission oil, the vehicle will need to be standing level. If possible position the vehicle over an inspection pit, but failing this raise and support the vehicle at the front and rear on axle stands to allow access underneath the vehicle whilst at the same time keeping it level.
2 Remove the transmission undertray which is secured by bolts and pegs. Remove the transmission breather to ensure full draining.
3 Loosen the transmission drain plug using a suitable key, position a container under the plug, then remove the plug to drain the oil into the container (photos). When the oil has fully drained, refit the plug and wipe clean the area around the drain hole. Remove the container and dispose of the old oil (do not re-use it).
4 Refit the undertray.
5 Unscrew and remove the transmission filler/level plug (photo).

Fig. 6.1 Underside view of JB3 type transmission showing the filler/level plug (1) and the drain plug (2) (Sec 3)

3.5 Oil level/filler plug (arrowed) – NG9 and UN1 transmission

Fig. 6.2 JB3 transmission oil level requirement and filler/level plug (1) (Sec 3)

6

Fig. 6.3 NG9 and UN1 transmission oil level/filler plug (1), drain plug (2) and undershield (3) (Sec 3)

6 Slowly refill the transmission using the specified grade of oil until the oil overflows from the filler plug orifice. Wait a few minutes to allow any trapped air to escape and then, if possible, add more oil. Repeat this process two or three times until no more oil can be added and then, with the level right to the top of the plug orifice, refit the filler plug. Take care over this operation as this type of transmission may take quite some time to fill.
7 Refit the transmission breather, then lower the vehicle (where applicable).

4 Transmission - removal and refitting

JB3 transmission

1 The transmission can be removed together with or separate from the engine. Removal with the engine and their subsequent separation is dealt with in Chapter 1. The method described in this Section is for removal of the transmission only, and leaves the engine in position in the vehicle.
2 After disconnecting all the relevant attachments, controls and services, the transmission is removed upwards and out of

Fig. 6.5 Fabricated support bracket and support stud engagement - JB3 transmission (Sec 4)

the engine compartment. Due to the weight of the unit, it will be necessary to have some form of lifting equipment available, such as an engine crane or suitable hoist to enable the unit to be removed in this way.
3 Begin by disconnecting the battery negative terminal and then refer to Section 3 and drain the transmission oil.
4 Unclip and pull back the rubber sleeve from the gearchange link rod joint, then disconnect the joint (photo).
5 Undo the retaining bolts and remove the engine/transmission U-shaped steady bar.
6 Jack up and securely support the front of the car, then remove the front roadwheels.
7 Unclip and remove the inner wing lower shield on the left-hand side.
8 Refer to Chapter 8 and detach the right and left-hand driveshafts from the transmission.
9 Position a jack under the engine with an interposed block of wood to prevent damage and raise it to support the weight of the engine. Alternatively, the manufacturers recommend the use of a special tool (WN 103) as shown in Figs. 6.4 and 6.5. The support stud is hooked through a fabricated bracket bolted to the air cleaner mounting studs. The support bar legs rest in the drain channels on each side of the engine compartment.
10 Disconnect the clutch cable from the release lever and the support bracket on top of the transmission. Move the cable out of the way.

4.4 Gearchange link rod joint - JB3 transmission

4.12 Unbolt the angular piston/speed sensor wiring connector from the JB3 transmission

11 Extract the speedometer cable wire retaining clip from its locating holes in the rear engine mounting bracket and gearbox casing. Note the fitted direction of the clip. Withdraw the speedometer cable from the gearbox.
12 Unbolt and detach the angular position/speed sensor unit from the top of the clutch housing. Detach its wiring connector from the top of the transmission and move the wiring and sensor out of the way (photo). Note that the retaining bolts are of a specific shouldered type and should not be replaced with ordinary bolts.
13 Detach the ignition coil HT lead and move it out of the way.
14 Remove the air cleaner unit as described in Chapter 3.
15 Disconnect the reversing light switch lead and the two transmission earth leads. Note the routeings and detach the leads from their retaining clips on the transmission and place them out of the way.
16 Disconnect the choke cable from the carburettor (Chapter 3).
17 Unbolt and detach the engine/transmission stabilizer unit - see Fig. 6.6.
18 Unbolt and remove the protector plate from the clutch housing.
19 Loosen but do not remove the engine mounting bolts.
20 Unscrew the transmission mounting nuts (front and rear), and the nut from the rear engine mounting from above.
21 Referring to Fig. 6.8, unscrew and remove

Fig. 6.4 Special engine support tool (WN 103) - JB3 transmission (Sec 4)

Fig. 6.6 Unbolt the engine/transmission stabilizer - JB3 transmission (Sec 4)

Fig. 6.7 Rear engine nut (arrowed) -
JB3 transmission (Sec 4)

Fig. 6.8 Remove studs from positions A
and B - JB3 transmission (Sec 4)

4.23 Unscrew and remove the engine-to-
JB3 transmission bolts. Upper bolts
arrowed

the two studs using two nuts tightened against each other. A cranked spanner and a balljointed socket wrench will be needed to enable access.

22 Attach a suitable lift sling to the transmission and raise it so that the weight of the transmission is supported.

23 Undo the engine-to-transmission retaining bolts and withdraw them noting their lengths and positions (photo). These include the starter motor-to-clutch housing bolts, although the starter motor can be left attached to the engine by its end mounting bracket, and the solenoid wiring can be left attached.

24 Remove the front mounting, then slightly lower the engine. Withdraw the transmission from the engine ensuring that no pressure is applied to the input shaft, passing the 5th speed end housing between the sub-frame and the side members.

25 Raise the engine again to its normal position and twist the transmission to the left so that the final drive is free, then lift out the transmission.

26 Refitting is a reversal of the removal procedure, but note the following special points.

27 Before refitting the transmission unit, check that the driveshaft rollers are undamaged and that all the rollers are in position. Inspect the transmission differential

housing to ensure that no bearing rollers have fallen into it.

28 Smear the input shaft splines with grease, and ensure that no pressure is applied to the input shaft as the engine and transmission are reconnected.

29 Fit the two studs each side of the bellhousing before refitting the transmission to the engine (see Fig. 6.8).

30 When refitting the engine-to-transmission retaining bolts, ensure that the retaining bolt (V) in Fig. 6.9 is correctly located.

31 Refit the driveshafts as described in Chapter 8.

32 Tighten the respective fastenings to their specified torque wrench settings.

33 Refill the transmission with the correct grade of oil as described in Section 3.

NG9 transmission

34 The transmission may be removed on its own as described in this Section, or together with the engine as described in Chapter 1.

35 Remove the transmission undertray. This is secured by a single screw on the left-hand side and locating pegs at the rear and on the right-hand side (see photo 3.3B).

36 Undo the drain plug and drain the transmission oil into a suitable container for disposal (see photo 3.3C).

37 Disconnect the battery earth lead.

38 Place the car over an inspection pit or raise and support it at the front end on safety stands at a height sufficient to allow access underneath and sufficient to enable the transmission to be lowered and removed from underneath.

39 Disconnect and remove the exhaust downpipe.

40 Disconnect both driveshafts from the transmission as described in Chapter 1, Part B, Section 50.

41 Disconnect the speedometer cable from the transmission by gripping the retaining pin with a pair of pliers and pulling it outwards to release the cable (photo).

42 Disconnect the gearbox earth strap and the reversing light leads at the in-line connector.

43 Disconnect the gearchange linkage at the transmission end as described in Section 7.

44 Undo the retaining bolts and remove the transverse rod from the subframe (photo).

45 Disconnect the clutch cable at the release lever and support bracket on the top of the bellhousing. See Chapter 5 for details.

46 Undo the retaining bolts and remove the angular position/speed sensor from the top of the bellhousing.

47 Unscrew the starter motor mounting bolts to release the starter motor from the flywheel housing.

48 Unscrew and remove the bolts which connect the transmission to the engine

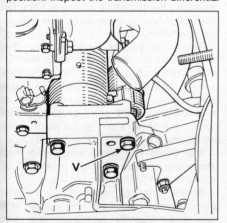

Fig. 6.9 Retaining bolt V must be correctly
located - JB3 transmission (Sec 4)

4.41 Disconnect the speedometer cable by
pulling on the retaining pin (arrowed) -
NG9 transmission

4.44 Unbolt the transverse rod -
NG9 transmission

6

4.48 Engine-to-NG9 transmission upper bolts (arrowed)

Fig. 6.12 Speedometer cable retaining clip - UN1 transmission (Sec 4)

(photo).

49 Support the engine using a jack or hoist and place a second jack, preferably of trolley type, under the transmission.

50 Disconnect the transmission flexible mountings and brackets.

51 Raise the transmission slightly to clear the crossmember during withdrawal to the rear.

52 Remove the transmission from under the car.

53 Refitting is a reversal of removal, but observe the following points.

54 Make sure that the clutch driven plate has been centralised, as described in Chapter 5.

55 On models with a pull-type clutch, ensure that the clutch release fork is correctly engaged with the release bearing before bolting the transmission in position.

56 Tighten all nuts and bolts to the specified

Fig. 6.13 UN1 transmission mountings and retaining bolts (arrowed) (Sec 4)

Fig. 6.10 Detach the exhaust downpipe – unbolt at points A and B - UN1 transmission (Sec 4)

torque and renew those of self-locking type.

57 Adjust the clutch cable (Chapter 5).

58 Fill the transmission with oil of the specified type.

UN1 transmission

59 The operations are similar to those described for the NG9 transmission, but the following differences must be taken into account.

60 Unbolt and remove the exhaust heat shield and unbolt the exhaust downpipe at the points indicated in Fig. 6.10.

61 Move the rigid cooling system pipes away from the clutch slave cylinder, then unbolt the slave cylinder and tie it up out of the way. There is no need to disconnect the hydraulic hose from the cylinder (see Chapter 5 for details).

62 When detaching the speedometer cable from the transmission, compress the clip shown in Fig. 6.12.

63 When the transmission is ready to be withdrawn, support it underneath with a trolley jack, and then undo the retaining bolts and remove the side mounting bracket on each side of the transmission see - Fig. 6.13.

Fig. 6.14 Location dowel locations (A and B) on clutch housing flange face - UN1 transmission (Sec 4)

Fig. 6.11 Detach the clutch slave cylinder (arrowed) - UN1 transmission (Sec 4)

Withdraw the transmission rearwards and downwards.

64 Refit in the reverse order of removal. When the transmission is being reconnected to the engine, align it with and engage it on the dowels on the mating flange - see Fig. 6.14. The splines of the clutch thrust pad bore, clutch shaft and the sunwheels of the differential should be lightly lubricated with a suitable grease.

65 Tighten the retaining nuts and bolts to the specified torque wrench settings where given.

66 On completion, top up the transmission oil level as described in Section 3 of this Chapter.

5 Transmission overhaul - general

Complete dismantling and overhaul of the transmission, particularly with respect to the differential and the bearings in the clutch and differential housing, entails the use of a hydraulic press and a number of special tools. For this reason it is not recommended that a complete overhaul be attempted by the home mechanic unless he has access to the tools required and feels reasonably confident. However, the transmission can at least be dismantled into its major assemblies without too much difficulty.

Before starting any repair work on the transmission, thoroughly clean the exterior of the casings using paraffin or a suitable solvent. Dry the unit with a lint-free rag. Make sure that an uncluttered working area is available with some small containers and trays handy to store the various parts. Label everything as it is removed.

After dismantling, all roll pins, circlips and snap-rings must be renewed, regardless of their condition, before reassembling.

Before starting reassembly all the components must be spotlessly clean and should be liberally lubricated with the recommended grade of gear oil during assembly.

1 Roller race
2 Secondary shaft
3 Roller
4 Roller spring
5 Snap-ring
6 2nd gear
7 3rd gear
8 Synchroniser ring
9 3rd/4th gear hub
10 4th gear
11 Washer
12 5th gear (secondary)
13 Washer
14 5th gear snap-ring
15 1st gear
16 1st/2nd gear hub
17 Primary shaft
18 Splined ring

19 Ball race
20 Snap-ring
21 Washer
22 5th gear ring
23 Needle race
24 5th gear (primary)
25 5th gear spring
26 5th gear hub
27 5th gear nut
32 Reverse shaft and
   gear
63 Oil baffle
64 Thrust washer
65 5th gear end bolt on
   secondary shaft
66 Shouldered washer
67 Retaining bolt and
   washer

Fig. 6.15 Exploded view of the primary and secondary shaft gear assemblies - JB3 transmission (Sec 5)

Fig. 6.16 Primary shaft components - NG9 transmission (Sec 5)

1 Roll pin   2 Special washer   3 Clutch shaft

6

1 Speedometer
   drivegear
2 Washer
3 5th gear
4 Thrust washer
5 Bearing
6 4th gear
7 Baulk ring
8 3rd/4th synchro
   unit and reverse
   gear
9 Spring clip
10 Roller
11 Circlip
12 Washer
13 Baulk ring

14 3rd gear
15 Washer
16 Circlip
17 Washer
18 2nd gear
19 Clip
20 Circlip
21 Baulk ring
22 1st/ 2nd synchro
   unit
23 Baulk ring
24 Circlip
25 Clip
26 1st gear
27 Bearing

Fig. 6.17 Secondary shaft components - NG9 transmission (Sec 5)

17 Thrust washer	28 4th gear baulk ring
18 Bearing	29 4th gear
19 Primary shaft	30 Split needle roller
20 3rd gear	bearing
21 Split needle roller	31 Thrust washer
bearing	32 Bearing
22 3rd gear baulk ring	33 Circlip
23 3rd/4th synchro unit	34 Oil seal
24 Roller	35 Roll pin
25 Roller spring clip	36 Clutch shaft
26 Circlip	38 Guide tube
27 Washer	39 O-ring

Fig. 6.18 Primary shaft components - UN1 transmission (Sec 5)

1 5th speed gear	7 1st gear baulk ring
2 Spacer plate	8 Circlip
3 Double taper roller	9 1st/2nd synchro unit
bearing	10 2nd gear baulk ring
4 1st gear	11 Synchro spring
5 Split needle roller	12 2nd gear
bearing	13 Split needle roller
6 Synchro spring	bearing

Fig. 6.19 Secondary shaft components - UN1 transmission (Sec 5)

6 Gear lever and remote control housing (JB3 transmission) - removal, refitting and adjustment

1 To remove the gear lever and remote control housing first jack up the front of the car and support it on axle stands.

2 From underneath, unhook the tension spring fitted between the gearchange rod and the stud on the vehicle floor (photo).

3 Slacken the clamp bolt securing the gearchange rod to the gear lever yoke and withdraw the yoke from the rod (photo).

4 Refer to Chapter 11 and remove the centre console.

5 With the console removed, undo the four bolts securing the remote control housing to the floor and withdraw the assembly from the car (photo). Recover the sealing gasket.

6 If necessary the gear lever assembly may

6.2 Gearchange rod tension spring

6.3 Gearchange rod and yoke

6.5 Gearlever remote control housing

1 Gearchange rod
2 Tension spring
3 Remote control housing
4 Gear lever knob
5 Rubber gaiter
6 Roll pin
7 Reverse stop release
8 Circlip
9 Gear lever
10 O-ring
11 Roll pin
12 Reverse stop release holder
13 Spring
14 Top cup
15 Damper
16 Half cup
17 Bottom cup
18 Half cup holder
19 Bellows
20 Limit stop
21 Roll pin
22 Stop

Fig. 6.20 Exploded view of the gear lever and remote control housing components (Sec 6)

6

be dismantled by referring to the component locations shown in Fig. 6.20. Note that the gear lever knob is bonded with adhesive to the lever.

7 Reassembly and refitting are the reverse of the above procedures. Adjust the gear lever as follows before tightening the yoke clamp bolt.

8 Select 2nd gear at the gearbox by moving the fork control shaft.

9 Move the gear lever so that the O-ring on the gear lever rests against the side of the remote control housing, as shown in Fig. 6.21. With the gear lever in this position leave a space of 5 mm (0.2 in) between the end of the gearchange rod and the fork of the gear lever yoke. Hold the components in this position and tighten the clamp bolt.

10 Check that all the gears can be selected and then refit the centre console. as described in Chapter 11, and lower the car to the ground.

Fig. 6.21 Position the gear lever so that the O-ring (10) rests against the side of the remote control housing (3) (Sec 6)

Fig. 6.22 Gear linkage adjustment (Sec 6)

1 Gearchange rod   C Gear lever yoke clamp
2 Gear lever yoke   V Clamp bolt

Fig. 6.23 Gearchange linkage (Sec 7)

7.1 Underside view showing gear selector rod, control rod and reverse cable (lever end)

7.2 Reverse gear interlock cable connection at the transmission

7 Gearchange linkage (NG9 and UN1 transmission) - removal and refitting

1 The system consists of two remote control rods and a cable to release a locking finger when the ring on the gear lever is lifted during selection of reverse gear (photo). This is part of an interlock device to prevent engagement of reverse gear when shifting from 3rd to 2nd.
2 To disconnect the controls from the transmission, first unscrew the cable retaining union nut (photo).
3 To disconnect the control rod at the transmission end, prise free the balljoint using suitable pliers inserted as shown and used as a lever (photo).
4 To detach the framed balljoint, undo the retaining bolts and disconnect the joint coupling (photos).
5 Disconnection of the linkage rods at the gear lever end will necessitate the removal of the exhaust system for access (Chapter 3). Disconnect both rods from the base of the gearchange lever. One rod is secured by a nut, the other by a ball socket which is simply prised apart.
6 The cable can be released after unclipping its stop and removing the sleeve.
7 Working inside the car, remove the centre console (Chapter 11).
8 Unscrew and remove the gear lever knob.
9 Extract the four screws from the bellows

7.3 Separating the control rod balljoint

7.4A Undo the retaining bolts (arrowed) . . .

7.4B . . . to separate the framed balljoint

7.11 Reconnecting the control rod balljoint

retainer and withdraw the bellows.
10 Withdraw the gear lever.
11 Refitting is a reversal of removal, but smear the threads of the cable union with

gasket cement before screwing it into the transmission casing. The balljoint connection can be reassembled using suitable grips as shown (photo).

Fault finding - manual transmission

Note: *It is sometimes difficult to decide whether it is worthwhile removing and dismantling the transmission for a fault which may be nothing more than a minor irritant. Transmissions which howl, or where the synchromesh can be beaten by a quick gearchange, may continue to perform for a long time in this state. A worn transmission usually needs a complete rebuild to eliminate noise because the various gears, if re-aligned on new bearings, will continue to howl when different bearing surfaces are presented to each other. The decision to overhaul, therefore, must be considered with regard to time and money available, relative to the degree of noise or malfunction that the driver has to suffer.*

Weak or ineffective synchromesh
- [ ] Synchro baulk rings worn, split or damaged
- [ ] Synchromesh units worn, or damaged

Jumps out of gear
- [ ] Gearchange mechanism worn
- [ ] Synchromesh units badly worn
- [ ] Selector fork badly worn
- [ ] Selector detent spring broken or jammed

Excessive noise
- [ ] Incorrect grade of oil in transmission or oil level too low
- [ ] Gearteeth excessively worn or damaged
- [ ] Intermediate gear thrust washers or spacers worn allowing excessive
- [ ] end play
- [ ] Worn bearings

Difficulty in engaging gears
- [ ] Worn synchromesh units
- [ ] Clutch fault
- [ ] Gear lever out of adjustment

Noise when cornering
- [ ] Wheel bearing or driveshaft fault
- [ ] Differential fault

Chapter 7 Automatic transmission

For modifications, and information applicable to later models, see Supplement at end of manual

Contents

Degrees of difficulty

Easy, suitable for novice with little experience	**Fairly easy,** suitable for beginner with some experience	**Fairly difficult,** suitable for competent DIY mechanic	**Difficult,** suitable for experienced DIY mechanic	**Very difficult,** suitable for expert DIY or professional

Specifications

General

Type	Three-speed, with computerised control
Type number	MJ3

Fluid

Capacity:	
From dry	6.0 litres (10.6 pints)
At fluid renewal	2.5 litres (4.4 pints)
Fluid type	Dexron type ATF

Torque wrench settings

	Nm	lbf ft
Driveplate-to-converter bolts	30	22
Fluid cooler pipe unions	19	14
Sump pan fixing screws	6	4
Filter retaining bolts	9	6
Torque converter housing-to-engine connecting bolts ...	54	40
Torque converter to crankshaft bolts	70	51
Mounting pad bolts	40	30

1 General description

The automatic transmission consists of three main assemblies: the torque converter, the final drive and the gearbox. A cutaway view of the transmission unit, with the three main assemblies sub-divided, is shown in Fig. 7.1.

The converter takes the place of the conventional clutch and transmits the drive automatically from the engine to the gearbox, providing increased torque when starting off.

Fully automatic gearchanging is provided without the use of a clutch, but override selection is still available to the driver.

The gearbox comprises an epicyclic geartrain giving three forward and one reverse

Fig. 7.1 Cutaway view of the MJ3 type automatic transmission (Sec 1)

Fig. 7.2 Sectional view showing the driveplate and torque converter assembly (Sec 1)

Fig. 7.3 Epicyclic gear train assembly (Sec 1)

C Internal ring gear   PS Planet wheel carrier   P Sunwheel   S Planet wheels

Fig. 7.4 Automatic transmission hydraulic control diagram (Sec 1)

gear, selection of which is dependent on the hydraulic pressure supplied to the respective clutches and brakes. The hydraulic pressure is regulated by the hydraulic distributor, and gear selection is determined by two solenoid valves. These are actuated by the electrically-operated governor/computer. The exact hydraulic pressure is regulated by a vacuum capsule and pilot valve operating according to engine loading.

The clutches (E1 and E2 in Fig. 7.4) and brakes (F1 and F2) are multi-disc oil bath type and, according to the hydraulic loading, engage or release the epicyclic geartrain components.

The governor is, in effect, a low output alternator which provides variable current to the computer. It is driven by a worm gear on the final drive pinion and its output depends on the vehicle speed and engine loading.

The computer or module is continually supplied with signals from the speed sensor, load potentiometer, multi-purpose switch, kickdown switch and its own control unit, and from this information it transmits signals to the pilot solenoid valves to select the correct gear range.

The kickdown switch is an integral part of the load potentiometer and a lower gear is selected when the pedal is fully depressed.

The multi-purpose switch is located on the rear of the transmission and is operated by the range selector lever. It controls the engine starting circuit, the reversing light circuit and the pilot solenoid valve circuit.

The load potentiometer is operated by the throttle valve and provides a variable voltage to the computer, dependent on the throttle position.

The speed sensor is mounted on the left-hand side of the transmission and it provides an output signal dependent on the speed of the parking pawl wheel, which is proportional to the speed of the car.

A vacuum capsule is connected directly to

the inlet manifold to regulate transmission fluid pressure according to engine loading.

The automatic transmission is a relatively complex unit and therefore, should problems occur, it is recommended that the fault be discussed with your Renault dealer, who should be able to advise you on the best course of action to be taken. Items that can be attempted by the home mechanic are given in the following Sections of this Chapter. To obtain trouble-free operation and maximum life expectancy from your automatic transmission, it must be serviced as described and not be subjected to abuse.

2 Maintenance

1 At the intervals specified in 'Routine maintenance' check the fluid level in the following way.

2 The engine and transmission should be cold. Start the engine and allow it to run for a few minutes in order to fill the torque converter and cooler with fluid.

3 With the selector lever in P and the engine idling, withdraw the dipstick, wipe it clean, re-insert it and withdraw it for the second time

Fig. 7.5 Automatic transmission fluid level dipstick location (Sec 2)

Fig. 7.6 Automatic transmission fluid level dipstick markings (Sec 2)

Fig. 7.7 Automatic transmission drain plug (3) (Sec 2)

Fig. 7.8 Automatic transmission fluid filter seal (J) (Sec 3)

Fig. 7.9 Automatic transmission fluid filter retaining bolt locations (Sec 3)

The fluid level should be between the 'min' and 'max' marks.

4 If necessary, top up with the specified fluid poured in through the dipstick guide tube.

5 The transmission will very rarely require topping-up, but if it does, check for leaks, probably at the torque converter or driveshaft oil seals in the transmission casing.

6 The transmission fluid should be drained, when cold, at the intervals specified in 'Routine maintenance'. Remove the dipstick then place a suitable container under the drain plug and remove the plug. When the fluid has drained, renew the fluid filter as described in Section 3.

7 Refit the drain plug, then fill the transmission to the specified level through the dipstick guide tube. Use only the specified type and quantity of fluid.

3 Fluid filter - renewal

The fluid filter should be renewed at the intervals specified in 'Routine maintenance' using the following procedure.

1 Drain the fluid as previously described, unbolt and remove the sump pan and gasket.

2 Undo the three filter unit retaining bolts and remove the filter.

4 Fit the new filter into position, ensuring that a new sealing ring is located as shown in Fig. 7.8. With reference to Fig. 7.9 initially locate the filter with the retaining bolt (1) to ensure that the filter is correctly positioned relative to the hydraulic control unit, then fit the remaining bolts (2 and 3) and tighten them to the specified torque wrench setting. Note that the number (2) bolt is shorter than the other two.

5 Clean the sump pan and check that the filter magnets are located as shown in Fig. 7.10, then refit the sump pan, ensuring that a new gasket is correctly located.

6 Check that the sump drain plug is tight, then refill the transmission as described in the previous Section.

4 Kickdown switch/load potentiometer - testing

1 The kickdown switch is incorporated in the load potentiometer on the throttle housing.

2 A defect in this unit is indicated by the gear shift speeds being constant, regardless of the position of the accelerator. On models fitted with an electronic fault warning lamp, the lamp will illuminate if a fault occurs in the transmission control system.

3 No further fault diagnosis is possible without the use of specialist test equipment. If a fault occurs, it is advisable to consult a Renault dealer who will have the specialist knowledge and tools available to rectify the fault.

5 Selector control lever and cable - removal, refitting and adjustment

1 Pull upwards on the selector lever handle to remove it from the lever.

2 Press the console trim to the left to release its retaining tags, whilst simultaneously lifting the console to remove it.

3 Raise and support the front of the vehicle on safety stands.

4 Remove the exhaust downpipe (Chapter 3), to provide access to the selector cable connections underneath.

5 Undo the four nuts securing the selector lever assembly to the floor.

6 Detach the selector light wire, then unclip the control cable from the relay unit balljoint.

7 Position a jack under the engine/transmission subframe, then unscrew the two

Fig. 7.10 Filter magnet locations (Sec 3)

Fig. 7.11 Removing selector lever console trim (Sec 5)

Fig. 7.12 Detach the control cable from the relay unit balljoint (Sec 5)

7

Fig. 7.13 Unclipping the control cable forward end from the mounting (Sec 6)

Fig. 7.14 Unclipping the control cable from the selector assembly case (Sec 5)

Fig. 7.15 Refit the control cable retaining clip as shown (Sec 5)

rear retaining bolts and lower the subframe by about 15 mm (0.6 in).

8 Unbolt and detach the transmission mounting on the right-hand side.

9 Detach the complete selector assembly.

10 To disconnect the cable for replacement, unclip it from the mounting at the forward end using a screwdriver. At the rear end, prise free the cover from the selector case, then unclip the joint from the bottom end of the lever and extract the retaining clip securing the cable to the case.

11 Refit in the reverse order of removal. Ensure that the rear retaining clip is fitted the correct way round as shown in Fig. 7.15.

Fig. 7.16 Prise free the cable lock clip from the mounting (Sec 5)

Fig. 7.17 Relocate the cable adjuster lock clip as shown (Sec 5)

12 To refit and adjust the control cable, relocate the right-hand transmission mounting (with cable attached). Raise the subframe and tighten its securing bolts.

13 Using a suitable screwdriver as shown in Fig. 7.16, prise the cable lock clip at the mounting, then pull the cable rearwards from the adjuster.

14 Position the automatic transmission and the selector lever in the 'D' position, then attach the cable to the relay unit balljoint. Allow the selector assembly to hang free under the vehicle, then reattach the cable adjuster lock clip as shown in Fig. 7.17.

15 Refit the selector assembly (with gasket) and reattach the selector light wire.

16 Refit the console and the selector lever handle. Check the lever for satisfactory engagement to complete.

6 Transmission oil seals - renewal

Torque converter oil seal

1 This is accessible after having removed the transmission (or engine) and the torque converter.

2 Tap the front face of the old seal at one point with a punch so that it tilts and can be extracted.

Fig. 7.18 Torque converter oil seal renewal – drive into position using a tube drift (Renault tool shown) (Sec 6)

3 Tap the new seal squarely into position using a suitable tube drift, having smeared its lips with petroleum jelly. Take care not to damage the shaft.

4 On refitting the torque converter, align it with the driveplate as shown in Fig. 7.24.

Driveshaft/transmission oil seals

5 The driveshaft removal and the oil seal removal details are given in Chapter 8.

7 Vacuum unit - removal and refitting

Note: *After removal and refitting of the unit, have the fluid pressure checked by a Renault dealer at the earliest opportunity.*

1 The transmission will have to be supported on a jack with a wooden block as an insulator so that the mounting can be removed to provide access to the vacuum unit.

2 Disconnect the vacuum pipe, remove the clamp plate and unscrew the unit.

3 Refitting is a reversal of removal. Lubricate the unit (black rubber) with fluid, screw the unit in by 2 1/2 to 3 turns, then fit the clamp plate. Have the fluid pressure checked and if necessary adjusted by a Renault dealer at the earliest opportunity.

Fig. 7.19 Vacuum unit and lockplate (2) (Sec 7)

Fig. 7.20 Disconnect the fluid cooler pipes at A and B (Sec 8)

Fig. 7.21 Remove the driveplate-to-torque converter bolts (V). Flywheel shown locked using Renault tool (Sec 8)

Fig. 7.22 Torque converter retaining bar in position (Renault tool shown) (Sec 8)

8 Automatic transmission - removal and refitting

1 A trolley jack will be useful during the removal and subsequent refitting of the transmission. Although not essential to drain the transmission fluid before removal, it is a task more easily achieved in the car and will help reduce the weight of the transmission.

2 Disconnect the battery earth lead.

3 Raise and support the vehicle at the front end on axle stands. Remove the front roadwheels.

4 Detach and remove the engine undershield.

5 Disconnect the angular position/speed sensor, the computer wiring plug, and the starter motor wiring. Unbolt and remove the starter motor (see Chapter 12).

6 Disconnect the vacuum pipe adjacent to the starter motor flange.

7 Disconnect the transmission fluid cooler pipes from the points indicated in Fig. 7.20. Plug them to prevent the ingress of dirt and fluid leakage.

8 Disconnect the driveshafts from the transmission as described in Chapter 8.

9 Detach and remove the exhaust downpipe as described in Chapter 3.

10 Working through the starter motor aperture, jam the driveplate to prevent it from turning, then undo the driveplate-to-torque converter retaining bolts. Loosen off each bolt in turn, then unscrew and remove them to detach the converter from the driveplate.

11 Unscrew and remove the upper engine-to-transmission bolts.

12 Disconnect the earth cable from the transmission.

13 Disconnect the selector control cable at the balljoint by levering it apart using a suitable screwdriver as shown in Fig. 7.12.

14 Position the trolley jack under the transmission to support its weight, then loosen off the engine/transmission subframe bolts and lower the subframe by about 15 mm (0.6 in).

15 Unbolt and remove the left-hand transmission mounting and support.

16 Remove the right-hand support.

17 Loosen off, but do not remove, the bolt securing the right-hand rubber pad, leaving the control cable attached.

18 Unscrew and remove the lower engine-to-transmission retaining bolts.

19 Lower the trolley jack and withdraw the transmission. Guide the computer out with the transmission. The engine should be supported safely on the front crossmember.

20 Secure the torque converter in position by bolting a retaining bar to a flange bolt hole as shown in Fig. 7.22.

21 Refitting is a reversal of removal, but observe the following points.

22 Check that the positioning dowels are in place before offering the transmission to the engine, also grease the recess in the crankshaft which accepts the torque converter.

23 Align the converter in relation to the driveplate, as shown in Fig. 7.24.

24 Tighten the driveplate bolts to the specified torque.

25 Tighten the exhaust flange bolts until the spring coils are coilbound.

26 Reconnect the driveshafts.

27 Check and top up the transmission fluid.

Fig. 7.23 Positioning dowels (Sec 8)

A Engine locating dowel
B Engine locating dowel
C Starter motor locating dowel

Fig. 7.24 Torque converter-to-driveplate alignment (Sec 8)

Fault finding - automatic transmission

1 Automatic transmission faults are almost always the result of low fluid level or incorrect adjustment of the selector control cable.
2 If these items are checked and found to be in order, the fault is probably internal and should be diagnosed by your Renault dealer who is specially equipped to pinpoint the problem and effect any necessary repairs.
3 Do not allow any defect in the operation of

the automatic transmission to go unchecked - it could prove expensive!
4 If the starter fails to function at any time, it is possible that the starter inhibitor switch is at fault but first check that (a) the selector control lever adjustment is correct and (b) the transmission wiring harness plugs and socket connections are secure. Check the starter circuit wiring for continuity to the switch plug.

The inhibitor switch is situated beneath the transmission computer unit and within the hydraulic section of the unit. The sump plate would have to be removed to gain access to the switch and this is therefore best entrusted to your Renault dealer.
5 The following guide to simple faults should be regarded as being the limit of fault diagnosis for the home mechanic.

Engine stalling or rough idling
☐ Leaking vacuum pipe

Loss of transmission fluid without visible leak
☐ Faulty vacuum unit

Violent gearchanges
☐ Faulty vacuum unit

'Creep' in N
☐ Selector cable requires adjustment

Slip in D or R
☐ Low fluid level

Incorrect gearchange speeds
☐ Throttle requires adjustment or kickdown switch/load potentiometer fault

Jerk at speed selection
☐ Fault in vacuum unit or pipe

No drive, or slipping during speed range changes
☐ Clogged fluid filter

Chapter 8
Driveshafts, hubs, roadwheels and tyres

For modifications, and information applicable to later models, see Supplement at end of manual

Contents

Degrees of difficulty

Easy, suitable for novice with little experience		Fairly easy, suitable for beginner with some experience		Fairly difficult, suitable for competent DIY mechanic		Difficult, suitable for experienced DIY mechanic		Very difficult, suitable for expert DIY or professional	

Specifications

Driveshafts
Type	Tubular with CV joint at each end
Inboard joint	GI 62 (tripod type) or RC 490 (tripod type)
Outboard joint	GE 86 or GE 76 (tripod type) or UF 95/Lobro (6-ball type)

Hubs
Front	Renewable split track ball bearing
Rear	Renewable split track roller bearing
Endfloat (maximum):	
Front	0 to 0.05 mm (0 to 0.002 in)
Rear	0 to 0.03 mm (0 to 0.001 in)

Roadwheels
Type	Pressed steel or light alloy
Size (depending on model)	5.5B 13 4 CH36
	5.5J 14 4 CH36
	5.5B 13 4 FH36
	5.5J 14 4 FH36
	5.5J 14 4 CH36
	6.5J 15 5 CH42

Tyres
Type	Radial ply, tubeless
Size (depending on model)	155 R 13T
	175/70 R 13T
	175/65 R 14H
	155/70 R 13T
	175/70 R 13H
	185/65 R 14H
	195/55 VR 15

Tyre pressures - cold*:	Front	Rear
Saloon models (except Turbo)	2.0 bar (29 lbf/in²)	2.2 bar (32 lbf/in²)
Savanna models:		
1.7 litre	2.0 bar (29 lbf/in²)	2.6 bar (37 lbf/in²)
2.0 litre	2.3 bar (33 lbf/in²)	2.6 bar (37 lbf/in²)
Turbo models	2.8 bar (40 lbf/in²)	2.5 bar (36 lbf/in²)

Allow for an increase of 0.3 bar (4 lbf/in²) when tyres are hot after running

8

Torque wrench settings

	Nm	lbf ft
Roadwheel bolts:		
Except Turbo	90	66
Turbo	100	74
Driveshaft nut	250	185
Rear hub nut	160	118
Rear stub axle bolts	75	55
Left-hand driveshaft inboard		
Flange retaining bolts (1.7 litre models)	25	18

1 General description

1 The driveshafts which transmit power from the transmission final drive to the front roadwheels incorporate a constant velocity (CV) joint at each end.
2 The inboard joint is of tripod type while the outboard joint is of tripod or six-ball type, depending upon car model.
3 The design and construction of the driveshaft components is such that the only repairs possible are renewal of the rubber bellows and renewal of the inner joint spiders. With the exception of the six-ball type, wear or damage to the outer constant velocity joints or the driveshaft splines can only be rectified by fitting a complete new driveshaft assembly.

2 Maintenance

1 A thorough inspection of the driveshafts and driveshaft joints should be carried out at the intervals given in 'Routine maintenance', using the following procedure.
2 Jack up the front of the car and support it securely on axle stands.
3 Slowly rotate the roadwheel and inspect the condition of the outer constant velocity joint rubber bellows. Check for signs of cracking, splits or deterioration of the rubber which may allow the grease to escape and lead to water and grit entry into the joint. Also check the security and condition of the retaining clips and

then repeat these checks on the inner joint bellows. If any damage or deterioration is found the joints should be attended to immediately.
4 Continue rotating the roadwheel and check for any distortion or damage to the driveshafts. Check for any free play in the outer joints by holding the driveshaft firmly and attempting to turn the wheel. Any noticeable movement indicates wear in the joints, wear in the constant velocity joint or wheel hub splines, a loose driveshaft retaining nut or loose wheel bolts. Carry out any necessary repairs with reference to the appropriate Sections of this, and other applicable Chapters of this manual.

3 Driveshafts (1.7 litre models) - removal and refitting

1 Remove the roadwheel trim plate, then loosen off the driveshaft nut and the wheel bolts (photo).
2 Jack up the car at the front and support it on axle stands. Remove the appropriate roadwheel.
3 Undo the two bolts securing the brake caliper to the hub carrier. Slide the caliper, complete with pads, off the disc and tie it up using string or wire from a suitable place under the wheel arch.
4 Unscrew and remove the driveshaft nut and washer.
5 Disconnect the steering arm from the stub axle at the balljoint as described in Chapter 10.
6 Unscrew but do not remove the shock absorber-to-hub carrier retaining bolt nuts. Use a suitable mallet to drive against the end

face of the bolts to release the serrated section under each bolt head from the shock absorber, then unscrew the nut from the upper bolt and remove the bolt. The lower bolt can be left in position (see photos 4.4 and 4.5A).
7 The procedure now varies according to whether the left-hand or right-hand driveshaft is being removed.

Left-hand driveshaft

8 Refer to Chapter 6 and drain the transmission oil.
9 Undo the three bolts securing the rubber bellows retaining plate to the side of the transmission casing (photo).
10 Pivot the hub carrier outwards at the top and simultaneously withdraw the driveshaft from the inner joint spider in the transmission housing.
11 Withdraw the outer constant velocity joint stub axle from the wheel hub and remove the driveshaft from the car. If the stub axle is a tight fit in the wheel hub, tap it out using a plastic mallet or use a suitable puller.

Right-hand driveshaft

12 Using a parallel pin punch of suitable diameter, drive out the roll pin securing the driveshaft inner joint yoke to the differential stub shaft (photo). Note that the roll pin is in fact two roll pins, one inside the other.
13 Pivot the hub carrier outwards at the top and simultaneously withdraw the driveshaft from the differential stub shaft. If the inner end of the driveshaft is difficult to withdraw carefully lever it free using a bar or screwdriver.
14 Proceed as described previously in paragraph 11.

3.1 Loosen off the driveshaft nut and the wheel bolts

3.9 Remove the bellows retaining bolts (left-hand driveshaft)

3.12 Drive out the roll pins securing the right-hand driveshaft

3.15A Align the roll pin holes when fitting the right-hand driveshaft (arrowed) . . .

3.15B . . . and fit new roll pins

4.2 Drive out the roil pins securing the driveshafts at their inboard ends

Refitting

15 Refitting the left-hand or right-hand driveshaft is basically a reverse of the removal procedure with reference to the following additional points:

(a) *Lubricate the driveshaft joint splines with molybdenum disulphide grease*

(b) *A rubber insulator washer may be fitted to the right-hand driveshaft at the transmission end, the details of which are described in Section 13. Where applicable, check that this washer is fitted. When fitting such driveshafts, press the shaft towards the differential housing to align the roll pin holes of the shafts. To ease roll pin insertion, a chamfer is machined in the roll pin hole at the top of*

4.4 Tap back the shock absorber-to-hub carrier bolts to expose their splines (arrowed)

a splined tooth on one side to provide a lead-in guide

(c) *On the right-hand side, position the inner joint splines so that the roll pin holes will align when the joint is pushed fully home (photos). Position the two roll pins so that their slots are 90° apart*

(d) *Ensure that all retaining nuts and bolts are tightened to the specified torque*

(e) *If the left-hand driveshaft has been removed, refer to Chapter 6 and refill the transmission with oil*

4 Driveshafts (2.0 litre models) - removal and refitting

1 Proceed as described in paragraphs 1 to 4 of the previous Section. On Turbo models it is possible to leave the brake caliper unit attached to the hub carrier, but take care not to stretch the hydraulic hose.

2 Use a parallel pin punch of suitable diameter to knock out the driveshaft roll pins at the transmission end (photo). Note that there are two roil pins fitted, one inside the other.

3 Detach the steering arm outer balljoint as described in Chapter 10.

4 Unscrew but do not remove the shock absorber-to-hub carrier bolt nuts. Use a suitable mallet to drift against the end face of the bolts to release the serrated section under

each bolt head from the shock absorber, then remove the upper nut and bolt only (photo).

5 Pivot the hub carrier outwards at the top and simultaneously withdraw the driveshaft from the transmission (photos).

6 Withdraw the outer end of the driveshaft from the hub carrier and remove the shaft unit from the car. If the shaft is a tight fit in the hub carrier, tap it out using a plastic mallet or use a suitable puller.

7 Refitting is a reversal of removal, but observe the following points.

8 Smear the inboard shaft splines with molybdenum disulphide grease.

9 Use new roll pins (photo) and seal their ends with suitable sealant (hard setting type).

10 On non-Turbo models fitted with the NG9 type transmission, the transmission end of the driveshaft is fitted with an insulating washer. This washer is available in two thicknesses. Ensure that the correct type is fitted and in position when assembling the driveshaft to the differential stub shaft. Refer to Section 13 for identification details.

11 Apply thread locking fluid to the threads (clean) for the caliper fixing bolts (where applicable).

12 Tighten all nuts and bolts to the specified torque. Renew the driveshaft self-locking nut.

13 Apply the footbrake two or three times to position the disc pads against the disc (where applicable).

14 Refill the transmission with oil.

8

4.5A Pivot the hub carrier as shown . . .

4.5B . . . and withdraw the driveshaft from the transmission

4.9 Fit new roll pins (arrowed)

5.16 General view of the type GI 62 left-hand driveshaft joint

5.17 Remove the circlip (arrowed)

Fig. 8.1 Sectional view of the type GI 62 inboard tripod joint – right-hand driveshaft (Sec 5)

1 Yoke	5 Bellows
2 Spider	6 Bellows retaining
3 Metal cover	ring
4 Bellows retaining	7 Driveshaft
spring	

5 Driveshaft bellows and spider (inboard tripod joint - type GI 62) - renewal

Right-hand driveshaft

1 Remove the driveshaft, as described in the appropriate earlier Section.

2 Remove the bellows retaining spring.

3 Cut the bellows along their length, and remove and discard them.

4 Lift the anti-separation plate tabs using pliers, then withdraw the yoke from the spider.

5 The needles, rollers and trunnions are matched in production so keep them as originally assembled by winding adhesive tape around the spider.

6 Remove the circlip, then use a three-legged puller to withdraw the spider. Do not tap the shaft out of the spider as the rollers will be marked and the needles damaged.

7 Lubricate the driveshaft and slide the new bellows with small retaining ring into position on the shaft.

8 Use a suitable tube drift to drive the spider onto the driveshaft, then the circlip to secure.

9 Distribute the grease pack supplied between the bellows and the yoke.

10 Remove the adhesive tape from the spider, then fit the spider to the yoke.

11 Insert a 2.5 mm (0.10 in) thick metal wedge, fabricated to the dimensions shown in Fig. 8.3. between the anti-separation plate and the yoke. Carefully tap the anti-separation plate tabs into their original positions with a soft metal drift, then remove the wedge.

12 Locate the bellows lips in the grooves in the driveshaft and the yoke.

13 Insert a rod under the bellows at the yoke end to restrict the amount of air retained in the bellows, and set the overall length of the bellows as shown in Fig. 8.4.

14 Remove the rod and fit the bellows retaining spring, taking care not to stretch the spring.

15 Refit the driveshaft as described in the appropriate earlier Section.

Left-hand driveshaft

Note: *Access to a hydraulic press with suitable mandrels and adaptors will be required to carry out the following operations*

16 Remove the driveshaft as described in the appropriate earlier Section (photo).

17 Using circlip pliers, extract the circlip securing the spider to the driveshaft (photo).

18 Using suitable adaptors on the press bed,

support the spider under the roller cups and press out the driveshaft.

19 Support the bearing at the small end of the bellows and press the driveshaft out of the bellows and bearing assembly.

20 Secure the driveshaft on the press bed using an arrangement similar to that shown in Fig. 8.5. This will avoid placing excessive load on the outer joint as the components are pressed back into place.

21 Position the new bellows and bearing assembly over the end of the driveshaft. Using a tube of suitable diameter as a mandrel, press the assembly onto the shaft until the distance from the rear face of the bearing to the end of the driveshaft is 148.5 mm (5.85 in)

Fig. 8.2 Lift the anti-separation plate tabs (C) as shown (Sec 5)

Fig. 8.3 Metal wedge used to retain shape of anti-separation plate (Sec 5)

R = 45 mm
6mm
40 mm

Fig. 8.4 Expel any trapped air by lifting bellows with a rod, then check distance A (Sec 5)

A = 752 to 154 mm (5.95 to 6.03 in)

Fig. 8.5 Arrangement of hydraulic press and manufacturer's tool for refitting left-hand driveshaft bellows and bearing (Sec 5)

Fig. 8.6 Left-hand driveshaft bellows and bearing setting dimension (Sec 5)

Manufacturer's tool for fitting bearing shown in position over end of driveshaft

Note that the progressive force generated by a press is the only satisfactory method of fitting this assembly. The lip edges of the bearing oil seal can easily be damaged by shock loads leading to subsequent oil leakage if a hammer is used.

22 Place the spider on the driveshaft, press it into place and refit the circlip.

23 Refit the driveshaft as described in the appropriate earlier Section.

6 Driveshaft bellows and spider (inboard tripod joint - type RC 490) - renewal

1 The procedure is as described in Section 5 for the type GI 62 joint fitted to the right-hand driveshaft, but with the following differences.

2 The bellows are attached to the yoke by a metal ring which must be cut off and renewed on reassembly.

3 There is no anti-separation plate and therefore the spider can be slid straight out of the yoke.

4 On some models there is no spider retaining circlip. When refitting the spider on these models, punch the end of the shaft at 3 points 120° apart to retain the spider, as shown in Fig. 8.8.

Fig. 8.11 Special bellows expander tools (Sec 7)

T.Av. 537-02   T.Av. 586-01

Fig. 8.7 Sectional view of the type RC 490 inboard tripod joint (Sec 6)

1 Yoke
2 Spider
3 Metal cover
4 Bellows retaining collar
5 Bellows
6 Bellows retaining ring
7 Driveshaft

Fig. 8.9 Expel any trapped air by lifting bellows with a rod, then check distance A (Sec 6)

A = 155.0 to 157.0 mm (6.05 to 6.12 in)

5 Set the overall length of the bellows as shown in Fig. 8.9.

6 Crimp the new bellows metal retaining ring as shown in Fig. 8.10.

7 Driveshaft bellows (outboard tripod joint) - renewal

Note: *If the bellows are to be renewed without removing the spider from the inner joint a special bellows expander tool will be required.*

Fig. 8.12 Sectional view of the outboard tripod joint (Sec 7)

1 Stub axle
2 Starplate retainer
3 Spider
4 Yoke
5 Bellows retaining clip
6 Bellows
7 Bellows retaining clip

Fig. 8.8 Peen the spider using a centre punch of 3 points 120° apart to secure (Sec 6)

Fig. 8.10 Secure the bellows retaining ring using crimping pliers (Sec 6)

Tool No. TAv 537-02 is required for the type GE 86 joint, and Tool No TAv 586-01 is required for the type GE 76 joint.

1 If the spider at the inboard end of the driveshaft is removed the outboard bellows can be slid off the shaft and renewed without the need for a special expander. The choice is with the home mechanic whether the extra work involved is worthwhile, so avoiding the need for the special tool. Note, however, that if working on a right-hand driveshaft fitted with a damper ring to reduce resonant vibrations, the bellows can only be removed from the outboard end.

Fig. 8.13 Lift the starplate arms (2) to remove the stub axle (Sec 7)

8

Fig. 8.14 Thrust button, spring and axial clearance shim (B) (Sec 7)

Fig. 8.15 Grip driveshaft in vice jaws as shown. Deburr any sharp edges at A (Sec 7)

Fig. 8.16 Slide the bellows onto the expander tool (Sec 7)

Fig. 8.17 Move bellows up and down the expander to stretch them prior to fitting on the yoke (Sec 7)

Fig. 8.18 Locate starplate (2) so that arms are positioned between spider rollers (Sec 7)

12 Locate the starplate so that each arm is centrally positioned between the spider rollers.

13 Insert the driveshaft yoke into the bell-shaped stub axle.

14 Tilt the shaft to engage one starplate arm in its slot and then use a screwdriver to engage the other two. Fit the thrust button shim (see Fig. 8.20).

15 Distribute the sachet of grease evenly between the bellows and the stub axle.

16 Locate the bellows lips in their grooves, insert a rod under the smaller diameter neck of the bellows to expel any trapped air.

17 Fit the retaining ring and spring clip to the bellows. On some models, crimped clips are used.

2 Remove the driveshaft as described in the relevant earlier Section.

3 Cut free the large diameter retaining clip from the bellows.

4 Pull back the bellows and wipe away as much grease as possible.

5 Prise up the starplate arms one by one and separate the stub axle from the driveshaft. Take care not to bend the starplate arms.

6 Retain the thrust button, spring and axial clearance shim.

7 To fit the new bellows, a special expander will be required,

8 Grip the driveshaft in the jaws of a vice and locate the expander on the end of the yoke. Deburr any edges at the joint - see Fig. 8.15.

9 Lubricate the expander and inside of the bellows and slide the bellows up the expander, making sure that the first fold is fully extended. Pull the bellows half way up the expander two or three times to stretch the rubber and then pull them right over the shaft yoke.

10 If the driveshaft has an intermediate bush, locate the bush in the shaft grooves.

11 Fit the spring and thrust button.

8 Driveshaft bellows (outboard six-ball type joint) - renewal

Note: *A bellows expander (Tool No TAv 537-02) will be needed for this operation*

1 If the spider at the inboard end of the driveshaft is removed, the outboard bellows can be slid off the shaft and renewed without the need for a special expander. The choice is with the home mechanic whether the extra work involved is worthwhile, so avoiding the need for the special tool.

Fig. 8.19 Grind end of screwdriver blade as shown to assist engagement of starplate arms (Sec 7)

A = 5 mm (0.195 in)   B = 3 mm (0.117 in)

Fig. 8.20 Fit the thrust button shim (Sec 7)

Fig. 8.21 Sectional views showing correct bellows and retaining clips fitting (Sec 7)

Fig. 8.22 Sectional view of the outboard six-ball type joint (Sec 8)

1 Stub axle   5 Ball hub
2 Driveshaft   6 Ball cage
3 Bellows   7 Circlip
4 Balls

2 Remove the driveshaft as described in the appropriate earlier Section.
3 Grip the driveshaft in the jaws of a vice and remove the clips, cut the bellows and remove and discard them.
4 Wipe away as much grease as possible.
5 Expand the circlip (7 - Fig. 8.23), at the same time tapping the ball hub(s) with a plastic mallet. Withdraw the driveshaft from the coupling.
6 Slide the bellows retaining ring (A - Fig. 8.24) onto the shaft, followed by the bellows (3).
7 Spread the grease supplied with the new bellows inside them.
8 Slide the coupling, complete with circlip,

Fig. 8.25 Using drilled rods to fit the bellows spring clip (Sec 8)

Fig. 8.26 Pressing off the anti-lock sensor target (Sec 9)

Fig. 8.23 Expand the circlip (7) and tap the ball hub (5) to remove the driveshaft (Sec 8)

onto the driveshaft until the circlip locks in its groove.
9 Locate the bellows so that their lips engage in the grooves of shaft and stub axle.
10 Fit the bellows retaining ring and the spring clip using drilled rods (see Fig. 8.25).

9 Driveshaft coupling joints - renewal

Inboard tripod joint - type GI 62

1 The spider assembly can be renewed on this type of joint and is supplied with a plastic retainer.
2 Removal and refitting operations are described in Section 5.

Inboard tripod joint - type RC 490

3 The spider and yoke can be renewed on this type of joint.
4 The spider is supplied with a plastic retainer and the removal and refitting procedure is described in Section 6.
5 The cover should be crimped to the yoke while the cover is under pressure and the yoke is fully home.
6 On cars fitted with the anti-lock braking system, the sensor target must be removed using a press before the cover is crimped.

Fig. 8.27 Sensor target relocated on driveshaft joint (Sec 9)

Fig. 8.24 Six-ball type driveshaft joint (Sec 8)

1 Six-ball coupling   A Bellows retaining
2 Driveshaft   ring
3 Bellows   B Circlip groove

When refitting the target, apply Loctite Scelbloc before pressing it into position.

Outboard tripod joint

7 The joint components may be renewed after dismantling as described in Section 7.

Outboard six-ball joint

8 The driveshaft or the stub axle/coupling may be renewed after separation, as described in Section 8.
9 Dismantling of the ball cage serves no purpose as individual spare parts are not available.

10 Front hub bearings (1.7 litre models) - renewal

Note: *Hub bearing renewal can only be achieved using suitable pullers, a press and some metal tubing of suitable diameter to press the old bearing out and the new bearing into the housing. For particulars read through before starting.*
1 Remove the front roadwheel trim plate on the side concerned, then loosen off the roadwheel bolts and the driveshaft nut.

Fig. 8.28 Front wheel hub puller tool (Renault type shown) (Sec 10)

8

Fig. 8.29 Inner bearing track ring puller (Renault type shown) (Sec 10)

2 Raise the car at the front and support it on axle stands. Remove the relevant roadwheel.
3 Remove the brake disc as described in Chapter 9.
4 Unscrew and remove the driveshaft nut and washer, then fit a suitable hub puller similar to that shown in Fig. 8.28. Withdraw the hub unit, then remove the puller from the hub.
5 To remove the inner bearing track ring, a puller of the type shown in Fig. 8.29 must be used.
6 Remove the hub carrier unit as described in Chapter 10.
7 Extract the bearing retaining ring from the carrier, then using a suitable tube drift, remove the bearing as shown in Fig. 8.30.

Fig. 8.32 Front hub bearing showing outer plastic protectors (A) and plastic ring (B) (Sec 10)

Fig. 8.34 Hub carrier installation – press on area indicated by arrows. Note thrust washer location (1) (Sec 10)

Fig. 8.30 Bearing removal from hub carrier using a tube drift (Sec 10)

Thoroughly clean the hub and driveshaft before fitting a new bearing.
8 Leave the plastic ring in the new bearing bore, but remove the outer plastic protectors. Press the bearing into the housing using a tube with an outside diameter of 71 mm, and a 66 mm bore, so that it only rests on the bearing outer track ring end face. Do not press on the bearing inner track ring or it will be damaged.
9 Remove the inner plastic protective ring, then locate the retaining ring.
10 Ensure that the thrust washer is in position on the hub then smear the bearing oil seal lips with a multi-purpose grease. Press the hub carrier onto the hub using a tube with an outside diameter of 48 mm and a bore of 43 mm in contact with the bearing inner track ring (Fig. 8.34).
11 Refit the hub carrier to the car in the reverse order of removal as described in

Fig. 8.33 Front hub bearing installation – press on areas indicated by arrows (Sec 10)

11.4 Forcing hub flange from bearing using roadwheel bolts and packing pieces

Fig. 8.31 Hub carrier and bearings (Sec 10)

Chapter 10. Tighten the retaining nuts and bolts to their specified torque wrench settings.

11 Front hub bearings (2.0 litre models) - renewal

Note: Refer to the note at the start of the previous Section. A T30 Torx bit will also be required
1 Proceed as described in paragraphs 1 to 3 of the previous Section.
2 Unscrew and remove the driveshaft nut and washer. Using a suitable Torx key inserted through the holes in the hub flange, unscrew the bolts securing the bearing assembly to the hub carrier.
3 Withdraw the hub flange and bearing assembly from the hub carrier and driveshaft.
4 Using two roadwheel bolts and two steel packing pieces, screw in the bolts gradually and evenly to force the hub flange from the bearing (photo).
5 To remove the inner bearing track ring from the hub flange a puller of the type shown in Fig. 8.29 will be required. Press to drift out the remaining inner bearing track ring from the bearing assembly and inspect the components for wear. Renew as necessary.
6 Fit the new bearing inner track ring to the hub flange and drive or press it home using a suitable tube having a bore of 41 mm.
7 Pack the bearing with grease then position it on the hub flange. Place the other inner track ring on the bearing and tap it into place with a hammer and suitable socket (photos).

11.7A Position the bearing on the hub flange. . .

11.7B . . . place the inner track ring on the bearing . . .

11.7C . . . and tap it into place

Fig. 8.35 Extracting the bearing assembly bolts using a Torx bit inserted through hub flange holes (B) (Sec 11)

8 Engage the bearing assembly with the driveshaft and tap it on until sufficient thread protrudes to enable the driveshaft nut to be screwed on two or three turns.

9 Refit the brake disc and caliper assembly as described in Chapter 9.

10 Tighten the driveshaft nut to draw the assembly into the hub carrier. Refit and tighten the bearing retaining bolts using the Torx tool inserted through the holes in the hub flange.

11 Refit the roadwheel, lower the car to the ground and tighten the driveshaft nut to the specified torque.

12 Rear hub bearings - renewal

Note: *On certain models, primarily the Renault 21 Turbo, the rear hubs and bearings cannot be separated, so the complete assembly will have to be renewed. Consult a Renault dealer for further information.*

1 Jack up the vehicle at the rear and support it on axle stands. Remove the relevant roadwheel.

2 Prise free and remove the hub cap (photo).

3 Remove the brake drum (non-Turbo models) or brake disc (Turbo models) as described in Chapter 9, Section 9 or 7 respectively. On 2.0 litre models, after removing the drum or disc, unscrew and remove the hub nut then remove the hub

(photo). Note than on 1.7 litre models the hub and drum are combined.

4 Extract the bearing retaining circlip from its groove in the hub bore, then using a suitable piece of tube with an outside diameter of 49 mm, press or drive out the bearing.

5 The circlip and hub nut must be renewed on reassembly.

6 Press the new bearing into position using a piece of tube with an outside diameter of 51 mm. Do not apply force to the inner race. When fitted, the bearing must be in contact with the shoulder in the hub/drum bore.

7 Locate the new circlip into its groove to secure the bearing.

8 Lubricate the stub axle with SAE 80 oil, then fit the hub/drum onto it.

9 Fit the new locknut and tighten it to the specified torque wrench setting.

10 Tap the hub cap into position and refit the brake drum/disc (Chapter 9).

11 Check that the wheel hub endfloat is as specified using a dial gauge, then adjust the brakes as described in Chapter 9.

12 Refit the roadwheel and lower the car to complete.

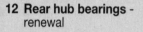

13 Driveshaft/differential oil seals - renewal

1 The driveshaft/differential oil seals can be renewed without having to remove the transmission from the car.

Fig. 8.36 Rear hub bearing components (Sec 12)

2 Refer to Section 3 or 4 as applicable, and detach the driveshaft from the transmission on the side concerned. It should not be necessary to remove the driveshaft from the hub carrier.

3 Remove the 0-ring seal from the differential stub shaft.

4 Prise and lever out the old oil seal from the

 8

12.2 Prising free the hub cap (2.0 litre model shown)

12.3 Rear hub nut (2.0 litre model)

Fig. 8.37 Rear hub bearing removal and refitting (Sec 12)

1 Removal – use 49 mm diameter tubing
2 Refitting – use 51 mm diameter tubing

Fig. 8.38 Driveshaft/differential oil seal removal method (Sec 13)

Fig. 8.39 Driveshaft oil seal identification on MJ3 automatic transmission models (Sec 13)

Fig. 8.40 Differential sunwheel/driveshaft insulation washer location in driveshaft – JB3 and NG9 transmission types (Sec 13)

differential housing, but take care not to damage the seal housing.

5 Before fitting the new oil seal into the housing, ensure that the replacement seal is the correct type by measuring its diameter. This is most important on MJ3 automatic transmission models, since on later models not only do the right-hand and left-hand seals differ in diameter, but the seal diameter was also enlarged - see Fig. 8.39.

6 Refitting is a reversal of the removal procedure. Lubricate the lips of the new seal with grease before driving it into position (photo). Renew the O-ring seal and lubricate it before fitting it onto the differential stub shaft (photo).

7 On 1.7 litre models fitted with the JB3 type transmission, and 2.0 litre models fitted with the NG9 type transmission, an insulator washer may be fitted at the differential sunwheel. The driveshaft butts against this washer, and when the driveshaft is refitted, it will need to be pressed in towards the differential to compress the washer and allow the retaining roll pins to be inserted. Two thicknesses of washer are available, and it is important that the correct type is fitted. The washer thickness is dependent on the differential sunwheel type as follows:

JB3 transmission

Sunwheel without shoulder - no washer fitted

Sunwheel with 3 mm shoulder - 5 mm thick washer fitted

Early models (left and right-hand)
– 42.2 mm diameter
Late models (left-hand) – 45.2 mm diameter
Late models (right-hand) – 43.7 mm diameter

NG9 transmission

Sunwheel with 1 mm thick shoulder - 3 mm thick washer fitted

Sunwheel with 3 mm thick shoulder - 5 mm thick washer fitted

8 Where applicable, ensure that this washer is fitted at the base of the driveshaft yoke before fitting the driveshaft.

9 Refit the driveshaft as described in Section 3 or 4 as applicable.

10 Top up the transmission oil level as described in Chapter 6 for manual transmissions or 7 for automatic transmissions.

14 Wheels and tyres - general care and maintenance

Wheels and tyres should give no real problems in use provided that a close eye is kept on them with regard to excessive wear or damage. To this end, the following points should be noted.

Ensure that tyre pressures are checked regularly and maintained correctly. Checking should be carried out with the tyres cold and not immediately after the vehicle has been in use. If the pressures are checked with the

P   Sunwheel
R   Insulating washer
A   Sunwheel shoulder width
B   Washer width

tyres hot, an apparently high reading will be obtained owing to heat expansion. Under no circumstances should an attempt be made to reduce the pressures to the quoted cold reading in this instance, or effective underinflation will result.

Underinflation will cause overheating of the tyre owing to excessive flexing of the casing, and the tread will not sit correctly on the road surface. This will cause a consequent loss of adhesion and excessive wear, not to mention the danger of sudden tyre failure due to heat build-up.

Overinflation will cause rapid wear of the centre part of the tyre tread coupled with reduced adhesion, harsher ride, and the danger of shock damage occurring in the tyre casing.

Regularly check the tyres for damage in the form of cuts or bulges, especially in the sidewalls. Remove any nails or stones embedded in the tread before they penetrate the tyre to cause deflation. If removal of a nail *does* reveal that the tyre has been punctured, refit the nail so that its point of penetration is marked. Then immediately change the wheel and have the tyre repaired by a tyre dealer. Do *not* drive on a tyre in such a condition, in many cases a puncture can be simply repaired by the use of an inner tube of the correct size and type. If in any doubt as to the possible consequences of any damage found, consult your local tyre dealer for advice.

Periodically remove the wheels and clean any dirt or mud from the inside and outside surfaces. Examine the wheel rims for signs of rusting, corrosion or other damage. Light alloy wheels are easily damaged by kerbing whilst parking, and similarly steel wheels may become dented or buckled. Renewal of the wheel is very often the only course of remedial action possible.

The balance of each wheel and tyre assembly should be maintained to avoid excessive wear, not only to the tyres but also to the steering and suspension components

13.6A Driving the new oil seal into its housing using a socket

13.6B Renew the O-ring seal on the differential stub shaft

Wheel imbalance is normally signified by vibration through the vehicles bodyshell, although in many cases it is particularly noticeable through the steering wheel. Conversely, it should be noted that wear or damage in suspension or steering components may cause excessive tyre wear. Out-of-round or out-of-true tyres, damaged wheels and wheel bearing wear/maladjustment also fall into this category. Balancing will not usually cure vibration caused by such wear.

Wheel balancing may be carried out with the wheel either on or off the vehicle. If balanced on the vehicle, ensure that the wheel-to-hub relationship is marked in some way prior to subsequent wheel removal so that it may be refitted in its original position.

General tyre wear is influenced to a large degree by driving style - harsh braking and acceleration or fast cornering will all produce more rapid tyre wear. Interchanging of tyres may result in more even wear, but this should only be carried out where there is no mix of tyre types on the vehicle. However, it is worth bearing in mind that if this is completely effective, the added expense of replacing a complete set of tyres simultaneously is incurred, which may prove financially restrictive for many owners.

Front tyres may wear unevenly as a result of wheel misalignment. The front wheels should always be correctly aligned according to the settings specified by the vehicle manufacturer.

Legal restrictions apply to the mixing of tyre types on a vehicle. Basically this means that a vehicle must not have tyres of differing construction on the same axle. Although it is not recommended to mix tyre types between front axle and rear axle, the only legally permissible combination is crossply at the front and radial at the rear. When mixing radial ply tyres, textile braced radials must always go on the front axle, with steel braced radials at the rear. An obvious disadvantage of such mixing is the necessity to carry two spare tyres to avoid contravening the law in the event of a puncture.

In the UK, the Motor Vehicles Construction and Use Regulations apply to many aspects of tyre fitting and usage. It is suggested that a copy of these regulations is obtained from your local police if in doubt as to the current legal requirements with regard to tyre condition. minimum tread depth, etc.

Fault finding - driveshafts, hubs, roadwheels and tyres

Vibration
☐ Driveshaft bent
☐ Worn CV joints
☐ Out of balance roadwheels

'Clonk' on taking up drive or on the over run
☐ Worn CV joints
☐ Worn splines on driveshaft, hub or differential sun wheels
☐ Loose driveshaft nut or wheel bolts

Noise or roar when cornering
☐ Worn hub bearings
☐ Loose driveshaft/hub nut

Rapid or uneven wear of tyre tread
☐ Out of balance roadwheels
☐ Distorted roadwheel
☐ Incorrect front wheel alignment

8

Notes

Chapter 9 Braking system

For modifications, and information applicable to later models, see Supplement at end of manual

Contents

Degrees of difficulty

Easy, suitable for novice with little experience	**Fairly easy,** suitable for beginner with some experience	**Fairly difficult,** suitable for competent DIY mechanic	**Difficult,** suitable for experienced DIY mechanic	**Very difficult,** suitable for expert DIY or professional

Specifications

General

Type .... Servo-assisted, hydraulic, dual circuit. Front disc and rear drum brakes on all models except Turbo which has discs all round. ABS standard on Turbo models, optional on some others. Handbrake operates on rear wheels.

Front brakes

Disc diameter:
- 1.7 litre models .... 238 mm (9.28 in)
- 2.0 litre non-Turbo models .... 265 mm (10.34 in)
- 2.0 litre Turbo models .... 285 mm (11.12 in)

Minimum disc thickness:
- 1.7 litre L481 models .... 10.5 mm (0.41 in)
- 1.7 litre L482, K481 and K482 models .... 18.0 mm (0.70 in)
- 2.0 litre non-Turbo models .... 17.7 mm (0.69 in)
- 2.0 litre Turbo models .... 19.0 mm (0.75 in)

Minimum pad thickness (including backing):
- 1.7 litre models .... 6.0 mm (0.23 in)
- 2.0 litre models .... 6.5 mm (0.25 in)

Maximum disc run-out .... 0.07 mm (0.003 in)

9

Rear drum brakes

Drum diameter:
  1.7 litre models:
    Saloon .... 180.25 mm (7.03 in)
    Savanna .... 228.5 mm (8.91 in)
  2.0 litre models .... 228.5 mm (8.91 in)
Maximum allowable drum diameter after refacing:
  1.7 litre models:
    Saloon .... 181.25 mm (7.07 in)
    Savanna .... 229.5 mm (8.95 in)
  2.0 litre models .... 229.5 mm (8.95 in)
Minimum lining thickness (including shoe) .... 2.5 mm (0.10 in)

Rear disc brakes

Disc diameter .... 255.0 mm (9.95 in)
Minimum disc thickness .... 9.5 mm (0.37 in)
Maximum disc run-out .... 0.07 mm (0.003 in)
Minimum pad thickness (including backing) .... 6.0 mm (0.23 in)

Hydraulic fluid

Type/specification .... Hydraulic fluid to SAE J1703F, DOT 3 or DOT 4

Torque wrench settings

	Nm	lbf ft
Master cylinder/servo bolts	13	9
Servo unit bolts	20	15
Front brake caliper:		
Caliper mounting bolts	100	73
Caliper bracket mounting bolts (Bendix IV type)	65	48
Caliper guide bolts (Bendix IVM type)	25	18
Caliper guide bolts (Girling type)	35	26
Rear brake caliper:		
Caliper mounting bolts	65	48
ABS system:		
Wheel sensor mounting bolt	8	6
Hydraulic control unit nuts	20	14
Hydraulic system:		
Bleed screws	7	5
Brake pipe unions and associated fittings	13	9

1 General description

The braking system is of four wheel dual circuit type. On all models except those fitted with ABS (anti-lock braking system), the circuits are split diagonally. On models fitted with ABS, the circuits are split front to rear.

The front brakes are of ventilated disc type, with automatically adjusted drum brakes at the rear. On Turbo models, and all models with ABS, four wheel disc brakes are fitted, with ventilated discs at the front, and solid discs at the rear.

All models have servo assistance and a brake compensator system to balance the system in accordance with pressure and loading.

The handbrake is cable operated to the rear brakes, adjustment being automatic.

The removal and refitting of some brake system components requires the use of Torx type keys, therefore it is advisable to read through the instructions for a particular task before commencing, and examine the items on the vehicle to assess the tool requirements.

Fig. 9.1 Brake circuit diagram – 1.7 litre models with fixed compensators (Sec 1)

Fig. 9.2 Brake circuit diagram – 1.7 litre models with compensator integral in wheel cylinders (Sec 1)

Fig. 9.3 Brake circuit diagram – 1.7 and 2.0 litre models with load dependent compensator (Sec 1)

Fig. 9.4 Brake circuit diagram – 2.0 litre ABS models with load dependent compensator (Sec 1)

2.2 Brake fluid reservoir and fluid levels

2 Maintenance

1 Regularly check the fluid level in the brake master cylinder reservoir. The need for topping-up should be very infrequent and then only a small quantity should be required to compensate for friction lining wear.
2 The fluid level should never be allowed to fall below the 'Minimum' level marking on the front face of the reservoir, or topped up beyond the 'Maximum' mark. Any loss of fluid will be due to a leak in the brake hydraulic system (or possibly the clutch hydraulic system on Turbo models, as both use the same reservoir) (photo).

Fig. 9.5 Lock the guide pins (8) when unscrewing the caliper guide bolts (7) – Girling type (Sec 3)

3 When topping-up use only clean fluid of the correct type which has been stored in an airtight container. On models equipped with ABS the following procedure is used for topping up. Switch on the ignition then depress the brake pedal several times to activate the ABS hydraulic pump. Wait until the pump stops (the pump is an electric motor under the brake fluid reservoir) then check the reservoir level and top up to between the minimum and maximum marks if necessary. 4 At the intervals specified in 'Routine maintenance' the following service operations should be carried out on the braking system.
5 With the car raised on a hoist, over an inspection pit or supported on ramps or axle stands, carefully inspect all the hydraulic pipes, hoses and unions for chafing, cracks, leaks and corrosion. Details will be found in Section 14.
6 Remove the front wheels and check the thickness of the front brake pads. Renew the

Fig. 9.6 Using a clamp to depress the caliper piston – Renault tool shown (Sec 3)

pads, as described in Section 3, if they are worn to the specified minimum thickness.
7 Remove the rear wheels and inspect the rear brake linings, or pads as applicable. With drum brakes it will be necessary to remove the brake drum to make a full inspection of the brake linings. The wheel cylinder can also be inspected for any signs of leakage at the same time.
8 Check the operation of the handbrake on each rear wheel and lubricate the exposed cables and linkages under the car.
9 Although not a specific manufacturer's service recommendation, it is advisable to renew the hydraulic fluid as described in Section 15. at the intervals specified in 'Routine maintenance'.

3 Front disc pads - inspection and renewal

1 Raise the front of the car and support it securely.
2 Remove the front roadwheels.
3 Inspect the thickness of the friction material on the disc pads (photo). If it has worn below the minimum specified, renew the pads in the following way according to type.

Girling type

4 Unscrew the caliper guide bolts using a ring

9

3.3 Front brake disc pad inspection window (Girling type)

3.5 Lift the caliper out of the way . . .

3.6A . . . and detach the sensor wire . . .

3.6B . . . and remove the brake pads
(Girling type)

3.11 Smear the bolt threads with locking
compound . . .

3.12 . . . fit and tighten them to the
specified torque (Girling type)

Fig. 9.7 Bendix IV type front brake pads
retaining clip (1) and wedge (2) (Sec 3)

spanner and an open-ended spanner to lock the guide pins.

5 Lift off the caliper and support it or tie it up out of the way (photo).

6 Disconnect the sensor wire. Remove the disc pads and discard them (photos).

7 Brush away all dust and dirt. but *avoid inhaling it as it is injurious to health.*

8 The piston should now be pushed fully into its cylinder. Do this using a flat bar or a clamp similar to the one shown in Fig. 9.6. As the piston is depressed, the fluid will rise in the reservoir, so anticipate this by syphoning some out beforehand. An old battery hydrometer or poultry baster is useful for this, but make sure that they are clean. Do not syphon out fluid by mouth.

9 Fit the new pads; the inboard one being the one with the sensor wire.

10 Locate the springs correctly, then the caliper.

11 Fit the guide bolts, having applied thread locking fluid to their threads (photo).

12 Tighten the bottom guide bolt and then the upper one to the specified torque (photo). Proceed to paragraph 23.

Bendix IV type

13 Disconnect the pad wear sensor wire, then press piston into its caliper by sliding the caliper outwards (see paragraphs 7 and 8).

14 Note their location, then remove the retaining clip and wedge from the caliper housing. Withdraw the pads together with

their anti-rattle springs. As they are removed, note the orientation of each pad. On the outer pad the wear groove is offset and towards the front of the car, whilst on the inner pad the offset groove is towards the rear. Brush away all dust and dirt, but avoid inhaling it as it is injurious to health.

15 If new pads are to be fitted, locate the anti-rattle springs as shown in Fig. 9.9, then push the piston fully into its cylinder, as described in paragraph 8.

16 Fit the brake pads into position ensuring that they are positioned as shown in Fig. 9.10.

Fig. 9.10 Pad locations in Bendix IV type
caliper (Sec 3)

B Pad grooves are offset as shown
V Pad with wear sensor wire to be on inside
D Retaining clip location (inboard side)
C Caliper bracket bolt

Fig. 9.8 Pad identification and orientation –
Bendix IV type (Sec 3)

Fig. 9.9 Anti-rattle spring (3) fitted to pad –
Bendix IV type (Sec 3)

3.19 Unscrew the caliper guide bolt using a Torx key (Bendix IV type) . . .

3.20 . . . remove the pads . . .

3.21 . . . and spring (noting its orientation)

The pad wear sensor wire must be on the inboard side.

17 Slide the wedge into position and then fit the retaining clip to the inboard side of the caliper. Proceed to paragraph 23.

Bendix IVM type

18 Detach the brake pad wear sensor wire. Pull the caliper body outwards by hand to compress the piston into its cylinder.
19 Undo the caliper guide bolt using a T40 Torx key (photo). With the guide bolt detached from the caliper bracket, pivot the caliper body upwards and hold it in position to enable the pads to be withdrawn.
20 Withdraw the pads from the caliper bracket (photo).
21 Brush away all dust and dirt, *but avoid inhaling it, as it is injurious to health.* Remove and clean the spring (photo). If new pads are being fitted push the piston fully into its cylinder as described in paragraph 8.
22 Refit in the reverse order of removal. Note that the pad with the wear sensor wire is fitted to the inboard side of the caliper. Tighten the guide bolt to the specified torque wrench setting.

All models

23 Renew the pads on the opposite wheel in a similar way.
24 Apply the footbrake several times to position the pads against the discs.
25 Fit the roadwheels and lower the car to the floor.
26 Top up the master cylinder reservoir to the correct level.

3.27A Pad wear sensor wire and retaining clip on caliper (arrowed)

27 Ensure that the pad wear sensor wire is correctly routed and located (photos).

4 Rear disc pads -
inspection and renewal

1 Raise the rear of the car, support it securely and remove the rear roadwheels.
2 Check the wear of the friction material on the pads. If it has worn below the minimum specified, renew the pads in the following way.
3 Disconnect the handbrake cable from the lever on the caliper, refer to Section 22.
4 Extract the two lockpins and then tap out the two sliding keys (photos).
5 Lift the caliper from the disc and tie it up out of the way.

3.27B Pad wear sensor connector (arrowed) and retainer on suspension strut (2.0 litre model)

6 Remove the disc pads and springs for inspection. Clean the caliper by carefully brushing away the dust and dirt, *but avoid inhaling it as it is injurious to health.*
7 Retract the piston fully into its cylinder prior to fitting new pads. Do this by turning the piston with the square section shaft of a screwdriver until the piston continues to turn but will not go in any further. As the piston goes in, the fluid level in the master cylinder reservoir will rise; anticipate this by syphoning out some fluid (see Section 3, paragraph 8). Finally set the piston so that the line (R - Fig. 9.11) is nearest to the bleed screw.

Fig. 9.11 Rear brake caliper piston orientation (Sec 4)

Line R to be nearest bleed screw

4.4A Extract the lock pins (arrowed) . . .

4.4B . . . and remove the sliding keys

9

4.8A Locate the pad springs . . .

4.8B . . . and fit the pads

Fig. 9.12 Front disc brake caliper components, showing piston dust excluder (5) and gaiters (6) (Sec 5)

8 Locate the springs onto the pads and fit the pads (photos).
9 Fit the caliper by engaging one end of the caliper between the spring clip and the keyway on the bracket, compress the springs and engage the opposite end.
10 Insert the first key, then insert a screwdriver in the second key slot and use it as a lever until the slot will accept the key.
11 Fit new key lockpins.
12 Renew the pads on the opposite wheel.
13 Reconnect the handbrake cable.
14 Apply the footbrake several times to position the pads against the discs.
15 Fit the roadwheels and lower the car to the floor.
16 Top up the master cylinder reservoir to the correct level.

Fig. 9.13 Removing the piston seal ring from the caliper bore (Sec 5)

5 Front disc brake caliper - removal, overhaul and refitting

1 Raise the front of the car and remove the roadwheel.
2 Release the flexible brake hose from the caliper by unscrewing it no more than a quarter of a turn.
3 Remove the brake pads as described in Section 3.
4 Undo the two caliper unit-to-hub carrier bolts, then withdraw the caliper from the brake disc (photos).
5 Unscrew the caliper from the flexible hose and then cap the end of the hose or use a brake hose clamp to prevent loss of fluid (photo).
6 Clean away external dirt from the caliper and remove the dust excluder and, where fitted, the retaining ring.
7 Eject the piston from the cylinder by applying air pressure to the fluid inlet hole. Only low air pressure is required such as is generated by a foot-operated tyre pump. Remove the piston seal ring from its groove in the caliper bore.
8 Inspect the surfaces of the piston and cylinder. If there is evidence of scoring or corrosion, renew the caliper cylinder assembly complete.
9 If the components are in good condition, remove the seal and wash them in clean

hydraulic fluid or methylated spirit - nothing else.
10 Obtain a repair kit which will contain all the necessary renewable items. Fit the new seal, using the fingers to manipulate it into its groove.
11 Dip the piston in clean hydraulic fluid and insert the piston into the cylinder.
12 On the Girling caliper, fit the dust excluder and retaining ring.
13 Screw the caliper onto the flexible hose and fit the caliper to its bracket, making sure that the piston is fully depressed into its cylinder.
14 Refit the brake pads as described in Section 3.
15 Tighten the flexible hose union and bleed the hydraulic circuit (Section 15).
16 Refit the roadwheel and lower the car.
17 Apply the footbrake two or three times to settle the pads.

6 Rear disc brake caliper - removal, overhaul and refitting

1 Raise the rear of the car and remove the roadwheel.
2 Disconnect the handbrake cable from the lever on the caliper (see Section 22).

5.4A Brake caliper-to-hub carrier bolts (arrowed) – Girling type

5.4B Brake caliper-to-hub carrier bolts (arrowed) – Bendix type

5.5 Brake hose clamp in position

Fig. 9.14 Unscrewing the rear caliper piston using a screwdriver (Sec 6)

Fig. 9.15 Rear caliper support bracket arm wedge dimensions (in mm) (Sec 6)

Fig. 9.16 Driving in the wedge to spread caliper support arm brackets (Sec 6)

3 Release the flexible brake hose from the caliper by unscrewing it by no more than a quarter of a turn.

4 Remove the caliper from the disc as described in Section 4.

5 Unscrew the caliper from the hose and cap the end of the hose or use a brake hose clamp to prevent loss of fluid.

6 Clean away external dirt from the caliper and grip it in the jaws of a vice fitted with jaw protectors.

7 Remove the dust excluder from around the piston and then unscrew the piston, using the square section shaft of a screwdriver. Once the piston turns freely but does not come out any further, apply low air pressure to the fluid inlet hole and eject the piston. Only low air pressure is required such as is generated by a foot-operated tyre pump.

8 Inspect the surfaces of the piston and cylinder bore. If there is evidence of scoring or corrosion, renew the caliper cylinder.

9 To remove the cylinder a wedge will have to be made in accordance with the dimensions shown in Fig. 9.15.

10 Drive the wedge in to slightly separate the support bracket arms and so slide out the cylinder which can be done once the spring-loaded locating pin has been depressed (Figs. 9.16 and 9.17).

11 If the piston and cylinder are in good condition, then the cylinder will not have to be removed from the support bracket but overhauled in the following way.

12 Remove and discard the piston seal and wash the components in methylated spirit.

13 Obtain a repair kit which will contain all the necessary renewable items. Fit the new seal using the fingers to manipulate it into its groove.

14 Dip the piston in clean hydraulic fluid and insert the piston into the cylinder.

15 Using the square section shaft of a screwdriver, turn the piston until it turns but will not go in any further. Set the piston so that the line (R - Fig. 9.11) is nearest the bleed screw.

16 Fit a new dust excluder.

17 If the handbrake operating mechanism is worn or faulty, dismantle it in the following way before renewing the piston seal.

18 Grip the caliper in a vice fitted with jaw protectors.

19 Refer to Fig. 9.18 and remove the dust excluder (1), the piston (2), dust cover (3), and the circlip (4).

20 Compress the spring washers (5) and pull out the shaft (6).

21 Remove the plunger cam (7), spring (8), adjusting screw (9), plain washer (10) and spring washer (5).

22 Refer to Fig. 9.19 and drive out the

sleeve (12) using a drift, and remove the sealing ring (11).

23 Clean all components and renew any that are worn.

24 Reassembly is a reversal of removal but observe the following points.

25 Drive in the sleeve (12) until it is flush with face (A) in Fig. 9.20.

26 Make sure that the spring washers are fitted as shown, convex face to convex face.

27 Align the piston as previously described.

28 Refit the caliper after screwing it onto the hydraulic hose. Tighten the hose union. Refit the disc pads.

29 Reconnect the handbrake cable.

30 Bleed the hydraulic circuit (Section 15).

31 Fit the roadwheel and lower the car.

32 Apply the footbrake several times and adjust the handbrake cable (Section 20).

Fig. 9.17 Depressing cylinder spring-loaded locating pin (E) – Renault tool shown (Sec 6)

9

Fig. 9.18 Exploded view of rear caliper (Sec 6)

1 Dust excluder	6 Shaft
2 Piston	7 Plunger cam
3 Rear dust cover	8 Spring
4 Circlip	9 Adjusting screw
5 Spring washers	10 Washer

Fig. 9.19 Using a puller to compress spring washers in rear caliper. Inset O-ring (11) on adjusting screw (Sec 6)

5 Spring washer	11 O-ring
6 Shaft	12 Sleeve

Fig. 9.20 Rear caliper sleeve (12) fitted flush with face (A) (Sec 6)

7.2 Remove rust deposits from outside edge of brake disc

7.17 Removing a rear brake disc

Fig. 9.21 Rear disc brake caliper bracket retaining bolts (A) (Sec 7)

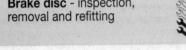

7 Brake disc - inspection, removal and refitting

Inspection

1 Whenever the disc pads are being checked for wear, take the opportunity to inspect the disc for deep grooving, scoring or cracks. Light scoring is normal.
2 Rust will normally build up on the edge of a disc and this should be removed periodically by holding a sharp tool against the disc whilst it is rotated (photo).
3 If there has been a history of brake judder, check the discs for run-out. Do this using a dial gauge or feeler blades between the disc and a fixed point while the disc is rotated. Run-out should be within the specified limit (see Specifications).
4 If the disc is grooved. cracked or distorted it must be renewed. Refinishing of a disc must not be carried out as this can cause the caliper piston to over-extend when the brakes are applied. If a new disc is being fitted, new brake pads must also be fitted to both sides of the car.

Front disc renewal

5 Raise the front of the car and remove the roadwheel.
6 Unscrew and remove the two caliper bracket bolts (see photos 5.4A and 5.4B).

7 Lift the caliper off the disc and tie it up out of the way.
8 Unscrew the disc fixing screws; these are of Torx type so a special bit will be required.
9 Remove the disc.
10 Clean any protective coating from the new disc and locate it on the hub.
11 Screw in and tighten the fixing screws.
12 Clean the threads of the caliper bracket fixing bolts, apply thread locking fluid to them, locate the caliper and screw in the bolts, tightening them to the specified torque.
13 Apply the brake pedal several times to position the pads up against the disc, fit the roadwheel and lower the car.

Rear disc renewal

14 Raise the rear of the car and remove the roadwheel.
15 Refer to Section 4 and remove the disc pads and disconnect the handbrake cable. Tie the caliper up out of the way.
16 Unscrew and remove the two caliper bracket bolts (A - Fig. 9.21) and lift off the caliper bracket.
17 Using a Torx bit, unscrew and remove the two disc fixing screws and remove the disc (photo).
18 Fitting the disc is a reversal of removal, but remove any protective coating from the new disc, and apply thread locking fluid to the threads of the caliper bracket bolts.
19 Apply the brake pedal several times and adjust the handbrake.
20 Refit the roadwheel and lower the car.

8 Rear brake shoes (Bendix type) - inspection and renewal

1 Raise the vehicle at the rear end, support on axle stands and remove the roadwheels.
2 To inspect the shoe linings the brake drum will need to be removed. One of two brake drum types will be fitted, a monoblock type or a steel disc type. Remove the drum as follows according to type.

Steel disc type drum

3 With the handbrake fully applied, unscrew and remove the two Torx retaining screws, release the handbrake and withdraw the drum (photo). If it is tight, try gently tapping it with a plastic or copper-faced hammer. If this fails, remove the blanking plug on the rear face of the backplate to allow access to the automatic adjuster. On some models access to the adjuster is obtained through a vacant wheel bolt hole in the drum. Using a suitable screwdriver and a length of rod as shown, release the adjuster and unscrew the knurled adjuster wheel (photo). With the adjuster fully retracted, the drum will be released.

Monoblock type drum

4 A hub cap and inertia extractor or slide hammer will be required to remove this type of drum. Prise free the hub cap. If the cap is tight, use an extractor as shown in Fig. 9.22

8.3A Unscrewing a rear brake drum Torx retaining screw

8.3B Showing method employed to release the automatic adjuster – drum removed for clarity

Rou. 943   Emb. 880

Fig. 9.22 Rear brake drum and hub cap removal tools – Renault tools shown (Sec 8)

Fig. 9.23 Press on handbrake operating lever to release stud (E) (Sec 8)

and withdraw it from the centre of the hub. Unscrew the hub flange nut, then with the handbrake fully released, withdraw the brake drum. If it is tight, loosen off the secondary handbrake cable, then insert a screwdriver through one of the wheel bolt holes in the drum and press the handbrake operating lever down to release the shoe stud (E in Fig. 9.23). Push the lever rearwards to assist. Remove the drum.

All drum types

5 Brush away dust and dirt, *taking care not to inhale it as it is injurious to health.*
6 If the shoe friction linings have worn down to or below the specified minimum, then the shoes should be renewed.
7 Obtain factory relined shoes, do not attempt to reline the old shoes as this seldom proves satisfactory. Tap off the hub dust cap,

Fig. 9.24 Disconnecting the upper return springs (1) – Bendix type (Sec 8)

unscrew the hub nut and remove the hub assembly.
8 Note carefully the position of the leading and trailing shoes and how the friction lining exposes more of the shoe web at one end than the other.
9 Note also into which holes in the shoe web the return springs engage.
10 Disconnect the upper and lower return springs.
11 Disconnect the handbrake cable from the trailing shoe.
12 Remove the two shoe hold-down springs. Do this by gripping the hold-down spring caps with a pair of pliers, then compressing the cap and spring. Simultaneously turn them through 90° to align the slotted hole in the cap with the T-head of the central retaining pin, then withdraw the cap and spring.
13 Remove the leading shoe and toothed adjuster quadrant, the trailing shoe and link unit.
14 When disconnecting the link from the trailing shoe, take care not to damage the automatic adjuster.
15 Remove the toothed adjuster quadrant and spring from the leading shoe.
16 While the shoes are removed. do not touch the brake pedal or the wheel cylinder pistons will be ejected. Keep the respective subassemblies together for reference during

Fig. 9.25 Brake shoe hold-down spring removal – Bendix type (Sec 8)

R Spring   T Retaining pin
E Backplate   4 Trailing brake shoe

reassembly, as the right and left-hand assemblies differ and must not be interchanged.
17 Assemble the link and spring to the trailing shoe as shown in Fig. 9.26, and the toothed adjuster quadrant and spring to the leading shoe as shown in Fig. 9.27. Move the knurled adjuster to the zero position.
18 Fit the new shoes by reversing the removal operations. Apply a smear of high melting-point grease to the shoe-rubbing high spots on the brake backplate, to the shoe lower anchor block recesses and to the end faces of the wheel cylinder pistons. Take care not to get any grease on the brake linings or the braking surfaces of the drum during reassembly.
19 When fitting the leading shoe ensure that the toothed adjuster quadrant engages with the link correctly before securing it.
20 When the brake shoes are fully refitted, adjust the diametrical position of the shoes before fitting the brake drum. To do this, turn the toothed adjuster quadrant to set the outside diameter of the brake shoes to the specified setting shown in Fig. 9.28.

9

Fig. 9.26 Trailing brake shoe adjuster (B) and spring (5) (Sec 8)

Fig. 9.27 Leading brake shoe toothed adjuster quadrant (C) and spring (6) (Sec 8)

Fig. 9.28 Provisional brake shoes adjustment – Bendix type (Sec 8)

C Toothed adjuster quadrant
X = 178.7 to 179.2 mm (6.97 to 6.99 in)

Fig. 9.29 Brake adjuster screw unit identification – Girling type (Sec 9)

Left-hand side – silver end piece (B)
Right-hand side – gold end piece (B)

21 Clean the interior of the drum and fit it, together with the hub, taking care not to damage the oil seal. Tighten the hub nut to the specified torque (Chapter 8).
22 Refit the dust cap over the nut.
23 Refit the backplate plug (if applicable).
24 Repeat the operations on the opposite wheel.
25 Depress the brake pedal a few times to operate the automatic adjuster mechanism, then adjust the handbrake (Section 20).

9 Rear brake shoes (Girling type) - inspection and renewal

1 Raise the vehicle at the rear end, support on axle stands and remove the roadwheels.
2 Repeat the operations described in Section 8, paragraphs 2 to 9.
3 Prise free and remove the upper and lower brake shoe return springs.
4 Disconnect the handbrake cable from the trailing shoe (photos).
5 Disconnect the tension spring and remove the adjuster lever.
6 Grip one of the shoe hold-down caps with a pair of pliers, depress the cap and turn it through 90° so that it will pass over the T-shaped head of the hold-down pin. Remove the cap, spring and pin. Remove the hold-down assembly from the other brake shoe in a similar manner.
7 Detach and withdraw the leading brake shoe and thrust link.
8 Remove the trailing brake shoe.
9 While the shoes are removed, do not touch

Fig. 9.30 Provisional brake shoes adjustment – Girling type (Sec 9)

D Toothed adjuster quadrant
X = 227.9 to 228.5 mm (8.89 to 8.91 in)

the brake pedal or the wheel cylinder pistons will be ejected.
10 Clean the backplate and inspect the brake assembly components. Keep the sub-assemblies separate, as the right and left-hand assemblies are different and must not be interchanged. The toothed adjuster screw units are colour-coded for identification as shown in Fig. 9.29. Clean the threads of the toothed adjusters and lightly grease them.
11 Apply a smear of high melting-point grease to the shoe-rubbing high spots on the brake backplate, to the shoe lower anchor block recesses and to the end faces of the wheel cylinder pistons.
12 Refitting is a reversal of the removal procedure. Take care not to get grease or oil onto the brake linings or the drum friction surface. Ensure that all connections are correctly and securely made (photo).
13 Prior to refitting the drum, adjust the diameter of the brake shoes to that specified in Fig. 9.30 by turning the toothed adjuster as required.
14 Refit the brake drums and carry out the operations given in paragraphs 21 to 25 of the previous Section to complete.

9.4A Girling type rear drum brake

1 Wheel cylinder
2 Upper return spring
3 Tension spring and adjusting lever
4 Shoe hold down spring unit

10 Rear wheel cylinder - removal, overhaul and refitting

1 Raise the rear of the car, support on axle stands and remove the roadwheel.
2 Remove the brake drum (according to type), as described in Section 8, paragraph 3 or 4 as applicable.
3 Prise and chock the upper ends of the brake shoes so that they are separated from the wheel cylinder pistons.
4 Clean the area around the hydraulic pipe union at the wheel cylinder connection on the inboard side of the backplate, then loosen off the union nut using a brake pipe spanner (photo).
5 Undo the two wheel cylinder mounting bolts and withdraw the cylinder. As the cylinder is withdrawn from the backplate, take care not to spill hydraulic fluid onto the brake linings or paintwork. Plug the hydraulic pipe to prevent spillage and the ingress of dirt.
6 If the wheel cylinder is defective, it must be renewed as a unit as no repair kits are available.
7 Refitting is a reversal of the removal procedure. Ensure that the hydraulic pipe connection at the wheel cylinder is clean. Do

9.4B Handbrake cable (arrowed) – Girling type rear drum brake

9.12 Reassembled Girling brake assembly

10.4 Brake pipe spanner

Fig. 9.31 Wheel cylinder mounting bolts (arrowed) (Sec 10)

12.2 Brake master cylinder (1), fluid reservoir (2) and low level warning switch (3) – 2.0 litre model shown

Fig. 9.32 Servo pushrod setting diagram (Secs 12 and 19)

X = 22.3 mm (0.87 in)
P Pushrod adjuster
L = 105 mm (4.10 in)
C Pedal pushrod adjuster clevis

not fully tighten the nut until after the mounting bolts have been fitted.

8 Adjust the outside diameter of the brake shoes as described in Section 8 or 9, as applicable, before refitting the drum.

9 Refit the roadwheel, lower the car, then bleed the brake hydraulic system as described in Section 15. On 1.7 litre models fitted with wheel cylinders which incorporate a compensator, the system cut-off pressure should be checked. This task requires the use of a special pressure measuring gauge and must therefore be entrusted to a Renault dealer.

11 Brake drum - inspection and renovation

1 Whenever the brake drums are removed to examine the shoe linings for wear, take the opportunity to inspect the interior of the drums for grooving, scoring or cracks.

2 The drums may be machined to renovate them provided both drums are done at the same time and the internal diameter will not be increased to more than the specified maximum.

12 Master cylinder (non-ABS models) - removal and refitting

1 Syphon the fluid from the master cylinder reservoir. Use a syringe, a clean battery hydrometer or a poultry baster to do this, never use the mouth to suck the fluid out through a tube.

2 Disconnect the leads from the low level switch and pull the reservoir upwards out of the sealing grommets (photo).

3 Note the locations of the hydraulic pipes and then disconnect them from the master cylinder by unscrewing the unions. Catch any fluid which may drain out.

4 Unbolt the master cylinder from the front face of the servo unit and remove it.

5 A faulty master cylinder cannot be overhauled, only renewed, due to the fact

that the internal roll pins cannot be extracted.

6 Before fitting the master cylinder, check the servo pushrod protrusion (X - Fig. 9.32). This must be as specified. Adjust if necessary by means of the pushrod nut.

7 Ensure that a new O-ring seal is fitted between the joint faces of the master cylinder and the servo unit.

8 Bolt the master cylinder into position and connect the fluid pipes.

9 Push the reservoir firmly into its grommets

10 Fill the reservoir with clean fluid and bleed the complete hydraulic system (Section 15).

11 Check that dimension L in Fig. 9.32 is as specified and adjust if necessary by loosening the locknut at the clevis (C), then turning the rod to suit. Retighten the locknut to complete.

13 Brake compensator - removal and refitting

1 Checking the operation of the brake compensator is not within the scope of the home mechanic as specialised equipment is required. However, a unit that is known to be faulty can be removed and renewed. It is important to ensure that the correct replacement compensator unit is obtained, as different types are fitted depending on model. Either a fixed or load-controlled type compensator will be fitted. On some models

Fig. 9.33 Master cylinder and O-ring seal (A) (Sec 12)

the fixed type compensator is integral with the rear wheel cylinders, and in this instance a fault in the compensator (or the cylinder) necessitates renewal of the relevant cylinder unit as described in Section 10.

2 The compensator unit on other models is located on the underside of the car, just to the right of centre, forward of the rear axle (photos).

13.2A Brake compensator – 2.0 litre non-Turbo model. Do not alter setting of nut (arrowed)

13.2B Brake compensator – 2.0 litre Turbo model. Do not alter setting of nut (arrowed)

9

13.2C Brake compensator – 1.7 litre model. Do not alter setting of nut (arrowed)

Fig. 9.34 Fixed type compensator unit and retaining bolt (arrowed) (Sec 13)

Fig. 9.35 Fixed type compensator and inlet unions (arrowed) (Sec 13)

3 Raise and support the vehicle at the rear on axle stands.

4 Clean the hydraulic pipe connections to the compensator, then undo the hydraulic pipe unions and disconnect the pipes. Plug them to prevent the ingress of dirt and leakage.

5 Unscrew and remove the compensator retaining bolt.

Fixed type compensator

6 Tilt the assembly, then withdraw it from the underside of the vehicle floor pan. Uncouple the compensator from the support.

Load-controlled type compensator

7 To remove this compensator, detach the control spring from the V-shaped profile, then pivot the compensator support and withdraw it from the underside of the car. Do not

14.1 Flexible-to-rigid hydraulic brake pipe connection and retainer bracket – check for security and condition

unscrew or reset the adjuster nut. Detach the compensator from its support.

All compensator types

8 Refitting for each type of compensator is a reversal of the removal procedure. Note that the hydraulic inlet pipe connections of the fixed type compensator are on the side with the smaller unions (see Fig. 9.35).

9 When the compensator is refitted, bleed the brake hydraulic system as described in Section 15.

10 On completion, have the compensator pressures checked by a Renault dealer as soon as possible.

14 Hydraulic pipes and hoses - inspection, removal and refitting

1 At intervals given in 'Routine maintenance' carefully examine all brake pipes, hoses, hose connections and pipe unions (photo).

2 First check for signs of leakage at the pipe unions. Then examine the flexible hoses for signs of cracking, chafing and fraying.

3 The brake pipes must be examined carefully and methodically. They must be cleaned off and checked for signs of dents, corrosion or other damage. Corrosion should be scraped off and, if the depth of pitting is significant, the pipes renewed. This is particularly likely in those areas underneath the vehicle body where the pipes are exposed and unprotected.

4 If any section of pipe or hose is to be removed, first unscrew the master cylinder reservoir filler cap and place a piece of

polythene over the filler neck. Secure the polythene with an elastic band ensuring that an airtight seal is obtained. This will minimise brake fluid loss when the pipe or hose is removed. On models fitted with ABS, ensure that the ignition is switched off and empty the accumulator by pumping the brake pedal twenty times. The brake pedal pressure should become hard.

5 Brake pipe removal is usually quite straightforward. The union nuts at each end are undone, the pipe and union pulled out and the centre section of the pipe removed from the body clips. Where the union nuts are exposed to the full force of the weather they can sometimes be quite tight. As only an open-ended spanner can be used, burring of the flats on the nuts is not uncommon when attempting to undo them. For this reason a self-locking wrench or special brake union split ring spanner should be used.

6 To remove a flexible hose, wipe the unions and brackets free of dirt and undo the union nut from the brake pipe end.

7 Next extract the hose retaining clip, or unscrew the nut, and lift the end of the hose out of its bracket. If a front hose is being removed, it can now be unscrewed from the brake caliper.

8 Brake pipes can be obtained individually, or in sets, from most accessory shops or garages with the end flares and union nuts in place. The pipe is then bent to shape, using the old pipe as a guide, and is ready for fitting to the car.

9 Refitting the pipes and hoses is a reverse of the removal procedure. Make sure that the hoses are not kinked when in position and also make sure that the brake pipes are securely supported in their clips. After refitting, remove the polythene from the reservoir and bleed the brake hydraulic system, as described in the next Section.

Fig. 9.36 Flexible brake hose (Sec 14)

A Taper seat (no washer used) B Union nut C End fittings

Fig. 9.37 Rigid brake pipe flare cross-section (Sec 14)

15 Brake hydraulic system - bleeding

Non-ABS systems

1 If the master cylinder or the pressure regulating valve has been disconnected and reconnected, then the complete system (both circuits) must be bled.

2 If a component of one circuit has been disturbed then only that particular circuit need be bled.

3 Bleed one rear brake and its diagonally opposite front brake. Repeat in this sequence on the remaining circuit if the complete system is to be bled.

4 Unless the pressure bleeding method is being used, do not forget to keep the fluid level in the master cylinder reservoir topped up to prevent air from being drawn into the system which would make any work done worthless (photo).

5 Before commencing operations, check that all system hoses and pipes are in good condition with all unions tight and free from leaks.

6 Take great care not to allow hydraulic fluid to come into contact with the vehicle paintwork as it is an effective paint stripper. Wash off any spilled fluid immediately with cold water.

7 As the system incorporates a vacuum servo, destroy the vacuum by giving several applications of the brake pedal in quick succession.

Bleeding - two man method

8 Gather together a clean jar and a length of rubber or plastic tubing which will be a tight fit on the brake bleed screws.

9 Engage the help of an assistant.

10 Push one end of the bleed tube onto the first bleed screw and immerse the other end in the jar which should contain enough hydraulic fluid to cover the end of the tube (photos).

11 Open the bleed screw one half a turn and have your assistant depress the brake pedal fully then slowly release it. Tighten the bleed screw at the end of each pedal downstroke to

15.4 Topping-up master cylinder reservoir – 1.7 litre model shown

obviate any chance of air or fluid being drawn back into the system.

12 Repeat this operation until clean hydraulic fluid, free from air bubbles, can be seen coming through into the jar. Tighten the bleed screw at the end of a pedal downstroke and remove the bleed tube.

13 Bleed the remaining screws in a similar way.

Bleeding - using one way valve kit

14 There are a number of one-man, one-way brake bleeding kits available from motor accessory shops. It is recommended that one of these kits is used whenever possible as it will greatly simplify the bleeding operation and also reduce the risk of air or fluid being drawn back into the system, quite apart from being able to do the work without the help of an assistant.

15 To use the kit, connect the tube to the bleed screw and open the screw one half a turn.

16 Depress the brake pedal fully and slowly release it. The one-way valve in the kit will prevent expelled air from returning at the end of each pedal downstroke. Repeat this operation several times to be sure of ejecting all air from the system. Some kits include a translucent container which can be positioned so that the air bubbles can actually be seen being ejected from the system.

17 Tighten the bleed screw, remove the tube and repeat the operations on the remaining brakes.

18 On completion, depress the brake pedal. If it still feels spongy repeat the bleeding operations as air must be trapped in the system.

Bleeding - using a pressure bleeding kit

19 These kits too are available from motor accessory shops and are usually operated by air pressure from the spare tyre.

20 By connecting a pressurised container to the master cylinder fluid reservoir, bleeding is then carried out by simply opening each bleed screw in turn and allowing the fluid to run out, rather like turning on a tap, until no air is visible in the expelled fluid.

21 By using this method, the large reserve of hydraulic fluid provides a safeguard against air being drawn into the master cylinder during bleeding which often occurs if the fluid level in the reservoir is not maintained.

22 Pressure bleeding is particularly effective when bleeding 'difficult' systems or when bleeding the complete system at a time of routine fluid renewal.

All methods

23 It may also be necessary to bleed the clutch hydraulic circuit (Chapter 5).

24 When bleeding is completed, check and top up the fluid level in the master cylinder reservoir.

25 Check the feel of the pedal. If it feels at all spongy, air must still be present in the system and further bleeding is indicated. Failure to bleed satisfactorily after a reasonable period of the bleeding operation, may be due to worn master cylinder seals.

26 Discard brake fluid which has been expelled. It is almost certain to be contaminated with moisture, air and dirt making it unsuitable for further use. Clean fluid should always be stored in an airtight container as it absorbs moisture readily (hygroscopic) which lowers its boiling point and could affect braking performance under severe conditions.

ABS system

27 On models fitted with ABS, the brake bleeding procedure should be carried out as follows.

9

15.10A Front brake bleed screw (under dust cap – arrowed) – 2.0 litre Turbo model shown

15.10B Rear drum brake bleed screw (under dust cap – arrowed) – 2.0 litre model shown

15.10C Rear disc brake bleed screw (under dust cap) – arrowed – 2.0 litre Turbo model

28 Before starting any dismantling or bleeding operations on the hydraulic circuit it is essential to first ensure that the ignition is switched off, and then to empty the pressure accumulator. To do this, depress the brake pedal twenty times so that the brake pedal pressure becomes noticeably hard. Ensure that the ignition is switched off at all times during the following procedure, except where switching on of the ignition is specified.

29 The front brake circuit must be bled first as follows. Ensure that the pressure accumulator is empty, and that the ignition is switched off.

30 The front circuit should be bled using a pressure bleeding kit as described previously for non-ABS models.

31 Ensure that the fluid reservoir is full, and open the compressed air valve on the bleeding equipment (where applicable).

32 Open the bleed screw on the right-hand wheel and wait for approximately 20 seconds for the hydraulic fluid to drain out. Close the bleed screw.

33 Repeat this procedure for the left-hand wheel.

34 The rear hydraulic circuit can now be bled as follows. Ensure that the pressure accumulator is empty (see paragraph 28), and that the ignition is switched off.

35 Connect one end of a hose to the bleed nipple on the right-hand wheel and immerse the other end in a suitable container, containing enough brake fluid to cover the open end of the hose.

36 It is most important to ensure that the following operations are carried out in the order given.

37 Open the bleed screw. Press down lightly on the brake pedal. Switch on the ignition.

38 Wait for a continuous stream of hydraulic fluid free from air bubbles to flow into the container, then release the brake pedal.

39 Tighten the bleed screw. Switch off the ignition.

40 Repeat this procedure for the left-hand wheel.

41 Pressurise the pressure accumulator by switching on the ignition and waiting for the pump to stop.

42 If necessary, top up the brake fluid level.

16 Vacuum servo unit - description and testing

1 A vacuum servo unit is fitted to the master cylinder, to provide power assistance to the driver when the brake pedal is depressed (photo).

2 The unit operates by vacuum obtained from the induction manifold and comprises, basically, a booster diaphragm and a non-return valve.

3 The servo unit piston rod acts as the master cylinder pushrod. The driver's braking effort is transmitted through another pushrod to the servo unit piston and its built-in control system. The servo unit piston does not fit tightly into the cylinder, but has a strong diaphragm to keep its edges in constant contact with the cylinder wall, so assuring an airtight seal between the two parts. The forward chamber is held under vacuum conditions created in the inlet manifold of the engine and, during periods when the brake pedal is not in use, the controls open a passage to the rear chamber so placing it under vacuum. When the brake pedal is depressed, the vacuum passage to the rear chamber is cut off and the chamber opened to atmospheric pressure. The consequent rush of air pushes the servo piston forward in the vacuum chamber and operates the main pushrod to the master cylinder. The controls are designed so that assistance is given under all conditions and, when the brakes are not required, vacuum in the rear chamber is established when the brake pedal is released. Air from the atmosphere entering the rear chamber is passed through a small air filter.

4 Operation of the servo can be checked in the following way.

5 With the engine off, depress the brake pedal several times.

6 Depress the brake pedal fully and hold it down. Start the engine and feel that the pedal moves down slightly.

7 Hold the pedal depressed with the engine running. Switch off the engine, holding the pedal depressed. The pedal should not rise nor fall.

8 Start the engine and run it for at least a minute. Switch off, then depress the brake pedal several times. The pedal travel should decrease with each application.

9 If the foregoing tests do not prove satisfactory, check the servo vacuum hose and non-return valve for security and leakage at the valve grommet.

10 If the brake servo operates properly in the test, but still gives less effective service on the road, the air filter through which air flows into the servo should be inspected. A dirty filter will limit the formation of a difference in pressure across the servo diaphragm.

11 The servo unit itself cannot be repaired and therefore a complete renewal is necessary if the measures described are not effective.

17 Vacuum servo air filter - renewal

1 Working under the facia panel, pull the dust excluder off the servo and slide it up the pushrod.

2 Using a scriber or similar tool, pick out the filter and cut it to remove it.

3 Cut the new filter as shown in Fig. 9.38 and push it neatly into position. Refit the dust excluding boot.

18 Vacuum servo non-return valve - renewal

1 Disconnect the vacuum hose from the connector on the front face of the servo unit.

2 Pull and twist the non-return valve elbow from its grommet.

3 Refitting is a reversal of removal; use a new grommet. A smear of rubber grease on the elbow spigot will ease its entry into the grommet. Do not force the elbow when fitting as it is possible to push the grommet into the interior of the servo.

16.1 Master cylinder and vacuum servo unit assembly – 1.7 litre model

Fig. 9.38 Vacuum servo air filter (Sec 17)

A Cut   F Filter location

Fig. 9.39 Vacuum servo non-return valve and grommet (Sec 18)

Fig. 9.40 Servo unit mounting nuts (arrowed) (Sec 19)

20.4 Handbrake cable central linkage with primary rod locknut arrowed

20.11 Handbrake cable endpiece (arrowed) – rear disc brake

19 Vacuum servo unit - removal and refitting

1 Remove the master cylinder, as described in Section 12.

2 Disconnect the vacuum hose from the servo unit.

3 Unscrew the trim panel under the facia on the driver's side. With the panel released, detach the fusebox from the hinged lid and remove the cigar lighter (Chapter 12). Disconnect the heater ventilation duct if necessary for access.

4 Disconnect the pushrod from the brake pedal by extracting the split pin and the clevis pin.

5 Working inside the car unscrew the brake servo mounting nuts.

6 Withdraw the servo from the engine compartment.

7 When refitting the servo unit and the master cylinder, check the pushrod dimensions (X and L) as described in Section 12 and Fig. 9.32.

20 Handbrake - adjustment

All models

1 The handbrake will normally be kept in adjustment by the action of the drum brake automatic adjuster or the self-adjusting action of the rear disc calipers.

2 The handbrake should only be adjusted when new brake linings, new handbrake cables, or a new handbrake lever has been fitted.

3 Raise the car at the rear and support it on axle stands.

4 Fully release the handbrake, then, working under the vehicle, loosen off the primary rod locknut and completely unscrew the central linkage (photo).

Drum brakes

5 Remove the two rear wheels, then the brake drum on each side.

6 Move the knurled automatic brake adjuster in each direction to ensure that it is operational, then loosen it off by 5 to 6 notches. Check that the cables slide freely and that the handbrake actuating lever is in contact with the brake shoes.

7 Now progressively tension the cables at the central adjuster so that the actuator lever of each rear brake unit starts to move at the 1st to 2nd notch position of the handbrake control lever travel. Retighten the primary rod locknut.

8 Fully release the handbrake, refit the brake drums and lower the vehicle.

9 Depress the brake pedal several times to settle the shoes. Apply the handbrake lever and check that it locks the rear wheels. The handbrake lever should fully apply the brakes when pulled over 9 notches.

Disc brakes

10 Remove the two rear wheels, then check that the handbrake actuating levers move without binding and move them as far as possible to the rear.

11 Progressively increase the tension of the cables from the central adjustment point. Adjust so that the cable end piece is just in contact with the actuator lever but does not actually move it (photo).

12 Now readjust the setting so that the actuating levers begin to move between the 1st and 2nd notch of the control lever travel, remaining lifted at the 2nd notch position. Retighten the primary rod locknut.

13 Refit the rear wheel and check the handbrake for satisfactory operation as described in paragraph 9, then lower the car.

21 Handbrake lever - removal and refitting

1 Chock the roadwheels, then fully release the handbrake.

2 Raise and support the vehicle at the rear on axle stands.

3 Working underneath the vehicle, extract the retaining clip from the cable clevis pin. Withdraw the clevis pin and detach the control rod from the central linkage.

4 Remove the trim cover from the safety belt anchors at the rear of the handbrake, then undo the two safety belt anchor bolts (photo).

5 Disconnect the handbrake switch wire, undo the handbrake lever retaining bolts, then withdraw the lever.

6 Refit in the reverse order of removal. Adjust the handbrake as described in Section 20 to give the correct lever travel.

22 Handbrake cables - removal and refitting

1 Raise the rear of the car and remove the rear roadwheels.

2 Fully release the handbrake.

3 On models with drum brakes, remove the drums and disconnect the cable(s) from the shoe lever(s).

4 On models with rear disc brakes, disconnect the cable(s) from the caliper lever(s).

5 If there is any difficulty in releasing the cable end fittings, slacken the adjuster on the handbrake primary rod right off.

6 Working at the central adjustment point, extract the clip, remove the clevis pin and disconnect the equaliser from the primary rod. Slip the cable out of the equaliser groove.

9

21.4 View showing handbrake lever (A), switch (B) and safety belt anchor bolts (C)

7 Disconnect the cables from their body clips.

8 Renew the cable by reversing the removal operations. Apply grease to the equaliser groove. Adjust as described in Section 20.

23 Brake pedal - removal and refitting

1 Remove the lower facia trim panel (see Section 19).

2 Disconnect the pushrod from the brake pedal arm by extracting the spring clip and pushing out the clevis pin (photo).

3 Disconnect the return and tension springs and remove the spring clip from the end of the pedal cross-shaft.

4 Push the cross-shaft out of the pedal bracket until the pedal can be removed.

5 Refitting is reversal of removal.

Fig. 9.41 Anti-lock braking system (ABS) layout (left-hand drive version shown) (Sec 25)

1 Hydraulic unit	5 Instrument panel
2 Computer	warning lights
3 Speed sensor	6 Compensator
4 Sensor target	7 Disc brake units

23.2 Brake pedal pushrod clevis pin (A) and stop-lamp switch (B)

24 Stop-lamp switch - adjustment

1 The stop-lamp switch should be adjusted by means of its locknut so that the stop-lamps come on when the switch plunger moves out about 1.0 mm (0.039 in) when the brake pedal is depressed (see photo 23.2).

25 Anti-lock braking system (ABS) - description

1 The hydraulic components used in this system are the same as those used in a conventional braking system but the following additional items are fitted. Refer to Fig. 9.41.

A speed sensor (3) on each wheel

Four targets (4) mounted at the front of the driveshafts and at the rear of the rear hubs (photo)

An electronic computer (2) comprising a self-monitoring system, a hydraulic unit (1) which incorporates a pressure regulating valve, and a high pressure pump

Two warning lamps are fitted to the instrument panel

2 The anti-lock braking system operates in the following way. As soon as the car roadspeed exceeds 6.0 kph (3.7 mph) the system becomes operational.

3 When the brakes are applied, the speed sensors detect the rapidly falling speed of any roadwheel which happens if it starts to lock. The computer operates a regulator valve to prevent hydraulic braking pressure rising and to reduce it until the particular roadwheel deceleration ceases.

4 As soon as this deceleration ceases, a reverse phase commences to again raise the hydraulic pressure to normal.

5 The anti-lock cycle can be repeated up to ten times per second.

6 In order to maintain even braking, one rear wheel locking will subject the opposite brake to the same pressure variation cycle.

7 The warning lamp indicates to the driver the fact that the system is non-operational.

25.1 ABS sensor target wheel (arrowed) on the front driveshaft

Should this happen, the normal braking system remains fully operational, but the fault in the ABS must be repaired at the earliest opportunity.

8 If the warning lamp illuminates intermittently, check that the wheel sensor lead connections are clean and secure.

9 The warning switch in the fluid reservoir is a two-stage type which first activates the handbrake warning lamp on the instrument panel when the fluid drops below the normal minimum level. If the fluid level continues to drop, the switch then activates a second warning lamp on the instrument panel.

10 When the second warning lamp is illuminated due to a further drop in the fluid level, the ABS continues to operate on the rear wheels only with normal braking to the front wheels.

11 In the event of both warning lamps operating simultaneously, it indicates that the pressure pump has a malfunction and is not working. Again the system will operate the rear wheel brakes only, with normal braking to the front wheels.

26 ABS wheel speed sensors - removal and refitting

Front wheel speed sensor

1 Unscrew the sensor retaining bolt and detach the sensor from the brake unit, and the lead from the strut (photos).

26.1A Front ABS sensor unit and retaining bolt

26.1B Front ABS sensor lead and attachment points (arrowed)

26.9 Rear ABS sensor and lead (arrowed)

Fig. 9.42 ABS sensor lead connection (2) in engine compartment (Sec 26)

2 Disconnect the sensor lead connector in the engine compartment adjacent to the top of the shock absorber turret. Detach the lead from its retainers and remove the sensor.

3 Refit in the reverse order of removal. Smear the sensor with a light coating of Molykote FB 180 grease before connecting it.

Front wheel speed sensor target

4 Remove the driveshaft as described in Chapter 8.

5 The sensor target can now be removed from the driveshaft by pressing it free as shown in Fig. 9.43.

6 Refit in reverse order of removal. Smear the target with Loctite Scelbloc before pressing it into position.

Rear wheel speed sensor

7 Raise and support the car at the rear on axle stands. Remove the roadwheel on the side concerned.

8 Undo the sensor retaining bolt and detach the sensor unit, then unclip the sensor cable from its retainers.

9 Detach the rear axle fairing to gain access to the sensor lead connector. Disconnect the lead and remove the sensor (photo).

10 Refit in the reverse order of removal. Lubricate the sensor with a light smear of Molykote FB 180 grease before fitting. Ensure that the lead connections are clean and secure.

27 ABS computer unit - removal and refitting

1 The ABS computer is located under the carpet on the outboard side of the front passenger seat. Fold back the carpet for access (photo).

2 Disconnect the battery earth lead.

3 Undo the two retaining bolts and remove the cover from the computer unit. Lift the unit from its housing and detach the lead connector. Handle the computer with care.

4 Refit in the reverse order of removal. Ensure that the lead is securely connected.

28 ABS hydraulic unit - removal and refitting

1 Disconnect the battery earth lead.

2 Depress the brake pedal twenty times in succession to reduce the pressure in the system. The pedal action will become hard.

3 Use a suitable syringe and empty the fluid from the reservoir (photo).

4 Disconnect the leads from the five connectors shown in Fig. 9.44. Also disconnect the earth lead and wiring mounting lug at (4).

5 Disconnect the clutch master cylinder hose and the rigid outlet pipes. Allow for fluid

Fig. 9.43 Pressing sensor target from a driveshaft (Sec 26)

spillage and clean any from adjacent paintwork and fittings. Plug the hose and pipes to prevent further leakage and the ingress of dirt.

6 Remove the lower facia trim panels and the lower steering column covers.

7 Remove the retaining clip and withdraw the brake pedal pushrod clevis pin.

8 Undo the retaining nuts securing the hydraulic unit to the bulkhead, then remove the hydraulic unit and its seal from the bulkhead.

9 Refit in the reverse order of removal. Ensure that the seal is correctly located when fitting

27.1 ABS computer unit location (carpet removed for access)

28.3 ABS hydraulic unit connections and reservoir

Fig. 9.44 ABS hydraulic unit lead connections (arrowed), earth lead mounting lug (4) and clutch master cylinder hose connection to the reservoir (5) (Sec 28)

Fig. 9.45 ABS hydraulic unit pipe identification (Sec 28)

Fig. 9.46 ABS hydraulic unit high pressure hose (I), pump retaining bolt (2), pump connector (1), reservoir mounting lug (7), and feed unit (E) – left-hand drive type shown (Sec 29)

Fig. 9.47 Locate spacer and new O-ring seal (6) to the take-off port and high pressure hose unions (1). Smear bolt threads (2) with locking fluid (Sec 29)

the hydraulic unit to the bulkhead. When connecting the hydraulic pipes, they should be positioned as shown in Fig. 9.45.

10 On completion, top up the brake fluid level and bleed the system as described in Section 15.

29 ABS master cylinder/amplifier unit - removal and refitting

1 Remove the hydraulic unit as described in the previous Section.
2 Disconnect and remove the reservoir low pressure hose.
3 Disconnect the high pressure hose and plug the take-off ports.
4 Disconnect and remove the hydraulic pump connector.
5 Undo the pump retaining bolt, and remove the feed unit assembly and the master cylinder low pressure hose.
6 Remove the mounting lug, then unclip the reservoir and remove it.
7 Disconnect the master cylinder pipes from the regulator unit and plug their take-off ports.
8 Undo the retaining bolts and remove the regulator unit.
9 Renew as necessary, no repairs are possible.
10 Ensure that all parts are clean during reassembly. Start by refitting the low pressure hose to the master cylinder unit, then locate the regulator unit and rigid pipe connections. Smear the mounting bolt threads with locking fluid.
11 Refit the feed unit, ensuring that the 'silent-bloc' bushes are in good order. Apply some locking fluid to the retaining bolt threads.

12 Locate the high pressure hose and new O-ring seals.
13 The reservoir can now be fitted, but ensure that the anchor cups are in good condition and fit a new O-ring seal to the take-off port.
14 Refit the reservoir mounting lug, the hydraulic pump and the master cylinder low pressure hoses to the reservoir. Smear the mounting lug retaining bolt threads with locking fluid before fitting.
15 Refit the hydraulic unit as described in Section 28.

30 ABS regulator unit - removal and refitting

1 Remove the hydraulic unit as described in Section 28.
2 Remove the reservoir mounting lug by undoing its retaining bolt, then unclip and remove the reservoir. Unclip the two low pressure hoses from the reservoir.
3 Remove the rigid hydraulic pipes from the master cylinder and regulator unit. Plug the take-off ports.
4 Undo the two retaining bolts and remove the regulator unit.
5 Refitting is a reversal of the removal procedure. Smear the retaining bolt threads with locking fluid before fitting, renew the take-off port O-ring seals and ensure that the anchor cups are in good condition.
6 Refit the hydraulic unit as described in Section 28.

31 ABS hydraulic feed unit - removal and refitting

1 The feed unit can be removed with the hydraulic unit in position, but in this instance, the four bolts securing the hydraulic unit in

position against the bulkhead must be removed in order to allow the pump retaining bolt removal.
2 Detach the wiring connector to the pressostat, then unscrew and remove the pressostat.
3 Detach the accumulator unit. If the hydraulic unit is in situ, release the pressure from the accumulator before removal. To do this follow the procedure given in Section 32 paragraph 1.
4 Disconnect the high pressure hose and plug its take-off port.
5 Undo the bolt securing the pump unit, then remove the feed unit. As it is withdrawn detach the pump-to-reservoir hose.
6 Refit in the reverse order of removal. Renew the high pressure hose O-ring seal and the bushes if they are worn or perished. Smear the threads of the feed unit bolt with locking fluid. The pressostat and the accumulator must also be fitted with new seals.
7 **Do not** switch on the ignition until after assembly is completed.

32 ABS accumulator - removal and refitting

1 Before removing the accumulator, ensure that the ignition is switched off, then pump the brake pedal twenty times to reduce the system pressure. The brake pedal operating pressure will increase. **Do not** switch the ignition on again until the accumulator is refitted.
2 Fit a suitable strap wrench over the accumulator (in a similar manner to that for oil filter removal), and remove the accumulator.
3 Refit in the reverse order of removal. Use a new O-ring seal.
4 Switch the ignition on, then when the pump is heard to stop, depress the brake pedal several times so that the pump is heard to restart and then stop again. Check the hydraulic fluid level in the reservoir and top up if necessary.

Fault finding - braking system

Before diagnosing faults from the following chart, check that any braking irregularities are not caused by:
- *Uneven and incorrect tyre pressures*
- *Wear in the steering mechanism*
- *Defects in the suspension and dampers*
- *Misalignment of the bodyframe*

Note: *Any suspected faults on the ABS should be referred to a dealer*

Pedal travels a long way before the brakes operate
- ☐ Air in hydraulic system
- ☐ Brake shoes set too far from the drums

Stopping ability poor, even though pedal pressure is firm
- ☐ Linings, discs or drums badly worn or scored
- ☐ One or more wheel hydraulic cylinders seized, resulting in some brake shoes not pressing against the drums (or pads against disc)
- ☐ Brake linings contaminated with oil
- ☐ Wrong type of linings fitted (too hard)

Car veers to one side when the brakes are applied
- ☐ Brake pads or linings on one side are contaminated with oil
- ☐ Hydraulic wheel cylinder on one side partially or fully seized
- ☐ A mixture of lining materials fitted between sides
- ☐ Brake discs not matched
- ☐ Unequal wear between sides caused by partially seized wheel cylinders

Pedal feels spongy when the brakes are applied
- ☐ Air is present in the hydraulic system

Pedal feels springy when the brakes are applied
- ☐ Brake linings not bedded into the drums (after fitting new ones)
- ☐ Master cylinder or brake backplate mounting bolts loose
- ☐ Severe wear in brake drums causing distortion when brakes are applied
- ☐ Discs out of true

Pedal travels right down with little or no resistance and brakes are virtually non-operative
- ☐ Leak in hydraulic system resulting in lack of pressure for operating wheel cylinders
- ☐ If no signs of leakage are apparent the master cylinder internal seals are failing to sustain pressure

Binding, juddering, overheating
- ☐ One or a combination of reasons given above
- ☐ Shoes installed incorrectly with reference to leading and trailing ends
- ☐ Broken shoe return spring
- ☐ Disc out-of-round
- ☐ Drum distorted
- ☐ Incorrect pedal or handbrake adjustment

Lack of servo assistance
- ☐ Vacuum hose disconnected or leaking
- ☐ Non-return valve defective or incorrectly fitted
- ☐ Servo internal defect

9

Notes

Chapter 10 Suspension and steering

For modifications, and information applicable to later models, see Supplement at end of manual

Contents

Degrees of difficulty

| **Easy,** suitable for novice with little experience 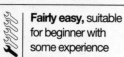 | **Fairly easy,** suitable for beginner with some experience | **Fairly difficult,** suitable for competent DIY mechanic | **Difficult,** suitable for experienced DIY mechanic | **Very difficult,** suitable for expert DIY or professional |

Specifications

Front suspension

Type	Independent by MacPherson struts with coil springs, integral telescopic shock absorbers and anti-roll bar
Toe setting:	
1.7 litre models	1.0 ± 1.0 mm (0.039 ± 0.039 in) toe-out
2.0 litre non-Turbo models	2.0 ± 1.0 mm (0.078 ± 0.039 in) toe-out
2.0 litre Turbo models	1.0 ± 1.0 mm (0.039 ± 0.039 in) toe-out
Underbody height (H1 minus H2 - see Fig. 10.18):	
1.7 litre models	84.0 ± 7.5 mm (3.28 ± 0.29 in)
2.0 litre non-Turbo models	98.0 ± 7.5 mm (3.82 ± 0.29 in)
2.0 litre Turbo models	119.0 ± 7.5 mm (4.64 ± 0.29 in)

Rear suspension

Type	Trailing arms with four-bar transverse link rods. Telescopic shock absorbers with coil springs on some models
Toe setting (all models)	2.0 to 5.0 mm (0.078 to 0.195 in) toe-in
Underbody height (H4 minus H5 - see Fig. 10.18):	
1.7 litre Saloon models	20.0 ± 7.5 mm (0.78 ± 0.29 in)
2.0 litre non-Turbo Saloon models	30.0 ± 7.5 mm (1.17 ± 0.29 in)
2.0 litre Turbo models	52.0 ± 7.5 mm (2.03 ± 0.29 in)
Savanna models	10.0 ± 7.5 mm (0.39 ± 0.29 in)

Steering

Type	Rack and pinion with collapsible safety column. Power assistance on some models
Power steering:	
Fluid type	Dexron type ATF
Fluid capacity	1.1 litres (1.9 pints)

10

Torque wrench settings

	Nm	lbf ft
Front suspension		
1.7 litre models:		
Lower suspension arm inboard pivot nuts	80	59
Lower balljoint clamp bolt nut	60	44
Anti-roll bar bearing nuts (to subframe)	30	22
Anti-roll bar bearing nuts (to arm)	30	22
Lower balljoint retaining nuts	75	55
Hub carrier-to-shock absorber bolts	80	59
Shock absorber upper retaining bolts	25	18
Shock absorber cup nut	60	44
2.0 litre models (where different from 1.7 litre models):		
Lower balljoint clamp bolt nut (Turbo models)	55	40
Anti-roll bar bearing nuts (to arm)	80	59
Lower balljoint retaining nuts	80	59
Hub carrier-to-shock absorber bolts	200	147
Rear suspension - all models		
Shock absorber top mounting	80	59
Shock absorber lower mounting	85	62
Rear axle mounting	85	62
Steering		
1.7 litre models:		
Steering arm (outer) balljoint nut	40	29
Suspension arm/hub carrier balljoint nut	60	44
Steering arm inner balljoint	50	37
Steering gear bolts	50	37
Steering wheel nut	40	29
Column universal joint coupling nuts	25	18
2.0 litre models (where different from 1.7 litre models):		
Steering arm adjuster sleeve locknuts:		
Outer locknut	35	26
Inner locknut	50	37
Steering arm bracket-to-rack:		
Bolts	40	29
Bolt locknuts	35	26
Steering arm-to-bracket bolts	35	26

1 General description

The front suspension is of independent type with coil springs and telescopic shock absorbers. An anti-roll bar is fitted to the front suspension on all models.

The rear suspension consists of a beam axle, trailing control arms and telescopic shock absorbers. On some models the shock absorber incorporates an external coil spring. Torsion bars and anti-roll bars are incorporated in the rear axle member on all models.

The steering gear is of rack and pinion type on all models, with power assistance fitted to some models. On some models the steering column incorporates a height adjustment mechanism.

Fig. 10.1 Suspension and steering layout – 1.7 litre transverse engine models (Sec 1)

Fig. 10.2 Suspension and steering layout – 2.0 litre longitudinal engine models (Sec 1)

Fig. 10.3 Power steering fluid reservoir – maintain fluid level 10 mm (0.4 in) above the grille (2) (Sec 2)

2 Maintenance

1 At the specified intervals, check all suspension flexible bushes for wear.
2 Occasionally check the condition and security of all steering and suspension nuts, bolts and components.
3 Inspect the struts and shock absorbers for signs of fluid leakage. If anything more than a slight weep from the top gland is evident, then the unit must be renewed.
4 If the car tends to roll on bends or dip under heavy braking, check the action of the struts and shock absorbers by pressing the corner of the car downwards and then releasing it. The up and down momentum of the car should be damped out immediately. If the car oscillates up and down several times, the condition of the particular unit should be checked after removal from the car.
5 Inspect the steering rack bellows for splits and loss of lubricant. Look particularly closely at the bottom of the bellows pleats when the steering is at full lock. Splits here can often pass unnoticed.
6 With the help of an assistant, check for wear in the steering arm end balljoints. Move

the steering wheel quickly a few degrees in each direction and observe the balljoints for shake or lost movement. If evident renew the balljoints.
7 Check the front suspension lower arm balljoint by inserting a lever carefully between the arm and the hub carrier and checking for vertical movement.
8 At the specified intervals, check the front wheel alignment.
9 On models with power-assisted steering, check the fluid level in the reservoir at the intervals specified in 'Routine maintenance'.
10 When necessary, top up the fluid level in the reservoir, but only use the specified fluid type (photo). The fluid level should be 10 mm (0.4 in) above the grille in the reservoir. Do not overfill or allow any dirt to enter the hydraulic system.

3 Front anti-roll bar - removal and refitting

1 With the weight of the vehicle on its wheels, undo the retaining bolts and detach the anti-roll bar from the subframe by removing its mounting block on each side (photos). Remove the engine undertray for access if necessary.

2.10 Topping-up the power steering fluid level – 2.0 litre model

2 Undo the retaining bolt nuts and remove the mounting block bracket from the suspension arm on each side (photo). On 2.0 litre models these nuts also secure the suspension arm lower balljoint and therefore, to prevent the joint from moving, refit a nut to one of the bolts whilst the anti-roll bar is removed from the vehicle.
3 On 2.0 litre models, remove the anti-roll bar from under the car. On 1.7 litre models, jack up the right-hand side of the car, support it on stands and remove the roadwheel. Withdraw the anti-roll bar from the right-hand side wheelarch.
4 Renew the rubber bushes if they are perished or worn.
5 Locate the anti-roll bar in position and refit the mounting blocks to the subframe. Do not fully tighten the bolts at this stage.

10

3.1A Anti-roll bar-to-subframe mounting – 1.7 litre model

3.1B Anti-roll bar-to-subframe mounting – 2.0 litre model

3.2 Anti-roll bar-to-suspension arm mounting – 2.0 litre model

Fig. 10.4 Sectional view showing front suspension and steering components on 1.7 litre models (Sec 4)

Fig. 10.5 Sectional view showing front suspension and steering components on 2.0 litre models (Sec 4)

6 On 1.7 litre models refit the roadwheel and lower the car to the ground.

7 Refit the mounting block brackets to the suspension arms on each side. It may be necessary to have an assistant push down on the front of the car to allow alignment of the mounting block bracket bolt holes. Once the bolts are engaged, release any pressure on the front of the car and tighten the nuts and bolts on all the mountings to the specified torque.

8 Where applicable, refit the engine undertray.

4 Front shock absorber and coil spring - removal and refitting

Note: *Overhaul of the shock absorber/coil spring unit must be entrusted to a Renault dealer*

1 Loosen off the front roadwheel bolts on the side concerned, raise the car at the front and support on axle stands. Remove the roadwheel.

2 On 2.0 litre models, disconnect the steering arm at the outboard end balljoint (see Section 12 for details).

3 Loosen off the two nuts on the shock absorber-to-hub carrier retaining bolts so that the end of each nut is flush with the end of its bolt (photo). Now tap the end face of each nut to drive the bolts out so that the serrated section under each bolt head is clear of the shock absorber. Remove the two nuts and withdraw the bolts.

4 Unscrew the three bolts securing the shock absorber strut to the upper mounting (photo).

5 Press down on the lower arm and remove the shock absorber/coil spring unit. Take care not to damage the driveshaft bellows as the unit is removed.

6 Dismantling of the coil spring/shock absorber unit is not considered a task to be undertaken by the home mechanic. The spring is fitted under a very high compression

loading and it is essential that special Renault tools are used for the removal and refitting of the spring. A normal coil spring compressor is not suitable, and any attempt at dismantling without the correct tools and specialist knowledge will probably result in damage and/or personal injury. It is therefore recommended that the strut is taken to a Renault dealer for dismantling and replacement as necessary.

7 Refitting is a reversal of the removal procedure. Ensure that the shock absorber-to-hub carrier bolts are fitted from the rear (with the nuts towards the front of the vehicle). Tighten the retaining bolts to their specified torque wrench settings.

4.3 Hub carrier-to-shock absorber retaining bolts – 1.7 litre model

4.4 Shock absorber upper mounting bolts (arrowed) – 2.0 litre non-Turbo model

Fig. 10.6 Front lower suspension arm
removal – 1.7 litre models (Sec 5)

3 Arm-to-subframe pivot bolts
A Balljoint plastic protection washer

5 Front lower suspension arm
- removal and refitting

1 Unscrew the retaining nuts and disconnect
the anti-roll bar from the lower suspension
arm. On 2.0 litre models, the retaining bolts
also secure the lower balljoint and one of the
nuts should be refitted once the anti-roll bar is

5.1A Front suspension arm outboard end –
1.7 litre model

1 Anti-roll bar mounting bolt
2 Balljoint retaining bolts

5.4A Front suspension arm front inboard
pivot mounting -1.7 litre model

Fig. 10.7 Front lower suspension arm
removal – 2.0 litre models (Sec 5)

1 Balljoint unit retaining nut
3 Arm-to-subframe pivot bolts
A Balljoint plastic protection washer

separated from the suspension arm to prevent
the balljoint from moving. Press downwards
on the anti-roll bar to separate it from the
suspension arm (photos).
2 Raise the vehicle at the front end and
support on axle stands.
3 Undo and remove the nut and washer, then
withdraw the clamp bolt securing the lower
suspension arm balljoint to the hub carrier
(photo).
4 Undo and remove the two nuts, washers
and pivot bolts securing the arm to the
subframe (photos).
5 Pull the arm down to disengage the

5.1B Front suspension arm outboard end –
2.0 litre Turbo model

5.4B Front suspension arm rear inboard
pivot mounting – 1.7 litre model

Fig. 10.8 Lower suspension arm inner pivot
bush renewal (Sec 5)

Remove/refit bush using 30 mm (1.18 in)
diameter tube for 1.7 litre models or 34 mm
(1.33 in) tube for 2.0 litre models.
Dimension 'A' between bush inner edges
must be as specified (see text)

balljoint, then lever it out of its inner pivot
mountings. Recover the balljoint washer.
6 If the inner pivot bushes are to be renewed
this can be done using suitable lengths of
tube and a press or wide-opening vice.
Renew the bushes one at a time so that the
distance between the bush inner edges is
maintained at 146.5 to 147.5 mm (5.77 to
5.81 in) for 1.7 litre models, or 189.5 to
190.5 mm (7.46 to 7.49 in) for 2.0 litre models
(see Fig. 10.8). Note that the front and rear
bushes differ on 2.0 litre models, so check
that correct replacements are obtained.

5.3 Lower suspension arm balljoint-to-hub
carrier clamp bolt – 2.0 litre model

10

5.4C Front suspension arm front inboard
pivot mounting – 2.0 litre model

5.4D Front suspension arm rear inboard pivot mounting – 2.0 litre model

7 Refitting the lower suspension arm is the reverse sequence to removal, bearing in mind the following points:
(a) Ensure that the plastic washer is in position over the balljoint shank before refitting the balljoint to the hub carrier
(b) Tighten all nuts and bolts to the specified torque, but do not tighten the pivot bolts and anti-roll bar clamp bolts until the car has been lowered to the ground and rolled back and forth to settle the suspension

6 Front lower suspension arm balljoint - removal and refitting

1 Proceed as described in the previous Section, paragraphs 1 to 5 inclusive, but do not fully remove the nuts and bolts securing the lower suspension arm to the subframe, only loosen them.
2 If the balljoint gaiter is damaged, or the joint is worn, it must be renewed as a unit. Unbolt it from the suspension arm for renewal.
3 Refitting is a reversal of the removal procedure. Ensure that the plastic protector washer is fitted to the balljoint and tighten the retaining bolts and nuts to the specified torque wrench settings.

8.3B Rear shock absorber lower mounting bolt – 1.7 litre Savanna

Fig. 10.9 Rear shock absorber unit, retaining bolts and washers (Sec 8)

Note: An external coil spring is fitted to the unit on some models

7 Front hub carrier - removal and refitting

1 Loosen the hub nut, then raise the car at the front and support it on safety stands. Remove the appropriate front wheel.
2 Remove the hub nut and recover the thrust washer.
3 Undo the two bolts securing the brake caliper to the hub carrier. Slide the caliper, complete with pads, off the disc and tie it up using string or wire from a convenient place under the wheel arch.
4 On 1.7 litre models, undo the locknut securing the steering arm balljoint to the hub carrier. Using a suitable separator tool (see Section 12), release the balljoint and move the steering arm to one side.
5 At the base of the hub carrier, undo and remove the nut and washer, then withdraw the balljoint clamp bolt (see photo 5.3).
6 Undo and remove the nuts and washers, then withdraw the two bolts securing the shock absorber to the upper part of the hub carrier.
7 Release the hub carrier from the shock absorber and then lift it, while pushing down

8.3C Rear shock absorber upper mounting bolt – 2.0 litre Saloon

8.3A Rear shock absorber upper mounting bolt – 1.7 litre Savanna

on the suspension arm, to disengage the lower balljoint. Withdraw the hub carrier from the driveshaft and remove it from the car. If the driveshaft is a tight fit in the hub bearings, tap it out using a plastic mallet, or use a suitable puller.
8 If the front hub bearings are to be renewed, refer to Section 10 or 11 (as applicable) of Chapter 8 for details.
9 Refitting is the reverse sequence to removal, bearing in mind the following points:
(a) Ensure that the mating faces of the disc and hub flange are clean and flat before refitting the disc (if applicable)
(b) Tighten all nuts and bolts to the specified torque

8 Rear shock absorber - removal and refitting

1 Jack up the rear of the car and support it on axle stands. Place a jack beneath the suspension trailing arm on the appropriate side of the car. Using the jack, raise the trailing arm slightly. Supplement the jack with an axle stand or blocks if necessary - ensure that the trailing arm is securely supported.
2 Remove the rear roadwheel on the side concerned.
3 Unscrew and remove the upper and lower rear shock absorber mounting bolts and remove the shock absorber (photos).

8.3D Rear shock absorber lower mounting bolt – 2.0 litre Saloon

4 Examine the shock absorber body for signs of damage or corrosion, and for any trace of fluid leakage. Check the piston rod for distortion, wear, pitting or corrosion along its entire length. On units that are not fitted with an external coil spring, test the operation of the shock absorber, while holding it in an upright position, by moving the piston rod through a full stroke and then through short strokes of 50 to 100 mm (2 to 4 in). In both cases the resistance felt should be smooth and continuous. If the resistance is jerky or uneven, or if there is any sign of wear or damage to the unit, renewal is necessary. Also check the condition of the upper and lower mounting bushes and renew them if there are any signs of deterioration or swelling of the rubber. Note that new shock absorbers are supplied complete with mounting bushes.

5 Before fitting a new shock absorber unit, hand pump the unit several times to ensure that it is fully primed.

6 Refit in the reverse order of removal. Smear the mounting bolt threads with thread locking compound before fitting. Do not fully tighten the retaining nut and bolt to the specified torque wrench setting until after the vehicle is lowered to the ground and is free-standing under its own weight.

9 Rear axle -
removal and refitting

1 A trolley jack and the aid of an assistant will be required to support and steady the axle unit during its removal and subsequent refitting.

2 Raise and support the vehicle at the rear on axle stands.

3 Remove the rear roadwheels.

4 Refer to Chapter 9 and disconnect the following brake system components from the rear axle:

(a) *The secondary handbrake cables*
(b) *The hydraulic brake lines*
(c) *The brake compensator (where applicable). On the load-controlled type compensator, take care not to change the setting of the preset adjuster nut (see Chapter 9)*

5 Unbolt and disconnect the rear shock absorbers at their top or bottom ends. Ensure that each trailing arm is well supported on a jack before removing the shock absorber mounting bolts, then slowly lower the jack until tension on the trailing arm is released.

6 Position the trolley jack under the centre of the axle and raise it to take the weight of the axle when the retaining bolts are removed. *It is important that the jack only supports the weight of the axle and is not raised to take the weight of the vehicle.*

7 Undo the retaining bolts on each side, check that the cables and hydraulic lines are clear, then carefully lower the axle unit and withdraw it from under the vehicle (photo).

Fig. 10.10 Rear axle components (Sec 9)

1 Axle beam unit   2 Link block   3 Anti-roll bars   4 Suspension bars

The aid of an assistant during this operation will be useful in steadying the axle as it is removed.

8 Refitting is a reversal of the removal procedure. Tighten the axle and shock absorber retaining bolts to their specified torque wrench settings, the latter only when the vehicle is lowered and standing under its own weight.

9 Reconnect the brake system components and bleed the hydraulic system with reference to the respective Sections of Chapter 9. On completion arrange to have the brake compensator adjustment checked at the earliest opportunity by a Renault dealer.

10 Rear axle torsion bars -
removal and refitting

Note: *Unless the rear axle is being replaced as a unit, the removal and refitting of the torsion bars (suspension and anti-roll bars) is a task best entrusted to a Renault dealer due to the special tools and setting procedures required. Read through this Section before starting so as to ensure awareness of the tool requirements and procedures involved*

1 Raise and support the vehicle at the rear on axle stands.

2 Remove the rear roadwheels.

3 Remove the rear shock absorbers (Section 8).

4 Prise off the cap (where fitted) from the outer face of the trailing arm mounting bracket and extract the clip (photo).

5 The suspension bar can now be withdrawn outwards using a slide hammer such as Renault tool Emb 880 or a suitable alternative.

6 Once the splines of the bar are free, the bar can be withdrawn completely from its location. Repeat this procedure for the opposite suspension bar.

7 Remove an anti-roll bar from one side using

9.7 Rear axle mounting bolts (arrowed) – 2.0 litre model

10.4 Remove cap from trailing arm mounting and extract clip (arrowed) – 2.0 litre model

10.7 Rear suspension anti-roll bar location (arrowed) – 2.0 litre Turbo model

Fig. 10.11 Suspension bar removal using a slide hammer (Sec 10)

1.7 litre Saloon   X = 496 mm (19.5 in)
2.0 litre Saloon   X = 485 mm (19.0 in)
1.7 and 2.0 litre Savanna
*   X = 475 mm (18.7 in)*

Fig. 10.12 Rear trailing arm setting – dimension 'X' should be set as specified in text according to model (Sec 10)

the slide hammer as described for the suspension bars (photo).

8 Remove the link block, then the remaining anti-roll bar.

9 Before refitting the torsion bars it is necessary to position the trailing arm so that the correct underbody height of the car is obtained when it is lowered onto its wheels. This is done as follows:

10 Measure the distance from the centre of the shock absorber lower mounting stud on the trailing arm to the centre of the shock absorber upper mounting bolt under the wheel arch. Move the trailing arm up or down as necessary until the distance (X) in Fig. 10.12 is exactly as follows according to model:

If it was necessary to move the arm up to achieve the setting, support it in this position using a jack. If it was necessary to pull the arm down, support it with a length of wood cut to length and small packing pieces. Take care over this procedure as this is a critical dimension and will determine the success of subsequent operations.

11 Repeat this procedure to set the opposite trailing arm in the same manner.

12 An alignment index mark on the end face of the suspension bar bearing is used to set the initial fitted position of the suspension bar.

If not already marked, an equivalent mark must also be made on the end face of the anti-roll bar bearing. This is achieved by aligning the hole centres as shown in Fig. 10.14 using a rule and making a mark adjacent to the bottom of a splined tooth.

13 The installation procedure for the bars now differs according to model.

1.7 litre Saloon models

14 Grease the splines of the left-hand anti-roll bar, then insert the bar so that the index mark on its end face is offset by five teeth to the index mark of the bearing end face, as shown in Fig. 10.15.

15 Fit the link block to the inner end of the anti-roll bar and centralise it within the V-section of the rear axle beam.

16 Now fit the opposing anti-roll bar with the index mark offset from its bearing end face index mark by five teeth in the opposite direction to the first anti-roll bar when viewed from the outer end.

17 Grease the left-hand suspension bar and fit it so that its index mark is offset by four teeth from its bearing index mark, as shown in Fig. 10.15. The link block on the inboard end of the anti-roll bars can be raised to ease engagement if necessary.

18 Repeat this procedure with the opposing

Fig. 10.13 End views of suspension bars showing identification marks (Sec 10)

1 Initial setting mark
G Left-hand suspension bar identification mark
D Right-hand suspension bar identification mark

Fig. 10.14 End view of fitted suspension and anti-roll bars (Sec 10)

1 Suspension bar alignment index mark
2 Anti-roll bar alignment index mark

Fig. 10.15 On 1.7 litre Saloon models, offset the left-hand anti-roll and suspension bars as shown (Sec 10)

A Suspension bar – offset by four teeth
B Anti-roll bar – offset by five teeth

Fig. 10.16 On 2.0 litre Saloon models, offset the left-hand anti-roll and suspension bars as shown (Sec 10)

A Suspension bar – offset by four teeth
B Anti-roll bar – offset by five teeth

Fig. 10.17 On Savanna models, offset the anti-roll and suspension bars as shown (Sec 10)

A Suspension bar – offset by 13 teeth
B Anti-roll bar – offset by 5 teeth

Fig. 10.18 Vehicle underbody height measuring points (Sec 11)

H1 Front wheel hub centreline to ground
H2 Front sidemember to ground (measured at wheel vertical centreline)
H4 Rear wheel hub centreline to ground
H5 Suspension bar centreline to ground

suspension bar, but align the index mark on the bar offset from its bearing end face index mark by four teeth in the opposite direction to the first suspension bar when viewed from its outboard end.

2.0 litre Saloon models

19 Proceed as described in paragraphs 14 to 18 inclusive, but when installing the suspension bars refer to Fig. 10.16 for the offset position of the left-hand bar relative to the bearing index mark. Offset the right-hand bar by an equal number of teeth in the opposite direction when viewed from the outer end.

Savanna models

20 Proceed as described in paragraphs 14 to 18 inclusive, but when installing the suspension bars refer to Fig. 10.17 for the offset position of the left-hand bar relative to the bearing index mark. Offset the right-hand bar by an equal number of teeth in the opposite direction when viewed from the outer end.

All models

21 Refit the shock absorbers as described in Section 8.
22 The vehicle body height must now be checked. Refit the roadwheels and lower the vehicle to the ground.
23 Roll the car back and forth and then bounce the body to settle the suspension. If the trailing arms were positioned correctly, as

described in paragraph 10, the car should now be standing level and at the correct height (see Section 11). If this is not the case, then the setting procedure will have to be repeated, noting that a deviation of 3 mm (0.12 in) either side of the specified dimension will alter the suspension bar position on the relevant side of the vehicle by one spline. This will have a corresponding effect on the underbody height; increasing or decreasing it by 3 mm (0.12 in).

11 Vehicle underbody height - checking and adjustment

1 Before carrying out the following checks, ensure that the fuel tank is full, the tyres are correctly inflated and the car is standing on level ground.
2 Refer to Fig. 10.18 and take measurements at the points shown. Having taken the appropriate measurements, subtract H2 from H1 and H5 from H4 and compare the results obtained with the settings given in the Specifications.
3 Only the rear underbody height is adjustable, and this is achieved by repositioning the rear suspension bars in their mounting bracket splines. Repositioning the torsion bars by one spline either way from their original position will alter the height on the side concerned by 3 mm (0.12 in). The procedure for doing this is described in Section 10.

4 If the front underbody height is not within the specified tolerance, this will be caused by a weakening of the front coil springs. If this is the case renewal is necessary and, to maintain the side-to-side tolerance, the springs should be renewed in pairs. This procedure is covered in Section 4.
5 If any alteration to the rear underbody height is made, it will be necessary to adjust the headlamp aim as described in Chapter 12 and, where applicable, to have the brake pressure regulating valve adjusted by a Renault dealer.

12 Steering arm outer balljoint - removal and refitting

1 Jack up the front of the car and support it on axle stands. Remove the appropriate front roadwheel.
2 Using a suitable spanner, slacken the balljoint locknut on the steering arm by a quarter of a turn (photos). Hold the steering arm with a second spanner engaged with the flats of the balljoint rod (1.7 litre models), or sleeve (2.0 litre models), to prevent it from turning.
3 Undo and remove the locknut securing the balljoint to the hub carrier (1.7 litre models) or the front shock absorber (2.0 litre models), and then release the tapered shank using a balljoint separator tool (photo).

10

12 2A View showing steering arm outer balljoint – 1.7 litre model

A Balljoint   C Locknut
B Retaining nut   D Flats on balljoint

12.2B View showing steering arm outer balljoint – 2.0 litre Turbo model

12.3 Steering arm balljoint separation – 2.0 litre model

12.4 Steering arm balljoint adjuster sleeve – 2.0 litre model. Measure the exposed thread length (arrowed) before disconnecting

Fig. 10.19 Balljoint removal – 2.0 litre model (Sec 12)

P Locknut   M Sleeve

Fig. 10.20 Steering arm inner balljoint assembly – 1.7 litre models (Sec 14)

1 End view of balljoint assembly
2 Side view of assembled thrust washer and lockplate
3 Lockplate

4 Count the number of exposed threads between the end of the balljoint and the locknut and record this figure (photo).
5 Unscrew the balljoint from the steering arm and unscrew the locknut from the balljoint.
6 Screw the locknut onto the new balljoint and position it so that the same number of exposed threads are visible as was noted during removal.
7 Screw the balljoint onto the steering arm until the locknut just contacts the arm. Now tighten the locknut while holding the steering arm as before.
8 Engage the shank of the balljoint with the hub carrier or shock absorber (as applicable) and refit the locknut. Tighten the locknut to the specified torque. If the balljoint shank turns while the locknut is being tightened, on 1.7 litre models place a jack under the balljoint and raise it sufficiently to push the tapered shank fully into the hub carrier. The tapered fit of the shank will lock it and prevent rotation as the nut is tightened. On 2.0 litre models, reverse this process by pressing down on the joint as the nut is tightened.
9 On completion, remove the jack, refit the roadwheel and lower the car to the ground.
10 Check the front wheel alignment, as described in Section 26.

13 Steering gear rubber bellows - removal and refitting

1.7 litre models

1 Remove the steering arm outer balljoint as described in Section 12.
2 If power steering is fitted, disconnect the bellows-to-bellows balance tube on the side concerned.
3 Release the retaining wire or the screw clips and slide the bellows off the rack and pinion housing and steering arm.
4 Lubricate the inner end of the bellows with rubber grease to assist fitting and position it over the steering arm and housing.
5 Using new clips or two or three turns of soft

iron wire, secure the bellows in position. Where applicable, refit the balance tube.
6 Refit the outer balljoint as described in Section 12.

2.0 litre models

7 Remove the two locknuts then unscrew the two bolts securing the steering arm bracket to the rack assembly. Slide the bracket clear of the rack.
8 Release the bellows retaining clips and slide the bellows off the rack and rack housing.
9 Fit the new bellows and secure with new clips.
10 Refit the steering arm bracket, tighten the bolts to the specified torque then fit the locknuts, also tightened to the specified torque.

14 Steering arm and inner balljoint (1.7 litre models) - removal and refitting

1 Remove the outer balljoint and rubber bellows, as described in Sections 12 and 13 respectively.
2 Hold the thrust washer with grips to prevent the rack turning and unscrew the inner balljoint housing with a suitable wrench. Remove the balljoint housing and steering

arm assembly under under the wheel arch.
3 With the components on the bench for inspection, identify the parts and note how they are fitted.
4 The steering arm and balljoint assembly may be refitted providing that it is in a satisfactory condition and that the balljoint serrations are undamaged. In both cases the lockplate and thrust washer must be renewed before refitting.
5 With new components of the correct type obtained, as necessary, reassemble as follows.
6 Refit the thrust washer and lockplate to the rack, ensuring that the two tabs on the lockplate are in line with the two flats on the end of the rack.
7 Apply a drop of locking compound to the threads of the balljoint and screw the balljoint housing and steering arm assembly into position. Tighten the housing securely.
8 Refit the rubber bellows and outer balljoint, as described in Sections 13 and 12 respectively.

1 Inner balljoint and steering arm assembly
2 Thrust washer and lockplate
3 Lockplate showing direction of fitting

Fig. 10.21 Steering arm inner balljoint components (Sec 14)

15 Steering arm (2.0 litre models) - removal and refitting

1 Remove the outer balljoint as described in Section 12.
2 Slacken the locknut securing the adjusting sleeve to the steering arm by quarter of a turn.
3 Count the number of exposed threads from the start of the threaded section on the steering arm to the locknut and record this figure.
4 Unscrew and remove the adjusting sleeve and the locknut from the steering arm.
5 Remove the two locknuts then unscrew the two bolts securing the steering arm bracket to the rack assembly. Slide the bracket clear of the rack.
6 Undo the locknut and remove the bolt securing the steering arm to the bracket. Withdraw the steering arm from the car.
7 Refitting is the reverse sequence to removal, bearing in mind the following points:
(a) Ensure that the same number of steering arm exposed threads are visible as recorded during removal
(b) Refit the outer balljoint as described in Section 12
(c) Tighten all nuts and bolts to the specified torque, where given

16 Manual steering gear (1.7 litre models) - removal and refitting

1 Jack up the front of the car and support it on axle stands. Remove both front roadwheels.
2 Unscrew the locknuts securing the steering arm outer balljoints to the hub carriers, then release them using a balljoint separator tool.
3 Mark the position of the intermediate shaft lower universal joint in relation to the rack and pinion housing and also the two halves of the universal joint in relation to each other. Where necessary, unclip and remove the plastic cover from the joint - see Section 23 (photo).
4 Undo the nut and remove the bolt securing

Fig. 10.22 Manual steering gear components – 1.7 litre models (Sec 16)

the lower part of the universal joint to the steering gear yoke.
5 Undo the two nuts and bolts securing the steering gear to the subframe, separate the universal joint and withdraw the steering gear sideways from under the wheel arch.
6 Refitting the steering gear is the reverse sequence to removal, bearing in mind the following points:
(a) Before fitting the steering gear unit into position, the pinion plunger setting must be checked for correct adjustment. To do this, prise back the lock tabs of the adjuster screw (A) in Fig. 10.23. Using a 10 mm hexagon key, tighten the plunger adjustment nut by one notch (1/8th of a turn), then check that the steering movement is free without any signs of

binding when moved from lock to lock. If necessary further adjustment can be made to a maximum of two notches. Secure the nut in the set position by peening over the lock tabs on each side
(b) Tighten all nuts and bolts to the specified torque
(c) When refitting the universal joint and steering gear yoke, align the marks made during removal. If no marks are present due to component renewal, set the steering wheel and steering gear to the straight-ahead position before fitting
(d) If the steering arms or outer balljoints have been removed, or their positions altered, check and adjust the front wheel alignment, as described in Section 26.

17 Power-assisted steering gear (1.7 litre models) - removal and refitting

1 Proceed as described in paragraphs 1 to 3 of the previous Section.
2 Clamp the power steering hoses at the reservoir end, then detach the hose support bracket. Disconnect the hoses at the reservoir and at the rotary valve on the high pressure pump.
3 Undo the engine rear mounting nut.
4 Unbolt and remove the engine undertray.

16.3 Remove the plastic cover for access to the universal joint – 1.7 litre model with manual steering

Fig. 10.23 Manual steering gear plunger adjuster lock tabs (A) – 1.7 litre models (Sec 16)

Fig. 10.24 Power steering gear and associated components – 1.7 litre models (Sec 17)

10

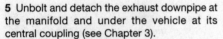

Fig. 10.25 Clamp the power steering hydraulic hoses (Renault tools shown) (Sec 17)

Fig. 10.26 Engine rear mounting nut – 1.7 litre models (Sec 17)

Fig. 10.27 Make alignment marks (arrowed) before disconnecting the gearchange control rod and lever – 1.7 litre models (Sec 17)

5 Unbolt and detach the exhaust downpipe at the manifold and under the vehicle at its central coupling (see Chapter 3).

6 Mark the relative fitted position of the gearchange control rod to the lever, then disconnect them - see Fig. 10.27.

7 Unbolt and remove the rear engine mounting cover plate, then undo the two engine mounting bolts and remove the mounting from the subframe. Raise the engine and transmission as high as possible.

8 Unscrew the two lower bolts securing the steering gear unit to the subframe. Move the rack to the left for access.

9 Unscrew and remove the steering gear unit upper retaining bolts, then, supporting the unit, withdraw it from the left-hand side, under the wheelarch.

10 Where a replacement steering gear unit is to be fitted, the steering arm outer balljoints can be removed and fitted to the new unit as described in Section 12.

11 When installing the steering gear unit, ensure that the engine and transmission are raised as high as possible. Refitting is a reversal of the removal procedure. but note the following significant points.

12 Align the positional index marks of the gearchange control rod and lever, and also the universal joint index marks.

13 Tighten the retaining nuts and bolts to their specified torque wrench settings.

14 When the power steering hoses are reconnected, top up the hydraulic fluid level to the grille line in the reservoir, then turn the steering fully from lock to lock, first with the engine switched off, then with it running. Top up the fluid level if required. Check for any signs of fluid leakage from the system hoses and connections.

15 Finally, check the steering geometry to complete (Section 26)

18 Manual and power-assisted steering gear (2.0 litre models) - removal and refitting

1 Disconnect the battery earth lead.

2 Unscrew the trim panel under the facia on the driver's side. With the panel released, detach the fusebox from the hinged lid and remove the cigar lighter (Chapter 12). Disconnect the heater ventilation duct if necessary for access.

3 Turn the steering to full right-hand lock and then unscrew the intermediate shaft-to-

Fig. 10.28 Rear engine mounting cover plate and retaining bolts (arrowed) – 1.7 litre models (Sec 17)

Fig. 10.29 Rear engine mounting bolts – 1.7 litre models (Sec 17)

Fig. 10.32 Power steering gear unit removal - 1.7 litre models (Sec 17)

Fig. 10.30 Power steering gear-to-subframe lower mounting bolts – 1.7 litre models (Sec 17)

Fig 10.31 Power steering gear upper retaining bolts – 1.7 litre models (Sec 17)

Fig. 10.33 Steering gear and associated components – 2.0 litre models (Sec 18)

18.8A View of right-hand end of power steering gear showing mounting bracket (arrowed) – 2.0 litre model

18.8B View of left-hand end of power steering gear showing mounting bracket (arrowed) – 2.0 litre model

18.9 Steering gear-to-shock absorber turret mounting – 2.0 litre model

18.12 Lower steering column universal joint viewed from vehicle interior – 2.0 litre model

steering wheel shaft universal joint coupling bolt and nut.

4 Raise and support the vehicle at the front on axle stands. Remove the front roadwheels. On Turbo models, unbolt and remove the heat shield from the turbocharger unit.

5 Disconnect the steering arm balljoints on each side as described in Section 12.

6 Disconnect the ignition coil wiring and the diagnostic plug and mounting at the bulkhead in the engine compartment.

7 Undo the locknuts and unscrew the steering arm bracket-to-rack bolts. Separate the bracket from the rack.

8 On models fitted with power steering, clamp the hydraulic hoses at the reservoir end, detach the hose support bracket, then disconnect the high pressure line from the valve union and the low pressure line from the pipe union (photos).

9 Undo the three steering unit-to-shock absorber turret nuts and withdraw the flange from the turret studs (photo).

10 Disconnect the relevant hoses, cables and wires as applicable from the steering unit.

11 Remove the PVC collar clip securing the bulkhead gaiter to the steering gear, where applicable.

12 Unscrew the retaining nuts from the main retaining clamps to the bulkhead, then

carefully pull the steering gear forwards and away from the bulkhead so that the column intermediate shaft universal joint coupling (to the pinion shaft) is exposed (photo). Mark the relative positions of the intermediate shaft coupling and the pinion shaft, undo the through-bolt nut and remove the bolt.

13 Withdraw the steering gear unit from the intermediate shaft coupling, then when free, withdraw the unit sideways from under the wheel arch. Take care not to damage the angular position/speed sensor on the transmission bellhousing as the unit is removed.

14 Refitting is a reversal of the removal procedure, but note the following points.

15 When reconnecting the intermediate shaft coupling, ensure that the alignment marks made when dismantling correspond.

16 Use a new PVC collar to secure the bulkhead gaiter to the steering gear, where applicable.

17 Tighten all fixings to their specified torque wrench settings. This includes the steering arm bracket-to-rack bolts (the rack being threaded).

18 When the unit is fitted on power steering models, reconnect the power steering hydraulic lines and then top up the fluid level in the power steering fluid reservoir. With the

Fig. 10.34 Steering column intermediate shaft-to-steering wheel shaft coupling bolt and nut (Sec 18)

Fig. 10.35 Steering arm bracket-to-rack bolts (A) – remove nuts first to allow bolts to be withdrawn (Sec 18)

Fig. 10.36 Detach the power steering hydraulic connections at the points indicated (Sec 18)

10

Fig. 10.37 Steering column locking lever setting diagram (Sec 20)

1 Nut	3 Lever
2 Ring nut	X = 30.0 mm (1.2 in)

engine switched off, turn the steering fully from right to left-hand lock, then back. Now start the engine and repeat the procedure. Recheck the level of the fluid in the reservoir and top up as necessary.

19 With the steering gear refitted, check the pinion adjustment as described in Section 16, paragraph 6(a).

20 Finally check and if necessary adjust the steering geometry as described in Section 26.

19 Steering gear and power steering pump - overhaul

1 In view of the special tools and skills required, it is not recommended that the steering gear or, where applicable, the power steering pump be dismantled or overhauled, but renewed by obtaining a new or factory reconditioned unit.

2 If new steering gear is being refitted, then centre the rack by placing a cardboard disc firmly on the pinion splines and count the number of turns required to turn the pinion from lock to lock. From full lock, turn the

Fig. 10.39 Steering wheel commutator screw (Sec 22)

21.2 Steering wheel pad removed for access to retaining nut

pinion half the number of turns counted and engage the pinion with the coupling (steering wheel in straight-ahead position).

20 Steering wheel height adjuster

1 The steering wheel height adjusting clamp lever can be adjusted for degree of tightness.

2 Remove the steering column shrouds.

3 Unscrew the locking lever nut (1 - Fig. 10.37) and lower the steering wheel as far as it will go. Remove the clamp lever.

4 Tighten the ring nut (2) and then refit the lever to its splined shaft so that (X) is 30.0 mm (1.2 in) from the column bracket.

5 Refit the nut and shrouds.

21 Steering wheel - removal and refitting

1 Set the front wheels in the straight-ahead position.

2 Ease off the steering wheel pad to provide access to the retaining nut (photo).

3 Using a socket and knuckle bar undo and remove the retaining nut and lockwasher.

4 Mark the steering wheel and steering column shaft in relation to each other and withdraw the wheel from the shaft splines. If it

22.7A Undo the retaining screw . . .

Fig. 10.38 Steering column components (Sec 22)

is tight, tap it upwards near the centre, using the palm of your hand. Refit the steering wheel retaining nut two turns before doing this, to stop it flying off.

5 Refitting is the reverse of removal, but align the previously made marks and tighten the retaining nut to the specified torque.

22 Steering column - removal, overhaul and refitting

1 Disconnect the battery earth lead.

2 Remove the steering wheel as described in the previous Section.

3 Detach and remove the lower facia panels and the steering column upper and lower shrouds (see Section 18).

4 Unscrew and remove the steering wheel commutator screw (see Fig. 10.39).

5 Unscrew and remove the steering column intermediate shaft-to-steering wheel shaft coupling bolt.

6 Relocate the steering wheel and its retaining nut temporarily (do not tighten the nut), then pull on the wheel to release the shaft and upper bush. The steering lock must be freed during this operation. Remove the steering wheel when the column shaft and bush are free.

7 The steering column lock/ignition switch unit must now be removed. Undo the retaining

22.7B . . . set key to the 'G' position and press retainer pin . . .

screw on the facia side, set the ignition key to the 'G' position, then depress the retaining pin on the underside of the unit and simultaneously withdraw the unit. Detach the wiring connector from the switch (photos).

8 Remove the steering column-to-dashboard retaining bolt, then the two nuts and two bolts securing the column support bracket (photo). Lower and remove the steering column.

9 The upper and lower column bushes can now be removed and renewed. Drive the bushes out using a suitable length of 35 mm (1.37 in) diameter tubing. Smear the new bushes with grease before driving them into position.

10 Refitting is a reversal of the removal procedure. When the steering column shaft is being fitted to the intermediate shaft universal joint coupling, align the flat section with the slot centreline (see Fiy. 10.41), then insert the key bolt.

11 Refit the steering wheel as described in Section 21.

<table><tr><td>**23**</td><td>**Steering column intermediate shaft** - removal and refitting</td></tr></table>

1.7 litre models

1 Detach and remove the lower trim panel from the facia on the driver's side (see Section 18).

Fig. 10.42 Intermediate shaft lower universal joint coupling bolt (1) (Sec 23)

22.7C . . . remove column lock/ignition switch unit

22.8 Steering column support bracket nuts and bolts (arrowed) – 2.0 litre model

Fig. 10.40 Steering column upper and lower bush locations (arrowed) (Sec 22)

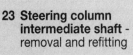

Fig. 10.41 Align column flat (A) with slot centreline when fitting the key bolt (Sec 22)

2 Turn the steering to full right-hand lock so that the upper column-to-intermediate shaft coupling bolt is positioned as shown in Fig. 10.34. Unscrew the nut and withdraw the bolt.

3 Remove the lower universal joint coupling bolt working from the engine compartment side of the bulkhead. On some models the lower coupling is covered by a protective shield, and this must be removed for access to the coupling. To remove the shield, carefully cut through the retaining clip and prise free the plastic clips. Be careful not to cut through the gaiter when removing the clip. Replace the foam seal when refitting.

4 With the coupling bolts removed, the intermediate shaft can be disengaged from the pinion at the lower end. and the column at the upper end, then removed. The bulkhead gaiter can be removed by undoing the three retaining nuts.

5 If the intermediate shaft is to be renewed,

Fig. 10.43 Lower universal joint protective shield components (Sec 23)

1 Shield
2 Clips (press-stud type)
3 Strap clip
4 Foam seal

A Cutting point for new seal
B Peel back protective paper from this face on new seal

10

Fig. 10.44 Measure the intermediate shaft to check for correct replacement (Sec 23)

1.7 litre models with manual steering – L = 455.5 to 457.5 mm (17.76 to 17.84 in)
1.7 litre models with power steering – L = 425.5 to 427.5 mm (16.59 to 16.67 in)
All 2.0 litre models – L = 306.5 to 308.5 mm (11.95 to 12.03 in)

ensure that the correct replacement type is obtained, as the shafts differ in length according to model - see Fig. 10.44.

6 Refitting is a reversal of the removal procedure. When fitting the shaft, align the coupling bolt holes so that the bolts can be slid into position without the need for force. Check the steering for satisfactory action on completion.

2.0 litre models

7 Proceed as described in paragraphs 1 and 2.
8 Raise and support the vehicle at the front end on axle stands.
9 Disconnect the steering arm balljoints as described in Section 12.
10 Unbolt but do not remove the steering gear unit, referring to Section 18 for details.
11 Withdraw the steering gear unit from the bulkhead just enough to allow the lower coupling bolt to be unscrewed and removed. Disengage the intermediate shaft from the lower and upper couplings and remove the shaft.
12 If required the gaiter can be removed from the bulkhead by undoing the three retaining nuts.
13 If the steering intermediate shaft is to be renewed, ensure that the correct replacement is obtained - see Fig. 10.44.
14 Refit in the reverse order to removal but note the following:
(a) Align the intermediate shaft coupling bolt holes correctly so that the bolts can be inserted without force
(b) Refit the steering gear unit as described in Section 18

(c) Reconnect the steering arm balljoints as described in Section 12
(d) On completion check that the steering action is satisfactory

24 Power steering pump - removal and refitting

1 On 1.7 litre models remove the alternator as described in Chapter 12.
2 Clamp the hydraulic hoses, then position a suitable container under the pump unit to catch the fluid. Detach the feed and high pressure hoses from the pump unit (photo).

Fig. 10.46 Power steering pump – 2.0 litre models (Sec 24)

A Tensioner bolt (for alternator drivebelt)
B Tensioner bolt (for power steering pump drivebelt)
C Pump mounting bolts
D Pump mounting bolt

Fig. 10.45 Power steering pump bolts (B) – 1.7 litre models (Sec 24)

3 On 1.7 litre models, undo the three retaining bolts and remove the pump unit.
4 On 2.0 litre models, refer to Fig. 10.46 and loosen off the drivebelt tensioner bolts of the alternator and power steering pump. Unscrew and remove the alternator lower retaining nut. Loosen bolts (C) and (D), also the pump rear mounting bolt (photo). Disengage the drivebelt, then remove the mounting bolts (C) and the rear mounting bolt. Withdraw the pump unit (photo).

Fig. 10.47 Sectional view of the power steering pump unit (Sec 24)

1 Pressure closure plate
2 Backplate
3 Stator
4 Shaft
5 Rotor
6 High pressure union

24.2 Power steering pump unit and hydraulic hose connections – 2.0 litre model

24.4A Power steering pump rear mounting bolt (arrowed) – 2.0 litre model

24.4B Removing the power steering pump unit – 2.0 litre model

5 In view of the special tools and skills required, it is not recommended that the power steering pump is dismantled or overhauled, but renewed by obtaining a new or factory reconditioned unit.

6 If the pump unit is to be renewed, the mounting bracket and pulley must be transferred to the new unit. As a special pulley withdrawal and refitting tool is required to change the pulley, it is a task best entrusted to a Renault dealer. Note that the mounting bracket must be in position when the pulley is fitted as it may not be possible to fit the bracket once the pulley is in position. In addition, the pulley position must be correctly set during assembly, or the drivebelt alignment will be incorrect.

7 Inspect the drivebelt and renew it if it is cracked or in poor general condition.

8 The refitting procedures for the power steering pump on both the 1.7 and 2.0 litre models are a reversal of the removal procedure, but note the following special points:

(a) On 1.7 litre models refit the alternator as described in Chapter 12

(b) Adjust the drivebelt tension(s) as described in Chapter 2

(c) Connect up the hydraulic system hoses, then top up the fluid level and bleed the system as described in Section 25

25 Power steering circuit - bleeding

1 This will only be required if any part of the hydraulic system has been disconnected.

2 Fill the reservoir to the brim with the specified fluid.

3 Turn the steering to full lock in both directions. Top up if required.

4 Start the engine and turn the steering slowly from lock to lock. Switch off and top up to the correct level.

26 Steering angles and front wheel alignment

1 Accurate front wheel alignment is essential to provide good steering and roadholding characteristics and to ensure slow and even tyre wear. Before considering the steering angles, check that the tyres are correctly inflated, that the front wheels are not buckled, the hub bearings are not worn or incorrectly adjusted and that the steering linkage is in good order, without slackness or wear at the joints.

2 Wheel alignment consists of four factors:

Camber, is the angle at which the road wheels are set from the vertical when viewed from front or rear of the vehicle. Positive camber is the angle (in degrees) that the wheels are tilted outwards at the top from the vertical.

Fig. 10.48 Camber angle diagram (Sec 26)

A Vertical
B Camber angle (positive)

Castor, is the angle between the steering axis and a vertical when viewed from each side of the vehicle. Positive castor is indicated when the steering axis is inclined towards the rear of the vehicle at its upper end.

Steering axis inclination, is the angle when viewed from the front or rear of the vehicle between vertical and an imaginary line drawn between the top and bottom strut mountings.

Toe, is the amount by which the distance between the front inside edges of the roadwheel rims differs from that between the rear inside edges. If the distance between the front edges is less than that at the rear, the wheels are said to toe-in. If the distance between the front inside edges is greater than that at the rear, the wheels toe-out.

3 Owing to the need for precision gauges to measure the small angles of the steering and suspension settings, it is preferable that measuring of camber and castor is left to a service station having the necessary equipment.

4 The camber and steering axis inclination angles are set in production and cannot be adjusted. Where they differ from those specified, suspect collision damage or gross wear in the steering or suspension components.

5 To check the front wheel alignment, first make sure that the lengths of both steering arms are equal when the steering is in the straight-ahead position. Adjust if necessary by releasing the steering arm end locknuts and turning the steering arms until the lengths of the exposed threads are equal on each side.

Fig. 10.49 Castor angle diagram (left-hand wheel) (Sec 26)

A Vertical
B Castor angle (positive)

6 Obtain a tracking gauge. These are available in various forms from accessory stores or one can be fabricated from a length of steel tubing suitably cranked to clear the sump and bellhousing and having a setscrew and locknut at one end.

7 With the gauge, measure the distance between the two wheel inner rims (at hub height) at the rear of the wheel. Push the vehicle forward to rotate the wheel through 180° (half a turn) and measure the distance between the wheel inner rims, again at hub height, at the front of the wheel. This last measurement should differ from the first by the appropriate toe-out according to specification (see Specifications).

8 Where the toe-out is found to be incorrect, refer to Section 12 and slacken the outer balljoint locknuts (1.7 litre models) or the nuts on either side of the steering arm adjuster

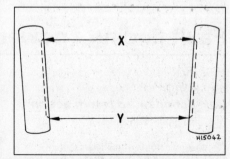

Fig. 10.50 Front wheel alignment diagram showing toe out (Sec 26)

X – Y = toe-out

10

sleeves (2.0 litre models). Turn the steering arms or adjuster sleeves equally, by no more than a quarter of a turn at a time, then re-check the alignment.

9 Turn each steering arm in the same direction when viewed from the centre line of the car otherwise the rods will become unequal in length. This would cause the steering wheel spoke position to alter and cause problems on turns with tyre scrubbing. On completion, tighten the steering arm locknuts without disturbing their setting, check that the balljoint is at the centre of its arc of travel.

27 Rear wheel alignment

1 All angles are set in production and cannot be adjusted
2 Rear wheel alignment can be checked as described for the front wheels, but any deviation from the specified limits indicates rear suspension damage or wear, as the toe-setting is not adjustable.

28 Steering column lock/ignition switch - removal and refitting

1 Disconnect the battery.
2 Remove the steering column shroud.
3 The lock/ignition switch assembly can now be removed as described in paragraph 7 of Section 22.
4 Refit in the reverse order of removal. On completion check for satisfactory operation of the steering, ignition and steering lock.

Fault finding - front suspension

Vehicle wanders
☐ Incorrect wheel alignment
☐ Worn front lower arm balljoints

Heavy or stiff steering
☐ Incorrect front wheel alignment
☐ Incorrect tyre pressures

Wheel wobble or vibration
☐ Roadwheels out of balance
☐ Roadwheel buckled
☐ Incorrect front wheel alignment
☐ Faulty shock absorber
☐ Weak coil spring

Excessive pitching or rolling on corners or during braking
☐ Faulty shock absorber
☐ Weak or broken coil spring

Tyre squeal when cornering
☐ Incorrect front wheel alignment
☐ Incorrect tyre pressures

Abnormal tyre wear
☐ Incorrect tyre pressures
☐ Incorrect front wheel alignment
☐ Worn hub bearing

Fault finding - rear suspension

Poor roadholding and wander
☐ Faulty shock absorber
☐ Weak coil spring (where applicable)
☐ Worn or incorrectly adjusted hub bearing
☐ Worn suspension arm bush

Fault finding - manual steering

Stiff action
☐ Lack of rack lubrication
☐ Seized steering arm end balljoints
☐ Seized suspension lower balljoint

Free movement at steering wheel
☐ Wear in steering arm balljoints
☐ Wear in rack teeth

Knocking when traversing uneven surface
☐ Incorrectly adjusted pinion plunger setting

Fault finding - power-assisted steering

The symptoms and reasons applicable to manual steering gear will apply plus the following:

Stiff action or no return action
☐ Slipping pump drivebelt
☐ Air in fluid
☐ Steering column out of alignment
☐ Castor angle incorrect due to damage or gross wear in bushes and mountings

Steering effort on both locks unequal
☐ Leaking seal in steering gear
☐ Clogged fluid passage within gear assembly

Noisy pump
☐ Loose pulley
☐ Kinked hose
☐ Low fluid level

Chapter 11 Bodywork and fittings

For modifications, and information applicable to later models, see Supplement at end of manual

Contents

Degrees of difficulty

Easy, suitable for novice with little experience	**Fairly easy,** suitable for beginner with some experience	**Fairly difficult,** suitable for competent DIY mechanic	**Difficult,** suitable for experienced DIY mechanic	**Very difficult,** suitable for expert DIY or professional 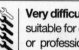

1 General description

The bodyshell and underframe are of all-steel welded construction, incorporating progressive crumple zones at the front and rear and a rigid centre safety cell. The assembly and welding of the main body unit is completed by computer-controlled robots, and is checked for dimensional accuracy using computer and laser technology.

The front and rear bumpers are of collapsible cellular construction to minimise minor accident damage and the front wings are bolted in position to facilitate accident damage repair.

2 Maintenance - bodywork and underframe

The general condition of a vehicle's bodywork is the one thing that significantly affects its value. Maintenance is easy, but needs to be regular. Neglect, particularly after minor damage, can lead quickly to further deterioration and costly repair bills. It is important also to keep watch on those parts of the vehicle not immediately visible, for instance the underside, inside all the wheel arches, and the lower part of the engine compartment.

The basic maintenance routine for the bodywork is washing - preferably with a lot of water, from a hose. This will remove all the loose solids which may have stuck to the vehicle. It is important to flush these off in such a way as to prevent grit from scratching the finish. The wheel arches and underframe need washing in the same way, to remove any accumulated mud, which will retain moisture and tend to encourage rust. Paradoxically enough, the best time to clean the underframe and wheel arches is in wet weather, when the mud is thoroughly wet and soft. In very wet weather, the underframe is usually cleaned of large accumulations automatically, and this is a good time for inspection.

Periodically, except on vehicles with a wax-based underbody protective coating, it is a good idea to have the whole of the underframe of the vehicle steam-cleaned, engine compartment included, so that a thorough inspection can be carried out to see what minor repairs and renovations are necessary. Steam-cleaning is available at many garages, and is necessary for the removal of the accumulation of oily grime, which sometimes is allowed to become thick in certain areas. If steam-cleaning facilities are not available, there are some excellent grease solvents available which can be brush-applied; the dirt can then be simply hosed off. Note that these methods should not be used on vehicles with wax-based underbody protective coating, or the coating will be removed. Such vehicles should be inspected annually, preferably just prior to Winter, when the underbody should be washed down, and any damage to the wax coating repaired. Ideally, a completely fresh coat should be applied. It would also be worth considering the use of such wax-based protection for injection into door panels, sills, box sections, etc, as an additional safeguard against rust damage, where such protection is not provided by the vehicle manufacturer.

After washing paintwork, wipe off with a chamois leather to give an unspotted clear finish. A coat of clear protective wax polish will give added protection against chemical

11

2.4A Use a thin gauge rod to clean out the door drain channels

2.4B Tailgate drain aperture – Savanna model

pollutants in the air. If the paintwork sheen has dulled or oxidised, use a cleaner/polisher combination to restore the brilliance of the shine. This requires a little effort, but such dulling is usually caused because regular washing has been neglected. Care needs to be taken with metallic paintwork, as special non-abrasive cleaner/polisher is required to avoid damage to the finish. Always check that the door and ventilator opening drain holes and pipes are completely clear, so that water can be drained out. Brightwork should be treated in the same way as paintwork. Windscreens and windows can be kept clear of the smeary film which often appears, by the use of proprietary glass cleaner. Never use any form of wax or other body or chromium polish on glass.

3 Maintenance - upholstery and carpets

Mats and carpets should be brushed or vacuum-cleaned regularly, to keep them free of grit. If they are badly stained, remove them from the vehicle for scrubbing or sponging, and make quite sure they are dry before refitting. Seats and interior trim panels can be kept clean by wiping with a damp cloth. If they do become stained (which can be more apparent on light-coloured upholstery), use a little liquid detergent and a soft nail brush to scour the grime out of the grain of the material. Do not forget to keep the headlining clean in the same way as the upholstery. When using liquid cleaners inside the vehicle, do not over-wet the surfaces being cleaned. Excessive damp could get into the seams and padded interior, causing stains, offensive odours or even rot.

HAYNES HiNT *If the inside of the vehicle gets wet accidentally, it is worthwhile taking some trouble to dry it out properly, particularly where carpets are involved. Do not leave oil or electric heaters inside the vehicle for this purpose.*

4 Minor body damage - repair

Repairs of minor scratches in bodywork

If the scratch is very superficial, and does not penetrate to the metal of the bodywork, repair is very simple. Lightly rub the area of the scratch with a paintwork renovator, or a very fine cutting paste, to remove loose paint from the scratch, and to clear the surrounding bodywork of wax polish. Rinse the area with clean water.

Apply touch-up paint to the scratch using a fine paint brush; continue to apply fine layers of paint until the surface of the paint in the scratch is level with the surrounding paintwork. Allow the new paint at least two weeks to harden, then blend it into the surrounding paintwork by rubbing the scratch area with a paintwork renovator or a very fine cutting paste. Finally, apply wax polish.

Where the scratch has penetrated right through to the metal of the bodywork, causing the metal to rust, a different repair technique is required. Remove any loose rust from the bottom of the scratch with a penknife, then apply rust-inhibiting paint to prevent the formation of rust in the future. Using a rubber or nylon applicator, fill the scratch with bodystopper paste. If required, this paste can be mixed with cellulose thinners to provide a very thin paste which is ideal for filling narrow scratches. Before the stopper-paste in the scratch hardens, wrap a piece of smooth cotton rag around the top of a finger. Dip the finger in cellulose thinners, and quickly sweep it across the surface of the stopper-paste in the scratch; this will ensure that the surface of the stopper-paste is slightly hollowed. The scratch can now be painted over as described earlier in this Section.

Repairs of dents in bodywork

When deep denting of the vehicle's bodywork has taken place, the first task is to pull the dent out, until the affected bodywork almost attains its original shape. There is little point in trying to restore the original shape

completely, as the metal in the damaged area will have stretched on impact, and cannot be reshaped fully to its original contour. It is better to bring the level of the dent up to a point which is about 3 mm below the level of the surrounding bodywork. In cases where the dent is very shallow anyway, it is not worth trying to pull it out at all. If the underside of the dent is accessible, it can be hammered out gently from behind, using a mallet with a wooden or plastic head. Whilst doing this, hold a suitable block of wood firmly against the outside of the panel, to absorb the impact from the hammer blows and thus prevent a large area of the bodywork from being "belled-out".

Should the dent be in a section of the bodywork which has a double skin, or some other factor making it inaccessible from behind, a different technique is called for. Drill several small holes through the metal inside the area - particularly in the deeper section. Then screw long self-tapping screws into the holes, just sufficiently for them to gain a good purchase in the metal. Now the dent can be pulled out by pulling on the protruding heads of the screws with a pair of pliers.

The next stage of the repair is the removal of the paint from the damaged area, and from an inch or so of the surrounding "sound" bodywork. This is accomplished most easily by using a wire brush or abrasive pad on a power drill, although it can be done just as effectively by hand, using sheets of abrasive paper. To complete the preparation for filling, score the surface of the bare metal with a screwdriver or the tang of a file, or alternatively, drill small holes in the affected area. This will provide a really good "key" for the filler paste.

To complete the repair, see the Section on filling and respraying.

Repairs of rust holes or gashes in bodywork

Remove all paint from the affected area, and from an inch or so of the surrounding "sound" bodywork, using an abrasive pad or a wire brush on a power drill. If these are not available, a few sheets of abrasive paper will do the job most effectively. With the paint removed, you will be able to judge the severity of the corrosion, and therefore decide whether to renew the whole panel (if this is possible) or to repair the affected area. New body panels are not as expensive as most people think, and it is often quicker and more satisfactory to fit a new panel than to attempt to repair large areas of corrosion.

Remove all fittings from the affected area, except those which will act as a guide to the original shape of the damaged bodywork (eg headlight shells etc). Then, using tin snips or a hacksaw blade, remove all loose metal and any other metal badly affected by corrosion. Hammer the edges of the hole inwards, in order to create a slight depression for the filler paste.

Wire-brush the affected area to remove the powdery rust from the surface of the remaining metal. Paint the affected area with rust-inhibiting paint, if the back of the rusted area is accessible, treat this also.

Before filling can take place, it will be necessary to block the hole in some way. This can be achieved by the use of aluminium or plastic mesh, or aluminium tape.

Aluminium or plastic mesh, or glass-fibre matting, is probably the best material to use for a large hole. Cut a piece to the approximate size and shape of the hole to be filled, then position it in the hole so that its edges are below the level of the surrounding bodywork. It can be retained in position by several blobs of filler paste around its periphery.

Aluminium tape should be used for small or very narrow holes. Pull a piece off the roll, trim it to the approximate size and shape required, then pull off the backing paper (if used) and stick the tape over the hole; it can be overlapped if the thickness of one piece is insufficient. Burnish down the edges of the tape with the handle of a screwdriver or similar, to ensure that the tape is securely attached to the metal underneath.

Bodywork repairs - filling and respraying

Before using this Section, see the Sections on dent, deep scratch, rust holes and gash repairs.

Many types of bodyfiller are available, but generally speaking, those proprietary kits which contain a tin of filler paste and a tube of resin hardener are best for this type of repair. A wide, flexible plastic or nylon applicator will be found invaluable for imparting a smooth and well-contoured finish to the surface of the filler.

Mix up a little filler on a clean piece of card or board - measure the hardener carefully (follow the maker's instructions on the pack), otherwise the filler will set too rapidly or too slowly. Using the applicator, apply the filler paste to the prepared area; draw the applicator across the surface of the filler to achieve the correct contour and to level the surface. As soon as a contour that approximates to the correct one is achieved, stop working the paste - if you carry on too long, the paste will become sticky and begin to "pick-up" on the applicator. Continue to add thin layers of filler paste at 20-minute intervals, until the level of the filler is just proud of the surrounding bodywork.

Once the filler has hardened, the excess can be removed using a metal plane or file. From then on, progressively-finer grades of abrasive paper should be used, starting with a 40-grade production paper, and finishing with a 400-grade wet-and-dry paper. Always wrap the abrasive paper around a flat rubber, cork, or wooden block - otherwise the surface of the filler will not be completely flat. During the

smoothing of the filler surface, the wet-and-dry paper should be periodically rinsed in water. This will ensure that a very smooth finish is imparted to the filler at the final stage.

At this stage, the "dent" should be surrounded by a ring of bare metal, which in turn should be encircled by the finely "feathered" edge of the good paintwork. Rinse the repair area with clean water, until all of the dust produced by the rubbing-down operation has gone.

Spray the whole area with a light coat of primer - this will show up any imperfections in the surface of the filler. Repair these imperfections with fresh filler paste or bodystopper, and once more smooth the surface with abrasive paper. Repeat this spray-and-repair procedure until you are satisfied that the surface of the filler, and the feathered edge of the paintwork, are perfect. Clean the repair area with clean water, and allow to dry fully.

 If bodystopper is used, it can be mixed with cellulose thinners to form a really thin paste which is ideal for filling small holes.

The repair area is now ready for final spraying. Paint spraying must be carried out in a warm, dry, windless and dust-free atmosphere. This condition can be created artificially if you have access to a large indoor working area, but if you are forced to work in the open, you will have to pick your day very carefully. If you are working indoors, dousing the floor in the work area with water will help to settle the dust which would otherwise be in the atmosphere. If the repair area is confined to one body panel, mask off the surrounding panels; this will help to minimise the effects of a slight mis-match in paint colours. Bodywork fittings (eg chrome strips, door handles etc) will also need to be masked off. Use genuine masking tape, and several thicknesses of newspaper, for the masking operations.

Before commencing to spray, agitate the aerosol can thoroughly, then spray a test area (an old tin, or similar) until the technique is mastered. Cover the repair area with a thick coat of primer; the thickness should be built up using several thin layers of paint, rather than one thick one. Using 400-grade wet-and-dry paper, rub down the surface of the primer until it is really smooth. While doing this, the work area should be thoroughly doused with water, and the wet-and-dry paper periodically rinsed in water. Allow to dry before spraying on more paint.

Spray on the top coat, again building up the thickness by using several thin layers of paint. Start spraying at one edge of the repair area, and then, using a side-to-side motion, work until the whole repair area and about 2 inches

of the surrounding original paintwork is covered. Remove all masking material 10 to 15 minutes after spraying on the final coat of paint.

Allow the new paint at least two weeks to harden, then, using a paintwork renovator, or a very fine cutting paste, blend the edges of the paint into the existing paintwork. Finally, apply wax polish.

Plastic components

With the use of more and more plastic body components by the vehicle manufacturers (eg bumpers. spoilers, and in some cases major body panels), rectification of more serious damage to such items has become a matter of either entrusting repair work to a specialist in this field, or renewing complete components. Repair of such damage by the DIY owner is not really feasible, owing to the cost of the equipment and materials required for effecting such repairs. The basic technique involves making a groove along the line of the crack in the plastic, using a rotary burr in a power drill. The damaged part is then welded back together, using a hot-air gun to heat up and fuse a plastic filler rod into the groove. Any excess plastic is then removed, and the area rubbed down to a smooth finish. It is important that a filler rod of the correct plastic is used, as body components can be made of a variety of different types (eg polycarbonate, ABS, polypropylene).

Damage of a less serious nature (abrasions, minor cracks etc) can be repaired by the DIY owner using a two-part epoxy filler repair material. Once mixed in equal proportions, this is used in similar fashion to the bodywork filler used on metal panels. The filler is usually cured in twenty to thirty minutes, ready for sanding and painting.

If the owner is renewing a complete component himself, or if he has repaired it with epoxy filler, he will be left with the problem of finding a suitable paint for finishing which is compatible with the type of plastic used. At one time, the use of a universal paint was not possible, owing to the complex range of plastics encountered in body component applications. Standard paints, generally speaking, will not bond to plastic or rubber satisfactorily. However, it is now possible to obtain a plastic body parts finishing kit which consists of a pre-primer treatment, a primer and coloured top coat. Full instructions are normally supplied with a kit, but basically, the method of use is to first apply the pre-primer to the component concerned, and allow it to dry for up to 30 minutes. Then the primer is applied, and left to dry for about an hour before finally applying the special-coloured top coat. The result is a correctly-coloured component, where the paint will flex with the plastic or rubber, a property that standard paint does not normally possess.

11

7.3 Door lock striker

Fig. 11.1 Bonnet hinges (A) and adjuster shim plates (B) (Sec 8)

8.2 Windscreen washer hoses T-piece connector

5 Major body damage - repair

Where serious damage has occurred, or large areas need renewal due to neglect, it means that completely new sections or panels will need welding in, and this is best left to professionals. If the damage is due to impact, it will also be necessary to check completely the alignment of the bodyshell structure. Due to the principle of construction, the strength and shape of the whole car can be affected by damage to one part. In such instances the services of an accident repair specialist or Renault dealer with special checking jigs are essential. If a body is left misaligned, it is first of all dangerous, as the car will not handle properly, and secondly uneven stresses will be imposed on the steering, engine and transmission, causing abnormal wear or complete failure. Tyre wear may also be excessive.

6 Maintenance - hinges and locks

1 Oil the hinges of the bonnet, boot or tailgate and door with a drop or two of light oil at regular intervals (see 'Routine maintenance').

2 At the same time, lightly oil the bonnet release mechanism and all door locks.
3 Do not attempt to lubricate the steering lock.

7 Door rattles - tracing and rectification

1 Check first that the door is not loose at the hinges, and that the latch is holding the door firmly in position. Check also that the door lines up with the aperture in the body. If the door is out of alignment, adjust it, as described in Section 15 or 22 as applicable.
2 If the latch is holding the door in the correct position, but the latch still rattles, the lock mechanism is worn and should be renewed.
3 If required the door striker can be adjusted for position by loosening with a suitable Torx key (photo).
4 Other rattles from the door could be caused by wear in the window operating mechanism, interior lock mechanism, or loose glass channels.

8 Bonnet - removal, refitting and adjustment

1 Open the bonnet and support it in the open position using the stay.

2 Disconnect the windscreen washer hose at the T-piece connector (photo).
3 Mark the outline of the hinges with a soft pencil, then loosen the four retaining bolts (photo).
4 With the help of an assistant, remove the stay, unscrew the four bolts and lift the bonnet off the car, together with any hinge shim plates.
5 Refitting is the reverse sequence to removal. Position the bonnet hinges within the outline marks made during removal, but alter its position as necessary to provide a uniform gap all round. Adjust the height of the lock mechanism if necessary, as described in Section 9.

9 Bonnet lock and release cable - removal, refitting and adjustment

Bonnet lock

1 Open and support the bonnet.
2 Remove the windscreen wiper arms (Chapter 12), then remove the grille panel from the base of the windscreen. This panel is secured by screws and clips (photos). Remove the seal and grille.
3 Unbolt and withdraw the bonnet lock (photo). Disconnect the cable.
4 Refitting is the reverse sequence to removal, but adjust the lock height so that the

8.3 Bonnet hinge bolts

9.2A Remove the grille retaining screws (arrowed) . . .

9.2B . . . and peel back seal to remove grille . . .

9.3 . . . for access to bonnet lock and cable

bonnet line is flush with the front wings and shuts securely without force.

Release cable

5 Remove the bonnet lock and disconnect the release cable from it, as described in paragraphs 1 to 3.
6 From inside the vehicle, detach and remove the lower facia panel on the driver's side.
7 Undo the release cable handle retaining bolt, unclip the cable and withdraw it through the bulkhead (photo).
8 Refit in the reverse order of removal. When reconnected, check for satisfactory operation prior to refitting the facia and grille panels.

10 Radiator grille - removal and refitting

1 Open the bonnet and support it in the raised position.
2 Undo the grille retaining screws, working from the front. Depending on type, tilt the grille and withdraw it from the vehicle, or if necessary lower the bonnet to allow sufficient clearance for grille removal.
3 Refit in the reverse order of removal. Engage the grille locating lugs before fitting the screws. When fitting a metal type grille, spring it into position between the bonnet (closed) and the bumper shield.

11.2 Front bumper side retaining bolts in engine compartment – Savanna model

Fig. 11.2 Adjust bonnet lock height with shims (C) and bonnet fitted height with rubber stops (D) (Sec 9)

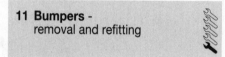

11 Bumpers - removal and refitting

Front bumper

1 Raise the vehicle at the front end and support it on axle stands.
2 Refer to Fig 11.4, (and photo) and remove the retaining screws and bolts from the points indicated. Note that screw (2) is accessible from the wheel arch side.
3 Repeat the procedure on the other side of the vehicle and remove the bumper.
4 Refit in the reverse order of removal. Check the bumper for correct alignment before fully tightening the retaining bolts and screws.

Rear bumper - Saloon

5 Raise and support the vehicle at the rear on axle stands.
6 Remove the trim panel from the left-hand side of the luggage area, then unscrew the bumper side fixing bolts.
7 Remove the mud baffle outer fastening.
8 Working from underneath the vehicle, undo the right-hand side fixing bolts from the wheel arch area, just to the rear of the fuel filler pipe.

Fig. 11.5 Rear bumper side retaining bolts in luggage area – Saloon model (Sec 11)

9.7 Bonnet release cable and handle (lower facia panel removed)

Fig. 11.3 Front grille retaining screw locations (Sec 10)

Fig. 11.4 Front bumper retaining screw and bolt locations (Sec 11)

Fig. 11.6 Rear bumper side fastening bolts in wheel arch – Saloon model (Sec 11)

11

Fig. 11.7 Rear bumper upper retaining screw locations – Savanna model (Sec 11)

Fig. 11.10 Underside fixings of early type spoiler (Sec 12)

3 Bolts   7 Bolt   8 Screw   9 Nut

Fig. 11.11 Early type spoiler assembly sequence (Sec 12)

1 Fit B to A   2 Fit C to A   3 Fit B to C

Fig. 11.8 Early (A) and late (B) type front spoiler (Sec 12)

Fig. 11.9 Front spoiler components – Turbo model (Sec 12)

1 Right and left-hand spoiler sections
2 Pop rivets
3 Shouldered screw (spoiler to wheel arch shield)
4 Bracket (to crossmember)
5 Bracket pop rivet
6 Clip
7 Screw
8 Pop rivet (spoiler to wheel arch shield)

9 Pull the bumper to the rear and remove it.
10 Refit in the reverse order of removal. Check for correct alignment before fully tightening the retaining bolts.

Rear bumper - Savanna

11 Proceed as described for the Saloon variants, but note the following additional points:
(a) Extract the foam plugs to gain access to the retaining bolts on the left-hand side of the luggage area
(b) Remove the plastic wheel arch protectors on each side
(c) Remove the upper retaining screws indicated in Fig. 11.7
12 Refitting is a reversal of the removal procedure. Check for correct alignment before fully tightening the retaining bolts.

12 Front spoiler (and brake cooling ducts - Turbo models) - removal and refitting

Front spoiler

1 The type of front spoiler fitted is dependent on the vehicle model. Refer to the accompanying illustrations for typical examples and their fixings. The earlier type spoiler is identified by its integral air intake grille.
2 Raise and support the vehicle at the front end on axle stands.

3 According to type, undo the retaining screws, nuts or bolts, and where necessary drill out the pop rivets. Withdraw the spoiler.
4 Where applicable, separate the two halves of the spoiler by drilling out the pop rivets and/or removing the retaining screws.
5 On Turbo models, disconnect the brake cooling ducts.
6 Refit in the reverse order of removal, noting the reassembly sequence for the early type spoiler as shown in Fig. 11.11.

Fig. 11.12 Underside fixings of late type spoiler (Sec 12)

1 Nuts   2 Pop rivet   3 Bolt

Fig. 11.13 Check for correct clip locations
on late type spoiler (Sec 12)

Fig. 11.14 Underside view of Turbo spoiler
and brake cooling duct (Sec 12)

3 Spoiler retaining screw
A Brake cooling duct retaining screw to
   spoiler

Fig. 11.15 Retaining clip on end of Turbo
spoiler (Sec 12)

Brake cooling ducts (Turbo models)

7 Brake cooling ducts are fitted to Turbo
models, the air being drawn in through the
grille in the front face of the spoiler
8 The ducts and protector shields are
secured by screws and bolts as shown in the
accompanying figures.
9 Removal of the shields will be necessary to
allow access when undertaking certain repair
and overhaul procedures on the front brakes
and suspension components.

13 Front wing -
removal and refitting

1 Remove the front indicator unit on the side
concerned as described in Chapter 12.
2 Working from underneath the vehicle, undo
the bumper retaining screws and bolts shown
in Fig. 11.18.

9   Left-hand cooling duct
10 Righthand cooling duct
11 Left-hand mounting
    bracket
12 Right-hand mounting
    bracket
13 Bracket
14 Spring nut
15 Screw

Fig. 11.16 Brake cooling ducts and associated fittings – Turbo model (Sec 12)

Fig. 11.17 Brake cooling duct and wheel
arch shield components (Sec 12)

11 and 12 Cooling duct mountings
13 Cooling duct-to-wheel arch shield bracket
14 Spring nut

Fig. 11.18 Underside view showing front
fixings (Sec 13)

1 Bolt   2 Bolt   3 Screw

Fig. 11.19 Front wing fixings (Sec 13)

5 Top edge screws   7 Wheel arch shield   8 Front bolts   10 Nuts
6 Scuttle grille screw   clips   9 Moulding screw   11 Sill screw

11

1	Door lock button	9	Trim
2	Door bin	10	Mirror inner trim
3	Speaker grille	11	Foam seal
4	Speaker unit	12	Grommet
5	Door catch release	13	Glass channel trim
6	Trim panel	14	Glass channel
8	Door rear view mirror	15	Insulator sheet

Fig. 11.20 Front door, trim panel and associated components (Sec 14)

3 Release the front end trim by undoing the retaining nut from within the indicator aperture.

4 Refer to Fig. 11.19 and remove the various retainers from the points indicated. Prise free the wheel arch protector shield retaining clips. To remove side retaining screw (8), pivot the bumper outwards for access.

5 When all the retainers are removed, heat the inner wing section in the area marked (A) using a hot air gun (a hair dryer will suffice), but take care not to burn the paint if the wing is to be re-used.

6 Refit in the reverse order of removal. If a new wing panel is being fitted, apply a suitable body sealant to the area marked (A).

7 Check for correct wing alignment before fully retightening the retaining bolts.

8 Check the indicators for correct operation on completion.

14 Door trim panels - removal and refitting

Front doors

1 Disconnect the battery earth lead.

2 Remove the door lock button by releasing its retainer as shown. Insert a suitable rod or a small screwdriver blade into the slot in the button and press to release the retainer (photo).

3 Undo the retaining screws and remove the lower trim/bin from the door panel (photo).

14.2 Door lock button removal

14.3 Door lower trim/bin retaining screws

14.4A Disconnect the door wiring connectors . . .

14.4B . . . to remove the switches and speakers

14.5A Undo the retaining screws . . .

14.5B . . . and detach the door catch release from the operating rod

14.6 Prise free the triangular trim panel

14.7 Removing a manual window regulator handle

14.8 Trim removal using a flat bladed tool with a forked end piece

4 Remove the door-mounted speaker unit and door switches, if applicable, as described in Chapter 12. Remove the speaker panel support and disconnect the wiring connectors (photos).

5 Undo the retaining screws and remove the door catch release (photos).

6 Prise free and remove the triangular trim panel from the door mirror adjuster (photo).

7 Where applicable, remove the door window regulator handle by prising free with a flat forked tool (photo).

8 Carefully prise free the trim panel from the door using a suitable tool as shown (photo).

9 Peel back the plastic insulator sheet from the inner door for access to the inner door fittings.

10 Refit in the reverse order of removal.

Rear doors

11 Proceed as described for the front door

trim panels, but ignore paragraphs 3. 4 and 6. Refer to Fig. 11.21.

15 Doors -
removal and refitting

1 Remove the trim panel and inner insulator sheet as described in Section 14, and disconnect the wiring from any retainers within the door. Withdraw the wiring harness from the door.

2 Release the door check strap by driving out the retaining pin with a drift (photo).

3 Support the door on blocks or with the help of an assistant.

4 Prise out the two caps covering each hinge pin, using a screwdriver.

5 Using a cranked metal rod suitable diameter as a drift, drive out the upper and

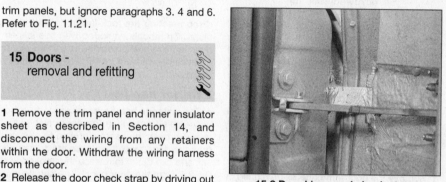

15.2 Door hinge and check strap

lower hinge pins. Note that the hinge pins are removed towards each other, ie downwards for the upper pin and upwards for the lower pin.

6 With the hinge pins removed, carefully lift off the door.

7 Renew the hinge pins and bushes whenever the door is removed. Note that there are two hinge pin types available - see Fig. 11.22. Ensure that correct replacements are obtained.

8 Refitting is a reversal of the removal procedure.

1 Lock button (inner)
3 Triangular trim (inner)
4 Door catch release handle
5 Trim panel
6 Window channel
7 Channel trim
8 Trim guard
9 Window glass guide
10 Insulator sheet (large)
11 Insulator sheet (small)
13 Triangular trim (outer)

Fig. 11.21 Rear door, trim panel and associated components (Sec 14)

Fig. 11.22 Door hinge pin types (Sec 15)

A Long pin   B Short pin

11

Fig. 11.23 Front door wiring harness routing and retaining clip locations (arrowed) (Sec 15)

Fig. 11.24 Rear door wiring harness routing and retaining clip locations (Sec 15)

Fig. 11.25 Front door lock, exterior handle and connecting rods (Sec 16)

1 Handle   2 Latch link   4 Link rod

9 If the door does not fit flush to the aperture, adjust by carefully bending the hinge arms using a suitable slotted lever bar. Ensure that the door wiring harness is correctly routed and secured - see Fig. 11.23 or 11.24 as applicable.

16 Door fittings -
removal and refitting

1 Remove the door trim panel as described in Section 14.
2 With the door trim panel removed, the following items can be removed from the door as required. Unless otherwise stated, the refitting details are a reversal of the removal procedures.

Central door locking

3 The solenoids can be removed after

disconnecting the lock link rods and wiring plugs. On models equipped with this system, door locking and unlocking is carried out by an infra red remote control device which is described in Chapter 12.

Exterior handle

4 The exterior handle is secured by a bolt accessible from within the door cavity. Undo the bolt, push the handle forward to release it from the door panel, then push the connecting link and clip down to release the upper end of the link from the door panel. The handle must be removed separately so that the clip is not damaged. Rotate the handle so that it is vertical, then disconnect the link.
5 If the link and its clips are separated, the amount by which the door handle opens will probably need adjustment. Refit the handle before clipping the link back in place.

Front door lock

6 Undo the two screws retaining the exterior handle, disconnect the link rod and remove the exterior handle.
7 Undo and remove the Torx screws securing the door lock, extract the rubber grommet, reach through the aperture and pull the lock towards the aperture. Detach the door catch

release control rod from the lock, then withdraw the lock unit.
8 Refit in reverse order, ensuring that the connecting links are securely attached. Check the operation of the lock before refitting the trim panel.

Rear door lock

9 Remove the door window glass as described in paragraphs 16 to 19.
10 Unscrew the window guide rail screws to enable the link to pass between the winder rail and the door.
11 Detach the horizontal link rod from its retaining clip, remove the link retaining fork and push it into the door body.
12 Undo the three Torx retaining screws from the door lock unit, then withdraw the lock through the inner door aperture. As it is being removed, detach the control link.
13 Refit in reverse order, ensuring that the connecting links are securely attached.

Door window regulator

14 On models with manually-operated windows, undo the bolts securing the regulator mechanism and cable to the door (photo) and manipulate the regulator out of the door aperture.
15 On models with electrically-operated windows, disconnect the motor wiring connectors, undo the bolts securing the motor to the door, and the bolts securing the mechanism to the door. Manipulate the assembly out of the door aperture (photo).

Fig. 11.26 Rotate the exterior handle and disengage it (Sec 16)

Fig. 11.27 Rear door lock, exterior handle and connecting rods (Sec 16)

1 Exterior handle	*5 Link*
2 Link rod	*6 Clip*
3 Wiring (central locking)	*10 Grommet*
	11 Latch control link

16.14 Manual door window regulator spindle and retaining bolt

1 Glass
2 Access holes (to glass fasteners)
3 Glass fasteners
4 Mechanism
5 Rail
6 Motor

Fig. 11.28 Front door electric window regulator mechanism components (Sec 16)

1 Glass
2 Access hole (for glass fasteners)

Fig. 11.29 Rear door window regulator mechanisms (electric type fitted) (Sec 16)

Fig. 11.30 Window glass (1) removal from front door (Sec 16)

Fig. 11.31 Window glass (1) removal from rear door (Sec 16)

400 mm

Fig. 11.32 Front door bottom channel-to-glass location (Sec 16)

Window glass

16 With the glass fully down, pull off the inner glass weatherstrip. No clips are used to retain it.
17 Raise the glass fully and unscrew the two bolts from the glass bottom channel, accessible through the holes (photo).
18 Lower the mechanism (manual or power-operated), at the same time holding the glass in the raised position.
19 Swivel the glass and withdraw it towards the outside of the door.
20 If the glass is removed from its bottom channel, reset it in the channel in accordance with the dimension given in Fig. 11.32 or 11.33 as applicable.
21 When the glass is refitted, wind the glass up and down to check for smoothness of operation. If required, the bottom of the guides can be moved to centralise the glass.

16.15 Electric door window regulator mechanism removal

16.17 Glass bottom channel bolt locations

700 mm

Fig. 11.33 Rear door bottom channel-to-glass location (Sec 16)

11

17.2A Electric mirror adjuster and retaining screws

17.2B Manual mirror adjuster and retaining screws

17.3A Manual mirror adjuster inner trim retaining screw (arrowed)

17 Door rear-view mirror - removal and refitting

1 On models fitted with electric rear-view mirrors, disconnect the battery earth lead, then remove the door speaker unit as described in Chapter 12. Reach through the speaker aperture and disconnect the wiring connector from the mirror.
2 Carefully prise free the plastic outer trim. Undo the mirror and mirror adjuster retaining screws. Withdraw the adjuster unit and peel back the insulation gasket (photos).
3 Extract the foam seal and on manual adjustment types, undo the inner trim

retaining screw. Undo the retaining nuts and remove the mirror (photos).
4 Refit in the reverse order of removal. Check for satisfactory operation on completion and adjust the mirror to suit.

18 Boot lid - removal and refitting

1 Open the boot lid and mark the outline of the hinges using a soft pencil. Remove the plastic hinge cover for access where applicable (photo).
2 With the help of an assistant, undo the two bolts each side securing the boot lid to the hinge and carefully lift the boot lid away. As it

is lifted clear, detach the number plate light and lock solenoid wiring connectors (where applicable).
3 Refitting is the reverse sequence to removal. Align the previously made outline marks or, if necessary, reposition the boot lid on each hinge to give a uniform gap all round.
4 To adjust the height of the boot lid, remove the trim panel for access, and reset the lock striker plate position to suit (photo).

19 Boot lid lock - removal and refitting

1 Open the boot lid and then remove the number plate and trim (photo).

Fig. 11.34 Disconnecting the rear view mirror wiring through the speaker aperture (Sec 17)

17.3B Manual mirror retaining studs (arrowed)

18.1 Boot lid hinge with plastic cover removed

Fig. 11.35 Boot lid and hinges. Remove hinge bolts (1). Do not remove bolts (2) unless absolutely necessary (Sec 18)

18.4 Boot lid lock striker plate

19.1 Boot lid lock shown with number plate and trim removed

19.2 Boot lid lock connecting link (arrowed)

19.4 Boot lid lock solenoid removal

20.2 Prising free a tailgate strut locking retainer

2 Unclip and remove the lock unit connecting link, undo the retaining screws, then tilt the lock and remove it (photo).
3 To remove the lock barrel, drive out the retaining pin (1.5 mm diameter), then extract the barrel.
4 Where applicable, to remove the boot lid lock solenoid, detach the wiring and the connecting rod, then release and remove the solenoid unit (photo).
5 Refit in the reverse order of removal. Check for satisfactory operation on completion.

20 Tailgate support struts (Savanna models) - removal and refitting

1 Raise and support the tailgate, with the aid of an assistant if both struts are to be removed.
2 Using a screwdriver, carefully lever out the locking retainer at the strut ball end fitting (photo).
3 Withdraw the strut from the ball pegs and remove it from the car. **Do not** attempt to repair a defective strut, renew it.
4 Refitting is the reverse sequence to removal.

21 Tailgate (Savanna models) - removal and refitting

1 Remove the rear side trim panel from the luggage area for access to the rear window washer reservoir on the left-hand side.
2 Detach the tailgate wiring harness connectors and earth leads (photos).
3 Disconnect the rear window washer pipe from the reservoir allowing for a small amount of spillage. Plug the pipe and reservoir connector to prevent continuous fluid spillage whilst detached.
4 Tie the pipe tailgate wiring harness to a suitable length of strong cord, so that as the wiring and pipe are withdrawn through the rear corner panel. the cord follows and can be untied once clear of the rear panel and left in situ. The process can then be repeated in

reverse order during refitting, the cord acting as a guide as it pulls the harness and pipe down through the corner panel.
5 Disconnect the support struts at the tailgate, as described in the previous Section.
6 Carefully prise free the headlining trim panel at the rear edge to gain access to the tailgate retaining nuts.
7 With the tailgate suitably supported, undo the retaining nuts and carefully remove the tailgate. Collect any adjustment shims from the hinges as they are withdrawn.
8 Refit in the reverse order or removal. Adjust the tailgate so that it is flush with the roof line using shims at the hinges.
9 If necessary, adjust the position of the tailgate striker as described in Section 22.

Fig. 11.36 Boot lid lock and barrel. Extract pin (arrowed) to remove barrel (Sec 19)

Fig. 11.37 Tailgate wiring harness connector location (1) behind rear side trim panel – Savanna models (Sec 21)

Fig. 11.38 Tailgate hinge retaining nuts are accessible on removing headlining trim panel (Sec 21)

21.2A Tailgate heated rear window element connector

21.2B Tailgate wiring harness and rubber gaiter

11

Fig. 11.39 Tailgate lock unit (Sec 22)

1 Retaining clip
2 Control lever
3 Barrel and return spring

22 Tailgate lock and associated fittings (Savanna models) - removal, refitting and adjustment

1 Open the tailgate and remove the rear trim panel from it.
2 Undo the retaining screws from the lock unit, then disengage the control link from the lock to allow the lock to be withdrawn.
3 To remove the lock barrel, prise free the retaining clip, remove the control lever and withdraw the barrel.
Take care not to lose the barrel return spring which may eject as the barrel is removed.
4 To remove the number plate/light panel, disconnect the lock link and the latch control from the handle. Undo the four retaining nuts and remove the panel. Disconnect the light wires as it is withdrawn.
5 Refitting is a reversal of the removal procedure. If the barrel return spring was removed, refit it as shown in Fig. 11.39 prior to inserting the lock barrel. Check for satisfactory operation.
6 If required, adjust the striker plate by loosening off its retaining screws and adjusting it as required. Retighten the screws to complete.

24.2 Centre console, speaker grille and retaining screws

23 Windscreen and fixed windows - removal and refitting

1 The removal and refitting of the windscreen and fixed windows (and the heated rear screen), are tasks which must be entrusted to a Renault dealer or a professional windscreen replacement specialist.
2 The glass is flush-mounted, and removal requires the use of a hot knife or wire to release the sealant plus the use of special bonding agents when refitting.

24 Centre console - removal and refitting

1 Disconnect the battery earth lead.
2 If fitted, remove the radio speaker unit as described in Chapter 12 (photo).
3 If fitted, lift out and remove the ashtray.
4 Unscrew and remove the console retaining screws.
5 Carefully prise free the gear lever gaiter from the console, pull it up and rotate it to allow it to pass over the gear lever. As the console is lifted clear, note any wiring

connections to the console-mounted switches and/or the cigar lighter, and detach them.
6 Refit in the reverse order of removal.

25 Luggage area side trim panel - removal and refitting

1 Untwist and remove the side trim retaining clips, then withdraw the panel.
2 The left-hand side panel also retains the rear window washer reservoir and it is therefore necessary to detach the wire from the pump unit and the fluid supply hose (see Chapter 12).
3 To remove the reservoir from the panel, simply prise open the panel sides to release the reservoir.
4 Refit in the reverse order of removal.

26 Facia panel - removal and refitting

1 Disconnect the battery earth lead.
2 Slide the front seats fully to the rear, or preferably unbolt and remove them to allow full access when removing the facia.
3 Remove the centre console as described in Section 24.
4 Undo the retaining screws from the positions indicated in Fig. 11.41 and remove the lower facia panels on the driver's side. Remove the fusebox from the hinged lid in the lower panel and disconnect the wiring multiplug connectors. Remove the relay plate from the fusebox area (see Chapter 12).
5 Remove the steering wheel and column as described in Chapter 10.
6 Remove the tweeter speaker from the facia on each side. To do this, prise free the small cover between the grilles, undo the retaining screw, then withdraw the speaker and disconnect the wire. Repeat the procedure

Fig. 11.40 Main facia panel and associated components – left-hand drive shown (Sec 26)

Fig. 11.41 Remove the lower facia panel retaining screws – left-hand drive shown (Sec 26)

26.9 Facia retaining nut – left-hand side viewed through tweeter speaker aperture

26.14 Facia panel centring peg (arrowed)

27.1A Seat rail rear retaining bolts (arrowed) . . .

27.1B . . . and front retaining bolt

and remove the speaker unit on the other side.

7 Remove the glovebox by releasing the retaining clip at the side of each pivot whilst simultaneously lifting and withdrawing the glovebox unit.

8 Detach and prise free the inner sill trim panel on each side. These panels are a press fit into securing clips which also retain the wiring harnesses each side. Disconnect the harnesses at their block connectors and also unbolt the earth wires on the left-hand side.

9 Undo the facia retaining nut on each side from the positions shown (photo).

10 Where applicable, disconnect and remove the manual choke control (see Chapter 3).

11 Disconnect the heater control panel (see Chapter 2).

12 Remove the three facia-to-heater unit mounting screws.

13 The facia unit is now ready to be withdrawn. An assistant will be required to help in supporting the weight of the unit and in guiding it clear. As it is withdrawn, disconnect the relevant wiring connectors from the rear

face of the facia panel. Note the routeing of the wiring harnesses and the radio antenna as they are disconnected to ensure that they are correctly located when reassembling.

14 Refitting is a reversal of the removal procedure. Engage the facia onto the centring peg and reconnect the wiring connectors, antenna lead and speedometer cable as the unit is relocated (photo).

27 Seats –
removal and refitting

Front seats

1 Move the seat to be removed fully forward, then undo the seat rail retaining bolts at the rear. Now slide the seat fully to the rear and undo the front rail retaining bolts (photos). Remove the seat.

2 Refit in the reverse order of removal.

Rear seat - saloon

3 Grip the seat retaining clip with a pair of

pliers and withdraw it from its location in the seat pivot. Remove the seat.

4 Refit in the reverse order of removal.

Rear 'intermediate' seat - Savanna

5 Tilt the seat forwards, unclip the gas support strut by prising free the balljoint retaining clip and detach the strut. Do not try to remove the clip from the balljoint.

6 Working from the inboard side of the seat, press down and remove the retaining clip using a screwdriver as shown in Fig. 11.43, or

A Mounting bar
B Seat frame
C Retaining clip

Fig. 11.42 Rear seat removal – Saloon model (Sec 27)

Fig. 11.43 Disconnecting a rear 'intermediate' seat retaining clip – Savanna model (Sec 27)

11

pivot down the trim cover and undo the hinge retaining bolts (photo).

7 Refit in the reverse order of removal.

Rear 'occasional' seat - Savanna

8 Undo the seat hinge bolts, fold the seat down and remove it.

9 Refit in the reverse order of removal.

28 Head rests

1 The headrests are adjustable for height simply by moving them up and down.

2 To remove them, twist the bevelled plinth at the base of the right-hand headrest stem while pulling the headrest upwards.

29 Seat belts - maintenance, removal and refitting

1 Periodically inspect the seat belts for

27.6 Rear 'intermediate' seat hinge trim cover removed – Savanna model

fraying or other damage. If evident, renew the belt.

2 The belts may be cleaned using warm water and liquid detergent. Do not use solvents of any kind.

3 If the car is involved in a front end collision and the belts have restrained the front or rear seat occupants, renew the belts.

4 When refitting, always maintain the original

29.5 Rear seat belt anchor bolt – Savanna model

fitted sequence of washers and spacers.

5 The rear seat belt lower anchor bolts are accessible after removing the seat back (photo). The upper anchor bolts can be reached after removing the trim panel (Section 25).

6 On some models, a buzzer warning system is fitted with a timer relay to prevent driving off with the seat belts unfastened.

Chapter 12 Electrical system

For modifications, and information applicable to later models, see Supplement at end of manual

Contents

Degrees of difficulty

Easy, suitable for novice with little experience | **Fairly easy,** suitable for beginner with some experience | **Fairly difficult,** suitable for competent DIY mechanic 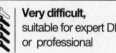 | **Difficult,** suitable for experienced DIY mechanic 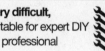 | **Very difficult,** suitable for expert DIY or professional

Specifications

General

System type	12 volt, negative earth
Battery type	Low maintenance or 'maintenance-free' sealed for life
Battery capacity	50 or 60 amp hr

Wiper blades

Front	Champion X-5103
Rear	Champion X-4503

Alternator

Make	Paris-Rhône or Ducellier
Type:	
Paris-Rhône (models without air conditioning)	A1 3N87, A1 3N88, A1 3N120 or A1 3N124
Paris-Rhône (air conditioned models only)	A14N73 or A14N76
Ducellier	516067
Maximum output	60 or 105* amps

air conditioned models only

Starter motor

Make/type number	Paris-Rhône D9E85, D9E771, D10E88 or D10E92

12

Bulbs (typical)

	Wattage
Headlamp	60/55
Front foglamp	55
Front sidelight	4
Direction indicators	21
Stop/tail	21/5
Reversing lamp	21
Rear foglamp	21
Rear number plate lamp	5
Interior lamps	10
Switch and panel illumination	1.2 or 2
Warning lamps	1.2 or 2

Fuses

Fuse No.	Application	Rating (amps)
1	Heating (and rear window wiper/washer on Savanna model)	20
2	Engine cooling fan, radio	10
3	Heated rear window	20
4	Clock and interior lights. Also radio*, electronic instrument panel (before ignition)	5
5	Windscreen wiper/park timer*	10
6	Flasher unit and hazard warning lights (Savanna and Turbo)	10
7	Side and tail lamps (left-hand side) and front foglamps*	5
8	Side and tail lamps (right-hand side)	5
9	Cigar lighter	10
10	Stop lamps	10
11	Instrument panel, reversing lamp*	10
12	Windscreen wiper	15
13	Rear foglamp	7.5
14	Not used	-
15	Air conditioning*	30
16	Electric door locks*, electric rear view mirrors*	25
17	Window winder (left-hand side)*	30
18	Window winder (right-hand side)*, sunroof*	30
19	Anti-lock brakes*	3

Fitting depends on model and territory

1 General description

The electrical system is of the 12 volt negative earth type, and consists of a battery, alternator, starter motor and related electrical accessories, components and wiring.

The battery, charged by the alternator which is belt-driven from the crankshaft pulley, provides a steady amount of current for the ignition, starting, lighting and other electrical circuits. The battery may be a low maintenance type of a maintenance-free 'sealed for life' type, according to model.

The starter motor is of the pre-engaged type incorporating an integral solenoid. On starting, the solenoid moves the drive pinion into engagement with the flywheel ring gear before the starter motor is energised. Once the engine has started, a one-way clutch prevents the motor armature being driven by the engine until the pinion disengages from the flywheel.

Further details of the major electrical systems are given in the relevant Sections of this Chapter.

Caution: Before carrying out any work on the vehicle electrical system, read through the precautions given in 'Safety First!' at the beginning of this manual and in Section 2 of this Chapter.

2 Electrical system - precautions

It is necessary to take extra care when working on the electrical system to avoid damage to semi-conductor devices (diodes and transistors), and to avoid the risk of personal injury. In addition to the precautions given in 'Safety First' at the beginning of this manual, observe the following items when working on the system.

1 *Always remove rings, watches, etc, before working on the electrical system.* Even with the battery disconnected, capacitive discharge could occur if a component live terminal is earthed through a metal object. This could cause a shock or nasty burn.

2 *Do not reverse the battery connections.* Components such as the alternator or any other having semi-conductor circuitry could be irreparably damaged.

3 If the engine is being started using jump leads and a slave battery, make the connections as shown in Fig. 12.1 and with

Fig. 12.1 Battery jump lead connections using a slave battery (Sec 2)

Note negative lead from slave battery connected to suitable earth point in engine compartment

Fig. 12.2 Remove battery cell covers (3) to top up electrolyte level (low maintenance type battery) (Sec 3)

reference to 'Safety first' at the beginning of this manual.

4 Never disconnect the battery terminals, or alternator wiring when the engine is running.

5 The battery leads and alternator wiring must be disconnected before carrying out any electric welding on the car.

6 Never use an ohmmeter of the type incorporating a hand cranked generator for circuit or continuity testing.

7 If an electronic instrument panel is fitted, refer to the precautionary notes given at the start of Section 24.

3 Maintenance

1 At the intervals given in 'Routine maintenance' the following service operations should be carried out on the electrical system components:

2 Check the operation of all the electrical equipment, ie wipers, washers, lights, direction indicators, horn, etc. Refer to the appropriate Sections of this Chapter if any components are found to be inoperative.

3 Visually check all accessible wiring connectors, harnesses and retaining clips for security, or any signs of chafing or damage. Rectify any problems encountered.

4 Check the alternator drivebelt for cracks, fraying or damage. Renew the belt if worn or, if satisfactory, check and adjust the belt tension. These procedures are covered in Chapter 2.

5 Check the condition of the wiper blades and if they are cracked or show signs of deterioration, renew them, as described in Section 28. Check the operation of the windscreen, tailgate and headlamp washers, as applicable, and adjust the nozzle setting if necessary.

6 Top up the battery, on models where this is necessary, using distilled water until the tops of the cell plates are just submerged. Clean the battery terminals and case and, if necessary, check the battery condition using the procedures described in Section 4.

7 Top up the washer fluid reservoir and check the security of the pump wires and water pipes.

8 It is advisable to have the headlamp aim adjusted using optical beam setting equipment.

9 While carrying out a road test, check the operation of all the instruments and warning lights and the operation of the direction indicator self-cancelling mechanism.

4 Battery - general

1 According to model the battery may be of the low maintenance type in which the cell covers may be removed to allow periodic topping-up in the conventional way, or of the maintenance-free type which do not require topping up. The maintenance-free battery has a sealed top cover which must not under any circumstances be removed. If the seals are broken the battery warranty will be invalidated.

2 On low maintenance batteries, periodically lift off the cover and check the electrolyte level. The tops of the cell plates should be just covered by the electrolyte. If not, add distilled or demineralized water until they are. Do not add extra water with the idea of reducing the intervals of topping-up. This will merely dilute the electrolyte and reduce charging and current retention efficiency.

3 If the electrolyte level needs an excessive amount of replenishment but no leaks are apparent, it could be due to overcharging as a result of the battery having been run down and then left to recharge from the vehicle rather than an outside source. If the battery has been heavily discharged for one reason or another it is best to have it continuously charged at a low amperage for a period of many hours. If it is charged from the car's system under such conditions, the charging will be intermittent and greatly varied in intensity. This does not do the battery any good at all. If the battery needs topping-up frequently, even when it is known to be in good condition and not too old, then the voltage regulator should be checked to ensure that the charging output is being correctly controlled. An elderly battery, however, may need topping-up more than a new one, because it needs to take in more charging current. Do not worry about this, provided it gives satisfactory service.

4 Keep the battery clean and dry all over by wiping it with a dry cloth. A dirty or damp top surface could cause tracking between the two terminal posts with consequent draining of power.

5 Periodically remove the battery and check the support tray clamp and battery terminal connections for signs of corrosion - usually indicated by a whitish green crystalline deposit. Wash this off with clean water to which a little ammonia or washing soda has been added. Then treat the terminals with petroleum jelly and the battery mounting with suitable protective paint to prevent further corrosive action.

6 On maintenance-free batteries access to the cells is not possible and only the overall condition of the battery can be checked using a voltmeter connected across the two terminals. On the low maintenance type a hydrometer can be used to check the condition of each individual cell. The table in the following Section gives the hydrometer readings for the various states of charge. A further check can be made when the battery is undergoing a charge. If, towards the end of the charge, when the cells should be 'gassing' (bubbling), one cell appears not to be, this indicates the cell or cells in question are probably breaking down and the life of the battery is limited.

5 Battery - charging

1 In winter when a heavy demand is placed on the battery, such as when starting from cold and using more electrical equipment, it may be necessary to have the battery fully charged from an external source. *Note that both battery leads must be disconnected before charging in order to prevent possible damage to any semi-conductor electrical components.*

2 The terminals of the battery and the leads of the charger must be connected *positive to positive* and *negative to negative*.

3 Charging is best done overnight at a 'trickle' rate of 1 to 1.5 amps. Alternatively, on low maintenance batteries, a 3 to 4 amp rate can be used over a period of 4 hours or so. Check the specific gravity in the latter case and stop the charge when the reading is correct. Maintenance-free batteries should not be charged in this way due to their design and construction. It is strongly recommended that you seek the advice of a Renault dealer on the suitability of various types of charging equipment before using them on maintenance-free batteries.

4 The specific gravities for hydrometer readings on low maintenance batteries are as follows:

Fully discharged	Electrolyte temperature	Fully charged
1.098	38°C (100°F)	1.268
1.102	32°C (90°F)	1.272
1.106	27°C (80°F)	1.276
1.110	21°C (70°C)	1.280
1.114	16°C (60°F)	1.284
1.118	10°C (50°F)	1.288
1.122	4°C (40°F)	1.292
1.126	-1.5°C (30°F)	1.296

12

6 Battery - removal and refitting

1 The battery is located in the engine compartment on the front right or left-hand corner, depending on model.

2 Open the bonnet and disconnect the battery negative (-) lead then the positive(+) lead in that order.

3 Unbolt the clamp from the lip at the base of the battery casing and lift the battery from its mounting platform (photo).

4 Refit by reversing the removal operations, connect the positive (+) lead and the negative (-) lead in that order.

5 On Renault original equipment batteries, the battery can be quickly disconnected simply by unscrewing the negative terminal thumbscrew through a few turns. There is no need to disconnect the cable from the battery terminal.

7 Alternator - precautions and maintenance

1 The alternator can be damaged if the following precautions are not observed.

2 Never connect the battery leads incorrectly.

3 Never run the engine with the alternator leads disconnected.

4 Do not pull off a battery lead as a means of stopping the engine.

5 When charging the battery from the mains, disconnect it from the car's electrical system or remove it.

6 When using electric welding equipment on the car, always disconnect both battery leads and the alternator leads.

7 Do not operate the starter motor if the engine earth lead is not connected.

8 Regularly inspect the condition of the alternator drivebelt and if frayed or cut, renew it, as described in Chapter 2.

Fig. 12.4 Front view of alternator installation on 2.0 litre engine (Sec 9)

A Belt tensioner adjuster bolt
B Belt tensioner
C Alternator mounting/pivot bolt

6.3 Battery retaining clamp and securing bolt – 1.7 litre model

9 The alternator has an integral voltage regulator.

8 Alternator - fault tracing and rectification

1 If the ignition warning lamp fails to illuminate when the ignition is switched on, first check the wiring connections at the rear of the alternator for security. If satisfactory, check that the warning lamp bulb has not blown and is secure in its holder. If the lamp still fails to illuminate check the continuity of the warning lamp feed wire from the alternator to the bulb holder. If all is satisfactory, the alternator is at fault and should be renewed or taken to an automobile electrician for testing and repair.

2 If the ignition warning lamp illuminates when the engine is running, ensure that the drivebelt is correctly tensioned (see Chapter 2), and that the connections on the rear of the alternator are secure. If all is so far satisfactory, check the alternator brushes and commutator, as described in Section 10. If the fault still persists, the alternator should be renewed, or taken to an automobile electrician for testing and repair.

3 If the alternator output is suspect even though the warning lamp functions correctly, the regulated voltage may be checked as follows:

4 Connect a voltmeter across the battery terminals and then start the engine.

9.3A Remove the rubber cover . . .

Fig. 12.3 Front view of alternator installation on 1.7 litre engine (Sec 9)

A Belt tensioner
B Alternator mounting/pivot bolt
C Adjuster bolt locking

5 Increase the engine speed until the reading on the voltmeter remains steady. This should be between 13.5 and 15 volts.

6 Switch on as many electrical accessories as possible and check that the alternator maintains the regulated voltage at between 13.5 and 15 volts.

7 If the regulated voltage is not as stated, the fault may be due to a faulty diode, a severed phase or worn brushes, springs or commutator. The brushes and commutator may be attended to, as described in Section 10, but if the fault still persists the alternator should be renewed, or taken to an automobile electrician for testing and repair.

9 Alternator - removal and refitting

1 Disconnect the battery earth lead.

2 On 2.0 litre models, access to the alternator is not good, but can be improved by raising the car at the front and removing the engine undershield to gain access from underneath, or by removing the radiator (see Chapter 2). If the former method is used, ensure that the vehicle is securely supported on axle stands.

3 Disconnect the leads from the terminals on the rear cover of the alternator (photos).

9.3B . . . and disconnect the leads from the rear of the alternator – 1.7 litre model

9.3C Detaching the alternator lead cover – 2.0 litre model

9.5A Alternator and adjuster/mounting bolts – 1 .7 litre model

9.5B Alternator and adjuster/mounting bolts – 2.0 litre model

4 Remove the drivebelt as described in Chapter 2.

5 Unscrew and remove the mounting and adjuster link bolts and lift the alternator from its mounting bracket (photos).

6 Refit by reversing the removal operations.

7 Tension the drivebelt as described in Chapter 2.

8 On 2.0 litre models, refit the radiator and top up the cooling system (Chapter 2) and/or refit the undershield as applicable.

10 Alternator brushes - removal, inspection and refitting

Note: *Due to the specialist knowledge and equipment required to test and repair an alternator accurately, it is recommended that,*

10.3 Alternator regulator and brush box assembly removal

10.4 Alternator brush box showing brush protrusion

if the performance is suspect the alternator be taken to an automobile electrician who will have the facilities for such work. It is, however, a relatively simple task to attend to the brush gear and this operation is described below.

1 On 1.7 litre engine models, brush removal can be carried out without removing the alternator from the engine, but in this instance the battery negative lead must first be disconnected, followed by the wiring connections to the alternator.

2 Remove the rear plastic cover.

3 Undo the two small bolts or nuts securing the regulator and brush box assembly to the rear of the alternator. Lift off the regulator and brush box, disconnect the electrical leads, noting their locations, then remove the regulator and brush box assembly from the alternator (photo).

4 Check that the brushes stand proud of their holders and are free to move without sticking (photo). If necessary clean them with a petrol-moistened cloth. Check that the brush spring pressure is equal for both brushes and gives reasonable tension. If in doubt about the condition of the brushes and springs compare them with new parts at a Renault parts dealer.

5 Clean the commutator with a petrol-moistened cloth, then check for signs of scoring, burning or severe pitting. If evident the commutator should be attended to by an automobile electrician.

6 Refitting the regulator and brush box assembly is the reverse sequence to removal.

Fig. 12.5 Paris-Rhône alternator components – models without air conditioning (Sec 10)

Fig. 12.6 Paris-Rhône alternator components – air conditioned models only (Sec 10)

12

Fig. 12.7 Ducellier alternator components (Sec 10)

12.3 Starter motor with heat shield (exhaust downpipe removed) – 1.7 litre model

11 Starter motor - testing in the car

1 If the starter motor fails to operate, first check the condition of the battery by switching on the headlamps. If they glow brightly then gradually dim after a few seconds, the battery is in an uncharged condition.
2 If the battery is satisfactory, check the starter motor main terminal and the engine earth cable for security. Check the terminal connections on the starter solenoid, located on top of the starter motor.
3 Access to the starter motor and the wiring connections is poor on all models; refer to Section 12 for details.
4 If the starter still fails to turn, use a voltmeter, or 12 volt test lamp and leads, to ensure that there is battery voltage at the solenoid main terminal (containing the cable from the battery positive terminal).
5 With the ignition switched on and the ignition key in position D, check that voltage is

reaching the solenoid terminal with the spade connector, and also the starter main terminal.
6 If there is no voltage reaching the spade connector, there is a wiring or ignition switch faulty. If voltage is available, but the starter does not operate, then the starter or solenoid is likely to be at fault.

12 Starter motor - removal and refitting

1 Disconnect the battery earth lead.
2 Access to the starter motor is poor on both the 1.7 and 2.0 litre models. In each case, access is best achieved from underneath, so raise and support the vehicle at the front on axle stands.
3 On 1.7 litre models, unbolt and disconnect the exhaust downpipe, and unbolt and remove the starter motor heat shield (photo).
4 On 2.0 litre models, detach and remove the engine undershield.
5 The procedure is now similar for both engine types.

6 Disconnect the electrical leads at the starter motor, noting their respective locations (photo).
7 Unscrew and remove the bolts securing the starter motor to the clutch housing, and also the rear support bracket bolts (photo). Withdraw the starter motor.
8 Note the position of the locating dowel in the upper rear bellhousing bolt hole and make sure that it is in place when refitting (photo).
9 Refitting the starter motor is the reverse sequence to removal, but on 2.0 litre models, tighten the bellhousing bolts before the support bracket bolts.

13 Starter motor - overhaul

Note: *Overhaul of the starter motor is normally confined to inspection and, if necessary, renewal of the brush gear components. Due to the limited availability of replacement parts, any other faults occurring on the starter usually result in renewal of the complete motor. However, for those wishing to dismantle the starter motor, this Section may be used as a guide. The procedure is essentially similar for all motor types and any minor differences can be noted by referring to the accompanying illustrations.*

1 Remove the starter motor from the car, as described in the previous Section.

12.6 Starter motor and lead connections (arrowed) – 2.0 litre model

12.7 Starter motor rear support bracket – 1.7 litre model

12.8 Refitting the starter motor – 1.7 litre model. Ensure that dowel (arrowed) is fitted to bellhousing

Fig 12.8 Paris-Rhône starter motor components – types D10E92 and D10E88 (Sec 13)

Fig. 12.9 Paris-Rhône starter motor components – type D9E85 (Sec 13)

Fig. 12.10 Paris-Rhône starter motor components – type D9E771 (Sec 13)

13.2A Starter motor and mounting support bracket – 1.7 litre model

13.2B Starter motor mounting support bracket – 2.0 litre model

13.3 Solenoid and wiring terminals on starter motor – 2.0 litre model

13.10 Starter motor pinion drive – 1.7 litre model

2 Undo the two nuts and remove the mounting support bracket from the rear of the motor.

3 Undo the nut and disconnect the lead from the solenoid terminal (photo).

4 Where fitted, remove the cap plate on the rear cover and the bolt and washers between rear cover and armature.

5 Tap out the engaging lever pivot pin from the drive end housing.

6 Undo the nuts securing the solenoid to the drive end housing.

7 Undo the through-bolts and withdraw the yoke, armature, solenoid and engaging lever as an assembly from the drive end housing.

8 Withdraw the solenoid and engaging lever, remove the rear cover with brushes, then slide the armature out of the yoke.

9 Slip the brushes out of their brush holders to release the rear cover.

10 If the pinion/clutch assembly is to be removed, drive the stop collar up the armature shaft and extract the circlip. Slide the stop collar and pinion clutch assembly off the armature (photo).

11 With the starter motor now completely

12

dismantled, clean all the components with paraffin or a suitable solvent and wipe dry.

12 Check that all the brushes protrude uniformly from their holders and that the springs all provide moderate tension. Check that the brushes move freely in their holders and clean them with a petrol-moistened rag if there is any tendency to stick. If in doubt about the brush length or condition, compare them with new components and renew if necessary. Note that new field brushes must be soldered to their leads.

13 Check the armature shaft for distortion and the commutator for excessive wear, scoring or burrs. If necessary, the commutator may be lightly skimmed in a lathe and then polished with fine glass paper.

14 Check the pinion/clutch assembly, drive end housing, engaging lever and solenoid for wear or damage. Make sure that the clutch permits movement in one direction only and renew the unit if necessary.

15 Accurate checking of the armature, commutator and field coil windings and insulation requires the use of special test equipment. If the starter motor was inoperative when removed from the car and the previous checks have not highlighted the problem, then it can be assumed that there is a continuity of insulation fault and the unit should be renewed.

16 If the starter is in a satisfactory condition, or if a fault has been traced and rectified, the unit can be reassembled using the reverse of the dismantling procedure.

14.1 Fuse box assembly. Note spare fuses on left together with fuse remover

14.5A The main relays . . .

Fig. 12.11 Relay units and identification (Sec 14)

1   Windscreen wiper timer
2   Door lock timer
3   Heated rear window
4   Lights on reminder buzzer
5   Flasher unit
6   Front foglight relay
7   Rear foglight (shunt)
8   Front foglight (shunt)
9   Headlight relay (where applicable)

14 Fuses and relays - general

Fuses

1 The main fuse box unit is located in a hinged panel mounted on the lower facia trim panel. Press the two retainers to allow the fuse panel unit to pivot outwards (photo).

2 To remove a fuse from its location simply lift it upwards and out. The wire within the fuse is clearly visible and it will be broken if the fuse is blown.

3 Always renew a fuse with one of an identical rating. Never renew a fuse more than once without tracing the source of the trouble. The fuse rating is stamped on top of the fuse and spare fuses are located in a holder within the cover.

14.5B . . . and the front foglamp relay

Fig. 12.12 ABS system relays and associated fittings in engine compartment (Sec 14)

A   Main relay
B   Auxiliary relay
C   Protective fuses (30 amps)
D   Diodes (in red based case)
E   Pump relay

4 If a fuse continues to blow, the fault in the circuit(s) that it covers must be traced and rectified without delay. Refer to the Specifications at the start of this Chapter for the fuse numbers, their ratings and circuits covered.

Relays

5 The main relay block is located on a plate behind the lower facia panel. Disconnect the battery earth lead, then remove the panel for access to the relays (photos).

6 Further relays are located in the engine compartment on some models, the most notable being the ABS relay assembly on Turbo models. These relays are housed behind the ignition module unit on the bulkhead and access is gained after removing the housing top cover (photo).

7 The various relays can be removed from their respective locations by carefully pulling them upwards and out.

8 If a system controlled by a relay becomes inoperative and the relay is suspect, operate the system and if the relay is functioning it should be possible to hear it click as it is energized. If this is the case the fault lies with the components or wiring of the system. If the relay is not being energized then the relay is

14.6 ABS relays location – Turbo model

16.6 Underside view of the column switches and retaining screws

not receiving a main supply voltage or a switching voltage, or the relay itself is faulty.
9 To remove the main relay plate unit, undo the retaining screws and remove it from the dowels.

15 Direction indicator and hazard flasher system - general

1 The flasher unit is located on the accessory plate situated behind the fuse panel see previous Section.
2 Should the flashers become faulty in operation, check the bulbs for security and make sure that the contact surfaces are not corroded. If one bulb blows or is making a poor connection due to corrosion, the system will not flash on that side of the car.
3 If the flasher unit operates in one direction and not the other, the fault is likely to be in the bulbs, or wiring to the bulbs. If the system will not flash in either direction, operate the hazard flashers. If these function, check the appropriate fuse and renew it if blown. If the fuse is satisfactory, renew the flasher unit.

16 Steering column switches - removal and refitting

1 Disconnect the battery earth lead.
2 Unscrew and remove the column shroud

Fig. 12.13 Steering column switches and wiring terminals (Sec 16)

A Windscreen wiper connector
1 Timed input   *3 Fast speed*   *5 Park/timer*   *7 Windscreen washer*
2 + feed after ignition *4 Slow speed*   *6 + feed after ignition*
B Lighting connector
1 Headlamp main beam   *3 + feed before ignition*
2 Headlamp dipped beam   *4 Side and tail lamps*
C Direction indicators and horn connector
1 Horn   *3 Horn feed + before ignition*   *5 Flasher*
2 Rear foglamp (if applicable) *4 Right-hand indicator*   *6 Left-hand indicator*
D Trip computer switch

retaining screws from their recessed locations in the lower shroud. The screws are of Torx type. Remove the upper and lower shrouds.
3 Where fitted, the remote radio volume control can be removed from the end of the wiper switch by simply lifting it clear and detaching its cable.
4 To remove the ignition switch, refer to Chapter 10.
5 Withdraw the ignition switch cover.
6 Undo the switch retaining screws from the switch concerned and withdraw the switch. Detach its wire connector to remove it (photo).
7 Refit in the reverse order of removal. Check the operation of the switches and their various functions to complete.

17 Switches (general) - removal and refitting

1 Disconnect the battery earth lead before disconnecting or removing a switch.
2 In most instances the switches and switch panels are held in position by plastic anchor tabs. If possible, reach behind the switch assembly and compress the tabs before prising the switch or plate from its location.
3 Withdraw the switch until the connecting plug can be disconnected (photo).
4 The interior and luggage area courtesy light switches are removed in a similar manner, but

17.3 Removing a facia switch

17.4A Door courtesy lamp switch and connector

17.4B Boot lamp switch – Saloon model

12

17.4C Luggage area lamp switch and wiring connector – Savanna model

the door courtesy lamp switch has a rubber cover which must be prised free from the support panel to allow the switch to be withdrawn and disconnected (photo).

5 Refit in the reverse order of removal.

18 Timing relays - general

1 Timing relays are fitted to control the duration of operation of the following:

Windscreen wiper (delay relay)
Electric door locks
Interior lights
Seat belt (buzzer) warning system (certain operating territories only)

Fig. 12.14 Timer relay with 2 to 4 second delay (Sec 18)

1 Opening switch
2 Earth
3 Closing switch
4 Motor
5 + feed before ignition (fuse)
6 Motor

2 Should a fault develop in a timing relay, renewal is the only solution, as repair is not possible.

19 Bulbs (exterior) - renewal

Headlamp bulb

1 Open the bonnet, turn the plastic cover on the rear of the headlamp through a quarter of a turn and remove it.

2 Pull off the wiring plug.

3 Release the bulbholder spring clip and withdraw the bulbholder assembly (photos).

4 When fitting the new halogen type bulb avoid touching it with the fingers.

 HAYNES HINT *If the halogen bulb is inadvertently touched, clean it with a tissue soaked in methylated spirit.*

5 On models with dual headlamps, the bulb renewal procedure is similar to that described above, but access is gained through the aperture in the top crossmember. After removing the plastic cover, release the clip and withdraw the bulbholder and lead. Detach the lead (photos).

Front parking lamp bulb

6 The bulb and holder are mounted in the headlamp reflector. Access is obtained as described for the headlamp bulb (photo).

Front direction indicator bulb

7 The bulb and holder are mounted in the direction indicator lamp reflector at the side of the headlamp. Twist the bulbholder through a quarter of a turn to remove it.

Side direction indicator bulb

8 Pull the lens free from the body panel, untwist the bulbholder from the lamp unit, then pull on the bulb to remove it from its holder (photo).

19.3A Headlamp bulbholder and retaining clip – single headlamp model

19.3B Headlamp bulbholder removal – single headlamp model

19.5A Dual headlamp bulbholder and retaining clip

19.5B Dual headlamp bulb removal

19.6 Front parking lamp bulb removal

19.8 Side direction indicator bulb replacement

19.10 Removing the access trim panel to renew a rear lamp bulb – Savanna model

19.11A Stop/tail and indicator lamp bulbs – Saloon model

19.11B Stop/tail and indicator lamp bulbs – Savanna model

Rear lamp bulbs

9 Open the boot lid or tailgate, as applicable.
10 Remove the access trim panel (photo).
11 Unclip and release the bulbholder from the rear of the lamp unit. Remove the bulb from the holder for renewal. To remove the holder unit, detach the wiring connector from it (photos).
12 If required, the lens can be removed by undoing its retaining nuts (photos).

Rear number plate lamp bulb

13 Compress the retaining clips and remove the lamp unit. Detach the bulbholder from the rear of the unit, then remove the bulb from the holder (photos).

Front foglamp bulb

14 Undo the retaining screws and withdraw the lamp unit from the car.
15 Remove the cover cap, release the spring clip and extract the bulbholder (photo). Do not handle the bulb with the fingers as it is a halogen type. Hold it with a tissue or cloth. If accidentally touched, wipe the bulb clean with a tissue soaked in methylated spirits.
16 Refit the bulb and lamp unit in the reverse order of removal, then check the beam alignment.
17 If necessary, adjustment to the beam alignment can be made by turning the adjuster screw as required (photo).

19.11C Reversing and foglamp bulbs – Saloon model

19.11D Reversing and foglamp bulbs – Savanna model

19.12A Lens retaining nuts removal from inside . . .

19.12B . . . allows lens removal – Saloon model

19.13A Rear number plate lamp (Saloon model) – compress clips at each end (arrowed) to remove

19.13B Number plate lamp removal – Savanna model

19.15 Front foglamp removed to show bulbholder

12

19.17 Front foglamp beam adjustment screw

20.1A Release the cover from the interior lamp unit frame . . .

20.1B . . . and then withdraw the unit frame

20.3 Combined interior lamp and map reading lamp unit removed to show wiring connections

20.4 Interior lamp and festoon bulb

20.5 Map-reading lamp bulbholder removal

20.6 General view of the interior/map reading lamp unit incorporating a sliding roof control switch and infra-red remote control unit

Fig. 12.15 Interior lamp retaining lugs (3) and map reading lamp retaining lugs (4) (Sec 20)

20.7 Boot lamp unit removal – Saloon model

20 Bulbs (interior) - renewal

Main interior lamp (standard type)

1 Insert a thin bladed tool around the periphery of the cover to compress and release the retaining clips, then lower the cover from the lamp unit frame. Detach and remove the frame unit from the roof. The festoon bulb can be removed from its holder for replacement (photos).

Map-reading and interior lamp

2 This unit can also retain the sliding roof control switch and the infra-red remote control unit, according to model.

3 Release the plastic cover from the front edge then undo the unit retaining screw on each side. Lower the unit from the roof and disconnect the appropriate wiring connectors (photo).

4 To renew the main interior light bulb, release the metal cover and pivot it down out of the way. Withdraw the festoon bulb from its holder (photo).

5 To remove the map-reading lamp, detach the wiring connector from the holder. Untwist and remove the holder to remove the bulb (photo).

6 To remove the lamp units from the frame, first detach and remove the infra-red remote control unit, then depress the lamp unit retaining lugs (photo).

Boot lamp bulb (Saloon models)

7 Open the boot lid, then reach through the access aperture, compress the lamp unit retaining clips and withdraw the lamp unit from the boot lid (photo).

8 Prise free the festoon bulb from its holder for replacement. To remove the unit, detach the wiring connector.

Luggage area lamp bulb (Savanna models)

9 Prise the lamp from its location and remove the festoon type bulb (photo).

20.9 Luggage area lamp removed –
Savanna models

21.2A Detach the headlamp rear cover . . .

21.2B . . . disconnect the wiring
connector . . .

Instrument panel bulbs

10 Remove the instrument panel, as described in Section 24.

11 The bulbholders can then be removed by twisting them and the wedge type bulbs removed simply by pulling them from their holders.

Fig. 12.16 Rear view of single headlamp unit (Sec 21)

1 Indicator lamp retaining spring
A and B Beam adjusting screws
C and D Bonnet height adjusters

21 Headlamps -
removal and refitting

Single headlamp unit

1 Disconnect the battery earth lead. Remove the battery if necessary for access.

2 Unscrew and remove the plastic cover from the rear of the headlamp unit, disconnect the wiring connector from the bulb and, where applicable, disconnect the remote control headlamp adjuster by untwisting at the balljoint (photos).

21.2C . . . and the headlamp adjuster
remote control joint (if applicable)

3 Release the retaining spring and withdraw the indicator unit. Disconnect its wiring connector (photos).

4 Remove the lower trim bar from the grille bumper by detaching its plastic retaining nut (photo).

5 Remove the upper and lower lamp unit retaining screws from the positions shown in Fig. 12.16 and the photograph. Remove the light unit (photo).

6 Refit in the reverse order of removal. When locating the headlamp into the body aperture, do not tighten the lower front retaining screw until the lamp unit is adjusted for position by the upper setting/retaining bolts. The lamp

21.3A Disengage the retaining spring
(arrowed) . . .

213B . . . and remove the front indicator
unit

21.4 Remove the lower trim plastic
retaining nut

21.5A Headlamp lower retaining screw

12

21.5B Removing a single headlamp unit

Fig. 12.17 Dual headlamp lower front retaining bolt (D) (Sec 21)

21.9A Dual headlamp unit upper retaining bolts

unit should be flush with the surrounding bodywork. When refitting is complete, check the lamps for satisfactory operation of beam alignment.

Dual headlamp unit

7 Proceed as described in paragraphs 1 to 3.
8 Remove the two retaining screws and withdraw the front grille. Removal of the bonnet will give improved access (Chapter 11).
9 Undo the two upper and the single front retaining bolts, then raise the headlamp unit for access to the lower front retaining bolt - see Fig. 12.17 (photos). Undo the bolt and withdraw the lamp unit.
10 Refit in the reverse order of removal, but note the special points given in paragraph 6.

22 Headlamp beam load adjuster

1 A sealed hydraulic beam-adjusting device is fitted on some models so that the headlamp beams may be adjusted (over and above the normal basic setting) to compensate for variations in the vehicle load and so prevent dazzle and improve road illumination.
2 The device consists of a rotary adjustment knob and an actuating unit at the headlamp.
3 The control knob should be set in accordance with the following conditions:
1   Drive alone or with front passenger, no luggage
2   Drive and four passengers, no luggage

3   Drive and four passengers plus luggage
4   Drive with luggage compartment full
4 The adjuster control and the connecting cable can be removed, but must be renewed if defective. Remove the lower facia panel, pull free the control knob, then undo the retaining nuts from within the control unit dish (photos).
5 Disconnect the control unit from the support bracket at the facia end, detach the balljoint from the rear of the headlamps, then feed the cables through to the interior from the engine compartment for removal (photo).
6 Refit in reverse order, and check for satisfactory operation.

23 Headlamp beam - alignment

1 It is recommended that the headlamp beam alignment is carried out by your dealer or a service station having the necessary optical beam setting equipment.
2 As a temporary measure the headlamp beam adjusting screws may be turned in the required direction. If a beam load adjuster is fitted ensure that its adjustment knob is set at the 'O' position. The headlamp beam adjuster screws are shown in Fig. 12.16. On dual headlamp models, the adjuster at the top corner is accessible through the top panel aperture (photo).

21.9B Dual headlamp unit front retaining bolt (arrowed)

22.4A Pull free the headlamp beam load adjuster knob . . .

22.4B . . . and undo the retaining nuts

22.5 Detach the beam load adjuster control unit

23.2 Headlamp beam adjuster screw – dual headlamp

Fig. 12.18 Instrument panel cowl screws (1) and panel screws (2) (Sec 24)

Fig. 12.19 Lift (3), then withdraw (4) the instrument panel from its aperture (Sec 24)

24 Instrument panel - removal and refitting

Note: *An electronic type instrument panel, is fitted to some models. This is identifiable from its LCD display zone and a tell-tale warning light zone. In the event of the instrument panel receiving a malfunction signal from a sensor, it will display an error code in lieu of the speed reading. The fault will need to be diagnosed and rectified without delay by a Renault dealer. This type of instrument panel is not repairable - only the illumination bulbs can be renewed. The following special precautionary points should be noted to avoid damaging an electronic instrument panel:*

(a) Ensure that the panel wiring connections and associated items are correctly connected
(b) Do not make any checks on the unit or the sensors and probes using a test lamp
(c) Do not disconnect the battery or the instrument panel feed fuse with the ignition switched on

The removal and refitting procedures for the electronic and conventional instrument panels are otherwise the same

1 Disconnect the battery earth lead.
2 Where applicable, lower the steering column to its lowest setting.
3 Unscrew and remove the four instrument panel cowl retaining screws (photo).
4 Depress the hazard warning and rear window demister switches, insert a suitable

screwdriver and depress the clips so that the cowl can be pivoted and removed (photos).
5 Unscrew the instrument panel retaining screws, then simultaneously lift and withdraw the panel outwards sufficiently to allow the wiring connectors and the speedometer cable to be detached from its rear face. As the panel is withdrawn get an assistant to feed the speedometer cable through the bulkhead from the engine compartment side just enough to allow the cable to be detached. Remove the instrument panel (photos).
6 Dismantling of the instrument panel is not recommended. Any tests or repairs which may be necessary should be entrusted to a Renault dealer. Illumination bulbs can be removed by untwisting the holder from the rear face of the panel (photo).

24.3 Instrument panel cowl retaining screws (arrowed)

24.4A Releasing the cowl retaining clips . . .

24.4B . . . to allow the cowl to be withdrawn

24.5A Instrument panel retaining screw

24.5B Speedometer cable (arrowed) and instrument panel wiring block connectors

24.6 Bulbholder removal from instrument panel

12

25.1A Horn and location bracket

25.1B Wind tone horn and compressor unit

26.2 Cigar lighter unit location on underside of panel

7 Refit in the reverse order of removal. Ensure that the wiring connections are correctly made and on completion check the operation of the various panel components.

25 Horns - removal and refitting

1 Electric or wind tone horns are fitted depending on model; in each case they are located on the forward chassis member (photos).
2 To remove the horn, disconnect the lead connector or air hoses (as applicable), then

27.3 Clock removal

undo the mounting bracket bolt and withdraw the horn.
3 Note that with the wind tone horns, the filter on the end of the compressor intake pipe should be kept clean.
4 Refit in the reverse order of removal.

26 Cigar lighter - removal and refitting

1 Disconnect the battery earth lead.
2 Remove the panel in which the cigar lighter is mounted for access to the rear of the unit (photo).
3 Disconnect the lead connector and bulb wire. Unclip the unit and remove it from the panel. Note that the illumination bulb is not renewable and therefore if this has blown or the unit is defective it must be renewed complete.
4 Refit in the reverse order of removal.

27 Clock - removal and refitting

1 On all models, the clock is a push-fit in its location aperture, and is retained by plastic compression catches.

2 To remove the clock, first disconnect the battery negative terminal.
3 Carefully ease the clock from its location using a thin blunt instrument (photo).
4 Disconnect the wiring connections and remove the clock from the car (photo).
5 Refitting is the reverse sequence to removal.

28 Wiper blades and arms - removal and refitting

1 The wiper blade is a snap fit in the groove at the end of the wiper arm.
2 Pull the wiper arm/blade away from the windscreen or tailgate glass until it locks, and pull the blade from the arm by giving the blade a sharp jerk (photo).
3 The wiper arm may be removed from its splined spindle by flipping up the nut cover, unscrewing the nut (photo) and prising the arm from the spindle. Before removing the arm, note the park position of the blade on the windscreen by marking with a felt tip pen or insulation tape which is easily removed. If the arm is tight, use two screwdrivers at opposite points under its eye as levers.
4 Refitting is a reversal of removal, but make sure that the alignment of the wiper blades and arms is correct.
5 Do not overtighten the wiper arm nuts.

27.4 Rear view of clock showing wiring connection and bulbholder

28.2 Windscreen wiper blade removal from wiper arm

28.3 Windscreen wiper arm-to-spindle nut

29.5 Windscreen wiper motor

30.3 Tailgate wiper motor – Savanna model

31.5 Pump unit removal from the tailgate washer reservoir – Savanna model

29 Windscreen wiper motor and linkage - removal and refitting

1 Remove the wiper arms and blades as described in the preceding Section.
2 Open the bonnet and disconnect the battery.
3 Prise free the scuttle grille-to-bonnet seal, undo the scuttle retaining bolts and screws and remove the scuttle and lower windscreen trim.
4 Unplug the wiper motor.
5 Unbolt the wiper motor and the wiper linkage mounting plates (photo).
6 Release the wiper arm (spindle) wheel boxes and withdraw the motor and linkage from the scuttle recess.
7 To remove the linkage from the wiper motor, undo the drive link nut and remove the three motor retaining screws.
8 When reassembling the linkage to the wiper motor, first ensure that the motor is switched off and set in the 'parked' position, with the connecting links aligned as shown in Fig. 12.20.
9 Refitting is otherwise a reversal of the removal procedure.

30 Tailgate wiper motor (Savanna models) - removal and refitting

1 Remove the wiper arm and blade.
2 Open the tailgate and remove the trim panel.
3 Unplug the wiper motor (photo).
4 Unscrew the wiper motor mounting bolts and remove the motor.
5 Refitting is a reversal of removal, but before bolting the motor into place, connect its plug and make sure that it is switched on and then off by means of its control switch so that it will be installed in the 'parked' position.

31 Windscreen, tailgate and headlamp washer systems

1 The windscreen washer reservoir is located in the engine compartment, and the tailgate washer reservoir (Savanna) is located in the left-hand side rear trim panel in the luggage area.
2 Check the reservoir(s) regularly and top up with a suitable cleaning fluid solution. Use a proprietary screen cleaning fluid in the water.

Do not use cooling system anti-freeze in the cleaning solution.
3 The adjustment of the washer jets is carried out by inserting a pin in the jet nozzle and moving it to obtain the desired jet pattern on the screen.
4 To remove the windscreen washer reservoir, first syphon out its contents, then remove the battery for access. Undo the retaining bolts, and withdraw the reservoir so that the pump leads and washer hoses can be disconnected.
5 To remove the tailgate reservoir, disconnect the washer hose, wiring lead and the pump, and detach the reservoir from the trim panel (photo).
6 Refit in the reverse order of removal and check for satisfactory operation on completion.
7 Where fitted, the headlight washer system uses the same fluid reservoir as the windscreen washers.

32 Engine oil level sensor

1 This device comprises a sensor unit mounted in the side of the cylinder block and a receiver unit at the instrument panel. It is not fitted to all models in the range.
2 If the sensor unit is to be removed for any reason, first partially drain the engine oil, then detach the wiring from the sensor. Unscrew and remove it.
3 Refit in reverse order, then top up the oil level and check the sensor for satisfactory

Fig. 12.20 Windscreen wiper motor and linkage (Sec 29)

1 Link arm   D Drive link nut
2 Link arm   E Motor retaining screws

Fig. 12.21 Engine oil level sensor location (C) (Sec 32)

Fig. 12.22 Engine oil level sensor and wiring terminals (arrowed) (Sec 32)

12

Fig. 12.23 Engine oil level receiver unit and wiring terminals (arrowed) (Sec 32)

operation as described in the driver's handbook.

4 The oil level receiver unit is mounted on the instrument panel. First remove the instrument panel unit for access as described in Section 24, then detach the receiver from it.

5 Once removed, the receiver can be checked by connecting the leads from an ohmmeter to the terminals on the rear face of the unit. The indicator needle should be seen to move.

6 Renew the receiver unit if it is defective and refit in the reverse order of removal.

33 Vehicle door locking - alternative systems

1 Each system enables the four doors, boot lid or tailgate (as applicable) and fuel filler cap to be unlocked.

Manual

2 Use the door key in the normal way to

Fig. 12.26 Electric window switch and terminals (Sec 34)

1	Motor	4	Lighting
2	Earth	5	Motor
3	+ feed after ignition		

Fig. 12.24 Fuel filler flap emergency release lever location (2) – Saloon (Sec 33)

unlock one front door then unlock the remaining doors by pulling up the locking knob.

3 The key opens the boot lid or tailgate (as applicable) and fuel filler flap.

Remote control

4 The door Is unlocked by pointing the remote control device at the infra red receiver which is mounted above the rear view interior mirror. The device has its own exclusive code for security reasons.

5 If the tell-tale lamp on the hand held sender unit does not illuminate, renew the batteries.

6 The fuel filler flap and the boot lid or tailgate (as applicable) are unlocked using the key.

Electric central door locking

7 This system enables all doors, fuel filler flap and boot lid or tailgate (certain versions) to be locked or unlocked using the key in a front door lock or the infra red remote control sender unit.

8 Alternatively, the doors can be locked or unlocked from inside the car using the switch on the centre console.

9 Should a fault develop which prevents the fuel filler flap opening, it may be unlocked

Fig. 12.27 Electric rear view door mirror and wiring connections (A, B and D) (Sec 35)

Fig. 12.25 Fuel filler flap emergency release lever location – Savanna (Sec 33)

(3) Access trim door
(4) Release lever

manually by pulling the lever which is hidden behind the trim panel at the side of the luggage compartment.

10 Access to the central locking system lock solenoids is described in Chapter 11.

34 Electric windows

1 Electrically-operated front and rear door windows are fitted to some models.

2 The control switches may be mounted in the centre console or in the door armrests. To remove a switch refer to Section 17.

3 Access to the window operating motors is described in Chapter 11.

35 Electric rear-view door mirror

1 The removal of this type of rear-view mirror is described in Chapter 11. If the mirror operation is defective in some way, remove the appropriate door trim panels and check the various wires and their connectors to ensure that they are secure and in good condition.

2 The various wiring connections and their identifications are shown in Fig. 12.27.

36 Radio/cassette player - general

1 All models are fitted with a stereo radio/cassette player as standard, but the type fitted is dependent on the vehicle model.

2 Similarly the speakers fitted and their locations are dependent on model. Speakers may be located in the console (woofer), in the facia upper corner above the ventilation grilles (tweeters), in the door panels, or in the rear parcel shelf.

3 All models are fitted with a roof-mounted radio aerial.

37.1 Insert U-shaped radio removal rods as shown to release side retaining clips . . .

37.2 . . . withdraw the unit and detach wiring and aerial connections

38.4 Aerial mounting nut viewed through headlining aperture

37 Radio/cassette player (Renault type) - removal and refitting

1 Insert two U-shaped rods of suitable gauge into the holes in the front face of the radio/cassette unit as shown (photo). Depress the retaining clips and simultaneously withdraw the radio/cassette unit.
2 Withdraw the unit sufficiently to disconnect the feed, earth, aerial and speaker leads (photo).
3 Refitting is a reversal of removal.

38 Radio aerial and speaker units - removal and refitting

Aerial

1 The radio aerial is roof-mounted above the windscreen and is a standard fitting on all models.
2 Remove the roof-mounted interior lamp unit as described in Section 20, and the radio/cassette unit as described in Section 37.
3 With the aerial lead disconnected from the radio, it will ease refitting if a suitable length of strong string or cord is tied to the end of the lead before it is withdrawn up through the windscreen pillar. The lower side trim and facia panel will also need to be removed for access during removal and refitting of the aerial lead.
4 Working through the small aperture in the headlining, unscrew the aerial mounting nuts while an assistant lifts off the aerial from outside the car (photo).
5 Carefully withdraw the aerial lead from the car, then once the radio/cassette end of the lead is clear, the string or cord can be detached from it.
6 Refit in the reverse order of removal. Trim the aerial on completion to obtain the best possible reception.

Speaker units

7 To remove the door or rear parcel shelf-mounted speaker units, untwist and remove the grille, undo the speaker retaining screws and withdraw the speaker. Detach the wires (photos).
8 To remove the tweeter speakers from their location above the vent grille, first prise free the intermediate trim panel. Undo the speaker unit retaining screw and withdraw the speaker. Detach the wire (photos).
9 Refit the speaker units in the reverse order of removal.

38.7A Untwist the door speaker grille . . .

38.7B . . . for access to the speaker mounting screws

38.7C Rear parcel shelf-mounted speaker

38.8A Remove the intermediate trim panel and screw

38.8B Withdraw the tweeter speaker from the facia

12

Fault finding - electrical system

No voltage at starter motor

☐ Battery discharged
☐ Battery defective internally
☐ Battery terminals loose or earth lead not securely attached to body
☐ Loose or broken connections in starter motor circuit
☐ Starter motor switch or solenoid faulty

Voltage at starter motor - faulty motor

☐ Starter brushes badly worn, sticking, or brush wires loose
☐ Commutator dirty, worn or burnt
☐ Starter motor armature faulty
☐ Field coils earthed

Starter motor noisy or rough in engagement

☐ Pinion or flywheel gear teeth broken or worn
☐ Starter motor retaining bolts loose

Alternator not charging*

☐ Drivebelt loose and slipping, or broken
☐ Brushes work, sticking, broken or dirty
☐ Brush springs weak or broken
If all appears to be well but the alternator is still not charging, take the car to an automobile electrician for checking of the alternator

Battery will not hold charge for more than a few days

☐ Battery defective internally
☐ Electrolyte level too low or electrolyte too weak due to leakage
☐ Plate separators no longer fully effective
☐ Battery plates severely sulphated
☐ Drivebelt slipping
☐ Battery terminal connections loose or corroded
☐ Alternator not charging properly
☐ Short in lighting circuit causing continual battery drain

Ignition light fails to go out, battery runs flat in a few days

☐ Drivebelt loose and slipping, or broken
☐ Alternator faulty

Fuel gauge gives no reading

☐ Fuel tank empty
☐ Electric cable between tank sender unit and gauge broken or loose
☐ Fuel gauge case not earthed
☐ Fuel gauge supply cable interrupted
☐ Fuel gauge unit broken

Fuel gauge registers full all the time

☐ Electric cable between tank unit and gauge earthed

Horn operates all the time

☐ Horn push either earthed or stuck down
☐ Horn cable to horn push earthed

Horn fails to operate

☐ Blown fuse
☐ Cable or cable connection loose, broken or disconnected
☐ Horn has an internal fault

Horn emits intermittent or unsatisfactory noise

☐ Cable connections loose
☐ Horn has internal fault

Lights do not come on

☐ If engine not running, battery discharged
☐ Light bulb filament burnt out or bulbs broken
☐ Wire connections loose, disconnected or broken
☐ Light switch shorting or otherwise faulty
☐ Blown fuse

Lights come on but fade out

☐ If engine not running, battery discharged

Lights give very poor illumination

☐ Lamp glasses dirty
☐ Reflector tarnished or dirty
☐ Lamps badly out of adjustment
☐ Incorrect bulb with too low wattage fitted
☐ Existing bulbs old and badly discoloured

Lights work erratically, flashing on and off, especially over bumps

☐ Battery terminals or earth connections loose
☐ Contacts in light switch faulty

Wiper motor fails to work

☐ Blown fuse
☐ Wire connections loose, disconnected or broken
☐ Brushes badly worn
☐ Armature worn or faulty
☐ Field coils faulty

Wiper motor works very slowly and takes excessive current

☐ Commutator dirty, greasy or burnt
☐ Drive to spindles bent or unlubricated
☐ Drive spindle binding or damaged
☐ Armature bearings dry or unaligned
☐ Armature badly worn or faulty

Wiper motor works slowly and takes little current

☐ Brushes badly worn
☐ Commutator dirty, greasy or burnt
☐ Armature badly worn or faulty

Wiper motor works but wiper blades remain static

☐ Linkage disengaged or faulty
☐ Drive spindle damaged or worn
☐ Wiper motor gearbox parts badly worn

Chapter 13 Supplement:
Revisions and information on later models

Contents

Degrees of difficulty

Easy, suitable for novice with little experience	**Fairly easy,** suitable for beginner with some experience	**Fairly difficult,** suitable for competent DIY mechanic	**Difficult,** suitable for experienced DIY mechanic	**Very difficult,** suitable for expert DIY or professional

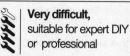

<table>
<tr><td>1</td><td>Introduction</td></tr>
</table>

This Supplement contains information which is additional to, or a revision of, the information contained in the first twelve Chapters.

The Sections in this Supplement follow the same order as the Chapters to which they relate. The Specifications are all grouped together at the beginning for convenience, but they too follow Chapter order.

It is recommended that before any work commences, reference is made to the appropriate Section(s) of this Supplement, in order to establish any changes to procedures or specifications, before reading the main Chapter(s). If no information on the relevant operation is contained in this Chapter, then the operation can be carried out using the information in the relevant original Chapter.

2 Specifications

1721 cc engine

Note: *Unless otherwise stated, the specifications and torque wrench settings are as given for the 1721 cc engine in Chapter 1.*

Engine type designation:
  Carburettor models F2N
  Fuel injection models F3N
Engine code numbers and compression ratios:
  Carburettor models:
    F2N 716 and F2N 750 . . . . 9.2 : 1
    F2N 752, F2N 754 and F2N 758 . . . . 9.5 : 1
  Fuel injection models:
    F3N 722, F3N 723 and F3N 726 . . . . 9.5 : 1

Torque wrench setting	Nm	lbf ft
Tensioner pulley nut (modified tensioner arrangement)	50	37

1965 cc engine

Note: *Unless otherwise stated, the specifications and torque wrench settings are as given for the 1721 cc engine in Chapter 1.*
Engine code number F2R 702
Compression ratio 8.4:1
Bore .... 82 mm
Stroke .... 93 mm
Capacity .... 1965 cc

1995 cc engine

Note: *Unless otherwise stated, the specifications and torque wrench settings are as given for the 1995 cc engine in Chapter 1. Note that these specifications are only applicable to the 8-valve engine. The specifications for the 12-valve engine are given under the next sub-heading in this Section.*
Engine type designation J7R
Engine code numbers and compression ratios:
  Non-Turbo models:
    J7R 746 and J7R 747 .... 9.25 : 1
  Turbo models:
    J7R 756 .... 8.5 : 1

Torque wrench settings

	Nm	lbf ft
Manually-adjusted timing belt tensioner pulley:		
Backplate retaining nut	20	15
Tensioner pulley nut	50	37
Cylinder head bolts (fitted with modified gasket) - non-Turbo models	See text	

1995cc 12-valve engine

Note: *Unless otherwise stated, the specifications and torque wrench settings are as given for the 1995 cc engine in Chapter 1.*
Engine type designation J7R
Engine code numbers .... J7R 740 and J7R 754
Compression ratio .... 9.3 : 1

Connecting rods and gudgeon pins

Gudgeon pin:
  Length .... 65.0 mm
  Diameter .... 23.0 mm

Piston rings

Piston-ring thickness:
  Top compression ring .... 1.5 mm
  Second compression ring .... 1.75 mm
  Oil control ring .... 3.0 mm

Cylinder head

Overall height .... 90.5 mm

Timing belt

Deflection .... See text

Valves

Stem diameter .... 7 mm
Head diameter:
  Small inlet valve .... 30.3 mm
  Large inlet valve .... 36.3 mm
  Exhaust valve .... 40.0 mm
Valve seat included angle - inlet and exhaust .... 90°
Valve seat width inlet and exhaust .... 1.7 mm
Valve guides:
  Bore .... 7 mm
  Outside diameter .... 12 mm
  Repair oversizes .... Not available
Valve clearances (cold):
  Inlet .... 0.15 to 0.20 mm
  Exhaust .... 0.20 to 0.25 mm

Lubrication system

Oil pressure (at 80°C):
  At idle .... 1.25 bars
  At 3000 rpm .... 3 bars
Oil capacity (with filter renewal) .... 5.5 litres

13

1995cc 12-valve engine (continued)

Torque wrench settings	Nm	lbf ft
Timing belt tensioner:		
Backplate retaining nut	20	15
Pulley retaining nut	50	37
Cylinder head bolts:		
Stage 1	20	15
Stage 2	Angle-tighten through 80°	Angle-tighten through 80°
Stage 3 Wait 3 minutes, then	Angle-tighten a further 80°	Angle-tighten a further 80°
Camshaft cover bolts	15	11
Rocker arm shaft retaining bolts	25	18
Camshaft sprocket retaining bolt	50	37
Rocker arm adjusting screw locknut	10	7
Sump retaining bolts	10	7
Oil pump		
Pump retaining bolts	40	30
Pump cover-to-body bolts	12	9
Crankcase stiffener bolts:		
7 mm bolts	15	11
10 mm bolts	40	30

2165 cc engine

Note: *Unless otherwise stated, the specifications and torque wrench settings are as given for the 1995 cc engine in Chapter 1.*

Engine type designation	J7T
Engine code numbers	J7T 754 and J7T 755
Compression ratio	9.2 : 1
Bore	88 mm
Stroke	89 mm

Cylinder liners
Height	148.5 mm

Crankshaft
Crankpin diameter	56.296 mm
Crankpin minimum regrind diameter	56.046 mm
Crankshaft endfloat	0.13 to 0.30 mm

Torque wrench setting	Nm	lbf ft
Big-end bearing cap nuts	65	48

Fuel and exhaust systems - 1721 cc carburettor models

Carburettor type
F2N 716, F2N 750 and F2N 752 engines	Solex 28/34 Z10
F2N 711, F2N 754 and F2N 758 engines	Solex 32/34 Z13
Code number application:	
F2N 716 engine	28/34 Z10 867, 913 or 970
F2N 750	28/34 Z10 926
F2N 752	28/34 Z10 927
F2N 711	32/34 Z 13 968
F2N 754 and F2N 758	32/34 Z13 967

Carburettor data

28/34 Z10 926:	Primary	Secondary
Venturi	20 mm	26 mm
Main jet	95	130
Air correction jet	155	180
Idle jet	48	45
Econostat	-	120
Enrichener	45	-
Accelerator pump injector	40	35
Needle valve	1.8	
Float level	33.5 ± 0.5 mm	
Defuming (degas) valve adjustment	2 ±1 mm	
Initial throttle opening (fast idle) adjustment	0.95 mm	
Choke pneumatic part-opening adjustment	2 ± 0.2 mm	
Idle speed	725 ± 25 rpm	
CO mixture	1 ± 0.5 %	

28/34 Z10 927:	Primary	Secondary
Venturi	20 mm	27 mm
Main jet	100	145
Air correction jet	200	190
Idle jet	49	50
Econostat	-	120
Enrichener	50	
Accelerator pump injector	40	35
Needle valve	1.8	
Float level	33.5 ± 0.5 mm	
Defuming (degas) valve adjustment	2 ± 1 mm	
Initial throttle opening (fast idle) adjustment	1 mm	
Choke pneumatic part-opening adjustment	2.2 ± 0.2 mm	
Idle speed	850 ± 50 rpm	
CO mixture	1.25 ± 0.5 %	

28/34 Z10 970:	Primary	Secondary
Venturi	20 mm	26 mm
Main jet	97.5	122.5
Air correction jet	200	145
Idle jet	47-49	45
Econostat	-	120
Enrichener	50	30
Accelerator pump injector	40	35
Needle valve	1.8	
Float level	33.5 mm	
Defuming (degas) valve adjustment	0.3 mm	
Initial throttle opening (fast idle) adjustment	0.95 mm	
Choke pneumatic part-opening adjustment	2.2 mm	
Idle speed	700 ± 25 rpm	
CO mixture	1 ± 0.5 mm	

32/34 Z13 967:	Primary	Secondary
Venturi	24 mm	27 mm
Main jet	115-117.5	137.5
Air correction jet	165	190
Idle jet	43-44	50
Econostat	-	120
Enrichener	50	-
Accelerator pump injector	40	35
Needle valve	1.8	
Float level	33.5	
Defuming (degas) valve adjustment	0.3 mm	
Initial throttle opening (fast idle) adjustment	0.75 mm	
Choke pneumatic part-opening adjustment	3.5 mm	
Idle speed	800 ± 50 rpm	
CO mixture	1.5 ± 0.5%	

32/34 Z13 968:	Primary	Secondary
Venturi	24 mm	27 mm
Main jet	120-122.5	137.5
Air correction jet	190	190
Idle jet	43-44	50
Econostat	-	120
Enrichener	40	-
Accelerator pump injector	40	35
Needle valve	1.8	
Float level	33.5 ± 0.5 mm	
Defuming (degas) valve adjustment	0.30 mm	
Initial throttle opening (fast idle) adjustment	0.8 mm	
Choke pneumatic part-opening adjustment	3.3 mm	
Idle speed	800 ± 50 rpm	
CO mixture	1.5 ± 0.5%	

13

Fuel and exhaust systems - 1721 cc single-point fuel injection models

General

System type	Bendix (Renix) Mono-point
Application (engine code)	F3N 722 and F3N 723

Fuel system data

Fuel pump type	Electric, situated underneath vehicle
Fuel pump pressure:	
Maximum	3 bars
Regulated pressure	1.2 ± 0.05 bars
Component resistances (approximate):	
Fuel injector	1.4 ohms (must be less than 10 ohms)
Coolant temperature sender:	
At 20°C	300 ohms
At 80°C	400 ohms
Fuel/air temperature sensor:	
At 0°C	260 ohms
At 20°C	290 ohms
At 40°C	320 ohms
Idle speed (not adjustable)	750 ± 50 rpm
CO mixture content (not adjustable)	Less than 0.5 %
Fuel grade	Unleaded fuel only, octane rating 95 RON minimum

Fuel and exhaust systems - 1721 cc multi-point fuel injection models

General

System type	Bendix (Renix) multi-point
Application (engine code)	F3N 726

Fuel system data

Fuel pump type	Electric, located underneath the vehicle
Fuel pump regulated pressure:	
Fuel pressure regulator vacuum hose connected	2.5 ± 0.2 bars
Fuel pressure regulator vacuum hose disconnected	3.0 ± 0.2 bars
Component resistances (approximate):	
Fuel injectors	2.5 ± 0.5 ohms
Coolant temperature sender (early models)	Refer to single-point injection system
Coolant temperature sender (later models):	
At 20°C	3500 ohms
At 80°C	350 ohms
Intake air temperature sensor (early models)	Refer to single-point injection system
Intake air temperature sensor (later models):	
At 0°C	7500 to 12 000 ohms
At 20°C	3000 to 4000 ohms
At 40° C	1300 to 1600 ohms
Idle speed (not adjustable)	800 ± 50 rpm
CO mixture content (not adjustable)	Less than 0.5 %
Fuel grade	Unleaded fuel only, octane rating 95 RON minimum

Fuel and exhaust systems - 1965 cc models

Carburettor type and code number ....

Solex 28/34 Z9 915

Carburettor data	Primary	Secondary
Venturi	20 mm	26 mm
Main jet	92.5	115
Air correction jet	190	200
Idle jet	41	40
Econostat	-	80
Enrichener	50	-
Accelerator pump injector	-	35
Needle valve	1.8	
Float level	33.5 ± 0.5 mm	
Initial throttle opening (fast idle) adjustment	1.3 mm	
Idle speed	700 ± 25 rpm	
CO mixture content	1.5 ± 0 5 %	

Fuel and exhaust systems - 1995 cc 8-valve models

Note: *These specifications are only applicable to the 1995 cc 8-valve engine. Specifications for the 1995 cc 12-valve engine are given under the next sub-heading in this Section.*

System type

Later non-Turbo (J7R 746 and J7R 747 engine) and Turbo (J7R 756 engine) models	Bendix (Renix) multi-point

Fuel system data

Fuel pump type	Electric, situated underneath the vehicle
Fuel pump regulated pressure:	
Fuel pressure regulator vacuum hose connected	2 ± 0.2 bars
Fuel pressure regulator vacuum hose disconnected	2.5 ± 0.2 bars
Component resistances (approximate):	
Fuel injector	2.5 ± 0.5 ohms
Coolant temperature sender - non-Turbo models:	
At 20°C	300 ohms
At 80°C	400 ohms
Coolant temperature sender - Turbo models:	
At 20°C	3000 to 4000 ohms
At 80°C	300 to 400 ohms
Intake air temperature sensor (early models):	
At 0°C	250 ohms
At 20°C	300 ohms
At 40°C	350 ohms
Intake air temperature sensor (later models):	
At 0°C	7500 to 12 000 ohms
At 20°C	3000 to 4000 ohms
At 40°C	1300 to 1600 ohms
Idle speed (not adjustable)	800 ± 50 rpm
CO mixture content	Less than 0.5 %
Fuel grade	Unleaded fuel only, octane rating 95 RON minimum

Fuel and exhaust systems - 1995 cc 12-valve models

System type

J7R 740 and 754 engines	Bendix (Renix) multi-point

Fuel system data

Fuel pump type	Electric, situated underneath vehicle
Fuel pump regulated pressure:	
Fuel pressure regulator vacuum hose connected	2.5 ± 0.5 bars
Fuel pressure regulator vacuum hose disconnected	3.0 ± 0.5 bars
Component resistances (approximate)	Refer to 1995 cc 8-valve engine details given above
Idle speed (not adjustable):	
Non-catalyst models (J7R 754 engine)	850 ± 50 rpm
Catalyst models (J7R 740 engine)	875 ± 50 rpm
CO mixture content:	
Non-catalyst models (J7R 754 engine)	1.8 ± 0.2 %
Catalyst models (J7R 740 engine) - not adjustable	Less than 0.5 %
Fuel grade:	
Non-catalyst models (J7R 754 engine)	Leaded or unleaded fuel, octane rating 95 RON minimum
Catalyst models (J7R 740 engine)	Unleaded fuel only, octane rating 95 RON minimum

Fuel and exhaust systems - 2165 cc models

System type

System type	Bendix (Renix) multi-point

Fuel system data

Fuel system data	Refer to 1995 cc 8-valve details given above

Ignition system

System type

Later Turbo models	Static (distributorless), computer-controlled
All other models	Breakerless, computer-controlled

Ignition timing

1721 cc carburettor models	3° to 5° BTDC at idle speed
1721 cc fuel injection models	Computer-controlled
1965 cc models	5° to 9° BTDC at idle speed
1995 cc models (8- and 12-valve engines)	Computer-controlled
2165 cc models	Computer-controlled

Spark plugs

1995 cc 12-valve models	Champion RC7BMC

13

Manual transmission

JB2 transmission

Application	1721 cc four-speed models
Ratios:	
1st	3.727 : 1
2nd	2.050 : 1
3rd	1.320 : 1
4th	0.903 : 1
Reverse	3.545 : 1
Final drive	3.294 : 1
Lubricant capacity	3.25 litres
Lubricant type/specification	Hypoid gear oil, viscosity SAE 80W, to API GL5

Automatic transmission

AR4 transmission

Type	Four-speed with computerised control
Lubrication:	
Transmission capacity:	
From dry	5.7 litres
At fluid renewal	4.0 litres
Final drive capacity:	
From dry	0.85 litres
At oil renewal	0.80 litres
Lubricant type:	
Transmission fluid	Dexron type ATF
Final drive oil	Tranself TRX 80 W 140 **only** (available from a Renault dealer)

Torque wrench settings

	Nm	lbf ft
Driveplate to torque converter bolts	35	26
Sump retaining bolts	10	7
Filter retaining bolts	5	4
Fluid cooler mounting bolts	20	15

Driveshafts, hubs, roadwheels and tyres

Tyres

Size (depending on model)	155/80 R 13, 165/80 R 13, 175/70 R 13, 175/65 R 13,175/65 R14,185/55 R 15 or195/55 R 15	
Tyre pressures - cold (bars/psi):	**Front***	**Rear**
185/55 R 15 tyres	2.3/33	2.3/33
155/80 R 13,165/80 R 13,175/70 R 13,175/65 R 14 and		
185/65 R 14 tyres	2.0/29	2.2/32
185/55 R 15 tyres**	2.3/33	2.3/33
195/55 R 15 tyres**:		
Normal use	2.2/32	2.0/29
High-speed use	2.5/36	2.3/33
Fully-laden	2.8/41	2.5/36

Note: *Pressures apply only to original-equipment tyres, and may vary if any other make or type is fitted; check with the tyre manufacturer or supplier for correct pressures if necessary.*
For models fitted with automatic transmission, add 0.1 bars (1.5 psi).
**Models with these tyres have a 'space-saver' spare wheel, fitted with a smaller tyre. The smaller spare tyre should run at 4.2 bars (67 psi). The vehicle should not be driven at speeds exceeding 50 mph with the space-saver spare wheel fitted*

Braking system

1995 cc 12-valve models

Front brake:	
Disc diameter	285 mm
Minimum disc thickness	19.0 mm
Minimum pad thickness (including backing plate)	6.5 mm
Maximum disc run-out	0.7 mm
Rear brake:	
Disc diameter	255 mm
Minimum disc thickness	9.5 mm
Minimum pad thickness (including backing plate)	6.0 mm
Maximum disc run-out	0.07 mm

Torque wrench setting

	Nm	lbf ft
Brembo brake caliper mounting bolts	70	52

Electrical system

Fuses (phase II models, mid-1989 onwards)

Fuse number	Application	Rating (amps)
1	Automatic transmission	5
2	Air conditioning	30
3	Air conditioning	30
4 to 6	Not used	-
7	Heater blower motor, rear screen wash/wipe	20
8	Radio, clock, alarm	10
9	Heated rear screen	20
10	Clock, interior lights, radio and instrument panel	10
11	Windscreen wiper	10
12	Direction indicators and hazard warning lamps	10
13	Left-hand sidelamps and front foglamps	5
14	Right-hand sidelamps	5
15	Cigar lighter, rear screen wiper	10
16	Stop-lamps, cruise control	10
17	Instrument panel, reversing lamps, alarm	10
18	Windscreen wiper	15
19	Rear foglamp	7.5
20	Engine cooling fan	20
21	Anti-lock braking system	3
22	Central locking system, electric mirrors, alarm	25
23	Left-hand electric windows	30
24	Right-hand electric windows	30

Note: *Not all fuses are fitted to all models.*

3 1721 cc engine

1 This Section contains information on the modifications which the 1721 cc (F2N) engine has undergone since its introduction. Operations which differ from those described in Chapter 1 are given below. If the relevant operation is not described below, it can be carried out using the original information given in Chapter 1.

1721 cc (F3N) engine - general information

2 The 1721 cc (F3N) engine is fitted to all fuel-injected 1.7 litre models in the range. Apart from the fuel system and manifolds, the engine is identical to the 1721 cc (F2N) engine covered in Chapter 1.

3 When working on the engine, refer to the information given in Chapter 1 for the 1721 cc engine, and also to the Specifications at the start of this Chapter. For all operations concerning the fuel and exhaust systems, including manifolds, refer to Section 10 or 11 of this Chapter (as applicable).

Timing belt covers - modification

4 On later 1721 cc models, a modified timing belt cover is fitted. On these models, the camshaft sprocket backing plate is replaced by a larger cover, and either a one- or two-piece outer cover is fitted.

Timing belt - removal and refitting

5 On some later 1721 cc engines a different timing belt tensioner arrangement is fitted, and the timing marks are slightly different. On these models, the tensioner pulley is the uppermost pulley, and the original tensioner pulley becomes an idler pulley. The camshaft sprocket timing mark aligns with a pointer on the timing belt outer cover. The removal and refitting procedures are as follows.

Removal

6 Referring to Chapter 1, Section 10, remove the alternator drivebelt. Rotate the crankshaft until the timing mark on the rim of the camshaft sprocket appears in the window in the top of the timing belt outer cover. Align the mark with the cover pointer, undo the retaining bolts and remove the outer cover.

7 Carry out the operations described in Chapter 1, Section 10, paragraphs 4 to 8, remembering that the idler pulley and tensioner pulley have swapped places. If there is no timing mark on the camshaft sprocket backing plate/timing cover, make one using a dab of paint prior to removing the timing belt.

Refitting

8 Referring to Chapter 1, Section 38, carry out the operations described in paragraphs 1 to 4, remembering that the tensioner and idler pulleys have swapped places.

9 The timing belt tension is set by moving the tensioner pulley against the belt. This can be done by screwing a 6 mm bolt through the threaded hole situated at the rear of the tensioner. Screw the bolt into position until it bears on the rear of the tensioner, then use the bolt to position the tensioner pulley as required.

10 Position the tensioner pulley so that the deflection at the mid-point of the rear run of the belt (between the auxiliary shaft sprocket and tensioner pulley) is 7.5 mm. Renault dealers use the special belt tensioning tool shown in Fig. 13.1 to measure the belt deflection. In the absence of this tool, an approximate setting may be achieved by measuring the belt deflection under firm thumb pressure.

11 With the belt correctly tensioned, hold the tensioner pulley stationary, and tighten the pulley retaining nut to the specified torque.

12 Remove the TDC locating rod. Refit the crankshaft pulley, then rotate the crankshaft through two complete turns in a clockwise direction. Reinsert the TDC locating rod, and check that the camshaft sprocket timing mark is correctly positioned.

Fig. 13.1 Using the special Renault belt-tensioning tool to check the timing belt deflection – 1721 cc engine (Sec 3)

13

Fig. 13.2 Timing belt and sprocket timing marks – 1965 cc (F2R) engine (Sec 4)

A Direction of rotation
B 6 mm bolt for adjusting the tensioner pulley
C Timing belt mark location
D Camshaft sprocket mark (right-hand line) and timing belt mark (left-hand line) locations
F Timing belt deflection measuring point

13 If all is well, recheck the belt deflection. If the belt deflection is being measured without the special Renault tool, the tension must be checked by a Renault dealer at the earliest possible opportunity. If the belt breaks or slips while the engine is running, extensive damage may result.

14 With the belt tension correctly set, refit all disturbed components as described in Chapter 1.

4 1965 cc engine

1965 cc (F2R) engine - general information

1 The 1965 cc (F2R) engine is of an identical construction to the 1721 cc (F2N) engine covered in Chapter 1. The bore and stroke have been increased to bring the capacity out to 1965 cc, and a different carburettor is fitted.
2 Operations which differ from those described in Chapter 1 are given below. If the relevant operation is not described below, it can be carried out using the information given for the 1721 cc engine in Chapter 1. Note that the specifications for the 1965 cc engine which differ from those for the 1721 cc engine are given at the start of this Chapter. For all operations concerning the fuel and exhaust systems, refer to Section 12 of this Chapter.

Fig. 13.3 Early (A) and later (B) types of sprocket and timing belt teeth profiles (Sec 5)

Timing belt - removal and refitting

3 The timing belt tensioner and timing mark arrangement fitted to later 1721 cc engines, described above in Section 3, is fitted to all F2R engines.
4 The timing belt can be removed and refitted as described in Section 3, referring to Fig. 13.2 for timing mark position information. Note that there are 59 teeth between the timing belt marks at D and C.

5 1995 cc engine (except 12-valve)

Note: For information on the 1995 cc 12-valve engine, refer to Section 6.

1 This Section contains information on the modifications which the 1995 cc engine has undergone since its introduction. Operations which differ to those described in Chapter 1 are given below. If the relevant operation is not described below, it can be carried out using the original information given in Chapter 1.

Timing belt and sprockets - modification

2 During the production run of the engine, the profile of the timing belt and sprocket teeth has been changed from a square profile on earlier models to a round profile on later models (see Fig. 13.3). When renewing the timing belt and/or sprockets, ensure that the replacement component is of the correct type. Do not under any circumstances interchange components with different teeth profiles.

Timing belt - removal and refitting

3 On later models, a manually-adjusted timing belt tensioner pulley is fitted in place of the spring-loaded tensioner used on earlier models. Timing belt removal and refitting is as described in Chapter 1, noting the points in the following paragraphs.
4 To release the tensioner, slacken the pulley backplate retaining nut and the large retaining nut. Pivot the pulley and backplate away from the belt to release the belt tension.
5 On refitting, with the belt correctly located

over the sprockets and the front run of the belt taut (see Chapter 1, Fig. 1.69), pivot the tensioner backplate towards the belt until the upper retaining nut is located at the mid-point of the backplate slot. Hold the backplate in this position, and tighten its retaining nut to the specified torque.
6 The timing belt tension is set by rotating the eccentric tensioner pulley using a peg spanner fitted to the two holes in the pulley centre. In the absence of the special Renault peg spanner (Mot. 1135), a home-made peg spanner can be fabricated. Alternatively, obtain two suitable diameter bolts, and insert these in the holes in the pulley hub; the pulley can then be rotated using a screwdriver or bar inserted between the bolts.
7 Using one of the tools described above, rotate the tensioner pulley towards the belt. Tension is correct when the deflection at the mid-point of the front run of the belt (between the camshaft sprocket and intermediate shaft sprocket, Point A in Fig. 1.69) is 10 ± 0.5 mm. Renault dealers use the belt-tensioning tool shown in Fig. 13.4 to measure the belt

Fig. 13.4 Using the special Renault belt-tensioning tool to check the timing belt deflection – 1995 and 2165 cc engines (Sec 5)

Fig. 13.5 Modified cylinder head tightening sequence – 1995 cc (8-valve) non-Turbo models (Sec 5)

deflection. In the absence of this tool, an approximate setting may be achieved by measuring the belt deflection under firm thumb pressure.

8 With the belt correctly tensioned, hold the tensioner pulley stationary, and tighten the large retaining nut to the specified torque.

9 Refit the crankshaft pulley, then rotate the crankshaft through two complete turns clockwise and recheck the belt deflection. If the belt deflection is being measured without the special Renault tool, the belt tension must be checked by a Renault dealer at the earliest possible opportunity. If the belt breaks or slips while the engine is running, extensive damage may result.

10 With the belt tension correctly set, check the valve timing and refit all disturbed components as described in Chapter 1.

Cylinder head gasket (non-Turbo models) - modification

11 On non-Turbo models, an improved non-asbestos gasket has been introduced by Renault, and the cylinder head bolt tightening sequence has been revised. The new gasket has been fitted in production since February 1992, and should be fitted to earlier models at overhaul, as follows.

12 Obtain a modified head gasket and a new set of cylinder head bolts from your Renault dealer.

13 Referring to Chapter 1, fit the new gasket and refit the cylinder head. Lubricate the threads and underside of the heads of the new head bolts sparingly, and screw them into position.

14 Working in the sequence shown in Fig. 13.5, tighten the head bolts to 20 Nm.

15 Once all the bolts have been tightened, working again in the specified sequence, angle-tighten the bolts through 105° using a socket and extension bar. It is recommended that an angle-measuring gauge is used during this stage of the tightening to ensure accuracy. If a gauge is not available, use a dab of white paint to make alignment marks between the bolt head and cylinder head prior to tightening; the marks can then be used to check that the bolt has been rotated sufficiently during tightening.

16 Working in the specified sequence, repeat

the operation described in paragraph 15 to tighten the bolts through a further 105°. Reassemble all other disturbed components using the information given in Chapter 1.

17 Note that when this method is used, the cylinder head bolts do not require any further tightening.

Sump (later Turbo models) - modification

18 On later Turbo engines, the sump arrangement has been altered. The new arrangement is the same as is fitted to the 1995 cc 12-valve engine. A small pressed-steel sump is bolted to a larger aluminium crankcase stiffener casting, which is in turn bolted to the base of the crankcase.

19 On these models the sump oil pump and crankcase stiffener casting can be removed as described in Section 6 for the 12-valve engine.

Oil cooler (Turbo models) - general information

20 On most Turbo models, an oil cooler is fitted to ensure the oil temperature remains constant even under extreme operating conditions. Refer to Section 6 of this Chapter for further information on the cooler.

---

6 1995 cc 12-valve engine

Note: *For information on the 1995 cc 8-valve engine, refer to Section 5.*

General information

1 In late 1989, a 12-valve version of the 1995 cc (J7R) engine was introduced into the Renault 21 range. This engine can be found in all TXI models, and has the engine code 7JR 740 (non-catalyst model) or 7JR 754 (with a catalytic converter).

2 The 12-valve engine is very similar to the earlier 8-valve engine covered in Chapter 1, the only major difference being the design of the cylinder head. On the 12-valve engine, there are three valves per cylinder, to improve efficiency: two inlet valves and one exhaust.

3 Operations which differ to those on the 8-valve 1995 cc engine covered in Chapter 1 are described below. If the operation is not described below, it can be carried out using the information given in Chapter 1 for the 1995 cc engine. Refer to Section 14 of this Chapter for details of the fuel and exhaust systems.

Timing belt - removal and refitting

Removal

4 Carry out the operations described in Chapter 1, Section 55, paragraphs 1 to 8, ignoring the remark about the camshaft sprocket timing mark aligning with the pointer in the timing belt cover viewing aperture.

5 Remove the crankshaft pulley, then temporarily refit the pulley bolt to the end of the crankshaft.

6 Rotate the crankshaft in a clockwise direction until the crankshaft sprocket Woodruff key, the camshaft sprocket and the intermediate shaft sprocket timing marks are positioned as shown in Fig. 13.6. In this position, all four pistons are at mid-stroke.

7 Slacken the tensioner pulley backplate retaining nut and the large pulley retaining nut, and pivot the pulley and backplate away from the belt to release the belt tension.

8 If the timing belt is to be re-used, use white paint or similar to mark the direction of rotation on the belt (if markings do not already exist) then slip the belt off the sprockets.

9 Check the timing belt carefully for any signs of uneven wear, splitting or oil contamination; renew it if there is the slightest doubt about its condition. If signs of oil contamination are found, trace the source of the oil leak and rectify it, then wash down the engine timing belt area and all related components to remove all traces of oil.

Refitting

10 Before refitting, thoroughly clean the timing belt sprockets, and check that the tensioner pulley rotates freely, without any sign of roughness. If there is any sign of roughness in the pulley bearing, then the tensioner assembly must be renewed.

11 Ensure all the sprocket timing marks are still positioned as shown in Fig. 13.6.

Fig. 13.6 Timing belt and sprocket timing marks – 1995cc 12-valve engine (Sec 6)

1 *Tensioner pulley retaining nut*
2 *Tensioner pulley backplate retaining nut*
3 *Tensioner pulley backplate*
P *Timing belt deflection measuring point*

13

Fig. 13.7 Timing belt markings – 1995 cc 12-valve engine (Sec 6)

Distance X (between marks 1 and 2) – 44 teeth
Distance Y (between marks 2 and 3) – 23 teeth

6.21a On 1995 cc 12-valve engines, the left-hand . . .

6.21b . . . and right-hand camshaft cover plastic covers are retained by two screws (arrowed) . . .

Manoeuvre the timing belt into position, ensuring that the arrows on the belt are pointing in the direction of rotation (clockwise when viewed from the right-hand end of the engine).

12 On the outside of the timing belt, there are three timing marks in the form of straight lines (see Fig. 13.7). These timing marks are painted on the belt to ensure the valve timing is correctly set.

13 Starting at the camshaft sprocket, align timing mark number 1 with the mark on the sprocket rim. Keeping the belt taut along its front run, so that all slack is on the tensioner pulley side of the belt, fit the belt over the intermediate shaft sprocket and crankshaft sprocket. Do not twist the belt sharply while refitting it, and ensure that the belt teeth are correctly seated on the sprockets.

14 If all is well, timing mark number 2 should align with the mark on the intermediate shaft sprocket, and timing mark number 3 should align with the mark on the crankshaft sprocket, indicating that the valve timing is correctly set. If not, disengage the belt and adjust the sprocket positions as required until all timing belt and sprocket marks are correctly aligned.

15 With the valve timing correctly set, pivot the tensioner backplate towards the belt until the upper retaining nut is located at the mid-point of the backplate slot. Hold the backplate in this position, and tighten its retaining nut to the specified torque.

16 The timing belt tension is then adjusted by rotating the eccentric tensioner pulley using a peg spanner fitted to the two holes in the pulley centre. In the absence of the special Renault peg spanner (Mot. 1135) a home-made peg spanner can be used. Alternatively, obtain two suitable diameter bolts and insert these in the pulley holes; the pulley can then be rotated using a screwdriver or bar inserted between the bolts.

17 Using one of the tools described above, rotate the tensioner pulley towards the belt until the deflection at the mid-point of the front run of the belt (between the camshaft sprocket and intermediate shaft sprocket, Point P in Fig. 13.6) is 10 ± 0.5 mm. Renault dealers use the special belt-tensioning tool shown in Fig. 13.4 to measure the belt deflection. In the absence of this tool, an approximate setting may be achieved by measuring the belt deflection under firm thumb pressure.

18 With the belt correctly tensioned, hold the tensioner pulley stationary, and tighten the large pulley retaining nut to the specified torque setting.

19 Remove the locating rod from the crankshaft, then rotate the crankshaft pulley through two complete turns in a clockwise direction. Refit the locating rod in position, and check that the sprocket timing marks are still correctly positioned. If all is well, recheck the belt deflection and adjust as necessary. If

the belt deflection is being checked without the special Renault tool, the belt tension must be checked by a Renault dealer at the earliest possible opportunity.

20 With the timing belt correctly tensioned, refit all disturbed components, referring to the information given in the relevant Chapters of this manual, and reconnect the battery earth terminal.

Cylinder head – removal and refitting

Removal

21 Undo the retaining screws and remove the three plastic covers from the camshaft cover. Each side cover is retained by two screws, and the rear cover is retained by three screws (photos).

22 Undo the two retaining bolts, and release the HT lead retaining bracket from the right-hand side of the camshaft cover (photo).

23 Undo the three retaining bolts and the single retaining nut, and release the accelerator cable bracket from the top of the camshaft cover (photo).

24 Slacken and remove the two nuts, and remove both the fuel hose retaining clamps from the left-hand side of the camshaft cover (photos).

25 Disconnect the breather hoses, then undo the three retaining nuts and lift off the camshaft cover along with its rubber seal

6.21c . . . and the rear cover is retained by three screws (arrowed)

6.22 Undo the two screws (arrowed) and free the HT lead bracket from the camshaft cover

6.23 Undo the retaining nut and bolts, and free the accelerator cable from the cover

6.24a Undo the two retaining nuts (arrowed) . . .

6.24b . . . and remove the fuel hose clamps from the left-hand side of the cover

6.25a Disconnect the two breather hoses . . .

(photos). Examine the seal for signs of damage or deterioration, and renew if necessary.

26 The cylinder head can then be removed as described in Section 56 of Chapter 1, noting that timing belt removal is as described above. It will also be necessary to disconnect the wiring connector from the knock sensor before removing the head, and to undo the bolts securing the dipstick and various brackets to the side of the head.

Refitting

27 Carry out the operations described in Chapter 1, Section 80, paragraphs 1 to 5.
28 Working in the sequence shown in Fig. 1.46, tighten the head bolts to their specified Stage 1 torque setting.
29 Again following the specified sequence, tighten the bolts through the specified Stage 2 angle using a socket and extension bar. It is recommended that an angle-measuring gauge is used during this stage of the tightening, to ensure accuracy. If a gauge is not available, make alignment marks between the bolt heads and the cylinder head with white paint; the marks can then be used to check that the bolt has been rotated through the correct angle during tightening.
30 Wait 3 minutes.
31 In the same sequence, repeat the operation described in paragraph 29 to tighten the bolts through the specified Stage 3 angle.
32 No further bolt tightening is required.
33 Refit the timing belt as described above, and check the valve clearances as described below.
34 Fit the camshaft cover to the cylinder head, ensuring that the seal is correctly located in the cover groove. Tighten the cover retaining bolts to the specified torque, starting with the outer bolts, tightening the centre bolt last.
35 Refer to Chapter 1, Section 56, paragraphs 1 to 8 and reconnect all applicable items.
36 Reconnect the breather hoses to the camshaft cover.
37 Refit the fuel hose retaining clamps to the cover, ensuring the hoses are correctly

routed, and securely tighten the clamp retaining nuts.
38 Refit the accelerator cable bracket to the cover, and securely tighten its retaining nut and bolts.
39 Refit the HT lead bracket to the side of the cover. Refit the three plastic covers, and tighten all the retaining bolts securely.

Cylinder head - dismantling, inspection and reassembly

Dismantling

40 With the cylinder head on the bench, remove the manifolds (if not already done) as described in Chapter 3.
41 Slacken the camshaft sprocket retaining bolt and remove it, along with its washer. To prevent the camshaft rotating as the bolt is slackened, a sprocket-holding tool will be required. In the absence of the special Renault tool, a substitute can be fabricated from two lengths of steel strip (one long, the other short) and three nuts and bolts. One nut and bolt form the pivot of a forked tool, with the remaining two nuts and bolts at the tips of the 'forks' to engage with the sprocket spokes.
42 With the retaining bolt removed, slide the sprocket off the end of the camshaft. If the Woodruff key is a loose fit, remove it for safekeeping.
43 Slacken all the rocker arm adjusting screws locknuts, and unscrew the adjusting

screws until valve spring pressure is relieved from the rocker arms.
44 Fully unscrew the rocker arm shaft retaining bolts, and lift the rocker arm assemblies away from the cylinder head, noting the correct fitted positions of the shaft locating pins. If the pins are a loose fit, remove them and store them safely. **Do not** under any circumstances remove the bolts from the rocker shaft.
45 The camshaft bearing caps should be marked 1 to 5, number 1 being at the timing belt end of the engine (photo). If identification marks do not already exist, make some using white paint or a marker pen. Also mark each cap to indicate which way round it is fitted. This will avoid the possibility of refitting the caps the wrong way round.
46 Lift off the bearing caps. Remove the camshaft from the cylinder head and discard its oil seal; a new seal must be used on refitting.
47 If necessary, the valves and associated components can be removed and cleaned as described in paragraphs 8 to 12 of Section 59 of Chapter 1.

Inspection

48 Examine the camshaft bearing surfaces and cam lobes for signs of wear ridges and scoring. Renew the camshaft if any of these conditions are apparent. Examine the condition of the bearing surfaces both on the camshaft journals and in the cylinder head and bearing caps. If the head bearing

6.25b . . . undo the retaining nuts and remove the camshaft cover

6.45 Identification numbers (arrowed) are cast into the top of each camshaft bearing cap

13

Fig. 13.8 On 1995 cc 12-valve engines, apply to the shaded areas of numbers 1 and 5 bearing caps (Sec 6)

Fig. 13.9 Ensure the locating pins (P) are correctly fitted to both the exhaust (upper) and inlet (lower) rocker shaft assemblies (Sec 6)

6.58 Ensure the collars and rocker arms are correctly positioned against the sides of the bearing caps prior to tightening the retaining bolts

surfaces are worn excessively, it may be necessary to renew the cylinder head. Consult a Renault dealer or engine reconditioning specialist.

49 Each rocker arm assembly can be dismantled by removing the retaining bolts one at a time and sliding the various components off the end of the shafts. Keep all components in their correct fitted order, making a note as each is removed, to ensure correct reassembly.

50 Examine the rocker arm surfaces which contact the camshaft lobes for wear ridges and scoring. Renew any rocker arms on which these conditions are apparent. Also ensure the rocker arm and shaft oilways are clear and free of blockages.

51 Examine the rocker arm and shaft bearing surfaces for wear ridges and scoring. If there are obvious signs of wear, the rocker arm and/or shaft must be renewed.

52 Refer to Chapter 1, Section 69 for information on cylinder head decarbonising, valve grinding and renovation, and to the Specifications at the start of this Chapter for relevant measurements.

Reassembly

53 Refit the valves and associated components as described in Chapter 1, Section 78, paragraphs 1 to 6.

54 Lubricate the bearings in the cylinder head with clean engine oil, and refit the camshaft.

55 Ensure the bearing cap and cylinder head mating surfaces are clean and dry, then apply a smear of sealant (Loctite 518 or equivalent) to the areas of bearing caps numbers 1 and 5 as shown in Fig. 13.8.

56 Refit the bearing caps to the cylinder head, using the identification marks to ensure that each is fitted in its original location.

57 Ensure that the rocker shaft locating pins are in position in each shaft. The exhaust shaft pin is located in the centre of the shaft at the bottom, and the inlet shaft pin is fitted to

the top of the shaft on the timing belt end (see Fig. 13.9).

58 Refit both rocker shafts to the camshaft bearing caps, and tighten the retaining bolts evenly and progressively to the specified torque. Before tightening the bolts, ensure that the rocker arms, springs and collars are correctly positioned against the sides of each bearing cap, and not trapped between the shaft and caps (photo). Note that the rocker arms must be fitted and the retaining bolts tightened as quickly as possible after fitting the bearing caps, before the sealant hardens.

59 Lubricate the lips of the new camshaft seal with clean engine oil. Drive the seal into position in the head, lips inwards, using a tubular drift (such as a socket) bearing only on the hard outer edge of the seal. Take care not to damage the seal lips during fitting.

60 Refit the Woodruff key (if removed), then locate the sprocket on the end of the camshaft, ensuring that the key is correctly engaged with the cutout in the camshaft end.

61 Clean the threads of the sprocket retaining bolt, and apply a coat of locking fluid to the threads.

62 Refit the sprocket retaining bolt and washer. Tighten the bolt to the specified torque, counterholding the sprocket with the tool used on removal.

63 Refit the cylinder head as described above.

Valve clearances - adjustment

64 Remove the camshaft cover as described earlier in this Section.

65 Referring to Section 82 of Chapter 1, carry

6.66 Camshaft sprocket timing marks (arrowed) should be aligned with the cylinder head surface

out the operations described in paragraphs 2 to 4.

66 With the camshaft timing mark aligned with the pointer on the timing belt cover, turn the crankshaft in a clockwise direction to align the first set of timing marks on the rear of the camshaft sprocket, one on either side of the rim, parallel with the cylinder head surface (photo).

67 In this position, adjust the corresponding three valves given in the table below. The valve clearances are given in the Specifications at the start of this Chapter. The valve locations can be determined from the position of the manifolds.

Camshaft sprocket timing marks	Adjust valves
1st marks	No 2 cylinder inlets and No 4 cylinder exhaust
2nd marks	No 1 cylinder inlets and No 2 cylinder exhaust
3rd marks	No 3 cylinder inlets and No 1 cylinder exhaust
4th marks	No 4 cylinder inlets and No 3 cylinder exhaust

68 Check the clearances of the three valves specified. Clearances are checked by inserting a feeler gauge of the correct thickness between the valve stem and the rocker arm adjusting screw. The feeler gauge should be a light, sliding fit. If adjustment is necessary, slacken the adjusting screw locknut and turn the screw as necessary until the feeler blade is a light sliding fit. Once the correct clearance is obtained, hold the adjusting screw and tighten the locknut (photo). Recheck the clearance and readjust if necessary

6.68 Adjusting an exhaust valve clearance – 1995 cc 12-valve engine

69 Rotate the engine so that the camshaft sprocket turns through 90° and the second set of sprocket timing marks are aligned with the cylinder head surface. Check the clearances of the next three specified valves.

70 Repeat the procedure for the third and fourth set of camshaft sprocket marks until all twelve valve clearances have been checked and, if necessary, adjusted. Finally refit the camshaft cover as described in paragraphs 35 to 39.

Sump - removal and refitting

71 On 12-valve engines, the sump arrangement has been altered. A small pressed-steel sump is bolted to a larger aluminium crankcase stiffener casting, which is in turn bolted to the base of the crankcase.

72 The sump can be removed as described in Chapter 1, Section 60, noting that there is no need to raise the engine. Refitting is as described in Chapter 1, Section 77, ignoring the remarks about the bolt types. Crankcase stiffener casting removal and refitting is described later in this Section.

Oil pump - removal and refitting

Removal

73 Remove the sump, referring to the information given above.

74 Remove the four bolts securing the oil pump strainer cover to the pump body. Lower the cover and recover the oil pump gears.

75 Undo the two bolts securing the pump body to the base of the crankcase, and remove the body from the crankcase. If the pump driveshaft is a loose fit, remove it and store it with the pump for safekeeping.

76 Inspect the oil pump components as described in Section 68 of Chapter 1.

Refitting

77 Check that the circlip on the pump end of

the driveshaft is in good condition and correctly located in its groove. Insert the driveshaft into the base of the crankcase, ensuring it is correctly engaged with the drive pinion.

78 Offer up the oil pump body, locating it on the end of the driveshaft. Refit the two bolts securing the pump to the base of the crankcase, and tighten them to the specified torque.

79 Refit the oil pump gears to the pump body, ensuring that the drivegear is correctly engaged with the driveshaft, and refit the cover. Tighten the cover retaining bolts to the specified torque.

80 Refit the sump, referring to the information given earlier.

Crankcase stiffener casting - removal and refitting

Removal

81 Remove the sump and oil pump as described earlier. Withdraw the dipstick from its tube.

82 Disconnect the wiring from the oil level sensor (where fitted) and remove the sensor from the side of the crankcase.

83 Where necessary, slacken and remove the bolt(s) securing the inlet manifold support stay(s) to the side of the stiffener casting.

84 Referring to Fig. 13.10, undo all the bolts securing the crankcase stiffener casting to the base of the crankcase Note that due to a lack of clearance, it may not be possible to withdraw all of the bolts; some of them will have to be removed with the stiffener.

85 With all the bolts slackened, release the stiffener casting from the base of the crankcase, and manoeuvre it out from underneath the vehicle. Withdraw the remaining retaining bolts from the stiffener, noting their locations. Discard the gasket: a new one must be used on refitting.

Refitting

86 Remove all traces of gasket from the stiffener casting and crankcase mating surfaces. Ensure the mating surfaces are clean and dry, and fit a new gasket to the top of the stiffener, using a few drops of sealing compound to hold the gasket in position.

87 Insert those bolts which could not be withdrawn due to a lack of clearance into position in the stiffener casting. This is important, since it will not be possible to insert them once the casting is manoeuvred into position.

88 Manoeuvre the casting assembly into position and, referring to Fig 13.10, insert the remaining bolts into their correct locations.

89 Tighten all the bolts lightly at first, then work around the casting and tighten each bolt to its correct torque setting.

90 Refit the oil pump and sump as described earlier in this Section.

Oil cooler - general information

91 An oil cooler is fitted to ensure that the oil temperature remains constant under extreme operating conditions. The oil cooler is mounted on the right-hand wing valance, and is cooled by engine coolant which is circulated through the cooler. The cooler is linked to the right-hand side of the cylinder block by two hoses. The oil filter, oil pressure switch and oil temperature sensor (as applicable) are also situated on the cooler rather than on the side of the cylinder block (photos).

6.91a The oil cooler is mounted onto the right-hand wing valance (oil pressure switch and temperature switch arrowed) . . .

6.91b . . . and is linked to the cylinder block by two hoses (arrowed)

Fig. 13.10 Crankcase stiffener casting bolt locations (Sec 6)

White circle = 6 mm sump bolts   *Black circle = 7 mm bolts*   *Triangles = 10 mm bolts*

13

92 When removing the engine, it will be necessary to unbolt the cooler assembly from the wing valance, disconnect the coolant hoses, and remove it with the engine. Alternatively, unscrew the feed and return pipe unions from the cooler and remove the engine, leaving the cooler in position in the vehicle. If the oil cooler feed and return hose unions are disturbed, discard the union O-rings, and fit new ones on refitting.

7 2165 cc engine

1 The 2165 cc (F7T) engine is of an identical construction to the 1995 cc engine covered in Chapter 1. The stroke has been increased to bring the capacity out to 2165 cc.
2 Operations which differ to those on the 1995 cc engine are described below. If the operation is not described below, it can be carried out using the information given in Chapter 1 and in Section 5 of this Chapter for the 1995 cc engine, noting that the specifications applicable to the 2165 cc engine are given at the start of this Chapter. Refer to Section 15 of this Chapter for details of the fuel and exhaust systems.

Sump (later models) modification

3 On later engines, the sump arrangement has been altered. The new arrangement is the same as is fitted to the 1995 cc 12-valve engine, with a small pressed-steel sump bolted to a larger aluminium crankcase stiffener casting, which is in turn bolted to the base of the crankcase.
4 On these models the sump, oil pump and crankcase stiffener casting can be removed using the information given in Section 6 for the 1995 cc 12-valve engine.

8 Cooling, heating and air conditioning systems

1 This Section contains information on modifications to the cooling, heating and air conditioning systems. Operations which differ to those described in Chapter 2 are given below. If the operation is not described below, it can be carried out using the original information given in Chapter 2.

Heater and ventilation controls (phase II models, mid-1989 onwards) - removal and refitting

2 From when the facelift phase II models were introduced, a revised heater control panel is fitted. The new panel is easily identified by its rotary control switches; earlier models have sliding controls for the heating and ventilation system. Removal and refitting is as follows.

Removal

3 Remove the centre console as described in Section 22.
4 Open up the fuse panel access flap on the driver's side lower facia panel, and unclip the fuse panel.
5 Undo the retaining screws and remove the driver's side lower facia panel from the facia assembly.
6 Undo the two screws and remove the small trim panel from the passenger side of the heater panel (inner edge of the glovebox).
7 Remove the radio/cassette player as described in Chapter 12.
8 Using a flat-bladed screwdriver, lift the four retaining clips and withdraw the storage compartment from the bottom of the centre facia panel.
9 Slacken and remove the four centre facia panel retaining screws (two at the top and two at the bottom) then undo the two nuts, located in the radio aperture, securing the panel to the heater unit.
10 Unscrew the two screws (one either side) securing the base of the centre facia panel to its mounting bracket.
11 Partially withdraw the centre panel from the facia until access can be gained to the heater/ventilation control retaining screws. Undo the two retaining screws, then depress the four retaining clips (two at the top and two at the bottom) and disengage the heater controls from the rear of the facia panel. The centre facia panel can then be manoeuvred out of the position, taking note of the correct routing of the radio wiring.
12 To remove the heater/ventilation controls, disconnect the wiring connector from the rear of the panel. Label each of the control cables, then remove the outer cable retaining clips and disconnect each inner cable from its control lever; the cables are a push fit in the levers. With the cables and wiring connector disconnected, the heater control panel can be removed from the facia. Do not attempt to dismantle the control panel.

Refitting

13 Refitting is a direct reversal of the removal procedure, noting the following points:
(a) *Use the marks made on the cables prior to removal to ensure each one is correctly reconnected.*
(b) *Prior to refitting the centre facia panel, check that each heater/ventilation control moves smoothly from fully open to fully closed. The cables are adjusted by repositioning the outer cable; release the retaining clip, reposition the cable as required, then secure it in position with the retaining clip.*
(c) *Ensure all components are securely retained by the retaining clips, and that all the screws are securely tightened.*

9 Fuel and exhaust systems - 1721 cc carburettor models

1 This Section contains information on modifications to the 1721 cc carburettor models. Operations which differ to those described in Chapter 3 are given below. If the operation is not described below, it can be carried out using the original information given in Chapter 3.

Fuel vapour separator - general information

2 On most models, a fuel vapour separator (sometimes called a de-aeration chamber) is fitted to the fuel line between the fuel pump and carburettor. The vapour separator ensures that the supply of fuel to the carburettor is kept at a constant pressure, and is free of air bubbles. Excess fuel is returned from the anti-percolation chamber to the fuel tank.
3 The separator has three hoses: an inlet from the fuel pump, and two outlets, of which one is the feed to the carburettor and the other a return to the fuel tank. If the hoses have to be disconnected for any reason, mark all hoses and unions to ensure that they are correctly reconnected.

Anti-percolation system - general information

4 Certain models may be fitted with an anti-percolation system. Its purpose is to reduce the underbonnet fuel temperature when the vehicle is stopped after a run. This prevents fuel percolation (vaporisation) occurring in the carburettor, so avoiding hot-start problems and fuel vapour emissions.
5 The main components of the system are an electric fan, air ducts leading to the carburettor, and the control circuitry. A temperature switch controls the electrical supply to the fan. If the temperature exceeds a certain value, the cooling fan operates, circulating fresh air around the carburettor to prevent vaporisation of the fuel in the carburettor float chamber. The system is either controlled by the cooling fan switch and operates off the radiator cooling fan via a duct, or is controlled by a separate temperature sensor located near the carburettor and operates off an auxiliary cooling fan located in the engine compartment.
6 No specific testing or repair procedures for the anti-percolation system were available at the time of writing.

Air cleaner housing - modification

7 On later models, a different air cleaner arrangement to that shown in Chapter 3 is fitted. The air cleaner housing is mounted on the left-hand side of the engine compartment, instead of on top of the carburettor and is

**Fig. 13.11 Carburettor adjustment points –
Solex 32/34 Z13 carburettor (Sec 9)**

A *Idle speed adjusting screw*
B *Mixture adjustment screw*
C *Fast idle actuator (power steering)*

linked to the carburettor via an intake duct. Air cleaner element renewal, and air cleaner housing removal and refitting, differ as follows.

Air cleaner - element renewal

8 Slacken and remove all the retaining screws. Lift the cover off the air cleaner housing and remove the filter element.
9 Wipe clean the inside of the filter housing and cover, and fit a new element.
10 Refit the cover, ensuring it is correctly seated, and securely tighten its retaining screws.

Air cleaner housing - removal and refitting

11 Remove the air cleaner element as described above.
12 Slacken the retaining clips (where fitted) and disconnect the hot-air intake, fresh-air intake hoses and the carburettor duct from the base of the filter housing.
13 Slacken and remove the retaining nuts and washers, and remove the housing from its mounting bracket.
14 If necessary, the various ducts and hoses can be removed once their retaining screws have been undone; the fresh-air intake duct is secured to the wing valance by a single retaining screw, and the air cleaner-to-

9.21 Removing the fuel inlet strainer

carburettor duct is secured to the carburettor by four retaining screws.
15 Refitting is a reversal of the removal procedure, ensuring all intake ducts are securely reconnected.

Solex 32/34 Z13 carburettor - general information

16 On some later models, a Solex 32/34 Z13 carburettor is fitted in place of the 28/34 Z10 carburettor. The 32/34 Z13 carburettor can be found on engines with the following codes: F2N 711, F2N 754 and F2N 758. On the F2N 754 engine, a manifold pre-heater system (described in greater detail later in this Section) is also fitted.
17 Both carburettors are virtually identical in operation. The only difference is that on the Z13, the opening of the secondary throttle valve is controlled by a vacuum diaphragm, instead of the mechanical linkage used on the Z10.
18 When working on the 32/34 Z13 carburettor, refer to the information given both in this Section and in Chapter 3 for the 28/34 Z10. The specifications for the 32/34 Z13 carburettor are given at the start of this Chapter. The locations of the idle speed adjusting screw and mixture screw are shown in Fig. 13.11.

Carburettor - overhaul and adjustment

Note: *The carburettor seen in the photographs is a Solex 28/34 Z10. As noted above, the Solex 32/34 Z13 is very similar.*

9.22 Removing the idling jet

19 Remove the carburettor as described in Chapter 3.
20 With the carburettor on a bench, thoroughly clean it externally with paraffin or degreasing agent.
21 Unscrew and remove the fuel inlet strainer (photo).
22 Unscrew the idling jet from the carburettor cover (photo).
23 Remove the heater retaining plate screw. Lift off the plate and withdraw the roll pin with the insulator, the terminal and the heater disc (photos). Be careful with the heater disc, it is very fragile.
24 Prise the defuming valve link rod out of the plastic bush (photo).

**Fig. 13.12 Carburettor heater components
– Solex 28/34 Z10 carburettor (Sec 9)**

1 *Roll pin*	5 *Retaining plate*
2 *Insulator*	a *Tongue*
3 *Terminal*	b *Slot*
4 *Heater disc*	

**9.23a Undo the retaining screw, then lift off
the retaining plate . . .**

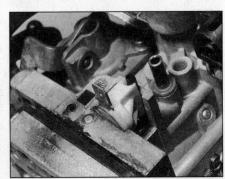

9.23b . . . and withdraw heater components

9.24 Disconnecting the defuming valve link

13

9.25a Undo the five retaining screws
(arrowed)

9.25b . . . and lift off the carburettor cover

9.26 Removing the float pivot pin

25 Remove the five screws which secure the carburettor cover. Lift off the cover with the float assembly and choke vacuum actuator attached (photos).
26 Remove the float pivot pin (photo). Remove the float assembly, the needle valve and the gasket.
27 Remove the idle circuit filter from the carburettor body (photo).
28 Pull the accelerator pump injector assembly from the body (photo)
29 Unscrew and remove the air correction jet/emulsion tube assemblies (photo).
30 Remove the main jets from the bottom of the emulsion tube wells by unscrewing them (photos).
31 Remove the idle mixture adjustment screw tamperproof cap. Screw the screw in

until it seats lightly, counting the **exact** number of turns required to do this, then unscrew it. On refitting, screw the screw in until it seats lightly, then back the screw off by the number of turns noted on removal, to return the screw to its original location.
32 If a complete overhaul is being undertaken, remove the various diaphragm covers so that the diaphragms can be examined and, if necessary, renewed.
33 Clean the jets, carburettor body assemblies, float chamber and internal drillings. An air line may be used to clear the internal passages once the carburettor is fully dismantled. Aerosol cans of carburettor cleaner are widely available, and can prove very useful in helping to clear internal passages of stubborn obstructions.

Warning: If high pressure air is directed into drillings and passages where a diaphragm is fitted, the diaphragm is likely to be damaged.
34 Use a straight-edge to check all carburettor body assembly mating surfaces for distortion.
35 On reassembly, renew any worn components, and fit a complete set of new gaskets and seals. A carburettor overhaul kit should be available from a Renault dealer or a carburettor specialist.
36 Reassembly is a reversal of the dismantling procedure. Ensure that all jets are securely locked in position, but take care not to overtighten them. Ensure all mating surfaces are clean and dry, and that all body sections are correctly assembled with their fuel and air passages correctly aligned. Working as described below, set the float height before assembling the carburettor. Carry out the necessary adjustment procedures before refitting the carburettor to the engine.

Float height adjustment

37 With the carburettor cover reassembled (including the gasket), invert the cover, and measure the distance from the gasket to the furthest point of the float assembly. The correct value is given in the Specifications. To adjust the float height setting, carefully bend the pivot arm (photo).

9.27 Removing the idle circuit filter from
the carburettor

9.28 Removing the accelerator pump
injector

9.29 Removing an air correction
jet/emulsion tube assembly

9.30a Unscrewing the main jet . . .

9.30b . . . and removing it from the
emulsion tube well

9.37 Measuring carburettor float level

9.39 Fast idle cam and adjustment screw

Fig. 13.13 Defuming valve adjustment – Solex 28/34 Z10 carburettor (Sec 9)

A   Gauge rod /for measuring throttle valve gap)
B   Adjustment screw

Defuming valve adjustment

38 Invert the reassembled carburettor. Open the throttle valve until the defuming valve just closes. Hold the throttle valve in this position and, using the shank of a twist drill, measure the clearance between the edge of the throttle valve and the carburettor bore. Compare this value to the clearance given in the Specifications. If necessary, adjust by turning the adjustment screw in the appropriate direction until the specified clearance is obtained (see Fig. 13.13 or 13.14).

Initial throttle opening (fast idle) adjustment

39 With the carburettor still inverted, operate the choke linkage to close the choke valve. Using the shank of a twist drill, measure the clearance between the edge of the throttle valve and the carburettor bore and compare this to the clearance given in the Specifications. If necessary, adjust by turning the screw which bears on the fast idle cam (photo).

Choke pneumatic part-opening adjustment

40 Operate the choke linkage to close the choke valve, and push the operating rod as far as it will go into the choke vacuum actuator.

Using the shank of a twist drill, measure the clearance between the edge of the choke valve and the bore, and compare this to the clearance given in the Specifications. If necessary, adjust by turning the screw situated in the centre of the vacuum actuator.

Secondary throttle link adjustment - 32/34 Z13 carburettor only

41 The link rod between the throttle vacuum actuator and the secondary throttle lever should be adjusted so that there is a small amount of play ('A' in Fig. 13.15) in both the fully-closed and fully-open positions.

Inlet manifold pre-heater system (F2N 754 engine) - general information, component removal and refitting

42 On the F2N 754 engine fitted with a 32/34 Z13 carburettor, an inlet manifold preheater system is fitted. The system consists of a heating element, fitted to the underside of the manifold, and a temperature switch which is screwed into the left-hand side of the manifold (see Fig. 13.16).

43 When the ignition is switched on and the engine is cold (below 63°C), the current flows through the closed manifold temperature switch contacts to the heater. This ensures

that the inlet manifold is warm enough to prevent fuel droplets condensing in the manifold, so improving driveability and reducing exhaust emissions when the engine is cold.

44 As soon as the manifold warms up to above 63°C, the switch contacts open and the power supply to the manifold heater is interrupted. Should the manifold temperature drop to below 56°C, the switch contacts close and the current flows again to the heating element, ensuring that the manifold temperature remains above 56°C at all times.

Manifold heater - removal and refitting

45 Disconnect the battery earth lead. Apply the handbrake, jack up the front of the car, and support it on axle stands. Access to the manifold heater can then be gained from underneath the vehicle, via the gap between the engine and engine compartment bulkhead.

Fig. 13.14 Defuming valve adjustment – Solex 32/34 Z13 carburettor (Sec 9)

A   Gauge rod (for measuring throttle valve gap)
B   Adjustment screw

Fig. 13.15 Throttle actuator link rod adjustment – Solex 32/34 Z13 carburettor (Sec 9)

A See text

Fig. 13.16 Inlet manifold pre-heater system components – F2N 754 engine (Sec 9)

1   Heating element
2   Inlet manifold
3   Temperature switch

13

46 Disconnect the wiring connector from the heater terminal, then slacken and remove the retaining screws. Withdraw the heater from the underside of the manifold along with its gasket. Inspect the gasket for signs of damage or deterioration, and renew if necessary.

47 Refitting is the reverse of the removal procedure.

Manifold heater temperature switch

48 Disconnect the wiring connector from the switch, and unscrew the switch.

49 Wipe clean the threads of the switch and those of the manifold. If a sealing washer is fitted, renew it whenever it is disturbed to prevent air leaks; if no sealing washer is fitted, apply a smear of sealant to the switch threads.

50 Refit the switch to the manifold, tightening it securely, and reconnect the wiring connector.

Solex 28/34 Z10 carburettor - modifications

Flat spot on acceleration

51 On models equipped with the 28/34 Z10 carburettor, there have been cases noted of a flat spot occurring under acceleration; this is caused by a lack of fuel as the carburettor changes from the primary to secondary throttle valve. Renault have overcome this problem by manufacturing a modified feed tube for the secondary valve idling circuit. However, fitting of the tube is a complex, fiddly task, and it is therefore recommended that it is entrusted to a Renault dealer.

Engine stalls immediately after starting when cold

52 To overcome the problem of the engine stalling immediately after starting when cold on earlier models, Renault have produced a modification kit for the carburettor. Fitting of the kit will overcome the problem, caused by the choke valve opening too quickly. Refer to your Renault dealer for further information.

10 Fuel and exhaust systems - 1721 cc single-point fuel injection models

Warning: Many of the procedures in this Chapter require the removal of fuel lines and connections, which may result in some fuel spillage. Before carrying out any operation on the fuel system, refer to the precautions given in Safety first! at the beginning of this manual and follow them implicitly. Petrol is a highly-dangerous and volatile liquid, and the precautions necessary when handling it cannot be overstressed.

Note: *Residual pressure will remain in the fuel lines long after the vehicle was last used; when disconnecting any fuel line,*

depressurise the fuel system as described in paragraphs 12 to 15.

1 There are two different types of fuel injection system fitted to the 1721 cc models in the Renault 21 range: a 'single-point' (single injector) system and a 'multi-point' (four-injector) system. This Section covers the singlepoint system. For information on the multi-point system, refer to Section 11.

General information

2 The fuel system consists of a fuel tank mounted under the rear of the car, an electric fuel pump and fuel filter also situated underneath the car, fuel feed and return lines, and the throttle body assembly (which incorporates the single fuel injector and the fuel pressure regulator), as well as the computer and the various sensors, electrical components and related wiring. The air cleaner contains a disposable paper filter element, and incorporates a flap valve air temperature control system. This allows cold air from the outside of the car and warm air heated by the exhaust manifold to enter the air cleaner in the correct proportions.

3 The fuel injection system also incorporates a closed-loop catalytic converter and an evaporative emission control system, and complies to the latest emission control standards. The system operates as follows.

4 The fuel pump transfers fuel from the tank to the fuel injector via a filter mounted next to the pump. Fuel supply pressure is controlled by the pressure regulator in the throttle body assembly, which allows excess fuel to return to the tank.

5 The electrical control system consists of the computer, along with the following sensors:

(a) *Throttle potentiometer - informs the computer of the throttle valve position and the rate of throttle opening/closing.*

(b) *Coolant temperature sensor - informs the computer of engine temperature.*

(c) *Fuel/air mixture temperature sensor - informs the computer of the temperature of the fuel/air mixture passing through the inlet manifold.*

(d) *Lambda sensor - informs the computer of the oxygen content of the exhaust gases (explained in greater detail later in this Section).*

(e) *Microswitch (no-load/full-load switch) - informs the computer when the throttle valve is fully-open or fully-closed*

(f) *Manifold absolute pressure (MAP) sensor - informs the computer of the load on the engine, expressed as manifold vacuum.*

(g) *Angular speed/position senso - informs the computer of engine speed and crankshaft position (see Chapter 4).*

6 All the above signals are compared by the computer. The computer selects the response appropriate to those values, and controls the fuel injector, varying its pulse width - the length of time the injector is held open to provide a richer or weaker mixture, as appropriate. The computer provides the best

settings for cranking, starting (with either a hot or cold engine), warm-up, idle, cruising and acceleration.

7 The computer also controls the engine idle speed via a stepper motor which is fitted to the throttle body. The motor pushrod rests against a cam on the throttle valve spindle. When the throttle valve is closed (accelerator pedal released), the computer uses the motor to vary the opening of the throttle valve and so control the idle speed.

8 The computer also manages the exhaust and evaporative emission control systems which are described in detail later in this Section, as well as the ignition system (see Section 16).

9 If there is an abnormality in any of the readings obtained from its various sensors, the computer has a back-up mode. On entering this mode, the computer ignores the sensor signal, and assumes a pre-programmed value which will allow the engine to continue running, albeit at reduced efficiency. If the computer enters this back-up mode, the warning light on the instrument panel will be illuminated, and the relevant fault code will be stored in the computer memory.

10 If the warning lamp is illuminated, the vehicle should be taken to a Renault dealer. A complete test of the engine management system can then be carried out, using a special electronic diagnostic test unit which is simply plugged into the system's diagnostic connector.

Fuel injection system - adjustments

11 As mentioned above, the idle speed and mixture adjustment are all controlled by the computer, and are not adjustable. Experienced home mechanics with a considerable amount of skill and equipment (including a tachometer and an exhaust gas analyser) may be able to check the exhaust CO level and the idle speed. However, if these are found to be in need of *adjustment,* the car **must** be taken to a Renault dealer for testing using the test equipment which is plugged into the diagnostic connector.

Fuel system - depressurisation

Note: *Refer to the warning note at the start of this Section before proceeding.*

Warning: The following procedure will merely relieve the pressure In the fuel system - remember that fuel will still be present in the system components, and take precautions accordingly before disconnecting any of them.

12 The fuel system referred to in this Section is defined as the fuel pump, the fuel filter, the fuel injector and the pressure regulator in the injector housing, and the metal pipes and flexible hoses of the fuel lines between these components. All these contain fuel, which will be under pressure while the engine is running and/or while the ignition is switched on. The pressure will remain for some time after the ignition has been switched off, and must be relieved before any of these components are disturbed for servicing work.

13 Disconnect the battery negative terminal.

14 On some models, a depressurisation valve is screwed into the side of the throttle body assembly, next to the fuel feed pipe union. To depressurise the system, unscrew the valve cap and depress the valve core using a suitable small screwdriver. Place a wad of rag around the valve to catch any fuel spray which may be released as the pressure is relieved. Once the pressure is relieved, screw the cap back onto the valve and tighten it securely.

15 Where there is no depressurisation valve, place a suitable container beneath the connection or union to be disconnected, and have a large rag ready to soak up any escaping fuel not being caught by the container. Slowly loosen the connection or union nut (as applicable) to avoid a sudden release of pressure, and position the rag around the connection to catch any fuel spray which may be expelled. Once the pressure is released, disconnect the fuel line. Insert plugs to minimise fuel loss, and to prevent the entry of dirt into the fuel system.

Fuel system pressure check

Note: *Refer to the warning note at the start of this Section before proceeding. A fuel pressure gauge will be required. If such a gauge is not available, the check must be performed by a Renault dealer.*

16 Depressurise the fuel system as described above, and connect a fuel pressure gauge into the fuel feed pipe to the throttle body.

17 Start the engine and measure the fuel system pressure with the engine idling. Compare it to the regulated pressure given in the Specifications at the start of this Chapter.

18 If necessary, the pressure can be adjusted via the screw in the centre of the base of the fuel pressure regulator cover. Remove the plug from the cover, and rotate the screw as required until the pressure is as specified. Once the correct pressure is obtained, stop the engine and refit the plug to the regulator cover.

19 Depressurise the fuel system, then remove the gauge and reconnect the fuel feed pipe.

Fuel pump and filter - removal and refitting

20 The fuel pump and filter arrangement is the same as that fitted to the 2.0 litre model. Refer to Part C of Chapter 3 for information on pump and filter removal and refitting, bearing in mind the information given in paragraphs 12 to 15 of this Section on depressurising the fuel system.

Air cleaner and element - removal and refitting

21 Refer to the information given in Part A of Chapter 3.

Throttle body assembly - removal and refitting

Note: *Refer to the warning note at the start of this Section before proceeding.*

Removal

22 Disconnect the battery negative terminal. Remove the air cleaner housing as described in Chapter 3.

23 Depress the retaining clips and disconnect the wiring connectors from the throttle potentiometer, the idle control stepper motor, the injector wiring loom connector and the microswitch.

24 Depressurise the fuel system as described in paragraphs 12 to 15.

25 Unscrew the union nuts, and disconnect the fuel feed and return pipes from the throttle body assembly. Plug the pipe ends and throttle body unions, to minimise fuel loss and prevent the entry of dirt into the fuel system.

26 Disconnect the accelerator cable from the throttle body as described in Chapter 3. Position the cable clear of the throttle body.

27 Slacken the retaining clip(s) and disconnect the various vacuum and breather hoses from the throttle body.

28 Slacken and remove the four nuts securing the throttle body assembly to the inlet manifold, then remove the assembly along with its gasket.

Refitting

29 Refitting is a reversal of the removal procedure, bearing in mind the following points:

(a) *Renew the gasket regardless of its apparent condition.*

(b) *Ensure the throttle body and inlet manifold mating surfaces are clean and dry, then fit the gasket and throttle body, and securely tighten the retaining nuts.*

(c) *Ensure the fuel pipe and throttle body unions are clean, then refit the pipes, tightening the union nuts securely.*

(d) *Ensure all hoses are correctly reconnected and, where necessary, that their retaining clips are securely tightened.*

(e) *On completion, start the engine and check the fuel pipe unions for signs of leakage.*

Fuel injector - removal and refitting

Note: *Refer to the warning note at the start of this Section before proceeding.*

Removal

30 Disconnect the battery negative terminal. Remove the air cleaner assembly as described in Chapter 3.

31 Depressurise the fuel system as described in paragraphs 12 to 15.

32 Disconnect the wiring connector from the top of the injector.

33 Slacken and remove the two retaining screws, and lift off the injector retaining plate and collar.

34 Withdraw the injector from the throttle body, along with both its sealing O-rings.

Refitting

35 Refitting is a reverse of the removal procedure, using new O-rings.

Fuel pressure regulator - removal and refitting

Note: *Refer to the warning note at the start of this Section before proceeding.*

Note: *The fuel pressure regulator should not be disturbed unless absolutely necessary. The regulator is adjustable via the screw in the base of the regulator cover. After refitting, the fuel system pressure should be checked and if necessary adjusted as described earlier in this Section.*

Removal

36 Remove the throttle body assembly as described earlier in this Section.

37 Using a marker pen, make alignment marks between the regulator cover and throttle body, then undo the three retaining screws. Lift off the cover, and recover the valve diaphragm, spring and spring seats, noting the orientation of each component.

38 Remove all traces of dirt, and examine the diaphragm for signs of splitting. If damage is found, it will be necessary to renew the complete fuel pressure regulator assembly.

Refitting

39 Refitting is a reverse of the removal procedure, ensuring that the diaphragm components are fitted the correct way around and the retaining screws are securely tightened.

40 Refit the throttle body, and check the fuel system pressure as described earlier in this Section.

Idle control stepper motor - removal and refitting

Removal

41 Disconnect the battery negative terminal. Remove the air cleaner assembly as described in Chapter 3 to improve access to the motor.

42 Depress the retaining clip and disconnect the wiring connector from the idle control stepper motor.

43 Undo the four retaining nuts and remove the motor from the throttle body.

Refitting

44 Refitting is a reverse of the removal procedure.

Throttle potentiometer - removal and refitting

Removal

45 Disconnect the battery negative terminal. To improve access, remove the air cleaner assembly as described in Chapter 3.

13

46 Depress the retaining clip and disconnect the wiring connector from the potentiometer.
47 Using a marker pen or a dab of paint, make alignment marks between the potentiometer and throttle body. Undo the two retaining screws, and remove the potentiometer from the throttle body.

Refitting

48 Refit the potentiometer, ensuring it is correctly engaged with the throttle valve spindle, and lightly tighten its retaining screws. Align the marks made before removal, then tighten the potentiometer retaining screws. If a new potentiometer is being installed, the potentiometer position must be set by a Renault dealer using the appropriate test equipment.
49 Reconnect the wiring connector, refit the air cleaner and reconnect the battery.

Fuel/air mixture temperature sensor - removal and refitting

Removal

50 The fuel/air mixture temperature sensor is screwed into the inlet manifold. To remove the sensor, first disconnect the battery negative terminal.
51 Disconnect the wiring connector from the sensor. Unscrew the sensor and remove it from the inlet manifold.

Refitting

52 Wipe clean the threads of the sensor and those of the manifold. If a sealing washer is fitted, renew it whenever it is disturbed to prevent air leaks; if no sealing washer is fitted, apply a smear of sealant to the sensor threads.
53 Refit the sensor to the manifold, tightening it securely, and reconnect the wiring connector.

Manifold absolute pressure (MAP) sensor - removal and refitting

Removal

54 The manifold absolute pressure (MAP) sensor is connected to the throttle body by a vacuum hose, and is mounted either on the engine compartment bulkhead or on the right-hand suspension mounting turret.
55 To remove the MAP sensor, disconnect the battery negative terminal, then trace the vacuum hose back from the throttle body to the sensor and disconnect it.
56 Unclip the MAP sensor from its mounting, disconnect the wiring connector, and remove the sensor from the engine compartment.

Refitting

57 Refitting is a reversal of the removal procedure.

Coolant temperature sensor - removal and refitting

Removal

58 The coolant temperature sensor is screwed into the front of the cylinder head.

Drain the cooling system, or be prepared for some coolant loss as the sensor is removed.
59 Disconnect the battery negative terminal, then disconnect the wiring connector from the coolant temperature sensor.
60 Unscrew the sensor, remove it from the head, and plug the sensor aperture to prevent the entry of dirt. If the cooling system has not been drained, work quickly to minimise coolant loss, and plug the aperture.

Refitting

61 Refitting is a reverse of the removal procedure. If a sealing washer is fitted, renew it to prevent coolant leaks; if no sealing washer is fitted, apply a smear of sealant to the sensor threads prior to refitting.

Microswitch (no-load/full-load switch) - removal and refitting

Removal

62 Disconnect the battery negative terminal. If necessary, to improve access to the microswitch, remove the air cleaner housing as described in Chapter 3.
63 Slacken and remove the two retaining screws, and remove the microswitch from the side of the throttle body.

Refitting

64 Refitting is a reverse of the removal procedure.

Computer - removal and refitting

Removal

65 The computer is located in a protective plastic box in the engine compartment. First disconnect the battery negative terminal.
66 Release the rubber retaining strap, and free the plastic box from its mounting plate.
67 Unclip the casing cover, then disconnect the computer wiring plug and withdraw the computer from the casing.

Refitting

68 Refitting is a reversal of removal, ensuring that the wiring plug is securely reconnected.

Manifolds - removal and refitting

69 The inlet and exhaust manifolds can be removed as described in Chapter 3, noting the following points.
(a) *Remove the exhaust gas recirculation pipe linking the manifolds. The pipe is secured to the exhaust manifold by two bolts, and to the inlet manifold by a union nut. On refitting, use a new EGR pipe gasket at the exhaust manifold.*
(b) *Remove the throttle body as described earlier in this Section, and disconnect the wiring connector(s) from the manifold sensor(s).*

Fig. 13.17 Exhaust system components – 1721 cc models with a catalytic converter (Secs 10 and 11)

1 Spacer	4 Downpipe (twin-pipe arrangement)	7 Exhaust clamp
2 Gasket	5 Catalytic converter	8 Silencer (up to mid-1989)
3 Downpipe (single-pipe arrangement)	6 Intermediate pipe	9 Silencer (mid-1989 on)
		10 Heat shields

Exhaust system - general information

70 The exhaust system is very similar to that fitted to earlier models, shown in Chapter 3, the only difference being that a catalytic converter is incorporated into the system. The catalytic converter is fitted between the downpipe and intermediate pipe (see Fig. 13.17). Refer to Section 9 of Chapter 3 for information on removal and refitting. Details of the catalytic converter are given at the end of this Section.

Exhaust emission control systems - general information, component removal and refitting

71 To minimise the amount of pollutants which escape into the atmosphere, these models are fitted with a catalytic converter, a lambda sensor and an exhaust gas recirculation (EGR) system.

Catalytic converter and lambda sensor

72 The catalytic converter is of the closed-loop type. A lambda sensor in the exhaust system provides the computer with constant feedback, enabling it to adjust the mixture to provide the best possible conditions for the converter to operate.

73 The lambda sensor's tip is sensitive to oxygen, and sends the computer a varying voltage depending on the amount of oxygen in the exhaust gases. If the intake air/fuel mixture is too rich, the exhaust gases are low in oxygen so the sensor sends a low-voltage signal, the voltage rising as the mixture weakens and the amount of oxygen in the exhaust gases rises. Peak conversion efficiency of all major pollutants occurs if the air/fuel mixture is maintained at the ratio of 14.7 parts (by weight) of air to 1 part of fuel (the 'stoichiometric' ratio). The sensor output voltage alters in a large step at this point, the computer using the signal change as a reference point, and correcting the intake air/fuel mixture accordingly by altering the fuel injector pulse width (opening duration).

74 Checking the lambda sensor's operation can be done only by attaching Renault diagnostic equipment to the sensor wiring, and checking that the voltage varies between appropriate values when the engine is running. **Do not** attempt to 'test' any part of the system with anything other than the correct test equipment.

EGR system

75 The EGR system consists of a pipe linking the exhaust manifold to the inlet manifold, and an EGR valve mounted on the inlet manifold. The valve is controlled by the computer via the same solenoid control valve as the evaporative emission system. The solenoid control valve is modulated on and off, allowing inlet manifold depression to act on the EGR valve diaphragm, and so open up the EGR pipe port in the inlet manifold. This allows the exhaust gases to pass from the exhaust manifold into the inlet manifold to be burnt again by the combustion process. This reduces the amount of unburnt hydrocarbons reaching the catalytic converter.

Lambda sensor - removal and refitting

Caution: The lambda sensor is - delicate it will not work if it is dropped or knocked, if its power supply is disrupted, or if any cleaning materials are used on it.

76 Disconnect the battery negative terminal.

77 The lambda sensor is either screwed into the side of the exhaust manifold, or is located underneath the vehicle, screwed into the top of the catalytic converter (depending on model). Remove the sensor as follows.

78 Where the sensor is screwed into the catalytic converter, firmly apply the handbrake, jack up the front of the vehicle and support it on axle stands.

79 Trace the wiring back from the sensor, releasing it from any retaining clips, to its wiring connectors. Disconnect the sensor wiring from the main loom. Unscrew the sensor from the exhaust manifold or catalytic converter, and remove it from the vehicle.

80 Refitting is a reverse of the removal procedure, noting the following points:

(a) Examine the sealing washer for signs of damage, and renew if necessary.

(b) Ensure the sensor and manifold/front pipe threads are clean, then apply a smear of high-temperature anti-seize compound to the sensor's threads. Refit the sensor and tighten it securely.

(c) Ensure the sensor wiring is correctly routed and secured in position with any relevant clips or ties.

EGR valve - removal and refitting

81 Disconnect the vacuum hose from the valve.

82 Undo the two retaining bolts, and remove the EGR valve from the inlet manifold along with its gasket. Discard the gasket; a new one must be used on refitting.

83 On refitting, ensure the valve and manifold mating surfaces are clean and dry, and fit the new gasket to the valve.

84 Refit the valve and gasket to the manifold, and securely tighten its retaining bolts. Reconnect the vacuum hose to the valve.

Evaporative emission control system - general information, component removal and refitting

85 To minimise the escape into the atmosphere of unburned hydrocarbons, an evaporative emissions control system is incorporated in the fuel injection system. The fuel tank filler cap is sealed, and a charcoal canister is mounted in the engine compartment to collect the petrol vapours generated in the tank when the car is parked. It stores them until they can be cleared from the canister (under the control of the computer, via the solenoid control valve and vacuum diaphragm) into the inlet tract, to be burned by the engine during normal combustion.

86 To ensure that the engine runs correctly when it is cold and/or idling, and to protect the catalytic converter from the effects of an over-rich mixture, the solenoid control valve is not opened by the computer until the engine has warmed up. The solenoid valve is then modulated on and off as required. When the valve is open, inlet manifold depression is allowed to act on the vacuum valve fitted to the line linking the canister to the manifold. The vacuum valve opens and allows the fuel vapours stored in the canister to be drawn into the manifold.

87 If the system is thought to be faulty, disconnect the hoses from the charcoal canister and solenoid control valves, and check that they are clear by blowing through them. If the solenoid valve or charcoal canister are thought to be faulty, they must be renewed.

Charcoal canister - removal and refitting

88 Disconnect the battery negative terminal.

89 Disconnect the hoses from the top of the canister. Release the rubber retaining strap and remove the canister from its mounting bracket. Store or dispose of the canister carefully - it may still contain fuel vapour.

90 Refitting is a reverse of the removal procedure.

Solenoid control valve - removal and refitting

91 The solenoid control valve is located on the right-hand side of the engine compartment, on the bulkhead.

92 Disconnect the battery negative terminal and disconnect the wiring connector from the valve.

93 Disconnect the vacuum hoses from the valve, noting their correct locations. Undo the two retaining nuts, and remove the valve from the engine compartment.

94 Refitting is a reverse of the removal procedure.

Charcoal canister vacuum valve - removal and refitting

95 The charcoal canister vacuum valve is situated next to the solenoid control valve.

96 Make identification marks on the three valve hoses, to ensure correct refitting. Disconnect the hoses and remove the vacuum valve from the engine compartment.

97 Refitting is a reverse of the removal procedure.

Unleaded petrol - general information and usage

98 As with all models equipped with a catalytic converter, these models must be run on unleaded fuel **only**. Fuel grade 95 RON (Premium unleaded) is suitable. Fuel grade 98 RON (Super unleaded) can also be used, though there is no advantage in doing so.

13

Leaded fuel must not be used, as it will seriously damage the catalytic converter.

Catalytic converter - general information and precautions

99 The catalytic converter is a reliable and simple device which needs no maintenance in itself, but there are some facts of which an owner should be aware if the converter is to function properly for its full service life.

(a) DO NOT use leaded petrol. Lead will poison the catalyst.

(b) Keep the ignition and fuel systems well-maintained. If the air/fuel mixture is allowed to become too rich due to neglect, the unburned surplus will enter and burn in the catalytic converter, overheating it.

(c) If the engine develops a misfire, drive the car as little as possible until the fault is cured. Misfiring will allow unburned fuel to enter the converter, which will result in its overheating, as noted above.

(d) DO NOT push- or tow-start the car - this will soak the catalytic converter in unburned fuel, causing it to overheat when the engine does start.

(e) DO NOT switch off the ignition at high engine speeds - ie do not 'blip' the throttle immediately before switching off.

Again, this will cause unburned fuel to enter the converter.

(f) DO NOT use fuel or engine oil additives - these may contain substances harmful to the catalytic converter.

(g) DO NOT continue to use the car if the engine burns oil to the extent of leaving a visible trail of blue smoke - the unburned carbon deposits will clog the converter passages.

(h) The catalytic converter operates at very high temperatures. DO NOT, therefore, park the car in dry undergrowth, or over long grass or piles of dead leaves.

(i) The catalytic converter is FRAGILE - do not drop it, or strike it with tools during servicing work. Do not ground it by driving over rough terrain.

(j) The catalytic converter, used on a well-maintained and well-driven car, should last for between 50 000 and 100 000 miles. From this point on, careful checks should be made at all specified service intervals of the CO level, to ensure that the converter is still operating efficiently. If the converter Is no longer effective, it must be renewed.

100 In some cases, particularly when the car is new and/or is used for stop/start driving, a sulphurous smell (like that of rotten eggs) may be noticed from the exhaust. This is common to many catalytic converter-equipped cars, and seems to be due to the small amount of sulphur found in some petrols reacting with hydrogen in the exhaust to produce hydrogen sulphide (H_2S) gas. This gas is toxic, but it is not produced in sufficient amounts to be a problem. Once the car has covered a few thousand miles, the problem should disappear - in the meanwhile, a change of driving style or of the brand of petrol used may effect a solution.

11 Fuel and exhaust systems - 1721 cc multi-point fuel injection models

⚠️ **Warning: Many of the procedures in this Chapter require the removal of fuel lines and connections, which may result in some fuel spillage. Before carrying out any operation on the fuel system, refer to the precautions given in Safety first! at the beginning of this manual, and follow them implicitly. Petrol is a highly-dangerous and volatile liquid, and the precautions necessary when handling it cannot be overstressed.**

Note: Residual pressure will remain in the fuel lines long after the vehicle was last used. When disconnecting any fuel line, depressurise the fuel system as described in Section 10 of this Chapter, ignoring the remark about the depressurisation valve.

1 There are two different types of fuel injection system fitted to the 1721 cc models in the Renault 21 range: a 'single-point' (single injector) system, and a 'multi-point' (four-injector) system. This Section covers the multi-point system. For information on the single-point system, refer to Section 10.

General information

2 The fuel system consists of a fuel tank mounted under the rear of the car, an electric fuel pump and fuel filter also situated underneath the car, fuel feed and return lines. The fuel pump supplies fuel to the fuel rail, which acts as a reservoir for the four fuel injectors which inject fuel into the inlet tracts. A fuel filter is incorporated in the feed line from the pump to the fuel rail, to ensure the fuel supplied to the injectors is clean. Fuel pressure is controlled by the pressure regulator mounted on the fuel rail.

3 The fuel injection system also incorporates a closed-loop catalytic converter and an evaporative emission control system.

4 The fuel pump mounted underneath the vehicle pumps fuel from the fuel tank to the fuel rail, via a filter mounted next to the pump. Fuel supply pressure is controlled by the pressure regulator in the fuel rail, which lifts to allow excess fuel to return to the tank when the optimum operating pressure of the fuel system is exceeded.

Fig. 13.18 Fuel injection system component locations – 1721 cc multi-point system (Sec 11)

1 Throttle housing
2 Throttle (no-load/full-load) switch
3 Manifold plenum chamber
4 Fuel pressure regulator
5 Diagnostic wiring connector
6 Intake air temperature sensor
7 Air cleaner housing
8 Manifold absolute pressure (MAP) sensor
9 Computer
10 Distributor
11 Idle speed auxiliary air valve
12 Ignition HT coil, power module and injection relay

5 The electrical control system consists of the computer, along with the following sensors:

(a) *Throttle (no-load/full-load) switch - informs the computer of the throttle valve position.*

(b) *Coolant temperature sensor - informs the computer of engine temperature.*

(c) *Intake air temperature sensor - informs the computer of the temperature of the air entering the inlet manifold.*

(d) *Lambda sensor - informs the computer of the oxygen content of the exhaust gases (explained in greater detail in Section 10.*

(e) *Pre-ignition (knock) sensor - informs the ECU if detonation ('pinking') is occurring.*

(f) *Manifold absolute pressure (MAP) sensor - informs the computer of the load on the engine.*

(g) *Angular position/speed sensor - informs the computer of the engine speed and crankshaft position.*

6 All the above signals are compared by the computer. Based on this information, the computer selects the response appropriate to those values, and controls the fuel injector (varying its pulse width - the length of time the injector is held open - to provide a richer or weaker mixture, as appropriate). The mixture and idle speed are constantly varied by the computer to provide the best settings for cranking, starting (with either a hot or cold engine), warm-up, idle, cruising and acceleration.

7 The computer also controls the engine idle speed via an auxiliary air valve. The air valve is connected to the air intake duct and to the throttle housing, downstream of the throttle valve. When the throttle valve is closed, the ECU controls the opening of the valve, which in turn regulates the amount of air entering the manifold, and so controls the idle speed.

8 The computer also controls the exhaust and evaporative emission control systems which are described in detail later in this Section, as well as the ignition system (see Section 16).

9 If there is an abnormality in any of the readings obtained from its various sensors, the computer has a back-up mode. On entering this mode, the computer ignores the sensor signal, and assumes a pre-programmed value which will allow the engine to continue running, albeit at reduced efficiency. If the computer enters this back-up mode, the warning lamp on the instrument panel will be illuminated, and a fault code will be stored in the computer memory.

10 If the warning lamp comes on, the vehicle should be taken to a Renault dealer. A complete test of the engine management system can then be carried out, using a special electronic diagnostic test unit which is simply plugged into the system's diagnostic connector.

Fuel injection system - adjustments

11 As mentioned above, the idle speed and mixture adjustment are all monitored and controlled by the computer, and are not adjustable. Experienced home mechanics with a considerable amount of skill and equipment (including a tachometer and an exhaust gas analyser) may be able to check the exhaust CO level and the idle speed. However, if these are found to be in need of *adjustment*, the car **must** be taken to a Renault dealer.

Fuel system - depressurisation

12 Refer to the information given in Section 10 of this Chapter, ignoring the remark about the depressurisation valve.

Fuel system pressure check

Note: *Refer to the warning note at the start of this Section before proceeding. A fuel pressure gauge will be required. If such a gauge is not available, the check must be performed by a Renault dealer.*

13 Disconnect the fuel feed hose from the fuel rail, bearing in mind the information on fuel system depressurisation given in Section 10. Connect a fuel pressure gauge into the feed pipe using a T-piece.

14 Disconnect the vacuum hose from the pressure regulator. Start the engine and measure the fuel system pressure with the engine idling. Reconnect the vacuum hose and note the pressure reading obtained. Compare both readings to the pressures given in the Specifications at the start of this Chapter.

15 If the pressure first recorded was too low, check the system carefully for leaks. If no leaks are found, with the engine idling, check the pump operating pressure by momentarily pinching the fuel return hose. If all is well, the pressure should rise to approximately 4 bars; if not, it is likely that the pump is faulty or the fuel filter blocked. First renew the filter and repeat the test; if there is no improvement, renew the fuel pump.

16 If the regulated pressure is low but the fuel pump operating pressure is satisfactory, the fuel pressure regulator is probably at fault.

17 Depressurise the fuel system, remove the gauge and remake the original connections.

Fuel pump and filter - removal and refitting

18 The fuel pump and filter arrangement is the same as is fitted to the 2.0 litre model. Refer to Part C of Chapter 3 for information on pump and filter removal and refitting, bearing in mind the information given in Section 10 on depressurising the fuel system.

Air cleaner and element - removal and refitting

Air cleaner - filter renewal

19 Slacken the retaining clip and disconnect the intake duct from the top of the air cleaner housing.

20 Release the retaining clips, lift off the air cleaner housing lid, and withdraw the filter element from the housing.

21 Wipe clean the inside of the filter housing and cover, and fit a new element.

22 Refit the cover, ensuring it is correctly seated, and secure it in position with its retaining clips. Reconnect the intake duct to the top of the housing.

Air cleaner housing - removal and refitting

23 Slacken the retaining clips, and disconnect both intake ducts from the air cleaner housing.

24 Unhook the two rubber retaining straps and remove the air cleaner housing from the engine compartment. If necessary, unbolt the air cleaner mounting bracket and remove it from the engine compartment.

25 Refitting is a reversal of the removal procedure, ensuring all intake ducts are securely reconnected.

Throttle housing - removal and refitting

Removal

26 Disconnect the battery negative terminal. Slacken the retaining clip and disconnect the intake duct from the throttle housing.

27 Disconnect the accelerator cable from the throttle housing, and disconnect the wiring connector from the throttle switch.

28 Release any pressure in the cooling system by removing the filler cap (engine cold). Slacken the retaining clips and disconnect the two coolant hoses from the throttle housing. Plug the hose ends to minimise coolant loss, and mop up any spilt coolant.

29 Slacken the retaining clips and disconnect the vacuum and breather hoses from the housing, noting their correct locations.

30 Undo the four retaining nuts securing the throttle housing to the inlet manifold. Withdraw the housing, and remove it along with its gasket(s) and insulating spacer (as applicable). Discard the gasket(s); new ones must be used on refitting.

Refitting

31 Ensure the manifold and throttle housing mating surfaces are clean and dry.

32 Where an insulating spacer is fitted, position a gasket on each side of the spacer, and fit the spacer and gaskets to the manifold studs. Where just a gasket was fitted, slide a new gasket into position on the manifold.

33 Refit the throttle housing, and securely tighten its retaining nuts.

34 Reconnect the vacuum and breather hoses to their correct locations on the housing.

35 Working quickly to minimise coolant loss, reconnect the coolant hoses to the housing, tightening their retaining clips securely.

36 Reconnect the accelerator cable and adjust it, referring to the information given in Chapter 3.

37 Connect the intake duct to the housing, and securely tighten its retaining clip.

13

38 Reconnect the throttle switch wiring connector and the battery negative terminal. Check the coolant level and top-up if necessary, as described in Chapter 2.

Manifold plenum chamber - removal and refitting

Removal

39 Carry out the operations described above in paragraphs 26 to 29. Free the accelerator cable from its bracket on the side of the plenum chamber.
40 Disconnect the vacuum and breather hoses from the plenum chamber, noting their fitted locations.
41 Slacken and remove the bolt securing the front of the chamber to its bracket on the cylinder head.
42 Slacken and remove the nuts and bolts securing the plenum chamber to the inlet manifold. Remove the plate from the plenum chamber studs, then lift off the plenum chamber. Remove the gasket and discard it; a new one must be used on refitting.

Refitting

43 Ensure the plenum chamber and manifold mating surfaces are clean and dry, and fit the new gasket over the manifold studs.
44 Lower the plenum chamber into position and refit the plate. Refit the retaining nuts and bolts, including the front bolt, and tighten them securely.
45 Reconnect the vacuum and breather hoses to their positions on the chamber. Carry out the operations described above in paragraphs 34 to 38.

Fuel rail and injectors - removal and refitting

Removal

46 Remove the manifold plenum chamber as described in paragraphs 39 to 42.
47 Disconnect the fuel feed and return hoses from the fuel rail, bearing in mind the information given in Section 10 on fuel system depressurisation. Plug the hose ends, to minimise fuel loss and prevent the entry of dirt into the system.
48 Disconnect the vacuum hose from the fuel pressure regulator.
49 Disconnect the wiring connectors from the four fuel injectors.
50 Slacken and remove the fuel rail retaining bolts, and carefully withdraw the fuel rail and injector assembly from inlet manifold. Recover the injector sealing rings.
51 If necessary, prise off the retaining clips, remove the injectors from the fuel rail, and recover the sealing rings.

Refitting

52 Refitting is a reversal of the removal procedure, noting the following points:
(a) Fit new O-rings to all disturbed injector unions.
(b) Apply a smear of engine oil to the O-rings,

to aid installation. Ease the injectors and fuel rail into position, ensuring that none of the O-rings are displaced.
(c) On completion, start the engine and check for fuel leaks.

Fuel pressure regulator - removal and refitting

Removal

53 The fuel pressure regulator is located on the left-hand end of the fuel rail. Disconnect the battery earth lead.
54 Disconnect the fuel return hose from the fuel pressure regulator, bearing in mind the information given in Section 10 on depressurising the fuel system.
55 Disconnect the vacuum hose from the regulator.
56 Undo the two bolts securing the fuel pressure regulator to the top of the fuel rail. Remove the regulator along with its O-ring. Examine the O-ring for signs of damage and deterioration, and renew if necessary.

Refitting

57 Fit the O-ring to the base of the regulator, and refit the regulator to the top of the fuel rail. Refit the regulator retaining bolts, and tighten them securely.
58 Reconnect the vacuum hose to the regulator.
59 Reconnect the fuel return hose, and securely tighten its retaining clip. Start the engine, and check the regulator for signs of leakage.

Idle speed auxiliary air valve - removal and refitting

Removal

60 The idle speed auxiliary air valve is attached to a bracket located on the left-hand side of the manifold plenum chamber. To remove the valve, first disconnect the battery negative terminal.
61 Disconnect the wiring connector from the top of the valve.
62 Slacken the clamp bolt, then release the valve from its mounting clamp. Disconnect the two hoses from the base of the valve, and remove the valve from the engine compartment.

Refitting

63 Refitting is a reversal of the removal procedure.

Throttle (no-load/full-load) switch - removal and refitting

Removal

64 The throttle switch is mounted on the side of the throttle housing. To remove the switch, first disconnect the battery negative terminal.
65 Depress the retaining clip and disconnect the wiring connector from the switch.
66 Using a marker pen or a dab of paint,

make alignment marks between the switch and throttle housing. Undo the two retaining screws, and remove the switch from the throttle body.

Refitting

67 Refit the switch, ensuring it is correctly engaged with the throttle valve spindle, and lightly tighten its retaining screws. Align the marks made before removal, then fully tighten the retaining screws. If a new switch is being installed, the switch position must be set using the special Renault test box.
68 Reconnect the wiring connector and reconnect the battery.

Intake air temperature sensor - removal and refitting

Removal

69 The intake air temperature sensor is screwed into the air cleaner-to-throttle housing duct. To remove the sensor, first disconnect the battery negative terminal.
70 Disconnect the wiring connector from the sensor, and unscrew the sensor from the duct.

Refitting

71 Refit the switch, tightening it securely. Reconnect the wiring connector and the battery.

Manifold absolute pressure (MAP) sensor - removal and refitting

72 Refer to Section 10.

Coolant temperature sensor - removal and refitting

73 Refer to Section 10.

Pre-ignition (knock) sensor - removal and refitting

74 Refer to the information given for the 1995 cc models in Part C of Chapter 3.

Computer - removal and refitting

75 Refer to Section 10.

Manifolds - removal and refitting

76 Although the inlet and exhaust manifolds are separate, they are retained by the same bolts and share the same gasket, and therefore are removed and refitted together.

Removal

77 Remove the manifold plenum chamber as described earlier in this Section.
78 Disconnect the fuel feed and return hoses from the fuel rail, bearing in mind the information given in Section 10 on fuel system depressurisation. Plug the hose ends, to minimise fuel loss and prevent the entry of dirt into the system.
79 Disconnect the wiring connectors from the four fuel injectors. Free the injector wiring

from any retaining clips or ties, and place it clear of the manifold.

80 Disconnect the downpipe from the exhaust manifold as described in Chapter 3. Where the lambda sensor is screwed into the manifold, trace the wiring back to its wiring connector, and disconnect it from the main wiring loom.

81 Slacken and remove the bolt(s) securing the exhaust manifold to its support bracket. Undo the retaining nuts, and withdraw the inlet manifold and exhaust manifold from the engine. Remove the manifold gasket and discard it; a new one must be used on refitting.

Refitting

82 Refitting is a reverse of the removal procedure, noting the following points:

(a) *Ensure that the manifold and cylinder head mating surfaces are clean and dry, and fit a new manifold gasket over the studs. Refit the manifolds and securely tighten the retaining nuts.*

(b) *Ensure that all hoses are reconnected to their original positions and are securely held (where necessary) by the retaining clips.*

Exhaust system - general information

83 Refer to Section 10.

Exhaust emission control systems - general information, component removal and refitting

84 Refer to Section 10, ignoring the information about the exhaust gas recirculation (EGR) system.

Evaporative emission control system - general information, component removal and refitting

85 Refer to Section 10.

Unleaded petrol - general information and usage

86 Refer to Section 10.

Catalytic converter - general information and precautions

87 Refer to Section 10.

12 Fuel and exhaust systems - 1965 cc models

1 The fuel and exhaust systems on the 1965 cc engine are basically the same as on the 1721 cc engine. One difference is the type of carburettor: 1965 cc models are fitted with a Solex 28/34 Z9.

2 When working on the fuel system, refer to the information given for 1721 cc models, both in Section 9 of this Chapter, and in Chapter 3. When working on the carburettor, refer to the

procedures given for the 28/34 Z10 carburettor, and to the Specifications at the start of this Chapter for details applicable to the 28/34 Z9 carburettor. Both carburettors are of a very similar construction.

3 The only major difference between the 1721 cc and 1965 cc models is in the air cleaner arrangement, which is as follows.

Air cleaner and element - removal and refitting

Air cleaner - filter renewal

4 Unscrew the wing nut, lift off the air cleaner cover, and withdraw the filter element from the housing.

5 Wipe clean the filter housing and lid, and fit a new element.

6 Refit the air cleaner lid, and tighten the wing nut.

Air cleaner housing - removal and refitting

7 Slacken the retaining clips (where fitted), and disconnect the intake ducts from the air cleaner housing.

8 Release the rubber retaining strap, and remove the air cleaner housing from the engine compartment. If necessary, the various intake ducts can then also be removed. Undo the three retaining screws, and remove the intake cover from the top of the carburettor along with its gasket.

9 Refitting is a reverse of the removal procedure. If the intake cover has been removed from the top of the carburettor, renew the gasket.

13 Fuel and exhaust systems - 1995 cc models

Note: *The information contained in this Section is only applicable to the 1995 cc 8-valve engine. For information on the 1995 cc 12-valve engine, refer to Section 14.*

Models with a catalytic converter - general information

1 Later non-Turbo 1995 cc models (J7R 746 and J7R 747 engines) and Turbo models (J7R 756 engine) are fitted a catalytic converter in the exhaust system. On these models, the fuel injection system also incorporates an evaporative emission control system, as well as the exhaust emission control system. The emission control systems are described in detail later in this Section. Other minor differences are as follows.

Fuel injection system - adjustments

2 On models with a catalytic converter, the idle speed is controlled in the same way as on earlier models, but it is no longer possible to adjust the idle mixture setting. The fuel injection computer has full control over the idle mixture. Using the information supplied by the lambda sensor (explained in detail in

Section 10), the computer constantly alters the mixture strength to provide the optimum fuel/air ratio for all operating conditions.

Exhaust system - general information

3 The exhaust system is very similar to that fitted to earlier models, shown in Chapter 3. The only difference is that a catalytic converter is incorporated into the system between the downpipe and intermediate pipe (see Fig. 13.19). Refer to Section 9 of Chapter 3 for information on removal and refitting. Details of the catalytic converter are given at the end of Section 10.

Unleaded petrol - general information and usage

4 Refer to Section 10.

Exhaust emission control systems - general information, component removal and refitting

5 Refer to the information given in Section 10 of this Chapter, ignoring references to the exhaust gas recirculation (EGR) system.

Evaporative emission control system (non-Turbo models) - general information, component removal and refitting

6 To minimise the escape into the atmosphere of unburned hydrocarbons, an evaporative emissions control system is incorporated in the fuel injection system. The fuel tank filler cap is sealed, and a charcoal canister is mounted in the engine compartment to collect the petrol vapours generated in the tank when the car is parked. It stores them until they can be cleared from the canister (under the control of the computer via the solenoid control valve) into the inlet tract, to be burned by the engine during normal combustion.

7 To ensure that the engine runs correctly when it is cold and/or idling, and to protect the catalytic converter from the effects of an over-rich mixture, the solenoid control valve is not opened by the computer until the engine has warmed up. The solenoid valve is then modulated on and off as required. When the valve is open, inlet manifold depression is allowed to act on the vacuum valve fitted to the top of the charcoal canister. The vacuum valve opens, and allows the fuel vapours stored in the canister to be drawn into the manifold.

8 If the system is thought to be faulty, disconnect the hoses from the charcoal canister and solenoid control valves, and check that they are clear by blowing through them. If the solenoid valve or charcoal canister are thought to be faulty, they must be renewed.

Charcoal canister - removal and refitting

9 Disconnect the battery negative terminal.

10 Disconnect the hoses from the top of the

13

canister. Release the rubber retaining strap, and remove the canister from its mounting bracket. Store (or dispose of) the canister carefully - it may still contain fuel vapour.

11 Refitting is a reverse of the removal procedure.

Solenoid control valve - removal and refitting

12 The solenoid control valve is mounted on the computer unit. To gain access to the valve, remove the plastic cover from the computer.

13 Disconnect the battery negative terminal. Disconnect the wiring connector from the valve.

14 Disconnect the vacuum hoses from the valve, noting their fitted locations. Undo the two retaining nuts, and remove the valve from the engine compartment.

15 Refitting is a reverse of the removal procedure.

Evaporative emission control system (Turbo models) - general information, component removal and refitting

16 To minimise the escape into the atmosphere of unburned hydrocarbons, an evaporative emissions control system is incorporated in the fuel injection system. The fuel tank filler cap is sealed, and a charcoal canister is mounted in the engine compartment to collect the petrol vapours generated in the tank when the car is parked. It stores them until they are drawn into the manifold intake duct by the depression created when the engine is under load. A restrictor is fitted to the hose linking the canister to the intake duct, to prevent the vapours leaking into the duct when the engine is stopped.

17 If the system is thought to be faulty, disconnect the hoses from the charcoal canister, and check that they are clear by blowing through them. If the charcoal canister is thought to be faulty, it must be renewed.

Charcoal canister - removal and refitting

18 Refer to the information given in paragraphs 9 to 11.

Fuel system pressure check

19 Refer to Section 11 of this Chapter.

14 Fuel and exhaust systems - 1995 cc 12-valve models

Note: *The information contained in this Section is only applicable to the 1995 cc 12-valve engine. For information on the 1995 cc 8-valve engine, refer to Section 13.*

1 The fuel and exhaust systems fitted to 1995 cc 12-valve models are very similar to those of the earlier models covered in Chapter 3. The only detail changes are to the manifold assemblies and the idle speed control valve. Non-catalyst (J7R 754) and catalyst (J7R 740) versions of the 12-valve engine have been available. Operations which differ on the 12-valve models are given below; where no information is given, the task can be carried out as described for the 1995 cc engine in Chapter 3.

Air cleaner and element - removal and refitting

Air cleaner - filter renewal

2 Slacken the retaining clip, and disconnect the intake duct from the top of the air cleaner housing.

3 Undo the four retaining screws, lift off the air cleaner housing lid, and withdraw the filter element from the housing.

4 Wipe clean the inside of the filter housing and cover, and fit a new element.

5 Refit the cover, ensuring it is correctly seated, and securely tighten its retaining screws. Reconnect the intake duct to the top of the housing.

Air cleaner housing - removal and refitting

6 Slacken the retaining clips, and disconnect both the upper and lower intake ducts from the air cleaner housing. Also disconnect the idle speed control valve hose from the side of the air cleaner housing.

7 The air cleaner housing can then be slid upwards off its mounting bracket. If necessary, unbolt the air cleaner mounting bracket and remove it from the engine compartment.

8 Refitting is a reversal of the removal procedure, ensuring the intake ducts and hose are securely reconnected.

Idle speed control valve - general information, removal and refitting

9 On 12-valve models, the idle speed control valve is mounted directly onto the inlet manifold, as opposed to the earlier set-up where it was linked to the manifold by a hose (photo).

10 To remove the valve, first disconnect the battery negative terminal.

11 Disconnect the wiring connector, then undo the two retaining bolts and remove the valve from the front of the manifold. Recover the gasket and discard it; a new one must be used on refitting.

Fig. 13.19 Exhaust system components – 1995 and 2165 cc models with a catalytic converter (Secs 13, 14 and 15)

1 *Downpipe*
2 *Lambda sensor*
3 *Heat shields*
4 *Sealing ring*

5 *Spacer*
6 *Catalytic converter*
7 *Silencer (4x4 models only)*

8 *Silencer (mid-1989 on)*
9 *Silencer (up to mid-1989)*
10 *Exhaust clamp*

14.9 On 1995 cc 12-valve models, the idle speed control valve is mounted onto the front of the inlet manifold

12 Refitting is a reversal of the removal procedure. Ensure that the valve and manifold mating surfaces are clean and dry, and use a new gasket.

Fuel rail and injectors - general information, removal and refitting

13 On 12-valve models, a modified fuel rail assembly is fitted. The main difference is that a pulse damper is screwed onto the top of the rail, to smooth out the pressure variations in the fuel system (see Fig. 13.20).

Removal

14 Disconnect the battery negative terminal. Undo the two retaining screws, and remove the plastic cover from the left-hand side of the camshaft cover.

15 Undo the three retaining bolts and single retaining nut, and disengage the accelerator cable bracket from the cover.

16 Disconnect the vacuum hose from the fuel pressure regulator, and disconnect the injector wiring connectors.

17 Bearing in mind the information given in Section 10 on depressurising the fuel system,

Fig. 13.21 Fuel pressure regulator – 1995 cc 12-valve engine (Sec 14)

6 Fuel pressure
     regulator
8 Fuel rail
9 Retaining bolt
10 O-ring
11 O-ring

Fig. 13.20 Fuel rail and injector assembly – 1995 cc 12-valve engine (Sec 14)

1 Injector retaining clip
2 Fuel injector
3 Fuel rail retaining bolt
4 Feed hose union
5 Return hose union
6 Fuel pressure regulator
7 Pulse damper
8 Fuel rail

disconnect the fuel feed and return hoses from the fuel rail.

18 Slacken and remove the three retaining bolts, and carefully withdraw the fuel rail and injector assembly from inlet manifold. Recover the injector sealing rings.

19 If necessary, prise off the retaining clips, remove the injectors from the fuel rail, and recover the sealing rings.

Refitting

20 Refitting is a reversal of the removal procedure, noting the following points:
(a) Fit new O-rings to all disturbed injector unions.
(b) Apply a smear of engine oil to the O-rings to aid installation, then ease the injectors and fuel rail into position, ensuring that none of the O-rings are displaced.
(c) On completion, start the engine and check for fuel leaks.

Fuel pressure regulator - removal and refitting

Removal

21 The fuel pressure regulator is located on the rear end of the fuel rail (see Fig. 13.21). Before removal, disconnect the battery negative terminal.

22 Disconnect the fuel feed hose from the fuel rail to depressurise the fuel system as described in Section 10. Once the pressure has been relieved, reconnect the hose and tighten its retaining clip.

23 Disconnect the vacuum hose from the regulator.

24 Undo the two bolts securing the fuel pressure regulator to the top of the fuel rail, and lift off the retaining plate. Remove the regulator along with its O-rings. Examine the O-rings for signs of damage and deterioration, and renew if necessary.

Refitting

25 Fit the O-rings to the base of the regulator, and refit the regulator to the top of the fuel rail. Refit the retaining plate and securely tighten the retaining bolts.

26 Reconnect the vacuum hose to the regulator.

27 Reconnect the battery, start the engine and check the regulator for signs of leakage.

Inlet manifold - removal and refitting

Removal

28 Disconnect the battery negative terminal. Disengage the power steering fluid reservoir from its mounting bracket, and place it clear of the manifold.

29 Undo the retaining screws, and disconnect the intake duct from the top of the throttle housing.

30 Disconnect the accelerator cable from the throttle housing, and position it clear of the manifold.

31 Disconnect the wiring connectors from the throttle switch, idle speed control valve and the air temperature sensor.

32 Undo the retaining bolt, and remove the support bracket from underneath the manifold.

33 Bearing in mind the information given in Section 10 on depressurising the fuel system, disconnect the fuel feed and return hoses from the fuel rail.

34 Disconnect the vacuum and breather hoses from the manifold, noting their fitted locations.

35 Undo the retaining nuts and withdraw the inlet manifold from the engine. Remove the manifold gasket and discard it; a new one must be used on refitting.

Refitting

36 Refitting is a reverse of the relevant removal procedure, noting the following points:
(a) Ensure that the manifold and cylinder head mating surfaces are clean and dry, and fit a new manifold gasket over the studs. Refit the manifold, and securely tighten its retaining nuts.
(b) Ensure that all hoses are reconnected to their original positions, and are securely held (where necessary) by the retaining clips.

13

Models with a catalytic converter - general information

37 Refer to Section 13 of this Chapter for information on all aspects of the fuel and exhaust systems which are affected by the fitting of a catalytic converter, noting that the evaporative emission control system on 12-valve models is the same as that fitted to Turbo models.

Fuel system pressure check

38 Refer to Section 11 of this Chapter.

15 Fuel and exhaust systems - 2165 cc models

1 All 2165 cc models are fitted with a catalytic converter, and have the same fuel, exhaust and evaporative emission control systems as non-Turbo 1995 cc models. All operations can be carried out using the information given in Section 13 of this Chapter, and in Chapter 3.

16 Ignition system

Ignition system - 1721 cc fuel injection models

1 On 1721 cc fuel injection models, the ignition system is controlled by the same computer as the fuel injection system; the computer unit shown in Chapter 4 is not fitted. On these models, the ignition HT coil is integral with a smaller power module, and is mounted on the left-hand side of the engine compartment. The power module does not contain a vacuum advance capsule; the ignition timing advance and coil charging time settings are automatically calculated by the computer, using the information received from its various sensors.

Ignition system - 1965 cc models

2 On 1965 cc models, the ignition system is the same as that fitted to earlier 1721 cc models. Refer to Chapter 4 for further information.

Ignition system - 1995 cc 12-valve models

3 On 1995 cc 12-valve models, the ignition system is the same as that described in Chapter 4 for 1995 cc 8-valve models.

Static (distributorless) ignition system (later Turbo models) - general information

4 On later Turbo models with a catalytic converter (J7R 756 engine), the ignition system is of the static (distributorless) type. On these models there is no distributor; instead, two ignition HT coils are fitted, each with two outputs.
5 Each ignition coil supplies two cylinders (one

coil supplies cylinders 1 and 4, and the other cylinders 2 and 3). Under control of the computer, the ignition system operates on the 'wasted spark' principle; each plug sparks twice for every cycle of the engine, once on the compression stroke and once on the exhaust stroke. The computer uses the inputs from the various sensors to calculate the required ignition advance and coil charging time.
6 On these models, both ignition HT coils are mounted on the end of the cylinder head (where the distributor would normally be) and a small power module is located in the centre of the bulkhead (where the HT coil is usually mounted).

17 Manual transmission

JB2 transmission - general information

1 The JB2 transmission is a four-speed unit which is fitted to some lower-specification 1721 cc models. The unit is very similar to the five-speed JB3 transmission fitted to all other 1721 cc models; the only major difference is that the absence of the fifth gear components means that a thinner rear cover is fitted.
2 Most operations on the JB2 transmission can be carried out using the information given in Part A of Chapter 6 for the JB3 transmission. Ignore all references to 5th gear components, and bear in mind the following points.

18 Automatic transmission

AR4 four-speed transmission - general information

1 From 1988 onwards, both 1995 cc and 2165 cc models have been available with the option of a four-speed automatic transmission. The AR4 transmission is computer-controlled,

Fig. 13.22 AR4 transmission filler tube location 'D' (Sec 18)

and is similar in operation to the three-speed MJ3 transmission described in Chapter 7. The hydraulic pressure in the AR4 transmission is controlled by the computer, via one of the many electrical solenoid valves. Note that there is no vacuum unit on the AR4 transmission.
2 Operations which differ to those on the MJ3 transmission are described below. Other operations can be carried out as described in Chapter 7.

AR4 transmission - routine maintenance

Transmission fluid level check

Note: *The fluid level checking procedure on the AR4 automatic transmission is particularly complicated, and the home mechanic would be well-advised to take the vehicle to a Renault dealer to have the work carried out, as special test equipment is necessary to carry out the check However, the following procedure is given for those who may have access to this equipment.*

3 The transmission fluid level should be checked every 6000 miles, or immediately if a transmission malfunction develops.
4 Remove the plug from the top of the filler tube 'D' on the right-hand side of the transmission (Fig. 13.22). Add 0.5 litre (1 pint) of the specified fluid to the transmission via the filler tube, using a clean funnel with a fine-mesh filter, then refit the plug.
5 Position the vehicle over an inspection pit, on a ramp, or jack it up and support it on axle stands, ensuring the vehicle remains level.
6 Connect the Renault XR25 test meter to the diagnostic socket, and enter 'DO4' then number '04'. With the selector lever in 'Park', run the engine at idle speed until the fluid temperature reaches 60°C.
7 With the engine still running, unscrew the level plug from the transmission (see Fig. 13.23). Allow the excess fluid to run out

Fig. 13.23 AR4 transmission drain and level plug locations (Sec 18)

A Final drive drain plug
B Final drive filler/level plug
C Transmission level plug (see text)

into a calibrated container for 20 seconds, then refit the plug. The amount of fluid should be more than 0.1 litre; if it is not, the fluid level in the transmission is incorrect.

8 If the level is incorrect, add an extra 1 litre (nearly 2 pints) of the specified fluid to the transmission, through the filler tube after removing the vent. Allow the transmission to cool down, then repeat the checking procedure again as described in the previous paragraphs. Repeat the procedure as required until more than the specified amount of fluid is drained as described in the previous paragraph, indicating that the transmission fluid level is correct, then securely tighten the level plug.

Final drive oil level check and renewal

9 On the AR4 transmission, the final drive is lubricated by its own separate oil bath. The final drive oil bath is sealed for life, and the oil level should never need to be checked, or the oil renewed.

10 For reference purposes, referring to Fig. 13.23, the final drive oil level is checked and topped-up via the filler/level plug 'A', and drained via the drain plug 'B'.

11 To check the oil level, position the vehicle over an inspection pit, or on a ramp or axle stands, ensuring that it remains level.

12 Wipe clean the area around the filler/level plug, unscrew the plug and remove it from the transmission. The oil level is correct when it is level with the bottom of the filler/level plug hole. If necessary, top-up with the specified type of oil until the oil trickles out of the hole. The level will be correct when the flow of oil ceases. If a large quantity of oil is added, refit the filler/level plug and take the vehicle on a short journey to distribute the oil around the final drive components, then recheck the oil level on return.

13 Wipe clean the level/filler plug, and examine the sealing washer for signs of damage or deterioration, renewing it if necessary. Refit the plug to the transmission, and tighten it securely.

Fig. 13.24 Filter is secured to the AR4 transmission by two bolts (1) (Sec 18)

Transmission fluid change and filter renewal

Note: *Special Renault test equipment is necessary to check the fluid level, and the home mechanic would be well-advised to take the vehicle to a Renault dealer to have the work carried out. If the task is to be undertaken, take great care not to introduce dirt into the transmission.*

14 The automatic transmission fluid and filter element should be renewed every 30 000 miles. The fluid should be changed when the transmission is cold.

15 Apply the handbrake, jack up the front of the vehicle, and support it on axle stands.

16 Place a container beneath the sump, and unscrew the fluid level plug from the transmission (see Fig. 13.23). Note that there is no transmission drain plug, and only a small amount of fluid will drain out of the level hole. When the flow of fluid stops, clean the threads of the level plug and refit it to the transmission, tightening it securely.

17 With the container still positioned underneath the transmission, slacken the sump retaining bolts slightly, and allow transmission fluid to drain into the container. When most of the fluid has drained, remove the retaining bolts completely, and lower the sump away from the transmission, tipping the contents of the sump into the container. Recover the sump seal from the base of the transmission.

18 Slacken and remove the filter retaining bolts, and remove the filter element from the base of the transmission, along with its sealing gasket. Discard the gasket; a new one must be used on refitting.

19 Position a new gasket on the top of the filter element, and offer the filter to the transmission. Refit the retaining bolts, ensuring the gasket is still correctly positioned, and tighten them to the specified torque.

20 Remove the magnet from inside the sump, and clean all traces of metal filings from it. The filings (if any) should be very fine; any sizeable chips of metal indicate a worn component in the transmission. Examine the sump seal for signs of damage or deterioration, and renew if necessary.

21 Ensure the seal is correctly located in the sump groove. Refit the sump to the transmission, tightening its retaining bolts to the specified torque.

Fig. 13.25 Prior to refitting the filter to the transmission, ensure the gasket (arrowed) is correctly located (Sec 18)

22 Lower the vehicle to the ground, then fill the transmission with the specified type and amount of fluid as described earlier in this Section.

23 Take the vehicle on a short journey, then recheck the transmission fluid level.

Fluid cooler (AR4 transmission) - general information, removal and refitting

General information

24 On the AR4 transmission, a fluid cooler is fitted to ensure the transmission fluid temperature remains constant, even under extreme operating conditions. The cooler is mounted on the right-hand side of the transmission. Engine coolant is circulated around the cooler, where it absorbs heat from the transmission fluid.

Removal

25 Using a hose clamp or similar, clamp both the fluid cooler coolant hoses to minimise coolant loss during the subsequent operation. Also release any pressure in the cooling system by removing the filler cap (engine cold).

26 Slacken the retaining clips and disconnect both coolant hoses from the fluid cooler, being prepared for some coolant spillage. Wash off any spilt coolant immediately with cold water, and dry the surrounding area before proceeding further.

27 Slacken and remove the two mounting bolts, and remove the cooler from the transmission. Recover the two O-rings which are fitted between the cooler and transmission, and discard them; new ones must be used on refitting. Also examine the cooler mounting bolt sealing washers for signs of damage or deterioration. and renew them if necessary.

Refitting

28 Lubricate the new O-rings with clean automatic transmission fluid, and locate one O-ring in each recess on the rear of the fluid cooler. Fit one sealing washer to each cooler mounting bolt.

29 Fit the fluid cooler on the side of the transmission housing, ensuring that both O-rings remain in position, and refit the mounting bolts. Tighten both mounting bolts to the specified torque.

30 Reconnect the coolant hoses to the fluid cooler, and securely tighten their retaining clips. Remove the hose clamp.

31 On completion, top-up the cooling system and check the transmission fluid level as described earlier in this Section.

AR4 transmission - removal and refitting

32 The AR4 transmission can be removed as described in Section 8 of Chapter 7, noting that it will also be necessary to carry out the following operations.

(a) Clamp the fluid cooler coolant hoses, and disconnect them from the fluid cooler.

13

(b) Unscrew the speedometer cable from the final drive housing.

(c) Unbolt the two support bars situated underneath the rear of the transmission.

(d) Before removing the retaining bolts, mark the position of the torque converter in relation to the driveplate. The marks can then be used to align the two on refitting.

(e) Before lowering the transmission out of position, make a final check that all the necessary wiring connectors and hoses have been disconnected.

33 Refit by reversing the removal operations.

Kickdown switch (all models) - general information

34 On most models, the kickdown switch is incorporated in the throttle potentiometer, as on earlier models. However, some models have a kickdown switch incorporated in the accelerator cable. The switch is situated at the pedal end of the outer cable, where it can be found behind the facia. The correct function of the switch can only be checked using special Renault equipment.

19 Driveshafts, hubs, roadwheels and tyres

New driveshafts - fitting

1 New driveshafts are supplied with cardboard protectors over the bellows. These protectors should be left in position until the driveshaft is correctly installed, then removed by hand. Do not use sharp-ended tools to remove the protectors, as there is a risk of damaging the bellows.

Driveshaft bellows renewal - general information

2 All driveshaft gaiters supplied by Renault are now made of a plastic material, as

Fig 13.26 General view of the Brembo rear brake caliper. Spring clip location (T) arrowed (Sec 20)

opposed to the early-type gaiters which were made of rubber. These later plastic bellows are stronger than the earlier rubber bellows, but are not as flexible and therefore cannot be expanded to pass over the driveshaft outer joint yoke (see Sections 7 and 8 of Chapter 8). Because of this, if the outer joint bellows is to be renewed, the inner joint assembly must first be removed, so that the original outer gaiter can be slid off the end of the driveshaft and the new one slid into position. Refer to Chapter 8 for further information.

Driveshaft coupling joint renewal - general information

3 Further to the information contained in Section 9 of Chapter 8, on some models it appears that the driveshaft coupling joint assemblies are no longer available separately. In such cases, the complete driveshaft will have to be renewed, even if only one joint is faulty. Refer to a Renault dealer or other specialist for further information on parts availability.

20 Braking system

Rear disc pads (Brembo caliper) - inspection and renewal

⚠ Warning: Renew both sets of rear brake pads at the same time - never renew the pads on only one wheel, as uneven braking may result. Note that the dust created by wear of the pads may contain asbestos, which is a health hazard. Never blow it out with compressed air, and don't inhale any of it. An approved filtering mask should be worn when working on the brakes. DO NOT use petroleum-based solvents to clean brake parts; use brake cleaner or methylated spirit only.

1 Chock the front wheels, then jack up the rear of the vehicle and support it on axle stands. Remove the rear roadwheels.

2 The pad thickness (friction material and backing plate) can be checked via the aperture in the caliper. However, it is recommended that the pads should be removed as follows for a thorough inspection.

Fig. 13.27 On refitting the pads to Brembo caliper, ensure the pad springs (R) are correctly seated as shown in the left-hand diagram (Sec 20)

3 Using a pair of pliers, disconnect the inner cable from the caliper handbrake lever, then remove the spring clip 'T' from the pad retaining pin (see Fig. 13.26).

4 Using a hammer and punch, tap the pad retaining pin out of the caliper, noting which way around it is fitted, and recover the anti-rattle spring.

5 Slacken and remove the caliper mounting bolts, then lift the caliper away from the disc and remove the brake pads from the caliper, noting the correct fitted locations of the pad springs.

6 First measure the thickness of each brake pad (friction material and backing plate). If either pad is worn at any point to the specified minimum thickness or less, all four pads must be renewed. The pads should also be renewed if any are fouled with oil or grease; there is no satisfactory way of degreasing friction material, once contaminated. If any of the brake pads are worn unevenly or fouled with oil or grease, trace and rectify the cause before reassembly. New brake pads and spring kits are available from Renault dealers.

7 If the brake pads are still serviceable, carefully clean them using a clean, fine wire brush or similar, paying particular attention to the sides and back of the metal backing. Clean out the grooves in the friction material, and pick out any large embedded particles of dirt or debris. Carefully clean the pad locations in the caliper body.

8 Before fitting the pads, check that the guide sleeves are free to slide easily in the caliper body, and that the rubber gaiters are undamaged. Brush the dust and dirt from the caliper and piston, but do not inhale it, as it is a health hazard. Inspect the dust seal around the piston for damage, and the piston for evidence of fluid leaks, corrosion or damage. If attention to any of these components is necessary, refer to the information given later in this Section.

9 If new brake pads are to be fitted, it will be necessary to retract the piston fully into the caliper bore by rotating it in a clockwise direction. In the absence of the special Renault tool (Fre. 1190), this may be achieved using a pair of circlip pliers or a suitable home-made peg spanner, which locates in the caliper piston holes. Provided that the master cylinder reservoir has not been overfilled with hydraulic fluid, there should be no spillage, but keep a careful watch on the fluid level while retracting the piston. If the fluid level rises above the 'MAX' level line at any time, the surplus should be syphoned off, or ejected via a plastic tube connected to the bleed screw. **Note:** *Do not syphon the fluid by mouth, as it is poisonous; use a syringe or an old poultry baster.*

10 Locate the inner brake pad in the caliper body, ensuring that its friction material is against the brake disc, then slide the outer pad into position in the caliper. Ensure that the pad springs are correctly positioned as shown in Fig. 13.27, then slide the caliper back into position on the disc.

11 Remove all traces of old locking compound from the threads of the caliper mounting bolts, and apply a few drops of fresh locking compound to each bolt. Refit both caliper bolts, and tighten them to the specified torque.

12 Position the anti-rattle spring in the caliper aperture, and slide the pad retaining pin into position, ensuring that it is fitted the correct way around, with the spring clip hole nearest the outer end.

13 Tap the retaining pin fully into position, ensuring that the pin passes through both the pad and anti-rattle spring holes, and secure it in position with the spring clip.

14 Depress the brake pedal repeatedly, until the pads are pressed into firm contact with the brake disc, and normal pedal pressure is restored.

15 Repeat the above procedure on the remaining rear brake caliper.

16 Reconnect the handbrake cables, and adjust the handbrake as described in Chapter 9, Section 20.

Rear disc brake caliper (Brembo type) - removal, overhaul and refitting

Note: *Hydraulic fluid is poisonous; wash off immediately and thoroughly in the case of skin contact, and seek immediate medical advice if any fluid is swallowed or gets into the eyes. Certain types of hydraulic fluid are inflammable, and may ignite when allowed into contact with hot components. When servicing any hydraulic system, it is safest to assume that the fluid IS inflammable, and to take precautions against the risk of fire as though it is petrol that is being handled. Hydraulic fluid is also an effective paint stripper, and will attack plastics; if any is spilt, it should be washed off immediately using copious quantities of fresh water. Finally, it is hygroscopic (it absorbs moisture from the air) - old fluid may be contaminated and unfit for further use. When topping-up or renewing the fluid, always use the recommended type, and ensure that it comes from a freshly-opened, previously-sealed container.*

Removal

17 Chock the front wheels, jack up the rear of the vehicle and support it on axle stands. Remove the relevant rear roadwheel.

18 Minimise fluid loss by first removing the master cylinder reservoir cap, and then tightening it down onto a piece of polythene to obtain an airtight seal. Alternatively, use a brake hose clamp, a G-clamp or a similar tool to clamp the flexible hose.

19 Clean the area around the caliper hose union, then loosen the brake hose union nut.

20 Remove the brake pads as described above.

21 Unscrew the caliper from the end of the brake hose. Plug the hose end, to minimise fluid loss and prevent the entry of dirt into the hydraulic system.

Overhaul

22 At the time of writing, it appears that very few spare parts are available for the Brembo rear brake caliper. The only components available are the caliper guide sleeves and gaiters, and the handbrake operating lever; the piston seal appears not to be available separately. If the piston seal is leaking, the complete caliper body assembly must therefore be renewed. Consult a Renault dealer for further information on parts availability. The guide sleeves should be examined as follows.

23 Withdraw the guide sleeves from the caliper body, and remove the rubber gaiters. Check the condition of the guide sleeves and their bores in the caliper body. Both sleeves should be undamaged and (when cleaned) a reasonably tight sliding fit in the body bores, if not, they must be renewed. The sleeves are available from Renault dealers as part of a kit which comes complete with gaiters and grease.

24 Apply the grease supplied in the repair kit, or a high-temperature brake grease or anti-seize compound, to the guide sleeves.

25 Fit the guide sleeves to the caliper body, and fit the new rubber gaiters, ensuring that they are correctly located in the grooves on both the sleeve and body.

Refitting

26 Screw the caliper fully onto the flexible hose union nut, then refit the brake pads as described earlier in this Section.

27 Securely tighten the brake hose union nut, and remove the brake hose clamp or polythene (as applicable).

28 Bleed the hydraulic system as described in Chapter 9. Note that, providing the precautions described were taken to minimise brake fluid loss, it should only be necessary to bleed the relevant rear brake.

29 Depress the brake pedal repeatedly until the pads are pressed into firm contact with the brake disc, and normal pedal pressure is restored.

Girling front brake caliper - removal and refitting

30 On the Girling front brake caliper, whenever the caliper retaining bolts have been slackened, they must be discarded and new bolts installed on fitting. New bolts are available from your Renault dealer, and are supplied with their threads already coated with locking compound.

31 Install the caliper and tighten both bolts to the specified torque setting (Chapter 9), starting with the lower bolt first.

Bendix front brake caliper - removal and refitting

32 On later Bendix front brake calipers, a curved retaining plate is fitted underneath the caliper retaining bolts. To avoid contact between the retaining plate and driveshaft gaiter when the steering is on full-lock, the

retaining plate must be installed so that its bend curves in towards the caliper body.

Bendix rear brake shoes - inspection and renewal

Note: *This procedure supersedes the information given in Section 8 of Chapter 9, unless otherwise stated.*

⚠ **Warning: Brake shoes must be renewed on both rear wheels at the same time - never renew the shoes on only one wheel as uneven braking may result Also, the dust created by wear of the shoes may contain asbestos, which is a health hazard. Never blow it out with compressed air, and don't inhale any of it. An approved filtering mask should be worn when working on the brakes. DO NOT use petroleum-based solvents to clean brake parts; use brake cleaner or methylated spirit only.**

Inspection

33 Chock the front wheels, then jack up the rear of the vehicle and support it on axle stands. Remove the rear roadwheels.

34 Remove the brake drums as described in Section 8 of Chapter 9.

35 Working carefully to avoid inhalation, remove all traces of brake dust from the brake drum, backplate and shoes.

36 Measure the thickness of each brake shoe (friction material and backing) at several points; if either shoe is worn at any point to the specified minimum thickness or less, all four shoes must be renewed as a set. Also, the shoes should be renewed if any are fouled with oil or grease; there is no satisfactory way of degreasing friction material, once contaminated.

37 If any of the brake shoes are worn unevenly, or fouled with oil or grease, trace and rectify the cause before reassembly.

38 To renew the brake shoes, proceed as described in the following paragraphs.

39 If all is well, ensure the handbrake lever stop peg is correctly located against the edge of each trailing shoe, then refit the brake drums as described in Chapter 9.

Renewal

40 Using a pair of pliers, remove the shoe retainer spring cups by depressing and turning them through 90°. With the cups removed, lift off the springs and withdraw the retainer pins.

41 Ease the shoes out one at a time from the lower pivot point, to release the tension of the return spring, then disconnect the lower return spring from both shoes.

42 Ease the upper end of both shoes out from their wheel cylinder locations, taking great care not to damage the wheel cylinder seals, and disconnect the handbrake cable from the trailing shoe. The brake shoe and adjuster strut assembly can then be manoeuvred out of position and away from the backplate. Do not depress the brake pedal until the brakes are reassembled; wrap a

13

Fig. 13.28 Correct fitted positions of Bendix rear brake components (Sec 20)

A   Leading shoe
B   Trailing shoe
C   Lower pivot point
F   Adjuster strut mechanism
1   Upper return spring
2   Lower return spring
3   Retaining pin, spring and spring cup
4   Adjuster strut-to-trailing shoe spring

strong elastic band around the wheel cylinder pistons to retain them.

43 With the shoe and adjuster strut assembly on a bench, make a note of the correct fitted positions of the springs and adjuster strut, to use as a guide on reassembly. Release the handbrake lever stop peg (if not already done), then carefully detach the adjuster strut bolt retaining spring from the leading shoe. Disconnect the upper return spring, then detach the leading shoe and return spring from the trailing shoe and strut assembly. Unhook the spring securing the adjuster strut to the trailing shoe, and separate the two.

44 If genuine Renault brake shoes are being installed, it will be necessary to remove the handbrake lever from the original trailing shoe, and install it on the new shoe. Secure the lever in position with the new retaining clip which is supplied with the brake shoes. All return springs should be renewed, regardless of their apparent condition; spring kits are also available from Renault dealers.

45 Withdraw the adjuster bolt from the strut, and carefully examine the assembly for signs of wear or damage, paying particular attention to the threads of the adjuster bolt and the knurled adjuster wheel, and renew if necessary. Note that left-hand and right-hand struts are not interchangeable - they are marked 'G' (gauche/left-hand) and 'D' (droit/right-hand) respectively. Also note that the strut adjuster bolts are not interchangeable; the left-hand strut bolt has a left-handed thread, and the right-hand bolt a right-handed thread. The left-hand bolt can be identified by the groove on its adjuster wheel

Fig. 13.29 Bendix rear brake left-hand adjuster strut bolt can be identified by groove (G) on adjuster wheel collar (Sec 20)

collar (Fig. 13.29). The right-hand bolt does not have a groove on the adjuster wheel collar, but the bolt itself is painted.

46 Ensure the components on the end of the strut are correctly positioned, then apply a little high melting-point grease to the threads of the adjuster bolt. Screw the adjuster wheel onto the bolt until only a small gap exists between the wheel and the head of the bolt, then install the bolt in the strut.

47 Fit the adjuster strut retaining spring to the trailing shoe, ensuring that the shorter hook of the spring is engaged with the shoe. Attach the adjuster strut to the spring end, then ease the strut into position in its slot in the trailing shoe.

48 Engage the upper return spring with the trailing shoe. Hook the leading shoe onto the other end of the spring, and lever the leading shoe down until the adjuster bolt head is correctly located in its groove. Once the bolt is correctly located, hook its retaining spring into the slot on the leading shoe.

49 Peel back the rubber protective caps, and check the wheel cylinder for fluid leaks or other damage. Ensure that both cylinder pistons are free to move easily. Refer to Chapter 9, if necessary, for information on wheel cylinder renewal.

50 Prior to installation, clean the backplate and apply a thin smear of high-temperature brake grease or anti-seize compound to all those surfaces of the backplate which bear on the shoes, particularly the wheel cylinder pistons and lower pivot point. Do not allow the lubricant to foul the friction material.

51 Ensure the handbrake lever stop peg is correctly located against the edge of the trailing shoe, and remove the elastic band fitted to the wheel cylinder.

52 Manoeuvre the shoe and strut assembly into position on the vehicle, and locate the upper end of both shoes with the wheel cylinder pistons. Attach the handbrake cable to the trailing shoe lever. Fit the lower return spring to both shoes, and ease the shoes into position on the lower pivot point.

53 Tap the shoes to centralise them with the backplate. Refit the shoe retainer pins and springs, and secure them in position with the spring cups.

54 Using a screwdriver, turn the strut adjuster wheel until the diameter of the shoes

is between 179.2 and 179.5 mm. This should allow the brake drum to just pass over the shoes.

55 Slide the drum into position over the linings, but do not refit the hub nut/retaining screws yet.

56 Repeat the above procedure on the remaining rear brake.

57 Once both sets of rear shoes have been renewed, adjust the lining-to-drum clearance by repeatedly depressing the brake pedal. When depressing the pedal, have an assistant listen to the rear drums, to check that the adjuster strut is functioning correctly; if so, a clicking sound will be emitted by the strut as the pedal is depressed.

58 Remove both the rear drums. Check that the handbrake lever stop pegs are still correctly located against the edges of the trailing shoes, and that each lever operates smoothly. If all is well, with the aid of an assistant, adjust the handbrake cable so that the handbrake lever on each rear brake assembly starts to move as the handbrake is moved between the first and second notch (click) of its ratchet mechanism. The stop pegs should still be in contact with the shoes when the handbrake is on the first notch of the ratchet, but no longer contact the shoes when the handbrake is on the second notch. Once the handbrake adjustment is correct, hold the adjuster nut and securely tighten the locknut.

59 Refit the brake drums. Securely tighten the drum retaining screws, or (when applicable) slide the thrustwashers into position, then refit the hub nuts, tightening them to the specified torque (Chapter 8).

60 When applicable, tap each hub cap into place in the centre of the brake drum.

61 On completion, check the hydraulic fluid level as described in Chapter 9.

21 Suspension and steering

Front suspension subframe - removal and refitting

Removal

1 Chock the rear wheels, firmly apply the handbrake, then jack up the front of the vehicle and support it on axle stands. Remove both front roadwheels.

2 While the subframe is removed from the vehicle, it will be necessary to support the weight of the engine and transmission assembly, to prevent unnecessary strain being placed on the mounting rubbers. This is best achieved using an engine support tool, as shown in Section 4 of Chapter 6. Alternatively, position a jack and block of wood beneath the engine, and raise the head of the jack until it is supporting the weight of the engine/transmission.

3 Slacken and remove the retaining nuts and bolts securing the balljoint to each lower suspension arm and, where necessary, the anti-roll bar retaining clamp nuts and bolts. Loosen the lower arm-to-subframe mounting bolts, and swing each lower arm downwards to disengage it from its balljoint.

4 Remove the exhaust system downpipe as described in Chapter 3.

5 On 1995 cc and 2165 cc models, slacken and remove the nuts securing the engine and transmission mountings to the subframe.

6 With the engine/transmission supported as described in paragraph 2, make a final check and release any cables or wiring from the subframe.

7 Undo the four subframe retaining bolts and washers. Carefully lower the subframe out of position, and remove it from underneath the vehicle.

Refitting

8 Manoeuvre the subframe into position, and refit its four retaining bolts and washers. On 1995 cc and 2165 cc models, when lifting the subframe into position, ensure that all the mounting rubber studs are correctly located in their subframe holes. With the subframe correctly positioned, securely tighten its mounting bolts.

9 On 1995 cc and 2165 cc models, refit the mounting rubber retaining nuts, and tighten them securely.

10 Refit the exhaust system downpipe as described in Chapter 3.

11 Lift up each lower arm, and refit the nuts and bolts securing the balljoint and anti-roll bar. Tighten them by hand only at this stage.

12 Remove the jack or engine support bar, and lower the vehicle to the ground.

13 With the vehicle resting on its wheels, rock the car gently to settle the disturbed suspension components in position, then tighten all disturbed lower arm fasteners to their specified torque settings (Chapter 10).

Front suspension subframe bushes - renewal

14 If the special Renault service tool Mot. 1 179 can be obtained, then it is possible to renew the subframe bushes with the subframe in position on the vehicle. Consult a Renault dealer for further information.

15 Without the special tool, the subframe must first be removed as described above. The bushes can then be renewed as follows. Note that the bushes should not be renewed individually - all four bushes should be renewed as a complete set.

16 Before removal, mark the position of the bush lugs on the subframe. Support the underside of the subframe. Using a hydraulic press and a suitable spacer, such as a socket, which bears on the hard metal insert of the bush, press the bush downwards and out of the subframe.

17 Apply a coat of soapy water to the new subframe bush to ease the installation process. Support the upper side of the subframe, then fit the new bush to the subframe, aligning its lugs with the marks made before removal (see Fig. 13.30). Press the bush fully into position until its shoulder abuts the underside of the subframe. Note that the maximum permissible clearance between the shoulder of the bush and the subframe is 0.3 mm (0.012 in).

18 Repeat the above procedure until all the bushes have been renewed, then refit the subframe to the vehicle as described above.

Manual steering gear - grating noise

19 If a grating noise is occasionally emitted from the steering gear as the steering wheel is turned, this is due to the steering gear anti-noise bush not being sufficiently lubricated. To lubricate the anti-noise bush, first obtain a sachet of Molykote 33 medium grease and a steering gaiter retaining clip from your Renault dealer. Cut the clip securing the gaiter to the opposite end of the steering gear from the pinion housing (left-hand end on right-hand drive models, right-hand end on left-hand drive models), and peel the gaiter back from the housing. Move the steering rack so that its exposed end is fully extended, then smear a light coat of the special grease all over the steering rack surface. Refit the gaiter to the housing, and secure it in position with the new retaining clip.

Steering column (phase II models, mid-1989 onwards) - removal and refitting

20 On phase II models (mid-1989 onwards), the steering column is removed as follows. (Phase II models are easily identified from inside by having rotary heater controls; earlier models have sliding controls for the heating and ventilation system.)

Removal

21 Remove the steering wheel as described in Chapter 10.

22 Open up the fuse panel access flap on the driver's side lower facia panel, and unclip the fuse panel.

23 Undo the retaining screws, and remove the driver's side lower facia panel from the facia assembly.

24 Slide back the cover from the radio control stalk, and slacken the clamp screw.

25 Slacken and remove the four retaining screws from the lower column shroud. Remove both the upper and lower shrouds from the steering column, and slide the radio control stalk out of its bracket.

26 Slacken the steering column switch clamp screw, then tap the screw to release the switch from the column. Disconnect the wiring connectors, and remove the switch assembly.

27 Trace the wiring back from the ignition switch, and disconnect it at the connector.

Fig. 13.30 Ensure all the subframe mounting bush lugs are correctly positioned, as shown in the relevant diagram (Sec 21)

A In-line engines   B Transverse engines

Release all the wiring from column retaining clips, noting its correct routing.

28 Make alignment marks between the column universal joint and intermediate shaft, then slacken and remove the universal joint coupling bolt. With the bolt removed, withdraw the key so that the steering column is locked in position.

29 Slacken and remove the five retaining nuts and bolts, and withdraw the column from the vehicle.

Fig. 13.31 Press each subframe bush into position until its shoulder abuts the subframe. Note that the maximum permitted clearance 'X' between the bush shoulder and subframe is 0.3 mm (Sec 21)

13

Refitting

30 Refitting is a reversal of the removal procedure, noting the following points:

(a) *On refitting, engage the universal joint with the intermediate shaft, aligning the mark made on removal, and engage the steering column tab with the facia panel.*

(b) *Securely tighten the column mounting nuts and bolts, but tighten the coupling bolt only finger-tight at this stage.*

(c) *Refit the column shrouds and the steering wheel.*

(d) *With the column shrouds and steering wheel fitted, position the column universal joint so that there is a suitable clearance between the base of the wheel and the steering column shrouds. Hold the joint in this position, and securely tighten the coupling bolt.*

22 Bodywork and fittings

Tailgate and support struts (Hatchback models) - removal and refitting

1 On Hatchback models, the tailgate and support struts can be removed and refitted as described in Sections 20 and 21 of Chapter 11, noting that the washer reservoir is located under the luggage compartment carpet, next to the spare wheel.

Tailgate lock and associated fittings (Hatchback models) - removal and refitting

Trim panel

2 Remove the outer access covers from the panel, to gain access to the two hidden retaining screws. Undo all the retaining screws, and remove the panel from the tailgate.

3 Refitting is a reversal of the removal procedure.

Tailgate lock

4 Open up the tailgate, and undo the two lock retaining bolts (photo). Withdraw the lock from the tailgate, and disconnect it from its control link.

5 On refitting, reconnect the lock to its control link, and locate the lock in position. Refit the retaining bolts, tightening them securely, and check the operation of the lock.

Lock barrel

6 Remove the trim panel as described above.

7 Slide out the retaining clip, then withdraw the barrel from the tailgate, disconnecting it from its control link (photo).

8 Refitting is a reversal of the removal procedure.

Central locking servo

9 Remove the trim panel as described above.

10 Disconnect the servo wiring connector, then undo the two retaining nuts and remove the servo unit, disconnecting it from its control link.

11 Refitting is a reversal of the removal procedure. Before refitting the trim panel, check the operation of the central locking system.

Centre console (phase II models, mid-1989 onwards) - removal and refitting

12 Phase II models (mid-1989 onwards) have a revised facia panel. The new panel is easily identified by its rotary heater and ventilation control switches; earlier models have sliding controls for the heating and ventilation system. Removal of the new console is as follows.

13 Disconnect the battery negative terminal.

14 On models with manual transmission, unclip the gearchange lever trim panel from the centre console, and fold the gaiter back over the gearchange lever. On models with automatic transmission, prise out the selector indicator panel from the centre console, disconnect the wiring connector from the panel switch, and remove it from the selector lever.

15 Undo the retaining screws securing the upper trim panel to the centre console, and remove the trim panel. disconnecting its wiring connectors as they become accessible.

16 Slacken and remove the centre console retaining screws, and carefully remove the console from the vehicle.

17 Refitting is a reverse of the removal procedure.

Facia panel (phase II models, mid-1989 onwards) - removal and refitting

18 From mid-1989 onwards, when the facelift phase II models were introduced, a revised facia is fitted. The new panel is easily identified by its rotary heater and ventilation control switches; earlier models have sliding controls for the heating and ventilation system. Removal and refitting is as follows.

Removal

19 Remove the heater panel as described in Section 8 of this Chapter.

20 Remove the steering column as described in Section 21.

21 Where applicable, remove the choke cable as described in Chapter 3.

22 Carefully prise both the left- and right-hand inner sill trim panels away from the vehicle, to gain access to the facia wiring connector. The panels are a push fit in their retaining clips. Note that it is not necessary to remove the panels, the front of each panel should be unclipped sufficiently until access to the wiring connectors can be gained.

23 Disconnect both the left-hand and right-hand facia wiring connectors. Disconnect the large connector situated behind the fuse panel, and the connector(s) clipped onto the heater unit, directly behind the radio aperture.

24 Reach up behind the panel, and disconnect the speedometer cable from the instrument panel.

25 Prise out the cover panel from the left-hand facia panel speaker, then undo the retaining screw and lift off the speaker grille. Remove the speaker and disconnect it from its wiring connectors to gain access to the upper facia retaining nut. Remove the right-hand speaker in the same way.

26 Undo both the left-hand and right-hand upper retaining nuts and lower retaining screws (one of each on each side).

27 The complete facia panel can then be removed from the vehicle. As the panel is manoeuvred out of position, make a note of the correct routing of all the wiring, releasing it from any relevant retaining clips. With the panel removed, recover the plastic locating peg from the bulkhead.

Refitting

28 Refitting is a reversal of the removal procedure, noting the following points:

(a) *Refit the plastic locating plug to the bulkhead. Manoeuvre the facia into position, ensuring the wiring is correctly routed and fed through the relevant facia apertures.*

(b) *Locate the facia on the retaining peg, then refit all the facia fasteners and tighten them securely.*

(c) *On completion, reconnect the battery and check that all the electrical components and switches function correctly.*

22.4 On Hatchback models, the tailgate lock is retained by two bolts

22.7 Hatchback tailgate lock barrel retaining clip 'A', control links 'B' and drain tube 'C'

23.1 On Hatchback models, the luggage compartment light is operated by a ball-type switch mounted on tailgate

23.3a On phase 11 models, withdraw the number plate lamp bulbholder (arrowed) . . .

23.3b . . . and pull out the bulb

23 Electrical system

Luggage area courtesy light switch (Hatchback models) - general information

1 On Hatchback models, a ball-type switch is mounted onto the tailgate to operate the luggage area courtesy light (photo). When the tailgate is opened, the ball in the switch falls to the opposite end of the switch, and opens the switch contacts. When the tailgate is shut, the ball returns to the bottom of the switch, and closes the switch contacts.

2 To remove the switch, first remove the trim panel from the tailgate as described in Section 22. The switch can then be unclipped from the tailgate and removed, once its wiring connector has been disconnected. Refitting is a reverse of the removal procedure, ensuring that the switch is fitted the right way up.

Rear number plate lamp bulb (phase II models, mid-1989 onwards) - renewal

3 On phase II models (mid-1989 onwards), the rear number plate lamp is an integral part of the tailgate/boot lid outer trim panel. On these models, to renew the bulb, remove the access panel from the tailgate boot lid to gain access to the rear of the lamp. Withdraw the bulbholder from the rear of the lamp, and remove the bulb. The bulb is of the capless (push-fit) type (photos). Fit the new bulb, refit the bulbholder, and clip the access panel back into position.

Instrument panel (phase II models, mid-1989 onwards) - removal and refitting

4 Phase II models (mid-1989 onwards) have a revised instrument panel, easily identified by the rotary heater and ventilation control switches; earlier models have sliding controls for the heating and ventilation system. Removal of the new panel is as follows.

Removal

5 Disconnect the battery negative terminal.
6 Undo the retaining screws, and lower the driver's side lower facia panel away from the facia.
7 Slacken and remove the four retaining screws securing the instrument panel shroud. Ease the shroud out of position, and remove it from the vehicle.
8 Reach up behind the panel, and disconnect the speedometer cable.
9 Slacken and remove the two upper retaining screws, and the two lower screws which are accessed from underneath the facia, one on each side of the steering column assembly.
10 With all four retaining screws removed, carefully ease the panel out from the facia, disconnecting the wiring connectors as they become accessible.

Refitting

11 Refitting is a reversal of the removal procedure. On completion, reconnect the battery and check the operation of all the panel warning lights to ensure they are functioning correctly.

Windscreen wiper arms - removal and refitting

12 To overcome a problem with the windscreen wiper arm retaining nuts working loose, modified retaining nuts are now available. Whenever the wiper arms are disturbed, the old

23.16 Tailgate wiper motor wiring connector 'A' and retaining bolts 'B' – Hatchback models

nuts should be discarded and the new, modified nuts fitted. The nuts should be tightened to a torque of 20 Nm (15lbf ft).

Tailgate wiper motor (Hatchback models) - removal and refitting

13 Remove the wiper arm as described in Chapter 12.
14 Unscrew the nut from the wiper motor spindle, and remove the trim cover.
15 Open up the tailgate, and remove the trim panel as described in Section 22.
16 Disconnect the wiring connectors, then undo the two retaining bolts and remove the motor from the tailgate (photo).
17 Refitting is a reversal of the removal procedure.

Windscreen, tailgate and headlamp washer systems (Hatchback models)

18 Refer to Section 31 of Chapter 12, noting that on Hatchback models, the tailgate washer reservoir is located underneath the luggage compartment carpet, next to the spare wheel.

Rear speakers (Hatchback models) - removal and refitting

19 Move the seat backrest forwards, then undo the five retaining screws and remove the trim cover from the speaker (photo).

23.19 On Hatchback models, to gain access to the rear speaker, undo the five retaining screws and remove the trim panel

13

20 Slacken and remove the four retaining screws, then lift out the speaker, disconnecting its wiring connectors as they become accessible (photos). If necessary, the speaker mounting can also be removed once its retaining screws have been removed.
21 Refitting is a reverse of the removal sequence.

Anti-theft alarm system - general information

22 Some models in the range are fitted with an anti-theft alarm system as standard equipment. The alarm is automatically armed and disarmed when the door locks are operated using the remote central locking transmitter.
23 At the time of writing, no information on the alarm system was available. Should the alarm system become faulty, the vehicle should be taken to a Renault dealer for attention.

23.20a Undo the four retaining screws (arrowed) . . .

23.20b . . . and withdraw the speaker, disconnecting the wiring (arrowed) as it becomes accessible

Electric sunroof - general information

24 Some models in the range are fitted with an electrically-operated sunroof as standard equipment. At the time of writing, no information on the sunroof was available. Should the sunroof become faulty, the vehicle should be taken to a Renault dealer for attention.

Diagram 1: Typical starting/charging, ignition, warning lights/gauges and engine cooling fan

14

Diagram 2: Typical engine management systems

Diagram 3: Typical engine management systems – 1721 cc single-point injection, and 1995 cc 12-valve models

WIRE COLOURS

Ba	White	So	Pink
Be	Blue	Ve	Green
Bj	Beige	Vi	Mauve
Cy	Clear		
Gr	Grey		
Jo	Yellow		
Ma	Brown		
No	Black		
Or	Orange		
Rg	Red		

KEY TO ITEMS

1 Battery
2 Ignition switch
3 Fuel injection computer
4 Lambda sensor
5 Injection locking relay
6 Fuel pump relay
7 Fuel pump
8 Map sensor
9 Electronic ignition power module
10 Distributor
11 Spark plugs
12 Fuel injector(s)
13 Air temperature sensor
14 Coolant temperature sensor
15 Pre-ignition sensor
16 TDC sensor
17 Idle speed regulator
22 Throttle (no load/full load) switch
23 Recirculation solenoid
24 Full throttle switch

1995cc 12 VALVE MULTI-POINT NON CATALYST/CATALYST

1721cc SINGLE-POINT CATALYST

14

Diagram 4: Typical engine management systems – Turbo models

Diagram 5: Typical exterior lighting

14

Diagram 6: Typical front and rear foglights, interior lighting

Diagram 7: Typical clock, horn, cigar lighter and wash/wipe

14

Diagram 8: Typical heated rear window, central locking and electric mirrors

Diagram 9: Typical electric windows, sunroof, trip computer and radio/cassette

14

Diagram 10: Typical anti-lock braking system and alarm

This is a guide to getting your vehicle through the MOT test. Obviously it will not be possible to examine the vehicle to the same standard as the professional MOT tester. However, working through the following checks will enable you to identify any problem areas before submitting the vehicle for the test.

Where a testable component is in borderline condition, the tester has discretion in deciding whether to pass or fail it. The basis of such discretion is whether the tester would be happy for a close relative or friend to use the vehicle with the component in that condition. If the vehicle presented is clean and evidently well cared for, the tester may be more inclined to pass a borderline component than if the vehicle is scruffy and apparently neglected.

It has only been possible to summarise the test requirements here, based on the regulations in force at the time of printing. Test standards are becoming increasingly stringent, although there are some exemptions for older vehicles. For full details obtain a copy of the Haynes publication Pass the MOT! (available from stockists of Haynes manuals).

An assistant will be needed to help carry out some of these checks.

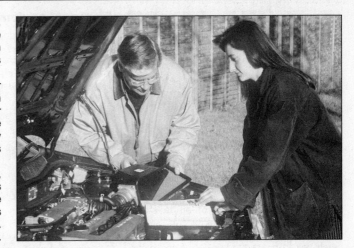

The checks have been sub-divided into four categories, as follows:

1 Checks carried out **FROM THE DRIVER'S SEAT**

2 Checks carried out **WITH THE VEHICLE ON THE GROUND**

3 Checks carried out **WITH THE VEHICLE RAISED AND THE WHEELS FREE TO TURN**

4 Checks carried out on **YOUR VEHICLE'S EXHAUST EMISSION SYSTEM**

---

1 Checks carried out **FROM THE DRIVER'S SEAT**

Handbrake

☐ Test the operation of the handbrake. Excessive travel (too many clicks) indicates incorrect brake or cable adjustment.

☐ Check that the handbrake cannot be released by tapping the lever sideways. Check the security of the lever mountings.

Footbrake

☐ Depress the brake pedal and check that it does not creep down to the floor, indicating a master cylinder fault. Release the pedal, wait a few seconds, then depress it again. If the pedal travels nearly to the floor before firm resistance is felt, brake adjustment or repair is necessary. If the pedal feels spongy, there is air in the hydraulic system which must be removed by bleeding.

☐ Check that the brake pedal is secure and in good condition. Check also for signs of fluid leaks on the pedal, floor or carpets, which would indicate failed seals in the brake master cylinder.

☐ Check the servo unit (when applicable) by operating the brake pedal several times, then keeping the pedal depressed and starting the engine. As the engine starts, the pedal will move down slightly. If not, the vacuum hose or the servo itself may be faulty.

Steering wheel and column

☐ Examine the steering wheel for fractures or looseness of the hub, spokes or rim.

☐ Move the steering wheel from side to side and then up and down. Check that the steering wheel is not loose on the column, indicating wear or a loose retaining nut. Continue moving the steering wheel as before, but also turn it slightly from left to right.

☐ Check that the steering wheel is not loose on the column, and that there is no abnormal

movement of the steering wheel, indicating wear in the column support bearings or couplings.

Windscreen and mirrors

☐ The windscreen must be free of cracks or other significant damage within the driver's field of view. (Small stone chips are acceptable.) Rear view mirrors must be secure, intact, and capable of being adjusted.

290mm

Seat belts and seats

Note: *The following checks are applicable to all seat belts, front and rear.*

☐ Examine the webbing of all the belts (including rear belts if fitted) for cuts, serious fraying or deterioration. Fasten and unfasten each belt to check the buckles. If applicable, check the retracting mechanism. Check the security of all seat belt mountings accessible from inside the vehicle.

☐ The front seats themselves must be securely attached and the backrests must lock in the upright position.

Doors

☐ Both front doors must be able to be opened and closed from outside and inside, and must latch securely when closed.

2 Checks carried out WITH THE VEHICLE ON THE GROUND

Vehicle identification

☐ Number plates must be in good condition, secure and legible, with letters and numbers correctly spaced – spacing at (A) should be twice that at (B).

☐ The VIN plate and/or homologation plate must be legible.

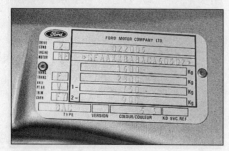

Electrical equipment

☐ Switch on the ignition and check the operation of the horn.

☐ Check the windscreen washers and wipers, examining the wiper blades; renew damaged or perished blades. Also check the operation of the stop-lights.

☐ Check the operation of the sidelights and number plate lights. The lenses and reflectors must be secure, clean and undamaged.

☐ Check the operation and alignment of the headlights. The headlight reflectors must not be tarnished and the lenses must be undamaged.

☐ Switch on the ignition and check the operation of the direction indicators (including the instrument panel tell-tale) and the hazard warning lights. Operation of the sidelights and stop-lights must not affect the indicators - if it does, the cause is usually a bad earth at the rear light cluster.

☐ Check the operation of the rear foglight(s), including the warning light on the instrument panel or in the switch.

Footbrake

☐ Examine the master cylinder, brake pipes and servo unit for leaks, loose mountings, corrosion or other damage.

☐ The fluid reservoir must be secure and the fluid level must be between the upper (**A**) and lower (**B**) markings.

☐ Inspect both front brake flexible hoses for cracks or deterioration of the rubber. Turn the steering from lock to lock, and ensure that the hoses do not contact the wheel, tyre, or any part of the steering or suspension mechanism. With the brake pedal firmly depressed, check the hoses for bulges or leaks under pressure.

Steering and suspension

☐ Have your assistant turn the steering wheel from side to side slightly, up to the point where the steering gear just begins to transmit this movement to the roadwheels. Check for excessive free play between the steering wheel and the steering gear, indicating wear or insecurity of the steering column joints, the column-to-steering gear coupling, or the steering gear itself.

☐ Have your assistant turn the steering wheel more vigorously in each direction, so that the roadwheels just begin to turn. As this is done, examine all the steering joints, linkages, fittings and attachments. Renew any component that shows signs of wear or damage. On vehicles with power steering, check the security and condition of the steering pump, drivebelt and hoses.

☐ Check that the vehicle is standing level, and at approximately the correct ride height.

Shock absorbers

☐ Depress each corner of the vehicle in turn, then release it. The vehicle should rise and then settle in its normal position. If the vehicle continues to rise and fall, the shock absorber is defective. A shock absorber which has seized will also cause the vehicle to fail.

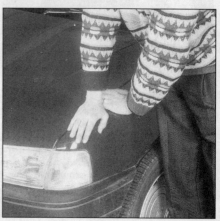

Exhaust system

☐ Start the engine. With your assistant holding a rag over the tailpipe, check the entire system for leaks. Repair or renew leaking sections.

3 Checks carried out
WITH THE VEHICLE RAISED AND THE WHEELS FREE TO TURN

Jack up the front and rear of the vehicle, and securely support it on axle stands. Position the stands clear of the suspension assemblies. Ensure that the wheels are clear of the ground and that the steering can be turned from lock to lock.

Steering mechanism

☐ Have your assistant turn the steering from lock to lock. Check that the steering turns smoothly, and that no part of the steering mechanism, including a wheel or tyre, fouls any brake hose or pipe or any part of the body structure.

☐ Examine the steering rack rubber gaiters for damage or insecurity of the retaining clips. If power steering is fitted, check for signs of damage or leakage of the fluid hoses, pipes or connections. Also check for excessive stiffness or binding of the steering, a missing split pin or locking device, or severe corrosion of the body structure within 30 cm of any steering component attachment point.

Front and rear suspension and wheel bearings

☐ Starting at the front right-hand side, grasp the roadwheel at the 3 o'clock and 9 o'clock positions and shake it vigorously. Check for free play or insecurity at the wheel bearings, suspension balljoints, or suspension mountings, pivots and attachments.

☐ Now grasp the wheel at the 12 o'clock and 6 o'clock positions and repeat the previous inspection. Spin the wheel, and check for roughness or tightness of the front wheel bearing.

☐ If excess free play is suspected at a component pivot point, this can be confirmed by using a large screwdriver or similar tool and levering between the mounting and the component attachment. This will confirm whether the wear is in the pivot bush, its retaining bolt, or in the mounting itself (the bolt holes can often become elongated).

☐ Carry out all the above checks at the other front wheel, and then at both rear wheels.

Springs and shock absorbers

☐ Examine the suspension struts (when applicable) for serious fluid leakage, corrosion, or damage to the casing. Also check the security of the mounting points.

☐ If coil springs are fitted, check that the spring ends locate in their seats, and that the spring is not corroded, cracked or broken.

☐ If leaf springs are fitted, check that all leaves are intact, that the axle is securely attached to each spring, and that there is no deterioration of the spring eye mountings, bushes, and shackles.

☐ The same general checks apply to vehicles fitted with other suspension types, such as torsion bars, hydraulic displacer units, etc. Ensure that all mountings and attachments are secure, that there are no signs of excessive wear, corrosion or damage, and (on hydraulic types) that there are no fluid leaks or damaged pipes.

☐ Inspect the shock absorbers for signs of serious fluid leakage. Check for wear of the mounting bushes or attachments, or damage to the body of the unit.

Driveshafts (fwd vehicles only)

☐ Rotate each front wheel in turn and inspect the constant velocity joint gaiters for splits or damage. Also check that each driveshaft is straight and undamaged.

Braking system

☐ If possible without dismantling, check brake pad wear and disc condition. Ensure that the friction lining material has not worn excessively, (A) and that the discs are not fractured, pitted, scored or badly worn (B).

☐ Examine all the rigid brake pipes underneath the vehicle, and the flexible hose(s) at the rear. Look for corrosion, chafing or insecurity of the pipes, and for signs of bulging under pressure, chafing, splits or deterioration of the flexible hoses.

☐ Look for signs of fluid leaks at the brake calipers or on the brake backplates. Repair or renew leaking components.

☐ Slowly spin each wheel, while your assistant depresses and releases the footbrake. Ensure that each brake is operating and does not bind when the pedal is released.

☐ Examine the handbrake mechanism, checking for frayed or broken cables, excessive corrosion, or wear or insecurity of the linkage. Check that the mechanism works on each relevant wheel, and releases fully, without binding.

☐ It is not possible to test brake efficiency without special equipment, but a road test can be carried out later to check that the vehicle pulls up in a straight line.

Fuel and exhaust systems

☐ Inspect the fuel tank (including the filler cap), fuel pipes, hoses and unions. All components must be secure and free from leaks.

☐ Examine the exhaust system over its entire length, checking for any damaged, broken or missing mountings, security of the retaining clamps and rust or corrosion.

Wheels and tyres

☐ Examine the sidewalls and tread area of each tyre in turn. Check for cuts, tears, lumps, bulges, separation of the tread, and exposure of the ply or cord due to wear or damage. Check that the tyre bead is correctly seated on the wheel rim, that the valve is sound and

properly seated, and that the wheel is not distorted or damaged.

☐ Check that the tyres are of the correct size for the vehicle, that they are of the same size and type on each axle, and that the pressures are correct.

☐ Check the tyre tread depth. The legal minimum at the time of writing is 1.6 mm over at least three-quarters of the tread width. Abnormal tread wear may indicate incorrect front wheel alignment.

Body corrosion

☐ Check the condition of the entire vehicle structure for signs of corrosion in load-bearing areas. (These include chassis box sections, side sills, cross-members, pillars, and all suspension, steering, braking system and seat belt mountings and anchorages.) Any corrosion which has seriously reduced the thickness of a load-bearing area is likely to cause the vehicle to fail. In this case professional repairs are likely to be needed.

☐ Damage or corrosion which causes sharp or otherwise dangerous edges to be exposed will also cause the vehicle to fail.

4 Checks carried out on YOUR VEHICLE'S EXHAUST EMISSION SYSTEM

Petrol models

☐ Have the engine at normal operating temperature, and make sure that it is in good tune (ignition system in good order, air filter element clean, etc).

☐ Before any measurements are carried out, raise the engine speed to around 2500 rpm, and hold it at this speed for 20 seconds. Allow

the engine speed to return to idle, and watch for smoke emissions from the exhaust tailpipe. If the idle speed is obviously much too high, or if dense blue or clearly-visible black smoke comes from the tailpipe for more than 5 seconds, the vehicle will fail. As a rule of thumb, blue smoke signifies oil being burnt (engine wear) while black smoke signifies unburnt fuel (dirty air cleaner element, or other carburettor or fuel system fault).

☐ An exhaust gas analyser capable of measuring carbon monoxide (CO) and hydrocarbons (HC) is now needed. If such an instrument cannot be hired or borrowed, a local garage may agree to perform the check for a small fee.

CO emissions (mixture)

☐ At the time of writing, the maximum CO level at idle is 3.5% for vehicles first used after August 1986 and 4.5% for older vehicles. From January 1996 a much tighter limit (around 0.5%) applies to catalyst-equipped vehicles first used from August 1992. If the CO level cannot be reduced far enough to pass the test (and the fuel and ignition systems are otherwise in good condition) then the carburettor is badly worn, or there is some problem in the fuel injection system or catalytic converter (as applicable).

HC emissions

☐ With the CO emissions within limits, HC emissions must be no more than 1200 ppm (parts per million). If the vehicle fails this test at idle, it can be re-tested at around 2000 rpm; if the HC level is then 1200 ppm or less, this counts as a pass.

☐ Excessive HC emissions can be caused by oil being burnt, but they are more likely to be due to unburnt fuel.

Diesel models

☐ The only emission test applicable to Diesel engines is the measuring of exhaust smoke density. The test involves accelerating the engine several times to its maximum unloaded speed.

Note: *It is of the utmost importance that the engine timing belt is in good condition before the test is carried out.*

☐ Excessive smoke can be caused by a dirty air cleaner element. Otherwise, professional advice may be needed to find the cause.

Introduction

A selection of good tools is a fundamental requirement for anyone contemplating the maintenance and repair of a motor vehicle. For the owner who does not possess any, their purchase will prove a considerable expense, offsetting some of the savings made by doing-it-yourself. However, provided that the tools purchased meet the relevant national safety standards and are of good quality, they will last for many years and prove an extremely worthwhile investment.

To help the average owner to decide which tools are needed to carry out the various tasks detailed in this manual, we have compiled three lists of tools under the following headings: *Maintenance and minor repair, Repair and overhaul*, and *Special*. Newcomers to practical mechanics should start off with the *Maintenance and minor repair* tool kit, and confine themselves to the simpler jobs around the vehicle. Then, as confidence and experience grow, more difficult tasks can be undertaken, with extra tools being purchased as, and when, they are needed. In this way, a *Maintenance and minor repair* tool kit can be built up into a *Repair and overhaul* tool kit over a considerable period of time, without any major cash outlays. The experienced do-it-yourselfer will have a tool kit good enough for most repair and overhaul procedures, and will add tools from the *Special* category when it is felt that the expense is justified by the amount of use to which these tools will be put.

Maintenance and minor repair tool kit

The tools given in this list should be considered as a minimum requirement if routine maintenance, servicing and minor repair operations are to be undertaken. We recommend the purchase of combination spanners (ring one end, open-ended the other); although more expensive than open-ended ones, they do give the advantages of both types of spanner.

☐ *Combination spanners: 10, 11, 12, 13, 14 and 17 mm*
☐ *Adjustable spanner - 35 mm jaw (approx)*
☐ *Engine sump/Gearbox drain plug key*
☐ *Set of feeler gauges*
☐ *Spark plug spanner (with rubber insert)*

☐ *Spark plug gap adjustment tool*
☐ *Brake bleed nipple spanner*
☐ *Screwdrivers: Flat blade and cross blade – approx 100 mm long x 6 mm dia*
☐ *Combination pliers*
☐ *Hacksaw (junior)*
☐ *Tyre pump*
☐ *Tyre pressure gauge*
☐ *Oil can*
☐ *Oil filter removal tool*
☐ *Fine emery cloth*
☐ *Wire brush (small)*
☐ *Funnel (medium size)*

Repair and overhaul tool kit

These tools are virtually essential for anyone undertaking any major repairs to a motor vehicle, and are additional to those given in the *Maintenance and minor repair* list. Included in this list is a comprehensive set of sockets. Although these are expensive, they will be found invaluable as they are so versatile - particularly if various drives are included in the set. We recommend the half-inch square-drive type, as this can be used with most proprietary torque wrenches. If you cannot afford a socket set, even bought piecemeal, then inexpensive tubular box spanners are a useful alternative.

The tools in this list will occasionally need to be supplemented by tools from the *Special* list:

☐ *Sockets (or box spanners) to cover range in previous list*
☐ *Reversible ratchet drive (for use with sockets)* **(see illustration)**
☐ *Extension piece, 250 mm (for use with sockets)*
☐ *Universal joint (for use with sockets)*
☐ *Torque wrench (for use with sockets)*
☐ *Self-locking grips*
☐ *Ball pein hammer*
☐ *Soft-faced mallet (plastic/aluminium or rubber)*
☐ *Screwdrivers:*
   Flat blade - long & sturdy, short (chubby), and narrow (electrician's) types
   Cross blade - Long & sturdy, and short (chubby) types
☐ *Pliers:*
   Long-nosed
   Side cutters (electrician's)
   Circlip (internal and external)
☐ *Cold chisel - 25 mm*
☐ *Scriber*

☐ *Scraper*
☐ *Centre-punch*
☐ *Pin punch*
☐ *Hacksaw*
☐ *Brake hose clamp*
☐ *Brake bleeding kit*
☐ *Selection of twist drills*
☐ *Steel rule/straight-edge*
☐ *Allen keys (including Torx type)*
☐ *Selection of files*
☐ *Wire brush*
☐ *Axle stands*
☐ *Jack (strong trolley or hydraulic type)*
☐ *Light with extension lead*
☐ *Torx bits*

Special tools

The tools in this list are those which are not used regularly, are expensive to buy, or which need to be used in accordance with their manufacturers' instructions. Unless relatively difficult mechanical jobs are undertaken frequently, it will not be economic to buy many of these tools. Where this is the case, you could consider clubbing together with friends (or joining a motorists' club) to make a joint purchase, or borrowing the tools against a deposit from a local garage or tool hire specialist. It is worth noting that many of the larger DIY superstores now carry a large range of special tools for hire at modest rates.

The following list contains only those tools and instruments freely available to the public, and not those special tools produced by the vehicle manufacturer specifically for its dealer network. You will find occasional references to these manufacturers' special tools in the text of this manual. Generally, an alternative method of doing the job without the vehicle manufacturers' special tool is given. However, sometimes there is no alternative to using them. Where this is the case and the relevant tool cannot be bought or borrowed, you will have to entrust the work to a franchised garage.

☐ *Valve spring compressor* **(see illustration)**
☐ *Valve grinding tool*
☐ *Piston ring compressor* **(see illustration)**
☐ *Piston ring removal/installation tool* **(see illustration)**
☐ *Cylinder bore hone* **(see illustration)**
☐ *Balljoint separator*
☐ *Coil spring compressors (where applicable)*
☐ *Two/three-legged hub and bearing puller*

Sockets and reversible ratchet drive

Valve spring compressor

Piston ring compressor

Piston ring removal/installation tool

Cylinder bore hone

Three-legged hub and bearing puller

Micrometer set

Vernier calipers

Dial test indicator and magnetic stand

Compression testing gauge

Clutch plate alignment set

Brake shoe steady spring cup removal tool

(see illustration)

☐ Impact screwdriver
☐ Micrometer and/or vernier calipers **(see illustrations)**
☐ Dial gauge **(see illustration)**
☐ Universal electrical multi-meter
☐ Cylinder compression gauge **(see illustration)**
☐ Clutch plate alignment set **(see illustration)**
☐ Brake shoe steady spring cup removal tool **(see illustration)**
☐ Bush and bearing removal/installation set **(see illustration)**
☐ Stud extractors **(see illustration)**
☐ Tap and die set **(see illustration)**
☐ Lifting tackle
☐ Trolley jack

Buying tools

For practically all tools, a tool factor is the best source, since he will have a very comprehensive range compared with the average garage or accessory shop. Having said that, accessory shops often offer excellent quality tools at discount prices, so it pays to shop around.

Remember, you don't have to buy the most expensive items on the shelf, but it is always advisable to steer clear of the very cheap tools. There are plenty of good tools around at reasonable prices, but always aim to purchase items which meet the relevant national safety standards. If in doubt, ask the proprietor or manager of the shop for advice before making a purchase.

Care and maintenance of tools

Having purchased a reasonable tool kit, it is necessary to keep the tools in a clean and serviceable condition. After use, always wipe off any dirt, grease and metal particles using a clean, dry cloth, before putting the tools away. Never leave them lying around after they have been used. A simple tool rack on the garage or workshop wall for items such as screwdrivers and pliers is a good idea. Store all normal spanners and sockets in a metal box. Any measuring instruments, gauges, meters, etc, must be carefully stored where they cannot be damaged or become rusty.

Take a little care when tools are used. Hammer heads inevitably become marked, and screwdrivers lose the keen edge on their blades from time to time. A little timely attention with emery cloth or a file will soon restore items like this to a good serviceable finish.

Working facilities

Not to be forgotten when discussing tools is the workshop itself. If anything more than routine maintenance is to be carried out, some form of suitable working area becomes essential.

It is appreciated that many an owner-mechanic is forced by circumstances to remove an engine or similar item without the benefit of a garage or workshop. Having done this, any repairs should always be done under the cover of a roof.

Wherever possible, any dismantling should be done on a clean, flat workbench or table at a suitable working height.

Any workbench needs a vice; one with a jaw opening of 100 mm is suitable for most jobs. As mentioned previously, some clean dry storage space is also required for tools, as well as for any lubricants, cleaning fluids, touch-up paints and so on, which become necessary.

Another item which may be required, and which has a much more general usage, is an electric drill with a chuck capacity of at least 8 mm. This, together with a good range of twist drills, is virtually essential for fitting accessories.

Last, but not least, always keep a supply of old newspapers and clean, lint-free rags available, and try to keep any working area as

Bush and bearing removal/installation set   Stud extractor set

Tap and die set

Whenever servicing, repair or overhaul work is carried out on the car or its components, observe the following procedures and instructions. This will assist in carrying out the operation efficiently and to a professional standard of workmanship.

Joint mating faces and gaskets

When separating components at their mating faces, never insert screwdrivers or similar implements into the joint between the faces in order to prise them apart. This can cause severe damage which results in oil leaks, coolant leaks, etc upon reassembly. Separation is usually achieved by tapping along the joint with a soft-faced hammer in order to break the seal. However, note that this method may not be suitable where dowels are used for component location.

Where a gasket is used between the mating faces of two components, a new one must be fitted on reassembly; fit it dry unless otherwise stated in the repair procedure. Make sure that the mating faces are clean and dry, with all traces of old gasket removed. When cleaning a joint face, use a tool which is unlikely to score or damage the face, and remove any burrs or nicks with an oilstone or fine file.

Make sure that tapped holes are cleaned with a pipe cleaner, and keep them free of jointing compound, if this is being used, unless specifically instructed otherwise.

Ensure that all orifices, channels or pipes are clear, and blow through them, preferably using compressed air.

Oil seals

Oil seals can be removed by levering them out with a wide flat-bladed screwdriver or similar implement. Alternatively, a number of self-tapping screws may be screwed into the seal, and these used as a purchase for pliers or some similar device in order to pull the seal free.

Whenever an oil seal is removed from its working location, either individually or as part of an assembly, it should be renewed.

The very fine sealing lip of the seal is easily damaged, and will not seal if the surface it contacts is not completely clean and free from scratches, nicks or grooves. If the original sealing surface of the component cannot be restored, and the manufacturer has not made provision for slight relocation of the seal relative to the sealing surface, the component should be renewed.

Protect the lips of the seal from any surface which may damage them in the course of fitting. Use tape or a conical sleeve where possible. Lubricate the seal lips with oil before fitting and, on dual-lipped seals, fill the space between the lips with grease.

Unless otherwise stated, oil seals must be fitted with their sealing lips toward the lubricant to be sealed.

Use a tubular drift or block of wood of the appropriate size to install the seal and, if the seal housing is shouldered, drive the seal down to the shoulder. If the seal housing is unshouldered, the seal should be fitted with its face flush with the housing top face (unless otherwise instructed).

Screw threads and fastenings

Seized nuts, bolts and screws are quite a common occurrence where corrosion has set in, and the use of penetrating oil or releasing fluid will often overcome this problem if the offending item is soaked for a while before attempting to release it. The use of an impact driver may also provide a means of releasing such stubborn fastening devices, when used in conjunction with the appropriate screwdriver bit or socket. If none of these methods works, it may be necessary to resort to the careful application of heat, or the use of a hacksaw or nut splitter device.

Studs are usually removed by locking two nuts together on the threaded part, and then using a spanner on the lower nut to unscrew the stud. Studs or bolts which have broken off below the surface of the component in which they are mounted can sometimes be removed using a stud extractor. Always ensure that a blind tapped hole is completely free from oil, grease, water or other fluid before installing the bolt or stud. Failure to do this could cause the housing to crack due to the hydraulic action of the bolt or stud as it is screwed in.

When tightening a castellated nut to accept a split pin, tighten the nut to the specified torque, where applicable, and then tighten further to the next split pin hole. Never slacken the nut to align the split pin hole, unless stated in the repair procedure.

When checking or retightening a nut or bolt to a specified torque setting, slacken the nut or bolt by a quarter of a turn, and then retighten to the specified setting. However, this should not be attempted where angular tightening has been used.

For some screw fastenings, notably cylinder head bolts or nuts, torque wrench settings are no longer specified for the latter stages of tightening, "angle-tightening" being called up instead. Typically, a fairly low torque wrench setting will be applied to the bolts/nuts in the correct sequence, followed by one or more stages of tightening through specified angles.

Locknuts, locktabs and washers

Any fastening which will rotate against a component or housing during tightening should always have a washer between it and the relevant component or housing.

Spring or split washers should always be renewed when they are used to lock a critical component such as a big-end bearing retaining bolt or nut. Locktabs which are folded over to retain a nut or bolt should always be renewed.

Self-locking nuts can be re-used in non-critical areas, providing resistance can be felt when the locking portion passes over the bolt or stud thread. However, it should be noted that self-locking stiffnuts tend to lose their effectiveness after long periods of use, and should then be renewed as a matter of course.

Split pins must always be replaced with new ones of the correct size for the hole.

When thread-locking compound is found on the threads of a fastener which is to be re-used, it should be cleaned off with a wire brush and solvent, and fresh compound applied on reassembly.

Special tools

Some repair procedures in this manual entail the use of special tools such as a press, two or three-legged pullers, spring compressors, etc. Wherever possible, suitable readily-available alternatives to the manufacturer's special tools are described, and are shown in use. In some instances, where no alternative is possible, it has been necessary to resort to the use of a manufacturer's tool, and this has been done for reasons of safety as well as the efficient completion of the repair operation. Unless you are highly-skilled and have a thorough understanding of the procedures described, never attempt to bypass the use of any special tool when the procedure described specifies its use. Not only is there a very great risk of personal injury, but expensive damage could be caused to the components involved.

Environmental considerations

When disposing of used engine oil, brake fluid, antifreeze, etc, give due consideration to any detrimental environmental effects. Do not, for instance, pour any of the above liquids down drains into the general sewage system, or onto the ground to soak away. Many local council refuse tips provide a facility for waste oil disposal, as do some garages. If none of these facilities are available, consult your local Environmental Health Department, or the National Rivers Authority, for further advice.

With the universal tightening-up of legislation regarding the emission of environmentally-harmful substances from motor vehicles, most vehicles have tamperproof devices fitted to the main adjustment points of the fuel system. These devices are primarily designed to prevent unqualified persons from adjusting the fuel/air mixture, with the chance of a consequent increase in toxic emissions. If such devices are found during servicing or overhaul, they should, wherever possible, be renewed or refitted in accordance with the manufacturer's requirements or current legislation.

Note: It is antisocial and illegal to dump oil down the drain. To find the location of your local oil recycling bank, call this number free.

Buying spare parts

Spare parts are available from many sources, for example: Renault garages, other garages and accessory shops, and motor factors. Our advice regarding spare parts is as follows.

Officially appointed Renault garages – These will be the best source for parts which are peculiar to your car, and are otherwise not generally available (eg complete cylinder heads, internal gearbox components, badges, interior trim, etc.). It is also the only place at which you should buy parts if your car is still under warranty – non-Renault components may invalidate the warranty. To be sure of obtaining the correct parts, it will always be necessary to give the storeman your car's vehicle identification number, and if possible to take the old part along for positive identification. Remember that many parts are available under a factory exchange scheme –

any parts returned should always be clean! It obviously makes good sense to go straight to the specialists on your car for this type of part, as they are best equipped to supply you.

Other garages and accessory shops – These are often very good places to buy materials and components needed for the maintenance of your car (eg oil filters, spark plugs, bulbs, drivebelts, oils and greases, touch-up paint, filler paste, etc). They also sell general accessories, usually have convenient opening hours, charge lower prices and can often be found not far from home.

Motor factors – Good factors will stock all the more important components which wear out relatively quickly (eg clutch components, pistons, valves, exhaust systems, brake cylinders/pipes/hoses/seals/ shoes and pads, etc.). Motor factors will often provide new or reconditioned components on a part exchange basis – this can save a considerable amount of money.

Vehicle identification numbers

Modifications are a continuing and unpublicised process in vehicle manufacture, quite apart from their major model changes. Spare parts manuals and lists are compiled on a numerical basis, the individual vehicle numbers being essential for correct identification of the component concerned.

When ordering spare parts it will usually be necessary to quote the numbers on the oval plate under all circumstances and often those on the manufacturer's plate. If engine or gearbox parts are being ordered, the engine plate or gearbox plate numbers will be needed. The paint code may be required if the colour of the car is not easily described. All these numbers with the exception of those on the gearbox plate are located in readily visible places in the engine compartment. The gearbox plate is affixed to the transmission housing.

The model type code numbers used in some Chapters of this manual appear on the manufacturer's plate – eg L485 identifies a 2.0 litre Turbo model.

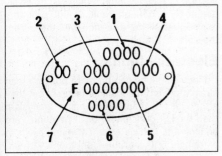

Oval identification plate information

1 Factory symbol
2 Transmission type
3 Equipment number
4 Optional equipment fitted (in production)
5 Fabrication number
6 Original paint reference (not all models)
7 Place of manufacture (Factory)

Manufacturer's information plate identification

10 Vehicle type
11 Chassis number
12 Gross vehicle weight
13 Gross total weight (loaded vehicle and loaded trailer)
14 Maximum permissible front axle loading
15 Maximum permissible rear axle loading

Engine plate

7 Engine type   9 Engine number
8 Engine suffix

Engine plate location (B) transverse (1.7 litre) engine

Engine plate location (B) - longitudinal (2.0 litre) engine

Alternative paint code plate location (D)

Introduction

The vehicle owner who does his or her own maintenance according to the recommended schedules should not have to use this section of the manual very often. Modern component reliability is such that, provided those items subject to wear or deterioration are inspected or renewed at the specified intervals, sudden failure is comparatively rare. Faults do not usually just happen as a result of sudden failure, but develop over a period of time. Major mechanical failures in particular are usually preceded by characteristic symptoms over hundreds or even thousands of miles. Those components which do occasionally fail without warning are often small and easily carried in the vehicle.

With any fault finding, the first step is to decide where to begin investigations. Sometimes this is obvious, but on other occasions a little detective work will be necessary. The owner who makes half a dozen haphazard adjustments or replacements may be successful in curing a fault (or its symptoms), but he will be none the wiser if the fault recurs and he may well have spent more time and money than was necessary. A calm and logical approach will be found to be more satisfactory in the long run. Always take into account any warning signs or abnormalities that may have been noticed in the period preceding the fault – power loss, high or low gauge readings, unusual noises or smells, etc – and remember that failure of components such as fuses or spark plugs may only be pointers to some underlying fault.

The pages which follow here are intended to help in cases of failure to start or breakdown on the road. There is also a Fault Diagnosis Section at the end of each Chapter which should be consulted if the preliminary checks prove unfruitful. Whatever the fault, certain basic principles apply. These are as follows:

Verify the fault. This is simply a matter of being sure that you know what the symptoms are before starting work. This is particularly important if you are investigating a fault for someone else who may not have described it very accurately.

Don't overlook the obvious. For example, if the vehicle won't start, is there petrol in the tank? (Don't take anyone else's word on this particular point, and don't trust the fuel gauge either!) If an electrical fault is indicated, look for loose or broken wires before digging out the test gear.

Cure the disease, not the symptom. Substituting a flat battery with a fully charged one will get you off the hard shoulder, but if the underlying cause is not attended to,the new battery will go the same way. Similarly, changing oil-fouled spark plugs for a new set will get you moving again, but remember that the reason for the fouling (if it wasn't simply an incorrect grade of plug) will have to be established and corrected.

Don't take anything for granted. Particularly, don't forget that a 'new' component may itself be defective (especially if it's been rattling round in the boot for months), and don't leave components out of a fault diagnosis sequence just because they are new or recently fitted. When you do finally diagnose a difficult fault, you'll probably realise that all the evidence was there from the start.

Electrical faults

Electrical faults can be more puzzling than straightforward mechanical failures, but they are no less susceptible to logical analysis if the basic principles of operation are understood. Vehicle electrical wiring exists in extremely unfavourable conditions – heat, vibration and chemical attack and the first things to look for are loose or corroded connections and broken or chafed wires, especially where the wires pass through holes in the bodywork or are subject to vibration.

All metal-bodied vehicles in current production have one pole of the battery 'earthed', ie connected to the vehicle bodywork, and in nearly all modern vehicles it is the negative (–) terminal. The various electrical components – motors, bulb holders, etc – are also connected to earth, either by means of a lead or directly by their mountings. Electric current flows through the component and then back to the battery via the bodywork. If the component mounting is loose or corroded, or if a good path back to the battery is not available, the circuit will be incomplete and malfunction will result. The engine and/or gearbox are also earthed by means of flexible metal straps to the body or subframe; if these straps are loose or missing, starter motor, generator and ignition trouble may result.

Assuming the earth return to be satisfactory, electrical faults will be due either to component malfunction or to defects in the current supply. Individual components are dealt with in Chapter 12. If supply wires are broken or cracked internally this results in an open-circuit, and the easiest way to check for this is to bypass the suspect wire temporarily with a length of wire having a crocodile clip or suitable connector at each end. Alternatively, a 12V test lamp can be used to verify the presence of supply voltage at various points along the wire and the break can be thus isolated.

If a bare portion of a live wire touches the bodywork or other earthed metal part, the electricity will take the low-resistance path thus formed back to the battery: this is known as a short-circuit. Hopefully a short-circuit will blow a fuse, but otherwise it may cause burning of the insulation (and possibly further short-circuits) or even a fire. This is why it is inadvisable to bypass persistently blowing fuses with silver foil or wire.

Spares and tool kit

Most vehicles are supplied only with sufficient tools for wheel changing; the *Maintenance and minor repair* tool kit detailed in *Tools and working facilities*, with the addition of a hammer, is probably sufficient for those repairs that most motorists would consider attempting at the roadside. In addition a few items which can be fitted without too much trouble in the event of a breakdown should be carried. Experience and available space will modify the list below, but the following may save having to call on professional assistance:

- [ ] *Spark plugs, clean and correctly gapped*
- [ ] *HT lead and plug cap – long enough to reach the plug furthest from the distributor*
- [ ] *Distributor rotor*
- [ ] *Drivebelt(s) – emergency type may suffice*
- [ ] *Spare fuses*
- [ ] *Set of principal light bulbs*
- [ ] *Tin of radiator sealer and hose bandage*
- [ ] *Exhaust bandage*
- [ ] *Roll of insulating tape*
- [ ] *Length of soft iron wire*
- [ ] *Length of electrical flex*
- [ ] *Torch or inspection lamp (can double as test lamp)*
- [ ] *Battery jump leads*

- [ ] *Tow-rope*
- [ ] *Ignition waterproofing aerosol*
- [ ] *Litre of engine oil*
- [ ] *Sealed can of hydraulic fluid*
- [ ] *Emergency windscreen*
- [ ] *Wormdrive clips*
- [ ] *Tube of filler paste*

If spare fuel is carried, a can designed for the purpose should be used to minimise risks of leakage and collision damage. A first aid kit and a warning triangle, whilst not at present compulsory in the UK, are obviously sensible items to carry in addition to the above. When touring abroad it may be advisable to carry additional spares which, even if you cannot fit them yourself, could save having to wait while parts are obtained. The items below may be worth considering:

- [ ] *Clutch and throttle cables*
- [ ] *Cylinder head gasket*
- [ ] *Alternator brushes*
- [ ] *Tyre valve core*

One of the motoring organisations will be able to advise on availability of fuel, etc, in foreign countries.

Engine will not start

Engine fails to turn when starter operated

- [ ] Flat battery (recharge use jump leads or push start)
- [ ] Battery terminals loose or corroded
- [ ] Battery earth to body defective
- [ ] Engine earth strap loose or broken
- [ ] Starter motor (or solenoid) wiring loose or broken
- [ ] Ignition/starter switch faulty
- [ ] Major mechanical failure (seizure)
- [ ] Starter or solenoid internal fault (see Chapter 12)

Starter motor turns engine slowly

- [ ] Partially discharged battery (recharge, use jump leads, or push start)
- [ ] Battery terminals loose or corroded

- [ ] Battery earth to body defective
- [ ] Engine earth strap loose
- [ ] Starter motor (or solenoid) wiring loose
- [ ] Starter motor internal fault (see Chapter 12)

Starter motor spins without turning engine

- [ ] Flywheel gear teeth damaged or worn
- [ ] Starter motor mounting bolts loose

Engine turns normally but fails to start

- [ ] Damp or dirty HT leads and distributor cap (crank engine and check for spark)
- [ ] No fuel in tank (check for delivery)
- [ ] Fouled or incorrectly gapped spark plugs (remove, clean and regap)
- [ ] Other ignition system fault (see Chapter 4)
- [ ] Other fuel system fault (see Chapter 3)

A simple test lamp is useful for checking electrical faults

Carrying a few spares may save you a long walk!

☐ Poor compression (see Chapter 1)
☐ Major mechanical failure (eg camshaft drive)

Engine fires but will not run

☐ Air leaks at carburettor or inlet manifold
☐ Fuel starvation (see Chapter 3)
☐ Ignition fault (see Chapter 4)

Engine cuts out and will not restart

Engine cuts out suddenly – ignition fault

☐ Loose or disconnected LT wires
☐ Wet HT leads or distributor cap (after traversing water splash)
☐ Coil failure (check for spark)
☐ Other ignition fault (see Chapter 4)

Engine misfires before cutting out – fuel fault

☐ Fuel tank empty
☐ Fuel pump defective or filter blocked (check for delivery)

Crank engine and check for spark. Note use of insulated tool

☐ Fuel tank filler vent blocked (suction will be evident on releasing cap)
☐ Carburettor needle valve sticking
☐ Carburettor jets blocked (fuel contaminated)
☐ Other fuel system fault (see Chapter 3)

Engine cuts out – other causes

☐ Serious overheating
☐ Major mechanical failure (eg camshaft drive)

Engine overheats

Ignition (no-charge) light illuminated

☐ Slack or broken drivebelt – re-tension or renew (Chapter 2)

Ignition warning light not illuminated

☐ Coolant loss due to internal or external leakage (see Chapter 2)
☐ Thermostat defective
☐ Low oil level
☐ Brakes binding
☐ Radiator clogged externally or internally
☐ Engine waterways clogged
☐ Ignition timing incorrect or automatic advance malfunctioning
☐ Mixture too weak
Note: *Do not add cold water to an overheated engine or damage may result*

Low engine oil pressure

Note: *Low oil pressure in a high-mileage engine at tickover is not necessarily a cause for concern. Sudden pressure loss at speed is far more significant. In any event check the gauge or warning light sender before condemning the engine.*

Gauge reads low or warning light illuminated with engine running

☐ Oil level low or incorrect grade
☐ Defective gauge or sender unit
☐ Wire to sender unit earthed
☐ Engine overheating
☐ Oil filter clogged or bypass valve defective
☐ Oil pressure relief valve defective
☐ Oil pick-up strainer clogged
☐ Oil pump worn or mountings loose
☐ Worn main or big-end bearings

Engine noises

Pre-ignition (pinking) on acceleration

☐ Incorrect grade of fuel
☐ Ignition timing incorrect
☐ Distributor faulty or worn
☐ Worn or maladjusted carburettor
☐ Excessive carbon build-up in engine

Whistling or wheezing noises

☐ Leaking vacuum hose
☐ Leaking carburettor or manifold gasket
☐ Blowing head gasket

Tapping or rattling

☐ Worn valve gear
☐ Worn timing chain or belt
☐ Broken piston ring (ticking noise)

Knocking or thumping

☐ Unintentional mechanical contact (eg fan blades)
☐ Worn drivebelt
☐ Peripheral component fault (generator, water pump, etc)
☐ Worn big-end bearings (regular heavy knocking, perhaps less under load)
☐ Worn main bearings (rumbling and knocking, perhaps worsening under load)
☐ Piston slap (most noticeable when cold)

Length (distance)

Inches (in)	x 25.4	= Millimetres (mm)	x 0.0394	= Inches (in)
Feet (ft)	x 0.305	= Metres (m)	x 3.281	= Feet (ft)
Miles	x 1.609	= Kilometres (km)	x 0.621	= Miles

Volume (capacity)

Cubic inches (cu in; in³)	x 16.387	= Cubic centimetres (cc; cm³)	x 0.061	= Cubic inches (cu in; in³)
Imperial pints (Imp pt)	x 0.568	= Litres (l)	x 1.76	= Imperial pints (Imp pt)
Imperial quarts (Imp qt)	x 1.137	= Litres (l)	x 0.88	= Imperial quarts (Imp qt)
Imperial quarts (Imp qt)	x 1.201	= US quarts (US qt)	x 0.833	= Imperial quarts (Imp qt)
US quarts (US qt)	x 0.946	= Litres (l)	x 1.057	= US quarts (US qt)
Imperial gallons (Imp gal)	x 4.546	= Litres (l)	x 0.22	= Imperial gallons (Imp gal)
Imperial gallons (Imp gal)	x 1.201	= US gallons (US gal)	x 0.833	= Imperial gallons (Imp gal)
US gallons (US gal)	x 3.785	= Litres (l)	x 0.264	= US gallons (US gal)

Mass (weight)

Ounces (oz)	x 28.35	= Grams (g)	x 0.035	= Ounces (oz)
Pounds (lb)	x 0.454	= Kilograms (kg)	x 2.205	= Pounds (lb)

Force

Ounces-force (ozf; oz)	x 0.278	= Newtons (N)	x 3.6	= Ounces-force (ozf; oz)
Pounds-force (lbf; lb)	x 4.448	= Newtons (N)	x 0.225	= Pounds-force (lbf; lb)
Newtons (N)	x 0.1	= Kilograms-force (kgf; kg)	x 9.81	= Newtons (N)

Pressure

Pounds-force per square inch (psi; lbf/in²; lb/in²)	x 0.070	= Kilograms-force per square centimetre (kgf/cm²; kg/cm²)	x 14.223	= Pounds-force per square inch (psi; lbf/in²; lb/in²)
Pounds-force per square inch (psi; lbf/in²; lb/in²)	x 0.068	= Atmospheres (atm)	x 14.696	= Pounds-force per square inch (psi; lbf/in²; lb/in²)
Pounds-force per square inch (psi; lbf/in²; lb/in²)	x 0.069	= Bars	x 14.5	= Pounds-force per square inch (psi; lbf/in²; lb/in²)
Pounds-force per square inch (psi; lbf/in²; lb/in²)	x 6.895	= Kilopascals (kPa)	x 0.145	= Pounds-force per square inch (psi; lbf/in²; lb/in²)
Kilopascals (kPa)	x 0.01	= Kilograms-force per square centimetre (kgf/cm²; kg/cm²)	x 98.1	= Kilopascals (kPa)
Millibar (mbar)	x 100	= Pascals (Pa)	x 0.01	= Millibar (mbar)
Millibar (mbar)	x 0.0145	= Pounds-force per square inch (psi; lbf/in²; lb/in²)	x 68.947	= Millibar (mbar)
Millibar (mbar)	x 0.75	= Millimetres of mercury (mmHg)	x 1.333	= Millibar (mbar)
Millibar (mbar)	x 0.401	= Inches of water (inH₂O)	x 2.491	= Millibar (mbar)
Millimetres of mercury (mmHg)	x 0.535	= Inches of water (inH₂O)	x 1.868	= Millimetres of mercury (mmHg)
Inches of water (inH₂O)	x 0.036	= Pounds-force per square inch (psi; lbf/in²; lb/in²)	x 27.68	= Inches of water (inH₂O)

Torque (moment of force)

Pounds-force inches (lbf in; lb in)	x 1.152	= Kilograms-force centimetre (kgf cm; kg cm)	x 0.868	= Pounds-force inches (lbf in; lb in)
Pounds-force inches (lbf in; lb in)	x 0.113	= Newton metres (Nm)	x 8.85	= Pounds-force inches (lbf in; lb in)
Pounds-force inches (lbf in; lb in)	x 0.083	= Pounds-force feet (lbf ft; lb ft)	x 12	= Pounds-force inches (lbf in; lb in)
Pounds-force feet (lbf ft; lb ft)	x 0.138	= Kilograms-force metres (kgf m; kg m)	x 7.233	= Pounds-force feet (lbf ft; lb ft)
Pounds-force feet (lbf ft; lb ft)	x 1.356	= Newton metres (Nm)	x 0.738	= Pounds-force feet (lbf ft; lb ft)
Newton metres (Nm)	x 0.102	= Kilograms-force metres (kgf m; kg m)	x 9.804	= Newton metres (Nm)

Power

Horsepower (hp)	x 745.7	= Watts (W)	x 0.0013	= Horsepower (hp)

Velocity (speed)

Miles per hour (miles/hr; mph)	x 1.609	= Kilometres per hour (km/hr; kph)	x 0.621	= Miles per hour (miles/hr; mph)

Fuel consumption*

Miles per gallon (mpg)	x 0.354	= Kilometres per litre (km/l)	x 2.825	= Miles per gallon (mpg)

Temperature

Degrees Fahrenheit = (°C x 1.8) + 32   Degrees Celsius (Degrees Centigrade; °C) = (°F - 32) x 0.56

It is common practice to convert from miles per gallon (mpg) to litres/100 kilometres (l/100km), where mpg x l/100 km = 282

A

ABS (Anti-lock brake system) A system, usually electronically controlled, that senses incipient wheel lockup during braking and relieves hydraulic pressure at wheels that are about to skid.

Air bag An inflatable bag hidden in the steering wheel (driver's side) or the dash or glovebox (passenger side). In a head-on collision, the bags inflate, preventing the driver and front passenger from being thrown forward into the steering wheel or windscreen.

Air cleaner A metal or plastic housing, containing a filter element, which removes dust and dirt from the air being drawn into the engine.

Air filter element The actual filter in an air cleaner system, usually manufactured from pleated paper and requiring renewal at regular intervals.

Air filter

Allen key A hexagonal wrench which fits into a recessed hexagonal hole.

Alligator clip A long-nosed spring-loaded metal clip with meshing teeth. Used to make temporary electrical connections.

Alternator A component in the electrical system which converts mechanical energy from a drivebelt into electrical energy to charge the battery and to operate the starting system, ignition system and electrical accessories.

Alternator (exploded view)

Ampere (amp) A unit of measurement for the flow of electric current. One amp is the amount of current produced by one volt acting through a resistance of one ohm.

Anaerobic sealer A substance used to prevent bolts and screws from loosening. Anaerobic means that it does not require oxygen for activation. The Loctite brand is widely used.

Antifreeze A substance (usually ethylene glycol) mixed with water, and added to a vehicle's cooling system, to prevent freezing of the coolant in winter. Antifreeze also contains chemicals to inhibit corrosion and the formation of rust and other deposits that would tend to clog the radiator and coolant passages and reduce cooling efficiency.

Anti-seize compound A coating that reduces the risk of seizing on fasteners that are subjected to high temperatures, such as exhaust manifold bolts and nuts.

Anti-seize compound

Asbestos A natural fibrous mineral with great heat resistance, commonly used in the composition of brake friction materials. Asbestos is a health hazard and the dust created by brake systems should never be inhaled or ingested.

Axle A shaft on which a wheel revolves, or which revolves with a wheel. Also, a solid beam that connects the two wheels at one end of the vehicle. An axle which also transmits power to the wheels is known as a live axle.

Axle assembly

Axleshaft A single rotating shaft, on either side of the differential, which delivers power from the final drive assembly to the drive wheels. Also called a driveshaft or a halfshaft.

B

Ball bearing An anti-friction bearing consisting of a hardened inner and outer race with hardened steel balls between two races.

Bearing

Bearing The curved surface on a shaft or in a bore, or the part assembled into either, that permits relative motion between them with minimum wear and friction.

Big-end bearing The bearing in the end of the connecting rod that's attached to the crankshaft.

Bleed nipple A valve on a brake wheel cylinder, caliper or other hydraulic component that is opened to purge the hydraulic system of air. Also called a bleed screw.

Brake bleeding

Brake bleeding Procedure for removing air from lines of a hydraulic brake system.

Brake disc The component of a disc brake that rotates with the wheels.

Brake drum The component of a drum brake that rotates with the wheels.

Brake linings The friction material which contacts the brake disc or drum to retard the vehicle's speed. The linings are bonded or riveted to the brake pads or shoes.

Brake pads The replaceable friction pads that pinch the brake disc when the brakes are applied. Brake pads consist of a friction material bonded or riveted to a rigid backing plate.

Brake shoe The crescent-shaped carrier to which the brake linings are mounted and which forces the lining against the rotating drum during braking.

Braking systems For more information on braking systems, consult the *Haynes Automotive Brake Manual*.

Breaker bar A long socket wrench handle providing greater leverage.

Bulkhead The insulated partition between the engine and the passenger compartment.

C

Caliper The non-rotating part of a disc-brake assembly that straddles the disc and carries the brake pads. The caliper also contains the hydraulic components that cause the pads to pinch the disc when the brakes are applied. A caliper is also a measuring tool that can be set to measure inside or outside dimensions of an object.

Camshaft A rotating shaft on which a series of cam lobes operate the valve mechanisms. The camshaft may be driven by gears, by sprockets and chain or by sprockets and a belt.

Canister A container in an evaporative emission control system; contains activated charcoal granules to trap vapours from the fuel system.

Canister

Carburettor A device which mixes fuel with air in the proper proportions to provide a desired power output from a spark ignition internal combustion engine.

Carburettor

Castellated Resembling the parapets along the top of a castle wall. For example, a castellated balljoint stud nut.

Castellated nut

Castor In wheel alignment, the backward or forward tilt of the steering axis. Castor is positive when the steering axis is inclined rearward at the top.

Catalytic converter A silencer-like device in the exhaust system which converts certain pollutants in the exhaust gases into less harmful substances.

Catalytic converter

Circlip A ring-shaped clip used to prevent endwise movement of cylindrical parts and shafts. An internal circlip is installed in a groove in a housing; an external circlip fits into a groove on the outside of a cylindrical piece such as a shaft.

Clearance The amount of space between two parts. For example, between a piston and a cylinder, between a bearing and a journal, etc.

Coil spring A spiral of elastic steel found in various sizes throughout a vehicle, for example as a springing medium in the suspension and in the valve train.

Compression Reduction in volume, and increase in pressure and temperature, of a gas, caused by squeezing it into a smaller space.

Compression ratio The relationship between cylinder volume when the piston is at top dead centre and cylinder volume when the piston is at bottom dead centre.

Constant velocity (CV) joint A type of universal joint that cancels out vibrations caused by driving power being transmitted through an angle.

Core plug A disc or cup-shaped metal device inserted in a hole in a casting through which core was removed when the casting was formed. Also known as a freeze plug or expansion plug.

Crankcase The lower part of the engine block in which the crankshaft rotates.

Crankshaft The main rotating member, or shaft, running the length of the crankcase, with offset "throws" to which the connecting rods are attached.

Crankshaft assembly

Crocodile clip See Alligator clip

D

Diagnostic code Code numbers obtained by accessing the diagnostic mode of an engine management computer. This code can be used to determine the area in the system where a malfunction may be located.

Disc brake A brake design incorporating a rotating disc onto which brake pads are squeezed. The resulting friction converts the energy of a moving vehicle into heat.

Double-overhead cam (DOHC) An engine that uses two overhead camshafts, usually one for the intake valves and one for the exhaust valves.

Drivebelt(s) The belt(s) used to drive accessories such as the alternator, water pump, power steering pump, air conditioning compressor, etc. off the crankshaft pulley.

Accessory drivebelts

Driveshaft Any shaft used to transmit motion. Commonly used when referring to the axleshafts on a front wheel drive vehicle.

Driveshaft

Drum brake A type of brake using a drum-shaped metal cylinder attached to the inner surface of the wheel. When the brake pedal is pressed, curved brake shoes with friction linings press against the inside of the drum to slow or stop the vehicle.

Drum brake assembly

E

EGR valve A valve used to introduce exhaust gases into the intake air stream.

EGR valve

Electronic control unit (ECU) A computer which controls (for instance) ignition and fuel injection systems, or an anti-lock braking system. For more information refer to the *Haynes Automotive Electrical and Electronic Systems Manual.*

Electronic Fuel Injection (EFI) A computer controlled fuel system that distributes fuel through an injector located in each intake port of the engine.

Emergency brake A braking system, independent of the main hydraulic system, that can be used to slow or stop the vehicle if the primary brakes fail, or to hold the vehicle stationary even though the brake pedal isn't depressed. It usually consists of a hand lever that actuates either front or rear brakes mechanically through a series of cables and linkages. Also known as a handbrake or parking brake.

Endfloat The amount of lengthwise movement between two parts. As applied to a crankshaft, the distance that the crankshaft can move forward and back in the cylinder block.

Engine management system (EMS) A computer controlled system which manages the fuel injection and the ignition systems in an integrated fashion.

Exhaust manifold A part with several passages through which exhaust gases leave the engine combustion chambers and enter the exhaust pipe.

Exhaust manifold

F

Fan clutch A viscous (fluid) drive coupling device which permits variable engine fan speeds in relation to engine speeds.

Feeler blade A thin strip or blade of hardened steel, ground to an exact thickness, used to check or measure clearances between parts.

Feeler blade

Firing order The order in which the engine cylinders fire, or deliver their power strokes, beginning with the number one cylinder.

Flywheel A heavy spinning wheel in which energy is absorbed and stored by means of momentum. On cars, the flywheel is attached to the crankshaft to smooth out firing impulses.

Free play The amount of travel before any action takes place. The "looseness" in a linkage, or an assembly of parts, between the initial application of force and actual movement. For example, the distance the brake pedal moves before the pistons in the master cylinder are actuated.

Fuse An electrical device which protects a circuit against accidental overload. The typical fuse contains a soft piece of metal which is calibrated to melt at a predetermined current flow (expressed as amps) and break the circuit.

Fusible link A circuit protection device consisting of a conductor surrounded by heat-resistant insulation. The conductor is smaller than the wire it protects, so it acts as the weakest link in the circuit. Unlike a blown fuse, a failed fusible link must frequently be cut from the wire for replacement.

G

Gap The distance the spark must travel in jumping from the centre electrode to the side

Adjusting spark plug gap

electrode in a spark plug. Also refers to the spacing between the points in a contact breaker assembly in a conventional points-type ignition, or to the distance between the reluctor or rotor and the pickup coil in an electronic ignition.

Gasket Any thin, soft material - usually cork, cardboard, asbestos or soft metal - installed between two metal surfaces to ensure a good seal. For instance, the cylinder head gasket seals the joint between the block and the cylinder head.

Gasket

Gauge An instrument panel display used to monitor engine conditions. A gauge with a movable pointer on a dial or a fixed scale is an analogue gauge. A gauge with a numerical readout is called a digital gauge.

H

Halfshaft A rotating shaft that transmits power from the final drive unit to a drive wheel, usually when referring to a live rear axle.

Harmonic balancer A device designed to reduce torsion or twisting vibration in the crankshaft. May be incorporated in the crankshaft pulley. Also known as a vibration damper.

Hone An abrasive tool for correcting small irregularities or differences in diameter in an engine cylinder, brake cylinder, etc.

Hydraulic tappet A tappet that utilises hydraulic pressure from the engine's lubrication system to maintain zero clearance (constant contact with both camshaft and valve stem). Automatically adjusts to variation in valve stem length. Hydraulic tappets also reduce valve noise.

I

Ignition timing The moment at which the spark plug fires, usually expressed in the number of crankshaft degrees before the piston reaches the top of its stroke.

Inlet manifold A tube or housing with passages through which flows the air-fuel mixture (carburettor vehicles and vehicles with throttle body injection) or air only (port fuel-injected vehicles) to the port openings in the cylinder head.

J

Jump start Starting the engine of a vehicle with a discharged or weak battery by attaching jump leads from the weak battery to a charged or helper battery.

L

Load Sensing Proportioning Valve (LSPV) A brake hydraulic system control valve that works like a proportioning valve, but also takes into consideration the amount of weight carried by the rear axle.

Locknut A nut used to lock an adjustment nut, or other threaded component, in place. For example, a locknut is employed to keep the adjusting nut on the rocker arm in position.

Lockwasher A form of washer designed to prevent an attaching nut from working loose.

M

MacPherson strut A type of front suspension system devised by Earle MacPherson at Ford of England. In its original form, a simple lateral link with the anti-roll bar creates the lower control arm. A long strut - an integral coil spring and shock absorber - is mounted between the body and the steering knuckle. Many modern so-called MacPherson strut systems use a conventional lower A-arm and don't rely on the anti-roll bar for location.

Multimeter An electrical test instrument with the capability to measure voltage, current and resistance.

N

NOx Oxides of Nitrogen. A common toxic pollutant emitted by petrol and diesel engines at higher temperatures.

O

Ohm The unit of electrical resistance. One volt applied to a resistance of one ohm will produce a current of one amp.

Ohmmeter An instrument for measuring electrical resistance.

O-ring A type of sealing ring made of a special rubber-like material; in use, the O-ring is compressed into a groove to provide the sealing action.

O-ring

Overhead cam (ohc) engine An engine with the camshaft(s) located on top of the cylinder head(s).

Overhead valve (ohv) engine An engine with the valves located in the cylinder head, but with the camshaft located in the engine block.

Oxygen sensor A device installed in the engine exhaust manifold, which senses the oxygen content in the exhaust and converts this information into an electric current. Also called a Lambda sensor.

P

Phillips screw A type of screw head having a cross instead of a slot for a corresponding type of screwdriver.

Plastigage A thin strip of plastic thread, available in different sizes, used for measuring clearances. For example, a strip of Plastigage is laid across a bearing journal. The parts are assembled and dismantled; the width of the crushed strip indicates the clearance between journal and bearing.

Plastigage

Propeller shaft The long hollow tube with universal joints at both ends that carries power from the transmission to the differential on front-engined rear wheel drive vehicles.

Proportioning valve A hydraulic control valve which limits the amount of pressure to the rear brakes during panic stops to prevent wheel lock-up.

R

Rack-and-pinion steering A steering system with a pinion gear on the end of the steering shaft that mates with a rack (think of a geared wheel opened up and laid flat). When the steering wheel is turned, the pinion turns, moving the rack to the left or right. This movement is transmitted through the track rods to the steering arms at the wheels.

Radiator A liquid-to-air heat transfer device designed to reduce the temperature of the coolant in an internal combustion engine cooling system.

Refrigerant Any substance used as a heat transfer agent in an air-conditioning system. R-12 has been the principle refrigerant for many years; recently, however, manufacturers have begun using R-134a, a non-CFC substance that is considered less harmful to

the ozone in the upper atmosphere.

Rocker arm A lever arm that rocks on a shaft or pivots on a stud. In an overhead valve engine, the rocker arm converts the upward movement of the pushrod into a downward movement to open a valve.

Rotor In a distributor, the rotating device inside the cap that connects the centre electrode and the outer terminals as it turns, distributing the high voltage from the coil secondary winding to the proper spark plug. Also, that part of an alternator which rotates inside the stator. Also, the rotating assembly of a turbocharger, including the compressor wheel, shaft and turbine wheel.

Runout The amount of wobble (in-and-out movement) of a gear or wheel as it's rotated. The amount a shaft rotates "out-of-true." The out-of-round condition of a rotating part.

S

Sealant A liquid or paste used to prevent leakage at a joint. Sometimes used in conjunction with a gasket.

Sealed beam lamp An older headlight design which integrates the reflector, lens and filaments into a hermetically-sealed one-piece unit. When a filament burns out or the lens cracks, the entire unit is simply replaced.

Serpentine drivebelt A single, long, wide accessory drivebelt that's used on some newer vehicles to drive all the accessories, instead of a series of smaller, shorter belts. Serpentine drivebelts are usually tensioned by an automatic tensioner.

Serpentine drivebelt

Shim Thin spacer, commonly used to adjust the clearance or relative positions between two parts. For example, shims inserted into or under bucket tappets control valve clearances. Clearance is adjusted by changing the thickness of the shim.

Slide hammer A special puller that screws into or hooks onto a component such as a shaft or bearing; a heavy sliding handle on the shaft bottoms against the end of the shaft to knock the component free.

Sprocket A tooth or projection on the periphery of a wheel, shaped to engage with a chain or drivebelt. Commonly used to refer to the sprocket wheel itself.

Starter inhibitor switch On vehicles with an

automatic transmission, a switch that prevents starting if the vehicle is not in Neutral or Park.

Strut See MacPherson strut.

T

Tappet A cylindrical component which transmits motion from the cam to the valve stem, either directly or via a pushrod and rocker arm. Also called a cam follower.

Thermostat A heat-controlled valve that regulates the flow of coolant between the cylinder block and the radiator, so maintaining optimum engine operating temperature. A thermostat is also used in some air cleaners in which the temperature is regulated.

Thrust bearing The bearing in the clutch assembly that is moved in to the release levers by clutch pedal action to disengage the clutch. Also referred to as a release bearing.

Timing belt A toothed belt which drives the camshaft. Serious engine damage may result if it breaks in service.

Timing chain A chain which drives the camshaft.

Toe-in The amount the front wheels are closer together at the front than at the rear. On rear wheel drive vehicles, a slight amount of toe-in is usually specified to keep the front wheels running parallel on the road by offsetting other forces that tend to spread the wheels apart.

Toe-out The amount the front wheels are closer together at the rear than at the front. On front wheel drive vehicles, a slight amount of toe-out is usually specified.

Tools For full information on choosing and using tools, refer to the *Haynes Automotive Tools Manual*.

Tracer A stripe of a second colour applied to a wire insulator to distinguish that wire from another one with the same colour insulator.

Tune-up A process of accurate and careful adjustments and parts replacement to obtain the best possible engine performance.

Turbocharger A centrifugal device, driven by exhaust gases, that pressurises the intake air. Normally used to increase the power output from a given engine displacement, but can also be used primarily to reduce exhaust emissions (as on VW's "Umwelt" Diesel engine).

U

Universal joint or U-joint A double-pivoted connection for transmitting power from a driving to a driven shaft through an angle. A U-joint consists of two Y-shaped yokes and a cross-shaped member called the spider.

V

Valve A device through which the flow of liquid, gas, vacuum, or loose material in bulk may be started, stopped, or regulated by a movable part that opens, shuts, or partially obstructs one or more ports or passageways. A valve is also the movable part of such a device.

Valve clearance The clearance between the valve tip (the end of the valve stem) and the rocker arm or tappet. The valve clearance is measured when the valve is closed.

Vernier caliper A precision measuring instrument that measures inside and outside dimensions. Not quite as accurate as a micrometer, but more convenient.

Viscosity The thickness of a liquid or its resistance to flow.

Volt A unit for expressing electrical "pressure" in a circuit. One volt that will produce a current of one ampere through a resistance of one ohm.

W

Welding Various processes used to join metal items by heating the areas to be joined to a molten state and fusing them together. For more information refer to the *Haynes Automotive Welding Manual*.

Wiring diagram A drawing portraying the components and wires in a vehicle's electrical system, using standardised symbols. For more information refer to the *Haynes Automotive Electrical and Electronic Systems Manual*.

Note: *References throughout this index relate to Chapter•page number*

Haynes Manuals – The Complete List

Title	Book No.
ALFA ROMEO	
Alfa Romeo Alfasud/Sprint (74 - 88)	0292
Alfa Romeo Alfetta (73 - 87)	0531
AUDI	
Audi 80 (72 - Feb 79)	0207
Audi 80, 90 (79 - Oct 86) & Coupe (81 - Nov 88)	0605
Audi 80, 90 (Oct 86 - 90) & Coupe (Nov 88 - 90)	1491
Audi 100 (Oct 76 - Oct 82)	0428
Audi 100 (Oct 82 - 90) & 200 (Feb 84 - Oct 89)	0907
AUSTIN	
Austin Ambassador (82 - 84)	0871
Austin/MG Maestro 1.3 & 1.6 (83 - 95)	0922
Austin Maxi (69 - 81)	0052
Austin/MG Metro (80 - May 90)	0718
Austin Montego 1.3 & 1.6 (84 - 94)	1066
Austin/MG Montego 2.0 (84 - 95)	1067
Mini (59 - 69)	0527
Mini (69 - Oct 96)	0646
Austin/Rover 2.0 litre Diesel Engine (86 - 93)	1857
BEDFORD	
Bedford CF (69 - 87)	0163
Bedford Rascal (86 - 93)	3015
BL	
BL Princess & BLMC 18-22 (75 - 82)	0286
BMW	
BMW 316, 320 & 320i (4-cyl) (75 - Feb 83)	0276
BMW 320, 320i, 323i & 325i (6-cyl) (Oct 77 - Sept 87)	0815
BMW 3-Series (Apr 91 - 96)	3210
BMW 3-Series (sohc) (83 - 91)	1948
BMW 520i & 525e (Oct 81 - June 88)	1560
BMW 525, 528 & 528i (73 - Sept 81)	0632
BMW 5-Series (sohc) (81 - 93)	1948
BMW 1500, 1502, 1600, 1602, 2000 & 2002 (59 - 77)	0240
CITROEN	
Citroen 2CV, Ami & Dyane (67 - 90)	0196
Citroen AX Petrol & Diesel (87 - 94)	3014
Citroen BX (83 - 94)	0908
Citroen CX (75 - 88)	0528
Citroen Visa (79 - 88)	0620
Citroen Xantia Petrol & Diesel (93 - Oct 95)	3082
Citroen ZX Diesel (91 - 93)	1922
Citroen ZX Petrol (91 - 94)	1881
Citroen 1.7 & 1.9 litre Diesel Engine (84 - 96)	1379
COLT	
Colt 1200, 1250 & 1400 (79 - May 84)	0600
DAIMLER	
Daimler Sovereign (68 - Oct 86)	0242
Daimler Double Six (72 - 88)	0478
DATSUN (see also **Nissan**)	
Datsun 120Y (73 - Aug 78)	0228
Datsun 1300, 1400 & 1600 (69 - Aug 72)	0123
Datsun Cherry (71 - 76)	0195
Datsun Pick-up (75 - 78)	0277
Datsun Sunny (Aug 78 - May 82)	0525
Datsun Violet (78 - 82)	0430
FIAT	
Fiat 126 (73 - 87)	0305
Fiat 127 (71 - 83)	0193
Fiat 500 (57 - 73)	0090
Fiat 850 (64 - 81)	0038
Fiat Panda (81 - 95)	0793
Fiat Punto (94 - 96)	3251
Fiat Regata (84 - 88)	1167
Fiat Strada (79 - 88)	0479
Fiat Tipo (88 - 91)	1625
Fiat Uno (83 - 95)	0923
Fiat X1/9 (74 - 89)	0273
FORD	
Ford Capri II (& III) 1.6 & 2.0 (74 - 87)	0283
Ford Capri II (& III) 2.8 & 3.0 (74 - 87)	1309
Ford Cortina Mk IV (& V) 1.6 & 2.0 (76 - 83)	0343
Ford Cortina Mk IV (& V) 2.3 V6 (77 - 83)	0426
Ford Escort (75 - Aug 80)	0280
Ford Escort (Sept 80 - Sept 90)	0686
Ford Escort (Sept 90 - 97)	1737
Ford Escort Mk II Mexico, RS 1600 & RS 2000 (75 - 80)	0735
Ford Fiesta (inc. XR2) (76 - Aug 83)	0334
Ford Fiesta (inc. XR2) (Aug 83 - Feb 89)	1030
Ford Fiesta (Feb 89 - Oct 95)	1595
Ford Granada (Sept 77 - Feb 85)	0481
Ford Granada (Mar 85 - 94)	1245
Ford Mondeo 4-cyl (93 - 96)	1923
Ford Orion (83 - Sept 90)	1009
Ford Orion (Sept 90 - 93)	1737
Ford Sierra 1.3, 1.6, 1.8 & 2.0 (82 - 93)	0903
Ford Sierra 2.3, 2.8 & 2.9 (82 - 91)	0904
Ford Scorpio (Mar 85 - 94)	1245
Ford Transit Petrol (Mk 1) (65 - Feb 78)	0377
Ford Transit Petrol (Mk 2) (78 - Jan 86)	0719
Ford Transit Petrol (Mk 3) (Feb 86 - 89)	1468
Ford Transit Diesel (Feb 86 - 95)	3019
Ford 1.6 & 1.8 litre Diesel Engine (84 - 96)	1172
Ford 2.1, 2.3 & 2.5 litre Diesel Engine (77 - 90)	1606
FREIGHT ROVER	
Freight Rover Sherpa (74 - 87)	0463
HILLMAN	
Hillman Avenger (70 - 82)	0037
Hillman Minx & Husky (56 - 66)	0009
HONDA	
Honda Accord (76 - Feb 84)	0351
Honda Accord (Feb 84 - Oct 85)	1177
Honda Civic 1300 (80 - 81)	0633
Honda Civic (Feb 84 - Oct 87)	1226
Honda Civic (Nov 91 - 96)	3199
HYUNDAI	
Hyundai Pony (85 - 94)	3398
JAGUAR	
Jaguar E Type (61 - 72)	0140
Jaguar MkI & II, 240 & 340 (55 - 69)	0098
Jaguar XJ6, XJ & Sovereign (68 - Oct 86)	0242
Jaguar XJ6 & Sovereign (Oct 86 - Sept 94)	3261
Jaguar XJ12, XJS & Sovereign (72 - 88)	0478
JEEP	
Jeep Cherokee Petrol (93 - 96)	1943
LADA	
Lada 1200, 1300, 1500 & 1600 (74 - 91)	0413
Lada Samara (87 - 91)	1610
LAND ROVER	
Land Rover 90, 110 & Defender Diesel (83 - 95)	3017
Land Rover Discovery Diesel (89 - 95)	3016
Land Rover Series IIA & III Diesel (58 - 85)	0529
Land Rover Series II, IIA & III Petrol (58 - 85)	0314
MAZDA	
Mazda 323 fwd (Mar 81 - Oct 89)	1608
Mazda 626 fwd (May 83 - Sept 87)	0929
Mazda B-1600, B-1800 & B-2000 Pick-up (72 - 88)	0267
MERCEDES-BENZ	
Mercedes-Benz 190 & 190E (83 - 87)	0928
Mercedes-Benz 200, 240, 300 Diesel (Oct 76 - 85)	1114
Mercedes-Benz 250 & 280 (68 - 72)	0346
Mercedes-Benz 250 & 280 (123 Series) (Oct 76 - 84)	0677
Mercedes-Benz 124 Series (85 - Aug 93)	3253
MG	
MGB (62 - 80)	0111
MG Maestro 1.3 & 1.6 (83 - 95)	0922
MG Metro (80 - May 90)	0718
MG Midget & AH Sprite (58 - 80)	0265
MG Montego 2.0 (84 - 95)	1067
MITSUBISHI	
Mitsubishi 1200, 1250 & 1400 (79 - May 84)	0600
Mitsubishi Shogun & L200 Pick-Ups (83 - 94)	1944
MORRIS	
Morris Ital 1.3 (80 - 84)	0705
Morris Marina 1700 (78 - 80)	0526
Morris Marina 1.8 (71 - 78)	0074
Morris Minor 1000 (56 - 71)	0024
NISSAN (See also **Datsun**)	
Nissan Bluebird 160B & 180B rwd (May 80 - May 84)	0957
Nissan Bluebird fwd (May 84 - Mar 86)	1223
Nissan Bluebird (T12 & T72) (Mar 86 - 90)	1473
Nissan Cherry (N12) (Sept 82 - 86)	1031
Nissan Micra (K10) (83 - Jan 93)	0931
Nissan Micra (93 - 96)	3254
Nissan Primera (90 - Oct 96)	1851
Nissan Stanza (82 - 86)	0824
Nissan Sunny (B11) (May 82 - Oct 86)	0895
Nissan Sunny (Oct 86 - Mar 91)	1378
Nissan Sunny (Apr 91 - 95)	3219
OPEL	
Opel Ascona & Manta (B Series) (Sept 75 - 88)	0316
Opel Ascona (81 - 88)	3215
Opel Astra (Oct 91 - 96)	3156
Opel Corsa (83 - Mar 93)	3160
Opel Corsa (Mar 93 - 94)	3159
Opel Kadett (Nov 79 - Oct 84)	0634
Opel Kadett (Oct 84 - Oct 91)	3196
Opel Omega & Senator (86 - 94)	3157

Title	Book No.
Opel Rekord (Feb 78 - Oct 86)	0543
Opel Vectra (88 - Oct 95)	3158
PEUGEOT	
Peugeot 106 Petrol & Diesel (91 - June 96)	1882
Peugeot 205 (83 - 95)	0932
Peugeot 305 (78 - 89)	0538
Peugeot 306 Petrol & Diesel (93 - 95)	3073
Peugeot 309 (86 - 93)	1266
Peugeot 405 Petrol (88 - 96)	1559
Peugeot 405 Diesel (88 - 96)	3198
Peugeot 406 Petrol & Diesel (96 - 97)	3394
Peugeot 505 (79 - 89)	0762
Peugeot 1.7 & 1.9 litre Diesel Engines (82 - 96)	0950
Peugeot 2.0, 2.1, 2.3 & 2.5 litre Diesel Engines (74 - 90)	1607
PORSCHE	
Porsche 911 (65 - 85)	0264
Porsche 924 & 924 Turbo (76 - 85)	0397
PROTON	
Proton (89 - 97)	3255
RANGE ROVER	
Range Rover V8 (70 - Oct 92)	0606
RELIANT	
Reliant Robin & Kitten (73 - 83)	0436
RENAULT	
Renault 5 (72 - Feb 85)	0141
Renault 5 (Feb 85 - 96)	1219
Renault 9 & 11 (82 - 89)	0822
Renault 12 (70 - 80)	0097
Renault 15 & 17 (72 - 79)	0763
Renault 18 (79 - 86)	0598
Renault 19 Petrol (89 - 94)	1646
Renault 19 Diesel (89 - 95)	1946
Renault 21 (86 - 94)	1397
Renault 25 (84 - 86)	1228
Renault Clio Petrol (91 - 93)	1853
Renault Clio Diesel (91 - June 96)	3031
Renault Espace (85 - 96)	3197
Renault Fuego (80 - 86)	0764
Renault Laguna (94 - 96)	3252
ROVER	
Rover 111 & 114 (95 - 96)	1711
Rover 213 & 216 (84 - 89)	1116
Rover 214 & 414 (Oct 89 - 92)	1689
Rover 216 & 416 (Oct 89 - 92)	1830
Rover 618, 620 & 623 (93 - 97)	3257
Rover 820, 825 & 827 (86 - 95)	1380
Rover 2000, 2300 & 2600 (77 - 87)	0468
Rover 3500 (76 - 87)	0365
Rover Metro (May 90 - 94)	1711
SAAB	
Saab 90, 99 & 900 (79 - Oct 93)	0765
Saab 9000 (4-cyl) (85 - 95)	1686
SEAT	
Seat Ibiza & Malaga (85 - 92)	1609
SIMCA	
Simca 1100 & 1204 (67 - 79)	0088
Simca 1301 & 1501 (63 - 76)	0199

Title	Book No.
SKODA	
Skoda Estelle 105, 120, 130 & 136 (77 - 89)	0604
Skoda Favorit (89 - 92)	1801
SUBARU	
Subaru 1600 (77 - Oct 79)	0237
Subaru 1600 & 1800 (Nov 79 - 90)	0995
SUZUKI	
Suzuki SJ Series, Samurai & Vitara (82 - 97)	1942
Suzuki Supercarry (86 - Oct 94)	3015
TALBOT	
Talbot Alpine, Solara, Minx & Rapier (75 - 86)	0337
Talbot Horizon (78 - 86)	0473
Talbot Samba (82 - 86)	0823
TOYOTA	
Toyota Carina E (May 92 - 97)	3256
Toyota Celica (Feb 82 - Sept 85)	1135
Toyota Corolla (fwd) (Sept 83 - Sept 87)	1024
Toyota Corolla (rwd) (80 - 85)	0683
Toyota Corolla (Sept 87 - 92)	1683
Toyota Corolla (Aug 92 - 97)	3259
Toyota Hi-Ace & Hi-Lux (69 - Oct 83)	0304
Toyota Starlet (78 - Jan 85)	0462
TRIUMPH	
Triumph Acclaim (81 - 84)	0792
Triumph Herald (59 - 71)	0010
Triumph Spitfire (62 - 81)	0113
Triumph Stag (70 - 78)	0441
Triumph TR7 (75 - 82)	0322
VAUXHALL	
Vauxhall Astra (80 - Oct 84)	0635
Vauxhall Astra & Belmont (Oct 84 - Oct 91)	1136
Vauxhall Astra (Oct 91 - 96)	1832
Vauxhall Carlton (Oct 78 - Oct 86)	0480
Vauxhall Carlton (Nov 86 - 94)	1469
Vauxhall Cavalier 1300 (77 - July 81)	0461
Vauxhall Cavalier 1600, 1900 & 2000 (75 - July 81)	0315
Vauxhall Cavalier (81 - Oct 88)	0812
Vauxhall Cavalier (Oct 88 - Oct 95)	1570
Vauxhall Chevette (75 - 84)	0285
Vauxhall Corsa (Mar 93 - 94)	1985
Vauxhall Nova (83 - 93)	0909
Vauxhall Rascal (86 - 93)	3015
Vauxhall Senator (Sept 87 - 94)	1469
Vauxhall Viva HB Series (ohv) (66 - 70)	0026
Vauxhall Viva & Firenza (ohc) (68 - 73)	0093
Vauxhall/Opel 1.5, 1.6 & 1.7 litre Diesel Engines (82 - 96)	1222
VOLKSWAGEN	
VW Beetle 1200 (54 - 77)	0036
VW Beetle 1300 & 1500 (65 - 75)	0039
VW Beetle 1302 & 1302S (70 - 72)	0110
VW Beetle 1303, 1303S & GT (72 - 75)	0159
VW Golf Mk 1 1.1 & 1.3 (74 - Feb 84)	0716
VW Golf Mk 1 1.5, 1.6 & 1.8 (74 - 85)	0726
VW Golf Mk 1 Diesel (78 - Feb 84)	0451
VW Golf Mk 2 (Mar 84 - Feb 92)	1081
VW Golf Mk 3 Petrol & Diesel (Feb 92 - 96)	3097

Title	Book No.
VW Jetta Mk 1 1.1 & 1.3 (80 - June 84)	0716
VW Jetta Mk 1 1.5, 1.6 & 1.8 (80 - June 84)	0726
VW Jetta Mk 1 Diesel (81 - June 84)	0451
VW Jetta Mk 2 (July 84 - 92)	1081
VW LT vans & light trucks (76 - 87)	0637
VW Passat (Sept 81 - May 88)	0814
VW Passat (May 88 - 91)	1647
VW Polo & Derby (76 - Jan 82)	0335
VW Polo (82 - Oct 90)	0813
VW Polo (Nov 90 - Aug 94)	3245
VW Santana (Sept 82 - 85)	0814
VW Scirocco Mk 1 1.5, 1.6 & 1.8 (74 - 82)	0726
VW Scirocco (82 - 90)	1224
VW Transporter 1600 (68 - 79)	0082
VW Transporter 1700, 1800 & 2000 (72 - 79)	0226
VW Transporter with air-cooled engine (79 - 82)	0638
VW Type 3 (63 - 73)	0084
VW Vento Petrol & Diesel (Feb 92 - 96)	3097
VOLVO	
Volvo 66 & 343, Daf 55 & 66 (68 - 79)	0293
Volvo 142, 144 & 145 (66 - 74)	0129
Volvo 240 Series (74 - 93)	0270
Volvo 262, 264 & 260/265 (75 - 85)	0400
Volvo 340, 343, 345 & 360 (76 - 91)	0715
Volvo 440, 460 & 480 (87 - 92)	1691
Volvo 740 & 760 (82 - 91)	1258
Volvo 850 (92 - 96)	3260
Volvo 940 (90 - 96)	3249
YUGO/ZASTAVA	
Yugo/Zastava (81 - 90)	1453

TECH BOOKS	
Automotive Brake Manual	3050
Carburettor Manual	3288
Diesel Engine Service Guide	3286
Automotive Electrical & Electronic Systems	3049
Automotive Engine Management and Fuel Injection Manual	3344
In-Car Entertainment Manual	3363
Automotive Tools Manual	3052
Automotive Welding Manual	3053

CAR BOOKS	
Automotive Fuel Injection Systems	9755
Car Bodywork Repair Manual	9864
Caravan Manual (2nd Edition)	9894
Haynes Technical Data Book (88 - 97)	1997
How to Keep Your Car Alive	9868
Japanese Vehicle Carburettors	1786
Small Engine Repair Manual	1755
SU Carburettors	0299
Weber Carburettors (to 79)	0393

C6684.CL04.04/97

Preserving Our Motoring Heritage

< The Model J Duesenberg Derham Tourster. Only eight of these magnificent cars were ever built – this is the only example to be found outside the United States of America

Almost every car you've ever loved, loathed or desired is gathered under one roof at the Haynes Motor Museum. Over 300 immaculately presented cars and motorbikes represent every aspect of our motoring heritage, from elegant reminders of bygone days, such as the superb Model J Duesenberg to curiosities like the bug-eyed BMW Isetta. There are also many old friends and flames. Perhaps you remember the 1959 Ford Popular that you did your courting in? The magnificent 'Red Collection' is a spectacle of classic sports cars including AC, Alfa Romeo, Austin Healey, Ferrari, Lamborghini, Maserati, MG, Riley, Porsche and Triumph.

A Perfect Day Out

Each and every vehicle at the Haynes Motor Museum has played its part in the history and culture of Motoring. Today, they make a wonderful spectacle and a great day out for all the family. Bring the kids, bring Mum and Dad, but above all bring your camera to capture those golden memories for ever. You will also find an impressive array of motoring memorabilia, a comfortable 70 seat video cinema and one of the most extensive transport book shops in Britain. The Pit Stop Cafe serves everything from a cup of tea to wholesome, home-made meals or, if you prefer, you can enjoy the large picnic area nestled in the beautiful rural surroundings of Somerset.

> John Haynes O.B.E., Founder and Chairman of the museum at the wheel of a Haynes Light 12.

< Graham Hill's Lola Cosworth Formula 1 car next to a 1934 Riley Sports.

The Museum is situated on the A359 Yeovil to Frome road at Sparkford, just off the A303 in Somerset. It is about 40 miles south of Bristol, and 25 minutes drive from the M5 intersection at Taunton.

Open 9.30am - 5.30pm (10.00am - 4.00pm Winter) 7 days a week, *except Christmas Day, Boxing Day and New Years Day*
Special rates available for schools, coach parties and outings Charitable Trust No. 292048